Portraits of Pioneers in Developmental Psychology

Portraits of Pioneers in Developmental Psychology

Edited by

Wade E. Pickren
Pace University

Donald A. Dewsbury
University of Florida

Michael Wertheimer
University of Colorado, Boulder

Sponsored by the Society for General Psychology, APA Division One

Psychology Press
Taylor & Francis Group

New York   London

Cover image provided by Wade E. Pickren.

Psychology Press
Taylor & Francis Group
711 Third Avenue
New York, NY 10017

Psychology Press
Taylor & Francis Group
27 Church Road
Hove, East Sussex BN3 2FA

© 2012 by Taylor & Francis Group, LLC
Psychology Press is an imprint of Taylor & Francis Group, an Informa business

Printed in the United States of America on acid-free paper
Version Date: 2011902

International Standard Book Number: 978-1-84872-895-0 (Hardback) 978-1-84872-896-7 (Paperback)

Library of Congress Cataloging-in-Publication Data

Portraits of pioneers in developmental psychology / editors, Wade E. Pickren,
    Donald A. Dewsbury, Michael Wertheimer.
        p. cm.
    Includes bibliographical references and index.
    ISBN 978-1-84872-895-0 (hbk. : alk. paper) -- ISBN 978-1-84872-896-7
    (pbk. : alk. paper)
        1. Developmental psychology--History. 2. Psychologists--Biography. I.
    Pickren, Wade E. II. Dewsbury, Donald A., 1939- III. Wertheimer, Michael.

    BF713.P67 2012
    155.092'2--dc23   2011034797

Visit the Taylor & Francis Web site at
http://www.taylorandfrancis.com

and the Psychology Press Web site at
http://www.psypress.com

Contents

Preface

With this volume, the series *Portraits of Pioneers in Psychology* takes a new direction in focusing on a specific area: developmental psychology. Previous volumes have included chapters on contributors to a variety of psychology's substantive areas of scholarship and practice. We now turn to a closer examination of specific areas within psychology with this volume, which features 16 key figures in developmental psychology. As with previous volumes, our aim is to have chapters that inform our readers about both the scholarly and personal lives of the psychologists included in the volume. The chapters have been constructed to be authoritative yet accessible. Our chapters include new insights, balanced perspectives, and new or little-known information about our subjects. Our objective is to make the chapters of interest to undergraduate students, graduate students, and faculty members in psychology. They should be of interest not only to psychologists, but also to scholars in many related fields. The chapters should be especially valuable in the field of the history of psychology. However, we believe they will also be useful in such courses as developmental psychology (child, adolescent, and lifespan), human development, and educational psychology. This volume represents a new direction for a series begun in 1991 by the Society for General Psychology and published as *Portraits of Pioneers in Psychology*. Now, each volume will focus on a particular subfield of psychology. For this volume, Donald Dewsbury and Michael Wertheimer continue to serve as coeditors. Wade Pickren has joined Dewsbury and Wertheimer and has undertaken primary responsibility for the volume.

Each of the 16 subjects made significant contributions to developmental psychology and thus are legitimately regarded as pioneers. Mamie Phipps Clark initiated the research that was later cited in the landmark *Brown v. Board of Education* litigation that helped end segregation in public schools; she also pioneered new community-based psychological interventions in New York City. Robert W. White pioneered a new approach to the study of persons across the lifespan and his contributions continue to be felt in many areas of psychology. Lois Barclay Murphy offered a distinctive perspective on the strengths of developing children; her work foreshadowed later developments in humanistic and positive psychology. Florence L. Goodenough pioneered new testing methods for children and was a leader of mid-20th century psychology, including the National Council of Women Psychologists. John Paul Scott hoped that his pioneering research on behavioral genetics would help diminish aggression and make a more peaceful world.

The chapters that make up the center of the book highlight the many contributions of European pioneers in developmental psychology: Jean Piaget, Charlotte Bühler, Heinz Werner, and Lev Vygotsky. The work of these Europeans has had an enduring influence on how we understand human development. Their contributions were carried forward in the United States by Joseph McVicker Hunt and in Brazil by Helena Antipoff. Both Hunt and Antipoff, as our chapters detail, interpreted the work of the Europeans to fit their respective contexts.

Arnold Gesell was in his time perhaps North America's best known authority on children. His film studies of children's development remain a landmark accomplishment. Lawrence Kohlberg pioneered the study of moral development across the lifespan and, as our chapter indicates, many of his questions about moral development arose in the context of his own life. While working with Kurt Lewin at the University of Iowa Child Welfare Station, Roger Barker was involved in the key studies on aggression and democratic leadership among children. From this foundation, Barker went on to study human development across the lifespan in a variety of settings and synthesized his findings into what became known as environmental or ecological psychology. Eleanor "Jackie" Gibson, of course, was one of the world's best known psychologists for her work on the "visual cliff." She was a lifelong researcher on questions of perception and development. Finally, Sidney Bijou had a long and productive career in which he delineated ways to improve the lives of children.

Consistent with the volumes in the Portraits of Pioneers in Psychology series, we have included a complete list of subjects and authors in an accompanying table. In addition, we have provided two descriptor terms for each of the subjects. We hope that this information will enable instructors who wish to supplement their courses in substantive areas of psychology to locate relevant chapters with ease. Our intent is to make the chapters both accessible and useful for instructors in psychology. At the conclusion of each chapter is a short list of suggested readings, annotated to help instructors guide students toward original sources.

The book owes its existence to the contributions of many people. We especially want to acknowledge the efforts of the chapter authors, as well as of our editor at Psychology Press/Taylor & Francis, Debra Riegert. Finally, we owe a deep debt of gratitude to our reviewers: Lawrence Balter (New York University), Barney Beins (Ithaca College), Brian Cox (Hofstra University), Harry Heft (Denison University), and Mark Mattson (Fordham University).

Wade E. Pickren
Donald A. Dewsbury
Michael Wertheimer

List of Contributors for Volumes I–VI

Earlier volumes of *Portraits of Pioneers in Psychology* were general in focus, and this is the first volume in a new direction for the *Pioneers* series.

Vol.	Author		Subject	
5	Ainsworth, M.	Bretherton, I.	Developmental	Personality
3	Allport, F. H.	Katz, D., et al.	Social	Personality
5	Anastasi, A.	Hogan, J. D.	Testing	Applied
5	Angell, J. R.	Dewsbury, D. A.	Systems	Administration
6	Arnold, M.	Shields, S. A.	Emotion	Personality
5	Asch, S.	McCauley, C. & Rozin, P.	Gestalt	Social
4	Bartlett, F. C.	Roediger, H. L., III	Memory	Cognitive
5	Bayley, N.	Rosenblith, J.	Developmental	Testing
4	Beach, F. A.	Dewsbury, D. A.	Comparative	Physiological
6	Bills, M.	Koppes, L., & Bauer, A. M.	Applied	Testing
3	Binet, A.	Fancher, R. E.	Testing	Personality
5	Bingham, W. vD.	Benjamin, L. T., Jr., & Baker, D. B.	I/O Psychology	Testing
2	Blatz, W. E.	Wright, M. J.	Developmental	Learning
5	Brunswik, E.	Kurz-Milcke, E., & Innis, N. K.	Perception	Systems
2	Burks, B. S.	King, D. B., et al.	Developmental	Genetics
1	Calkins, M. W.	Furumoto, L.	Gender	Self
1	Carr, H.	Hilgard, E. R.	Systems	Experimental
6	Cattell, J. McK.	Sokal, M.	Testing	Administration
6	Clark, K. B.	Jackson, J. P.	Race	Social
4	Cook, S. W.	Brigham, J. C.	Social	Personality
6	Dallenbach, K.	Evans, R. B.	Experimental	Sensory
3	Darwin, C.	Masterton, R. B.	Evolution	Comparative
2	Dewey, J.	Barone, D. F.	Systems	Philosophy
2	Dix, D.	Viney, W.	Clinical	Gender
2	Doll, E. A.	Doll, E. E.	Applied	Social
5	Downey, J. E.	Hogan, J. D., & Thompson, D. N.	Testing	Personality
3	Duncker, K.	King, D. B., et al.	Gestalt	Cognition
3	Ebbinghaus, H.	Boneau, C. A.	Memory	Experimental
3	Erickson, M.	Schiffman, H.	Hypnosis	Clinical
4	Eysenck, H.	Jensen, A. R.	Testing	Personality
2	Fechner, G. T.	Adler, H. E.	Perception	Experimental
3	Festinger, L.	Brehm, J. W.	Social	Cognition
1	Freud, S.	Beier, E. G.	Psychoanalysis	Personality
6	Fromm-Reichman, F.	Hornstein, G.	Psychoanalysis	Clinical
1	Galton, F.	McClearn, G.	Genetics	Testing
2	Gibson, J. J.	Reed, E. S.	Perception	Ecological
2	Gilbreth, L.	Perloff, R., & Naman, J. L.	Applied	Gender
5	Goldstein, K.	Pickren, W. E.	Physiological	Clinical
2	Graham, C.	Brown, J. L.	Perception	Learning
6	Griffith, C.	Green, C.	Sport	Education
2	Guthrie, E. R.	Prenzel-Guthrie, P.	Learning	Social

List of Contributors for Volumes I–VI *(Continued)*

Vol.	Author		Subject	
5	Hall, G. S.	Hogan, J. D.	Administration	Developmental
5	Harlow, H. F.	LeRoy, H. M.,& Kimble, G. A.	Comparative	Physiological
4	Hathaway, S. R.	Butcher, J. N.	Testing	Personality
2	Hebb, D. O.	Glickman, S. E.	Physiological	Comparative
1	Heidbreder, E.	Henle, M.	Systems	Cognition
4	Heider, F.	Malle, B. F., & Ickes, W.	Social	Gestalt
4	Helmholtz, H.	Adler, H. E.	Perception	Physiological
3	Hickock, L. P.	Bare, J. K.	Philosophy	Religion
2	Hollingworth, H.	Benjamin, L. T., Jr.	Applied	Clinical
1	Hollingworth, L. S.	Shields, S. A.	Gender	Testing
4	Hooker, E.	Kimmel, D. C., & Garnets, L. D.	Gender	Personality
4	Horney, K.	Paris, B.	Psychoanalysis	Gender
4	Hovland, C. I.	Shepard, R. N.	Learning	Social
1	Hull, C.. L.	Kimble, G. A.	Learning	Hypnosis
1	Hunter, W. S.	Cofer, C. N.	Experimental	Learning
1	James, W.	Ross, B.	Systems	Philosophy
1	Jastrow, J.	Blumenthal, A.	Experimental	Aesthetics
6	Jones, M. C.	Rutherford, A.	Developmental	Personality
1	Jung, C. G.	Alexander, I. E.	Psychoanalysis	Personality
4	Koch, S.	Finkelman, D., & Kessel, F.	Systems	Cognition
1	Köhler, W.	Sherrill, R.	Gestalt	Cognition
3	Krech, D.	Innis, N. K.	Learning	Social
3	Kuo, Z-Y.	Gottlieb, G.	Comparative	Developmental
1	Lashley, K. S.	Bruce, D.	Physiological	Comparative
5	Leibniz, G. W.	Fancher, R. E., & Schmidt, H.	Philosophical	Perceptual
3	Lewin, K.	Lewin, M. A.	Gestalt	Social
5	Lord, F. M.	Green, B. F.	Testing	Statistics
6	Maslow, A.	Coon, D.	Humanistic	Personality
5	McDougall, W.	Innis, N. K.	Systems	Learning
3	McGraw, M.	Dalton, T. C., & Bergenn, V. W.	Developmental	Physiological
5	Metzger, W.	Götzl, H.	Perception	Gestalt
5	Michotte, A.	Gavin, E. A.	Perception	Phenomenology
2	Milgram, S.	Blass, T.	Social	Personality
4	Müller, G. E.	Sprung, L., & Sprung, H.	Experimental	Learning
4	Münsterberg, H.	Benjamin, L. T., Jr.	Applied	Forensics
2	Murchison, C.	Thompson, D.	Administration	Social
6	Murray, H. A.	Barenbaum, N.	Personality	Clinical
3	Nissen, H. W.	Dewsbury, D. A.	Comparative	Evolution
6	Paterson, D. G.	Baker, D. B.	Counseling	Personality
1	Pavlov, I. P.	Kimble, G. A.	Learning	Physiological
3	Piaget, J.	Zigler, E., & Gilman, E.	Developmental	Cognition
1	Puffer, E.	Scarborough, E.	Gender	Aesthetics
5	Ratliff, F.	Werner, J. S., & Spillmann, L.	Perception	Experimental

List of Contributors for Volumes I–VI *(Continued)*

Vol.	Author		Subject	
2	Rhine, J. B.	Feather, S.	Parapsychology	Perception
4	Robertson, G. C.	King, D. B.	Philosophy	Physiological
3	Rogers, C. R.	Lakin, M.	Clinical	Humanistic
6	Sanford, E. C.	Goodwin, C. J.	Experimental	Administration
2	Schiller, P. H.	Dewsbury, D. A.	Comparative	Learning
4	Schneirla, T. C.	Tobach, E.	Comparative	Learning
2	Sechenov, I. M.	Kimble, G. A.	Learning	Physiological
6	Shakow, D.	Cautin, R.	Clinical	Education
3	Skinner, B. F.	Bjork, D. W.	Learning	Applied
4	Spearman, C. E.	Jensen, A. R.	Testing	Cognition
3	Spence, K. W.	Kimble, G. A.	Learning	Systems
4	Sperry, R. W.	Puente, A. R.	Physiological	Comparative
2	Stern, W.	Lamiell, J. T.	Personality	Testing
6	Stone, C. P.	Pickren, W. E.	Comparative	Physiological
4	Stumpf, C.	Sprung, H., & Sprung, L.	Perception	Aesthetics
1	Sullivan, H. S.	Chatelaine, K. L.	Psychoanalysis	Clinical
4	Sumner, F. C.	Guthrie, R. V.	Race	Education
4	Terman, L.	Crosby, J. R., & Hastorf, A. H.	Testing	Developmental
1	Thorndike, E. L.	Thorndike, R. I.	Learning	Testing
3	Thurstone, L. L.	Jones, L. V.	Testing	Personality
6	Tinbergen, N.	Dewsbury, D. A.	Comparative	Ethology
1	Titchener, E. B.	Evans, R. B.	Experimental	Systems
1	Tolman, E. C.	Gleitman, H.	Learning	Systems
2	Tomkins, S. S.	Alexander, I. E.	Personality	Emotion
1	Tryon, R. C.	Schlesinger, K.	Genetics	Learning
6	Turner, C. H.	Abramson, C.	Comparative	Sensory
5	Tyler, L.	Fassinger, R. E.	Testing	Counseling
3	Underwood, B. J.	Freund, J. S.	Experimental	Learning
4	Upham, T.	Fuchs, A. H.	Systems	Philosophy
5	Washburn, M. F.	Viney, W., & Burlingame-Lee, L.	Comparative	Systems
1	Watson, J. B.	Brewer, C. L.	Systems	Learning
1	Wertheimer, M.	Wertheimer, M.	Gestalt	Cognition
2	Witmer, L.	McReynolds, P.	Clinical	Comparative
5	Wolfe, H. K.	Benjamin, L. T., Jr.	Experimental	Education
6	Woodworth, R. S.	Winston, A. S.	Experimental	Systems
3	Wundt, W. M.	Blumenthal, A. L.	Experimental	Cultural
2	Yerkes, R. M.	Dewsbury, D. A.	Comparative	Testing

Foundations of Human Experience

WADE E. PICKREN

A psychology of human development was woven from multiple strands of theory, practice, and changing demographics in Europe and North America. The 19th century was an era of grand theories about human nature and human society, as exemplified in the writings of Karl Marx, August Comte, Charles Darwin, and Sigmund Freud, among others. The rise of manufactory capitalism as part of the Industrial Revolution helped create changes in the distribution of population, as millions moved to cities to work in factories. Home and work life was also impacted, as the modern nuclear family characteristic of Western societies gradually emerged and became the norm, if not the only expression of family relationships and modes of living. Questions about the status and role of children in modern industrializing societies arose, with compulsory schooling and legislation forbidding child labor spreading fitfully across both Europe and North America throughout the 19th and into the 20th century. Improvements in the understanding and treatment of disease led to slow but marked increases in life expectancy, with attendant questions about the life course and life stages. By the end of the 19th century, these various strands began to be woven together into an emergent science about human development, focused first on children and their development. In the first few decades of the 20th century, a pragmatic approach to developmental issues was fostered by a new cadre of philanthropic organizations that viewed an understanding of the child and human development as central to managing large and increasingly diverse societies. All of these strands together were important in constructing the field of developmental psychology.

The rich theoretical traditions of the 19th century shaped the more narrowly focused theories and practices of the early cohorts of developmental psychologists. For example, the ideas of Karl Marx, filtered through the Bolshevik Revolution in Russia and embedded in the new institutions of the Soviet Union, found expression in the work of Lev Vygotsky and his colleagues (see Chapter 7). But it was the ideas and writings of Charles Darwin that provided the greatest theoretical impetus for a psychology of human development.

Developmental psychology became diverse in topic, subspecialties, and reach, but the notion that children could be understood as holding the key to understanding human linkages with an evolutionary past grew from the writings of Darwin. Thus, as the new field of scientific psychology emerged in the last quarter of the

19th century, questions of the development of human characteristics became of interest to these new scientists.

Darwin was not the first theorist or scientist to address human development, especially that of children. Jean-Jacques Rousseau (1712–1778) was an advocate of developmentally appropriate education for children in *Émile, or On Education* (1762). Rousseau divided human development into three stages, each with unique developmental characteristics. Friedrich Froebel (1782–1852) originated the idea of a kindergarten, a term he coined and applied in 1840 to the Play and Activity Institute he founded in Germany in 1837. He emphasized the importance of the child learning through activities, in which he anticipated many later developmental and educational theorists, including two subjects in this volume, Lev Vygotsky (Chapter 7) and Helena Antipoff (Chapter 4).

Biographies of infants and young children were one way to describe child development. Two notable examples from Germany include those of philosopher Dietrich Tiedemann in 1787 and Wilhelm Preyer in 1881. In 1877 Darwin published an account of his son William's development based on observations made much earlier. In the United States, Millicent Shinn gave an intensive account of her niece's development in *The Biography of a Baby* (1900).

Still, it was the work of Darwin or, perhaps more accurately, interpretations of Darwin that inspired ideas about human, particularly child development among the first generation of the new scientific psychologists, especially in America (Noon, 2005; O'Donnell, 1985). G. Stanley Hall, notable for many accomplishments in the first generation of the New Psychologists, drew heavily upon evolutionary ideas, some of which were Darwinian, to extol the great promise of child study. Recapitulation theory, which owed more perhaps to German zoologist Ernst Haeckel than to Darwin, posited that the evolutionary history of a species is replayed in development. This idea that ontogeny (development) recapitulates phylogeny captured the imagination of many psychologists.

In the United States, the Child Study movement emerged in the late 19th century led by psychologist G. Stanley Hall. The movement is best understood in light of Progressive Era ideals of reform and rationalization of American life. Understanding the child, it was thought, would provide insight into how best to order an increasingly complex world and help make it possible to balance the social and the natural worlds. Psychologists and other social scientists of the era also saw this as an opportunity to gain cultural authority as experts who could contribute to the reform of society. Thus, these scientists became advocates for reform of child rearing, child hygiene, and child education. The last became especially important with the new compulsory schooling laws that led to a 1000% increase in the number of children in schools between 1890 and 1920.

The modes of scientific inquiry promoted by child study advocates centered on observation of the child, extensive questionnaires, and reports. Hall was a founder of the National Association for the Study of Childhood (NASC) in 1893, which was the leader in the promotion of these data-gathering efforts. Hall and the NASC introduced the use of the questionnaire, and nearly 200 distinct questionnaires were used over the next two decades to solicit information from thousands of school children about a wide variety of childhood fears, dreams, hopes, and behaviors.

All this activity, by psychologists, physicians, teachers, and other experts, aroused a kind of national fervor about childhood. President Theodore Roosevelt called the first White House Conference on Childhood in 1909 to develop ideas that could be used to sponsor legislation to improve the health and care of children. The Children's Bureau was established as part of the Department of Commerce and Labor in 1912. Hall even set up a Children's Institute at Clark in 1909. This was at a time when Hall was intensely interested in Freud's theories about childhood and sexuality. Hall established in the institute a section for the study of "Psychology, Pedagogy, and Hygiene of Sex." Although the institute was short-lived (1909–1914) and apparently little research was ever done there, it reflected Hall's intense interest in the importance of a scientific understanding of all aspects of childhood.

In 1904, Hall published what became a landmark, two-volume set on a newly minted developmental stage—adolescence. Hall, of course, coined the term and outlined its extensive implications for human development, as indicated by the title of the volumes: *Adolescence: Its Psychology and Its Relations to Physiology, Anthropology, Sociology, Sex, Crime, Religion, and Education.* Several of Hall's students at Clark University, including Arnold Gesell, Henry Goddard, and Lewis Terman, went on to become important contributors to the new science of child development.

The term used for much of this work was *genetic psychology*, indicating not the role of genes in human behavior, but genetic in the sense of origins of behavior. James Mark Baldwin (1861–1934), a psychologist educated at Princeton University, contributed two important books to the new genetic psychology, *Mental Development in the Child and the Race* (1895) and *Social and Ethical Interpretations in Mental Development* (1902). Baldwin's notion of the "dialectic of personal growth" suggested how children distinguish self from others and the implications of this realization for social and moral development. Baldwin's theorizing about child development in various domains, such as moral and cognitive development, later influenced Jean Piaget (see Chapter 6), Lawrence Kohlberg (see Chapter 16), and Lev Vygotsky (see Chapter 7).

Within the larger context of increasing urbanization, growth of professional expertise, and compulsory schooling with its demands for vastly expanded administrative and instructional structures, the new discourse on childhood and human development became part of the Progressive project of social reform. Notions about the importance of shaping children to continue the advance of humanity upward on the ladder of social evolution became incorporated into new programs of education, such as kindergartens and nursery schools.

The shift within the still young field of scientific psychology toward a science of prediction and control gave new importance to psychology's potential as an instrument of social management. It was this potential that the new philanthropies focused on when their attention turned to childhood and human development.

Although the work of Hall and his students was arguably the beginning of developmental psychology in North America, along with the theorizing of James Mark Baldwin, it was not until after the end of World War I that psychologists in North America began consistent research programs on development. This was an important part of the institutionalization of developmental psychology between the world wars. The additional, and critical, component was the injection of funding from newly established philanthropic foundations interested in supporting systematic research on childhood in the service of improving civil society and the social order (Bulmer & Bulmer, 1981).

Philanthropy and scientific research on child development were spurred by the nursery school movement, which began in England in the early 1900s. The movement caught on in the United States after World War I. Unlike the movement in England, American nursery schools began as part of colleges and universities, typically in the then new home economics programs. Psychology and education faculty members were initially adjunctive to these schools. Within a few years, however, academics began to see the potential of these schools as a place to study children scientifically. The Iowa Child Welfare Station at the University of Iowa was an early site of such study, with psychologist Bird Baldwin as its director. At the Merrill-Palmer School in Detroit, America's best known woman psychologist, Helen Thompson Woolley (1874–1947), was head of research, while at the psycho-clinic of Yale Hall's student psychologist–physician Arnold Gesell (1880–1961) was in charge (Varga, in press). Teachers College at Columbia University in New York was also an important setting for the emergence of systematic research on children's development. Typically, the research was interdisciplinary in these first laboratory-based clinics and institutes, so that physical, psychological, and nutritional aspects of growth were investigated, along with home care influences.

These efforts in the early 1920s provided a base for the expansion and then institutionalization of developmental psychology as a scientific subfield with academic psychology. The catalyst for both the expansion and institutionalization was the infusion of funds from private philanthropic foundations (Bulmer & Bulmer, 1981; Fisher, 1993; Kohler, 1991; Lomax, 1977). Beginning in the mid-1920s and continuing for the next 15–20 years, several new foundations (e.g., the Commonwealth Fund, the Rockefeller Foundation, and the Josiah Macy Jr. Foundation) provided significant funding, certainly far more than had ever been offered previously, for developmental research. The intent of the research funds often had an application rationale, such as to improve parent education. The funds supported a variety of initiatives, from fellowships for graduate study to direct support of laboratories, and included support for publishing. These were all crucial for creating the new field of developmental psychology (Kohler, 1987; Schlossman, 1981).

Perhaps the largest initiative came from one of the Rockefeller Foundation funds, the Laura Spelman Rockefeller Memorial (LSRM) (Bulmer & Bulmer, 1981). Psychologist Beardsley Ruml was the director of the memorial and in 1923 was given the task of spending $1 million of the funds yearly to benefit children. Social scientist Lawrence K. Frank was given the task of developing a plan to implement the program. Frank's plan focused on building a knowledge base about children through research. The practical result was the allocation of funds to establish independent research institutes at several universities across North America (Lomax, 1977; Pols, 1999).

With the funds, Teachers College at Columbia began the Child Development Institute and recruited Helen Thompson Woolley to become the director. While the Iowa Child Welfare Research Station was already well established, it received significant funds to supplement state support. New institutes were established in the next decade at the University of Toronto, University of Minnesota, and the University of California–Berkeley (Lomax, 1977; Smuts, 2006). It was at the Institute of Child Development at the University of Minnesota that Florence Goodenough (see Chapter 2) made her major contributions.

In an innovative move that was controversial at the time, the memorial required that the institutes be independent of existing academic departments, perhaps to prevent the diversion of funds to other purposes. This was an important safeguard, as research on children was not highly valued by academic psychologists, who were mostly male. Certainly, many of these male psychologists saw such work as women's work and did not want children around their laboratories.

An additional initiative supported by the LSRM was funds to establish a Committee on Child Development at the National Research Council in Washington, D.C. The committee was chaired by Robert S. Woodworth, then an experimental psychologist at Columbia University. Perhaps the most important function of the committee was the administration of a Fellows program. The fellowships provided crucial support for a number of graduate students to complete their doctorate in psychology, especially during the early years of the Great Depression (Smuts, 2006). Although the fellowships were open to both men and women, the recipients were mostly women. Several of these women went on to make highly significant contributions in both research and institutional leadership in developmental psychology.

Because knowledge dissemination was part of the mission of the Committee on Child Development, Woodworth and his colleagues were able to use funds from LSRM to host several conferences on child development, and these proved instrumental in institutionalizing the field. Out of these interdisciplinary conferences, one of the world's premier scientific organizations, the Society for Research in Child Development (SRCD), was created in 1933. The society then received funds from the General Education Board (Rockefeller Foundation) to initiate a new journal, *Child Development*, in 1935 (Smuts, 2006).

It was in this interwar period, then, that the field of scientific study of human development, focused first on children's development, became part of the landscape of American psychology. Although its greatest growth did not come for another two decades, these years were critical. Thus, the psychologists profiled in this volume provide the reader an opportunity to gain knowledge of the foundations of modern developmental psychology. These theorists and practitioners made contributions that continue to provide insight and inspiration today as developmental psychology grows as a science by and about the richness of the human experience.

REFERENCES

Baldwin, J. M. (1895). *Mental development in the child and the race*. New York: Macmillan. doi:10.1037/10003-000

Baldwin, J. M. (1902). *Social and ethical interpretations in mental development*. New York: Macmillan.

Bulmer, M., & Bulmer, J. (1981). Philanthropy and social science in the 1920s: Beardsley Ruml and the Laura Spelman Rockefeller Memorial, 1922–1929. *Minerva, 29,* 347–407. doi:10.1007/BF02192822.

Fisher, D. (1993). *Fundamental development of the social sciences: Rockefeller philanthropy and the Social Science Research Council.* Ann Arbor: University of Michigan Press.

Hall, G. S. (1904). *Adolescence: Its psychology and its relations to physiology, anthropology, sociology, sex, crime, religion and education* (2 vols.). New York: D. Appleton.

Kohler, R. E. (1987). Science, foundations, and American universities in the 1920s. *Osiris,* 2nd series, *3:* 135–164.

Kohler, R. E. (1991). *Partners in science: Foundations and natural scientists, 1900–1945.* Chicago: University of Chicago Press.

Lomax, E. (1977). The Laura Spelman Rockefeller Memorial: Some of its contributions to early research in child development. *Journal of the History of the Behavioral Sciences,* 13, 283–293. doi:10.1002/1520-6696(197707)13:3<283::AID-JHBS2300130309> 3.0.CO;2-J.

Noon, D. H. (2005). The evolution of beasts and babies: Recapitulation, instinct, and the early discourse on child development. *Journal of the History of Behavioral Sciences,* 41, 367–386. DOI 10.1002 /jhbs.20116.

O'Donnell, J. M. (1985). *The origins of behaviorism: American psychology, 1870–1920.* New York: New York University Press.

Pols, H. (1999). The world as laboratory: Strategies of field research developed by mental hygiene psychologists in Toronto, 1920–1940. In T. Richardson & D. Fisher (Eds.), *The development of the social sciences in the United States and Canada: The role of philanthropy* (pp. 115–142). Stamford, CT: Ablex.

Schlossman, S. L. (1981). Philanthropy and the gospel of child development. *History of Education Quarterly, 21,* 275–299. doi:10.2307/367699.

Smuts, A. B. (2006). *Science in the service of children, 1893–1935.* New Haven, CT: Yale University Press.

Varga, D. (in press). Look normal: The colonized child of developmental science. *History of Psychology, 14:* 137–157.

Editors

Wade E. Pickren is a professor and chair of psychology at Pace University in New York. He is the editor of *History of Psychology* and has served as historian of the American Psychological Association since 1998. He is a past president of the Society for the History of American Psychology (APA Division 26). He received his PhD in the history of psychology from the University of Florida. Wade is a widely respected author and editor of six books, numerous journal articles and book chapters, and has given conference presentations and invited talks on four continents. He is the coeditor of the book series Psychology in a Global Area.

Donald A. Dewsbury, coeditor and author of the chapter on John Paul Scott, is professor emeritus of psychology at the University of Florida. His PhD is from the University of Michigan and was followed by postdoctoral work with Frank Beach at the University of California, Berkeley. Through much of his career he has worked as a comparative psychologist, but in recent years his work has shifted to the history of psychology. He has served as the president of three APA divisions and the Animal Behavior Society. Dr. Dewsbury is the author or editor of 17 volumes, including *Comparative Animal Behavior, Comparative Psychology in the Twentieth Century, Evolving Perspectives on the History of Psychology,* and *Monkey Farm: A History of the Yerkes Laboratories of Primate Biology, 1930–1965.* He has also published over 360 articles and chapters.

Michael Wertheimer is professor emeritus at the University of Colorado at Boulder. He received his PhD in experimental psychology from Harvard University. He is coeditor of the first six volumes of the Portraits of Pioneers in Psychology series. Dr. Wertheimer is a past president of four APA divisions (general psychology, teaching of psychology, theoretical and philosophical psychology, and history of psychology) and the recipient of two national awards for the teaching of psychology. In 2000, APA's Division 26 presented him with a "lifetime achievement award for sustained, outstanding, and unusual contributions to the history of psychology."

Contributors

Bernard C. (Barney) Beins, author of the chapter on Jean Piaget, earned his PhD in experimental psychology from the City University of New York. He is currently a professor and chair of the Psychology Department at Ithaca College and formerly served as the director of pre-college and undergraduate programs at the American Psychological Association. Barney's professional interests include teaching by drawing connections between current psychological thought and historical theory and research and the scholarship of teaching and learning.

Regina Helena de Freitas Campos, author of the chapter on Helena Antipoff, earned her PhD at Stanford and is a professor of educational psychology at the Federal University of Minas Gerais (UFMG), Brazil. She established the Archives of the History of Brazilian Psychology at UFMG and is a member of the Work Group on the History of Psychology at the Brazilian Association for Research and Graduate Studies in Psychology.

Ben Harris, coauthor of the chapter on Arnold Gesell, is a professor of psychology and an affiliate professor of history at the University of New Hampshire. He works at the intersection of the history of psychology, history of medicine, and history of science. Ben's doctorate is in clinical psychology from Vanderbilt University and he has held fellowships in the history of science and medicine at the University of Pennsylvania and the University of Wisconsin, Madison. He is a former president of the Society for the History of Psychology and executive officer of the Cheiron Society.

Ann Johnson, author of the chapter on Florence L. Goodenough, earned her PhD in existential–phenomenological psychology from Duquesne University. She serves currently as the director of faculty development and a professor of psychology at the University of St. Thomas in St. Paul, Minnesota, where she teaches history and systems of psychology. Her research interests focus on second-generation women in the history of psychology (with Dr. Elizabeth Johnston) and the history of child psychology.

Elizabeth Johnston, author of the chapter on Lois Barclay Murphy, earned her PhD in Physiology from Oxford University and is currently a professor of psychology at Sarah Lawrence College. Her special interests include human perception of three-dimensional shape, binocular vision, and the perception of depth from motion. Elizabeth is the author of articles and book chapters on shape perception from stereopsis, sensorimotor integration, and combining depth information from different sources.

Edward K. Morris, author of the chapter on Sidney W. Bijou, earned his doctorate in psychology under Bijou's direction and the tutelage of William K. Redd at the University of Illinois. Since then, Edward has been a faculty member at the University of Kansas. His scholarly interests include the historical and conceptual foundations of behavior analysis, the field's relationships with biological and psychological sciences, and the possibilities of their integration. He was president of the Association for Behavior Analysis (ABA) and Division 25 of the American Psychological Association (APA), as well as the editor of *The Behavior Analyst* and two newsletters, *The Interbehaviorist* and *The Recorder*, the latter for Division 25. He is currently a fellow of ABA, APA, and the Association for Psychological Science.

Suzanne C. Ouellette, author of the chapter on Robert W. White, earned her PhD in psychology (personality processes and psychopathology) at the University of Chicago under the sponsorship of Eugene Gendlin and Salvatore R. Maddi. She also received an MA in theology from the Yale University Divinity School. Suzanne is currently on the faculty of the graduate school of the City University of New York within the Social/Personality, Environmental, and Developmental Psychology programs, and the Master of Arts in Liberal Studies (MALS) program. Her scholarly interests include the study of lives, narrative psychology, identity, and the necessary links between psychology and the arts and humanities.

Herbert L. Pick, Jr., author of the chapter on Eleanor Gibson, earned his PhD at Cornell University under the guidance of Richard Walk. He worked for Professors Walk and Gibson on investigation of perceptual learning. After a brief period at the University of Wisconsin, Herbert spent most of his career in the Institute of Child Development at the University of Minnesota focusing on perception and perceptual development. He has had a long-standing professional and intellectual interest in Soviet and Russian psychology. He has been able to make extended research visits there and to the Netherlands.

Alexandra Rutherford, author of the chapter on Mamie Phipps Clark, earned her PhD in history of psychology and clinical psychology at York University in Toronto under the direction of Ray Fancher. She is now an associate professor in the History and Theory of Psychology program at York. She is the author of *Beyond the Box: B. F. Skinner's Technology of Behavior From Laboratory to Life, 1950s–1970s* (University of Toronto Press, 2009) and coauthor with Wade Pickren of *A History of Modern Psychology in Context* (Wiley, 2010). Her current scholarship focuses on historical and contemporary issues in feminist psychology and she is the director of the Psychology's Feminist Voices project, see http://www.feministvoices.com.

M. M. Scott, author of the chapter on Roger Barker, is the Herman B. Wells Endowed Professor at Indiana University, and has taught human development, ecological psychology, and history of psychology for 35 years. She earned a PhD in psychology at Peabody College (now of Vanderbilt University). Her scholarly interests include theory of human development methods of oral history and other historical research methods.

John R. Snarey, author of the chapter on Lawrence Kohlberg, earned his doctorate in human development and psychology under the direction of Lawrence Kohlberg, with whom he worked for almost a decade. John is now a professor of human development and ethics at Emory University, where he teaches an annual graduate course on moral cognition, development, and education. John is a fellow of the American Psychological Association, a fellow of the American Educational Research Association, and a past president of the Association for Moral Education.

Jaan Valsiner, author of the chapter on Heinz Werner, is a cultural psychologist with a developmental axiomatic base that is brought to analyses of any psychological or social phenomena. Dr. Valsiner earned his PhD from Tartu Univeristy in 1976. He is the founding editor (1995) of the Sage journal *Culture & Psychology* and editor-in-chief of *Integrative Psychological and Behavioral Sciences*. In 1995 he was awarded the Alexander von Humboldt Prize for his interdisciplinary work on human development.

Fredric Weizmann, coauthor of the chapter on Arnold Gesell, is a senior scholar and professor emeritus in the psychology department at York University in Toronto. He received his PhD from The Ohio State University, specializing in clinical psychology, and then completed a postdoctoral research fellowship on infant cognitive development with J. McVicker Hunt at the University of Illinois. Before coming to York he taught at The Ohio State University, the University of Illinois, and Purdue University. His interests include the history of psychology and medicine as they pertain to child development and the history of eugenics and ideas of race.

William R. Woodward, author of the chapter on Charlotte Bühler, earned his MA under the direction of Julian Jaynes and his PhD at Princeton under the direction of George Rosen, the historian of public health. His biographical chapter on Jaynes appeared in *Reflections on the Dawn of Consciousness* (2006) is available through the Julian Jaynes Society website. Following a piece in *Integrative Psychology and Behavioral Science* (2007), he continues work on decolonialization. He has published on women's capacity building in the *Journal of Human Ontogenetics* (2009). His recent work on immigration and Russian women in psychology appeared in *History of Psychology* (2010). An article on Lotze's Gestalt metaphysics appears in *Idealistic Studies* (2010).

Anton Yasnitsky, author of the chapter on Lev Vygotsky, is currently a SSHRC postdoctoral fellow at York University in Toronto. Anton is primarily interested in the issues of integrative cultural and biosocial developmental science, specifically, the theory of cultural–historical development. These interests lead him to research on the social and intellectual history of Soviet, international and transnational psychology, the scientific legacy of the Vygotsky Circle, and application of cultural–historical psychology in the context of contemporary developmental and educational research. Anton served as a guest editor for a number of special issues of the *Journal of Russian and East European Psychology* as well as the Russian-language journal *Cultural–Historical Psychology*. Along with his collaborators (René van der Veer, Leiden University, and Michel Ferrari, University of Toronto) he is currently working on editing *The Cambridge Handbook of Cultural–Historical Psychology*.

1

Arnold Gesell: *The Maturationist*

FREDRIC WEIZMANN

York University

BEN HARRIS

University of New Hampshire

Arnold Gesell (1880–1961) was both a psychologist and a pediatrician. From the 1920s to the 1950s, his teaching and writing made him the foremost expert on parenting and child rearing until overtaken in popularity by his successor, Benjamin Spock. Although there is an institute that bears Gesell's name, his influence today comes not from his students or followers but rather from an idea that he popularized and embedded in the national psyche: the widespread belief that there is a timetable of child development, a set of age-related stages through which infants and children pass, with each stage being characterized by typical behaviors. Although others, most famously Sigmund Freud, had also proposed stage theories of child development, no one had documented or laid out the landmarks of development so precisely or so comprehensively. One still hears parents explain the behavior of their toddler by referring to "the terrible twos," or talk of a child "passing through a stage," and parents or professionals still speak of "developmental readiness" or "school readiness." These were ideas embodied in Gesell's books, which bore titles such as *The Mental Growth of the Preschool Child* (1925b) and *The Child From Five to Ten* (1977).

Figure 1.1   Arnold Gesell and infant. (Courtesy of Yale University, Harvey Cushing/John Hay Whitney Medical Library. With permission.)

1

SHAPED BY HIS FAMILY AND ENVIRONMENT

To write about this famous developmentalist, we begin by examining the development of his ideas, which were greatly influenced by his family, community, and schooling. Arnold Gesell was the oldest of five children, raised in a loving, tight-knit family. From his family, he developed the talents, work habits, and view of humankind that made him unique as a developmental theorist and researcher.

His father, Gerhard, had a photography business in Alma, Wisconsin, a Mississippi River town so small that it had only two streets. Gerhard documented the life of the town, its environs, and residents in studio portraits and outdoor photos. He pictured social clubs, individuals, and the working life of town and river. Arnold learned from him how to see adults and children *in context*, in settings that defined their lives and shaped their behavior. Looking at the artfully composed photographs by the father, one is struck by how much Arnold's theories put each child in a frame consisting of its age, family, and level of maturation.

The young Gesell also learned from his father humanitarian and republican values: As Arnold explained in a funeral oration in 1906, his father "hated all injustice, cruelty and oppression" (Gesell, 1906, p. 2). An orphan who had a "neglected and miserable childhood," the elder Gesell had come to the United States from Germany as a teenager and enlisted in the Union Army to defend the young republic (Gesell, 1906, p. 3). Having rejected the old world's reverence for monarchs, Arnold's father believed that Americans had begun to worship wealth as their new aristocracy. He believed, as did Arnold, that social solidarity and familial love should replace the love of material possessions.

While his father served as the family's patriarch, Arnold's mother, Christine, provided youthful energy and a desire for upward mobility. A former school teacher who married at age 18 (her husband was 35), she gave birth to Arnold 9 months later. Among her gifts to Arnold was a love of both learning and teaching. Always the teacher, she demonstrated that anything in life could be turned into a song, a poem, a school lesson, a play, or a family pageant, to be learned and taught—acted out—with a role for everyone.

In today's parlance, we would say that every day was full of teachable moments for the Gesell family (for a photo of the Gesell family, see Figure 1.2). And Arnold expressed this as an adult, publishing the architectural plans that he made for the bungalow he built in the desert when recovering from tuberculosis (Gesell, 1910). He also published a description of a baby basket he designed and built for train travel after his son was born. Unlike B. F. Skinner's account of his "Baby in a Box" (Skinner, 1945), Gesell's article was full of loving details about caring for the baby, both in and out of his invention (Gesell, 1911).

From parents and community, Arnold Gesell also learned to be upright, hard-working, and successful. His responsibilities were part of a vision in which both the individual and society were evolving. With the help of good habits and right living, humans were moving away from selfishness and ignorance toward socialist enlightenment. Consistent with this view, Arnold Gesell came to see each child as shaped by both heredity and environment, with habits and social influences intervening between the two. As Arnold's family nurtured him and served as a buffer between him and the outside world, so each child's abilities and habits would change how the world affected him or her. This philosophy, that maturation could be aided by a thoughtfully engineered environment, became one of Gesell's messages to the world. It also reflected his experience as a child and young adult and was part of the broader progressivism of his time. Unfortunately, as discussed in this chapter, it was a message that was often obscured and overshadowed in his writing and theorizing.

EDUCATION AND TRAINING

Born in 1880, Arnold was educated in Alma through high school. In his graduating class of six, he was charged with presenting a discussion of electricity. Characteristically inventive and independent, he designed and built a large electromagnet, connected it to a power source, turned it on, and lifted an iron into the air—suspending himself from its handle (Gesell, 1952; Program for Commencement, 1896).

To prepare for a career in education, Arnold enrolled in a nearby teachers' college, Stevens Point Normal School. There he combined his studies with captaining the second-string football team and editing the campus newspaper. Foreshadowing his success as a dispenser of advice based on rhetoric as much as on science, Gesell became a champion debater and speaker. In his second year he gave an oration on John Brown, the antislavery martyr. In it, one hears the voice of Gesell's father, rooting for the underdog and admiring Brown for battling the forces of oppression. According to Arnold, Brown's "deeds were neither actuated by revenge or ambition, nor tainted by vain or selfish desires, but prompted purely by a benevolent love for his oppressed fellow creatures to whose cries he opened his heart" (Gesell, 1898, p. 3).

The following year he won debate contests—first at home, next among all Wisconsin Normal Schools, and finally with winners from five Midwest states (Our Oratory, 1899). His oration, "The Spirit of Truth," expressed his optimism and belief in social evolution. "Although the past has been dark with despair," he noted, "the brighter era is fast coming, when man will develop, not by physical struggle, but by appeals to reason and to justice; not by catastrophe but by peaceful evolution" (Gesell, 1899, p. 77).

Two years of normal school courses qualified him to teach high school, which he did in the town of Stevens Point, Wisconsin, for 2 years. Next he enrolled at the University of Wisconsin–Madison, where he studied history with Frederick Jackson Turner and took courses in education and psychology. His senior thesis was historical, showing how colleges and universities developed in Wisconsin and Ohio—foreshadowing his career advocating school restructuring. At Madison he continued to excel as an orator and was elected president of the *Athenaean Debating Society*. Selected to deliver a commencement oration to a crowd of 2000, he spoke on the problem of child labor and its handling by British reformers.

At Wisconsin, the psychologist with the greatest influence on Gesell is someone ignored by biographers: Michael Vincent O'Shea, professor of education who taught Gesell while writing a text with the wonderfully progressivist title, *Education as Adjustment* (O'Shea, 1903). In O'Shea's classes, students were given the scientific evidence that supported the culturally popular ideas of progressive evolution and psychological recapitulationism.

Figure 1.2   Arnold Gesell Family Burlesque (Arnold Gesell with sword). Courtesy of the Wisconsin Historical Society [WHi 4597]. With permission.

In a course titled "Mental Development," Gesell was taught Herbert Spencer's (1862/1904) idea that both man and society were evolving upward. Although this was a distortion of Darwinian theory, it resonated with Gesell, who believed that socialism would arrive only after the birth of new generations of altruistic, group-minded individuals. At that time, the social order would no longer be based on selfishness. Greed would be replaced by the motives of cooperation and mutual aid.

Gesell also learned from O'Shea (1901) that childhood *recapitulates* the history of the human race. As he explained in an article assigned to students, "the child's body must … retrace the steps which have been taken in the creation of the human body throughout racial history; and we are coming to see that this is the method by which the Creator works in developing not only the corporeal part of man's nature but the mental as well" (O'Shea, 1901, p. 90). G. Stanley Hall, with whom Gesell did graduate work, was also a strong and influential propounder of this view.

Based upon this principle, Gesell's lifelong calling became observing, protecting, and guiding the child through the environment. As O'Shea explained, the job of the educator and psychologist is "helping [the child] along, more rapidly, aiding it to overcome obstacles along the way and preventing it from arrest of growth somewhere while en route" (O'Shea, 1901, p. 90). Upon such help depended the progress of the human race.

Gesell and G. Stanley Hall

Upon graduation, Gesell served as principal of Chippewa Falls High School for a year. He then won a fellowship to pursue a doctorate in education at Clark

University, studying with its president, G. Stanley Hall. As Gesell had learned from Professor O'Shea, Hall and his child study movement shared his own evolutionary view of human traits and emotions. Evolutionary theory provided the framework for Hall's thinking about development. In the late nineteenth century, the study of development was closely tied to evolutionary theory. (For a historical survey of the relationship between the study of embryological development and evolutionary theory, see Laubichler & Maienschein, 2007, especially Part I.) Embryologists studying biological development had documented the close resemblances among embryos of diverse species, relationships that provided key support for evolutionary theory. In an 1860 letter written to the American biologist Asa Grey, Darwin (1896, p. 131) wrote that embryological evidence provided "by far the strongest single class of facts in favor of" his theory. The growing popularity of evolutionary theory also coincided and overlapped with a general growth of interest in childhood development beginning in Europe during the last half of the nineteenth century.

As noted earlier, Hall was also a strong believer in recapitulationism. To prove that the developmental sequences through which the child and adolescent pass mirror the stages through which the human species and human civilization had passed, Hall's students used historical and observational data to show that lower instincts such as selfishness, fear of fire, and fear of water were replaced by higher ones as humans grew and societies became more advanced. At the highest level of development, one found a social order based on cooperation and mutual aid—similar to the utopias of American socialists, writings of the Russian anarchist Peter Kropotkin, and the teaching of several religious orders.

The idea of recapitulation itself fell out of favor after 1910 (e.g., Davidson, 1914; Gould, 1977; Rasmussen, 1991). In the post-1900 world of genetics and experimental embryology, there was little room for the idea that individual heredity and development were directly driven by the evolutionary history of the species. Gesell acknowledged and accepted these criticisms. In a tribute to his former teacher, Gesell (1925b, pp. 126–127) acknowledged that Hall "… exaggerated the doctrine of recapitulation." Gesell also went out of his way to deny explicitly the parallelism between the growth of culture and the growth of the individual espoused by Hall, stating that "such pretty parallelisms can nowhere be found except in the pages of a book" (Gesell & Ilg, 1943, p. 65).

Despite this difference, Gesell may be viewed as the inheritor of Hall's mantle. Hall had introduced the child study movement to the United States in the early 1880s, and it remained influential for the next quarter century (Siegel & White, 1982). The aim of this movement was to place knowledge about child development on a firm scientific basis and to use this knowledge to improve education and the welfare of children. Hall argued for the development of a scientific pedagogy built around child study and was a strong advocate for research in child development and education. Although not really a coherent movement, those associated with it were united in their conviction that empirical research provides a sound basis for achieving practical goals. The methods Hall and others used were not primarily based on experimentation but more on naturalistic methods including questionnaires, observations, journals, parental diaries, autobiographical accounts, physical measures, and other such data (Hulbert, 2003; Siegel & White, 1982; Smuts, 2008). Although he departed from Hall's recapitulation-based hereditarianism, Gesell continued to situate his developmental perspective in the context of evolutionary theory. Gesell's reliance on systematic observation, and his attempts to link empirical findings on child development to public policy also connect his work to Hall's.

In the spirit of Hall, Gesell wrote a dissertation on jealousy in animals and humans, viewed from a Darwinian perspective. In it, he offered a pedagogy of control for parents whose children showed an excess of the jealous instinct: "Develop in your children a robust spirit of self-worth…. Let them have a hobby … [as] a haven of consolation, when buffeted by rivalry … [so that they may] say after reflection, 'I am glad to be myself'" (Gesell, 1906, p. 487). This anticipated the mental hygiene movement, with its emphasis on a properly engineered environment for children.

Postdoctoral Explorations

In fall 1906, Gesell accepted a postdoctoral job that would seem odd today. He became a teacher at a boy's camp near Holderness, New Hampshire. Camp Asquam was a famous summer camp created by Winthrop Talbot, MD, in the 1880s. There, the sons of wealthy families were given a regimen of fresh air, sports, and outdoor culture. To Talbot, the benefits of this regimen could be seen and measured: in lung capacity, strength, and other developmental markers (Maynard, 1999). Hired to teach elementary school, Gesell joined the staff during an ill-fated attempt to run the camp year-round. Although he loved the outdoors, Gesell disparaged his boss's grandiose plans and disliked working there; he resigned in early 1907. Next, he moved to New York City and taught school at night from February to July 1907. Significantly, he lived at the East Side Settlement House, which provided health and social services to the urban poor (Harris, 1999).

What stunned Gesell in New York were the dreary, overcrowded slums. As he later explained to an audience of teachers in training, the contrast with rural New Hampshire could not be greater. On moving to New York, he wrote:

> It seemed that I was in another world. There was snow, but it was black, broken and rolled up in ugly clumps. No rest. Everywhere clangor, clanging, and pushing and hurrying. No mountains, unless you called those towering piles of steel and brick and mortar mountains. Everywhere people, people, people— on the sidewalks, in the street cars, descending into the bowels of the earth, for under my feet…. [h]umanity was being hurled north and south, at the rate of 40 miles in a pulsating monster. (Gesell, circa 1909)

Equally stunning to Gesell was the appearance, behavior, and sheer number of slum children:

> Have you ever entered a moldy old cellar infested—… uncanny sensation— the floor and every crevice in the wall is alive with vermin, and you wonder how so many creatures can thrive in such a sunless habitat. That was the sensation I had when I first entered [the slum]. It seems to swarm with these rats

of children. They go scampering across your path, block the sidewalk, fill the curbs, pour into the narrow streets, peering at you, out of windows above, creep up the fire escape, crawling behind garbage cans, clambering upon wagons and boxes, disappearing into hallways, hiding and chasing each other everywhere. Children everywhere, everywhere. (Gesell, circa 1909)

Despite the alien qualities of the poor, Gesell clung strongly to his meliorist environmentalism. Agreeing with progressivist photographer Jacob Riis, Gesell asserted that "defective nutrition lies at the basis of all forms of degeneracy. [The poor are] underclothed, underhoused, underfed" (Gesell, circa 1909). As a socialist, Gesell was outraged at the chasm between the living conditions for New York's rich and poor. What was needed was not a settlement house funded by the wealthy but a redistribution of wealth.[1]

Following his few months in New York, Gesell returned to college teaching in 1908, joining the faculty of Los Angeles State Normal School, where he was welcomed by Lewis Terman, a former classmate from Clark. (Terman later achieved fame through his development of the Stanford-Binet test, the first widely used standardized IQ test.) Soon Gesell met and married Beatrice Chandler, a fellow teacher with whom he coauthored a book, *The Normal Child and Primary Education* (Gesell & Gesell, 1912). Within a year, Arnold became interested in mentally retarded children and their place in the schools. He visited institutions that used intelligence tests to identify such children and began a lifelong friendship and collaboration with H. H. Goddard of the Vineland School in New Jersey (Harris, 1999).

The Turn to Medicine and to Yale

In 1909, Gesell decided that he needed a medical degree. Later in life, he presented his motives as scientific and altruistic: Medicine would help him know children better. Equally important, however, was his desire to be a leader in the new field of child hygiene. This had developed from the same impulse as campaigns for unadulterated milk, clean drinking water, and sanitary housing. Soon, the 20th century was declared "the century of the child" (Key & Franzos, 1909/2010; see also Richardson, 1989), and politicians joined public health authorities in a campaign for the future of the nation.

Gesell began his medical studies at his alma mater, the University of Wisconsin, in 1910. He then moved to Yale University in 1911 and received his MD in 1915. The lure of Yale was that it offered him an assistant professorship in its new Department of Education while he studied medicine. He was also given a room at a local pediatric clinic where he could screen children for psychological and educational problems. The work carried out at this "psycho-clinic" was a medicalized version of the work carried out by his friend Goddard at the Vineland School. Unlike Goddard, however, Gesell did not use psychological tests. Acting more like a teacher or pediatrician, he consulted with parents about the proper placement and treatment of their children (The Yale Psycho-Clinic, 1923).

Gesell's timing was perfect both in moving to medicine and in attending Yale. With the introduction of compulsory education, early 20th-century schools were overwhelmed by students who seemed uneducable. Connecticut had a reform-minded Board of Education, which pioneered the use of psychologists to help school systems cope with problem children. Thus, Gesell is credited with becoming the first school psychologist in the United States in 1915. Connecticut was also the birthplace of the mental hygiene movement, founded in 1908 to address the environmental causes of mental illness. (For a brief account of the origin and early years of the movement as seen through the work of one of its founders, Adolf Meyer, see Dreyer, 1976; for more extensive and critical accounts, see Horn, 1989; Richardson, 1989.) For reformers like Gesell, a psychologically supportive environment would reduce the incidence of mental illness, juvenile delinquency, school failure, and industrial conflict. To prevent the last of these ills, Gesell became a consultant to the management of a local rubber factors on how to manage mentally retarded workers.

Although Gesell's memoirs implied that his career developed naturally and without struggle, he was ambitious and skilled at acquiring status, influence, and advancement. In 1914, Lewis Terman engineered job offers for him from Stanford University and the State of California. With these offers in hand, Gesell induced Yale to appoint him full professor of child hygiene and the State of Connecticut to appoint him director of child hygiene.

In these positions, Gesell dealt with many children with various kinds of disabilities. Over the next few years he served on various commissions dealing with mental hygiene, "handicap," "deficiency," and "retardation" and made a number of influential policy recommendations. He encouraged the development of special education classes in the school system as well as special training for teachers dealing with exceptional children. He also worked to develop assessment tools to help identify and diagnose these children. Louise Bates Ames (1989, p. 17), Gesell's colleague and biographer, described Gesell's position on these issues as one that emphasized greater public responsibility in caring for and educating children with what would now be described as *special needs*. Like many progressives, in his earlier years Gesell had been an advocate of eugenic policies that targeted the "feeble-minded." By the early 1920s, however, his views had changed considerably. Gesell was now advocating that individuals with intellectual disabilities should not be kept in large institutions and should be integrated into the community to the extent possible (Weizmann, 2010). This was long before the policy of "normalizing" individuals with disabilities became generally accepted.

STUDYING THE NORMAL PRESCHOOL CHILD

During World War I, Gesell began conducting research on normal preschool children (a term generally credited to Gesell). This transformed his career and became the basis of the work for which he is best known. Even before the War, Gesell had argued that public hygiene programs focused on prevention and rooted in research on normal development should be implemented in schools. In 1919, Gesell recruited a small group of preschool children and began observing and charting their development at 10 different stages of growth from 6 months to 6 years of age. At the same time, he advocated that a nationwide network of nursery schools and kindergartens should be established employing experts in "child development," a biomedical version of child psychology. In his progressivist vision, such expertise would add social control to the chaotic school system and safeguard the mental health of the individual child.

As Gesell explained in *School and Society*, preschoolers needed to be placed under "medical oversight and educational observation" in kindergartens that would function as "a kind of Ellis Island" for elementary schools (Gesell, 1921, pp. 563, 559). Aligning himself with children's bureaus and illness prevention campaigns, Gesell warned that the malleability of the child's personality requires vigilance by both parents and teachers. "Mental hygiene, like charity, begins at home. But it does not end there," he cautioned. Preschools should educate parents in child rearing and offer children an individualized experience "to help strengthen the home and make up for its deficiencies" (Gesell, 1924).

Although his research population was small and ethnically narrow, Gesell increased the authority of his developmental norms by using motion pictures as illustrations. Inspired by Frank Gilbreth's time and motion studies, Gesell's film research began with helping to produce and direct a Pathé newsreel of the Yale clinic in 1923. Characteristically, he gained international fame as a filmmaker without acknowledging the preceding work of John B. Watson (Watson, 1923) or Myrtle McGraw (McGraw, 1935, 1939). From 1930 to 1948 selected babies and mothers were filmed while living in a photographic dome at Yale, creating a scientific version of the silent-era film *Baby's Day*.

These film records, plus observational reports from mothers, enabled Gesell to analyze the development of complex behavior and skills, to break them down into incremental steps, and to develop age norms related to the relevant developmental sequences. Initially, Gesell employed a sample of over 100 infants and young children. Over the years, he added to his sample size until it eventually included over 500. He focused on four areas: (1) motor development (e.g., postural adjustment, sitting, standing); (2) adaptive behavior (e.g., eye–hand coordination, reactions to objects); (3) language behavior (e.g., facial expression, babbling); and (4) personal-social behavior (e.g., toilet training, play, reactions to others). Gesell did not trust the psychometric methods employed in scoring intelligence tests and thus relied on qualitative judgments made by a clinical observer, not quantitative scores, to gauge a child's developmental level in each area. These judgments were combined (in ways that are somewhat unclear) to give an overall developmental age. Gesell assumed that these developmental sequences and the derived norms were representative of normal development, although all of the children studied were in fact White and middle class. These norms became the basis for the Gesell Behavior Tests and Developmental Schedules. Gesell and his associates continued to revise them over the years, culminating in Gesell's last work in the area, *Developmental Diagnosis* (Gesell & Armatruda, 1941). Gesell's students and associates continued to revise his tests even after his death in 1961.

Gesell's interest in mental testing was one he shared with his Clark colleagues and friends Terman and Goddard. Both were important figures in the history of intelligence testing. However, Gesell believed that conventional intelligence measures were too narrow. They measured intelligence in comparative terms, based only on how individuals did relative to other individuals, and also ignored some of the broader areas of adaptive behavior. Gesell (Gesell & Armatruda, 1941, pp. 114–16) was more interested in assessing developmental maturity, as indicated by the developmental level that individuals achieved in acquiring adaptive skills. He attempted to differentiate the scores obtained on his tests from those derived from intelligence tests by using the term developmental quotient (D.Q.) rather than IQ. However, the distinction was often ignored, and Gesell himself was not always clear in elaborating the difference (see Ames, 1989, chapter 9).

Although Gesell's reliance on clinical and qualitative measures provided inter- pretive flexibility, the sample of children that provided the data on which Gesell based his Developmental Schedules were limited and unrepresentative, and Gesell provided no statistical information about their reliability or validity of the Schedules. Despite improvements over the years, the statistical problems with the Schedules remained (e.g., Kaplan & Saccuzzo, 2009), and Gesell's tests are not widely used today. However, they did serve as an important foundation for the most widely used current measures of early development (Ames, 1989; Brooks & Weintraub, 1976).

GESELL AND WATSON

In his early popular writing, Gesell positioned himself between the heredi- tarian evolutionism of G. Stanley Hall—increasingly out of date—and the ultra-environmentalism of behaviorist John B. Watson. Because Watson's popular advice on child rearing competed with Gesell's in the 1920s, it is worth comparing them (for Watson's views of child rearing and the family, see Harris, 1984; for more on Watson generally, see Buckley, 1989). Methodologically, each man promised to supply behavioral norms that were lacking for infants and children. Using newborns from the Johns Hopkins University maternity ward, Watson began cataloging a nar- row slice of infant life: reflexes and emotional reactions. He also filmed his work to show to child study groups in a fund raising campaign (Harris, 1985). However, his firing by Johns Hopkins ended this research after 2 years. A popular author in the 1920s, Watson used rhetorical and photographic sleight of hand to disguise his lack of data (Watson, 1928b). Watson's ultra-environmentalism and fear of emotional involvement distorted his view of children and the family and resulted in advice that was antimaternal and affectively sterile. Its strength was its ability to catch the reader's attention by his irreverent view of the family and social institutions (e.g., Watson, 1928a). Religion crippled children by instilling fear, Watson said, and most mothers create dysfunctional adults by emotionally swaddling their children (Harris, 1984).

Gesell, by contrast, offered reassurance that parents could manage any ill effects of the environment. He did so using a mix of modern psychologi- cal concepts (classical conditioning) and pedagogical concepts from the nine- teenth century—such as character formation. Children's fears, he explained, are the result of learning, not inherited or the work of the devil. To reduce the child's vulnerability, he urged parents to "nourish the child's trustfulness in life" (Gesell, 1924, p. 16). If a fear takes hold, he explained, it cannot be driven out or cajoled away. Rather, it requires a combination of fortitude and fear-reducing experiences. Strengthen the child's spirit, he advised, by a regimen of mental health. Applying the ideas that mental hygienists brought back from WWI, he urged parents to "build up the morale of your child daily, beginning with his babyhood. He must meet pain, error, injustice, evil, all along the path to maturity, and his main business, when an adult, will be to meet them as a man" (Gesell, 1924, p. 82).

Turning to the child's personality, Gesell again mixed behaviorist concepts with the older psychology of William James and his peers. If a child became domineering or jealous or phobic, that "child should be and could be reconditioned … that is, given a new set of personality habits" (Gesell, 1925a, p. 16). Although Watson the behaviorist could have written that, Gesell added the reassurance of a maturationist and professor of child hygiene. And he did so with grace and benevolence:

> A child, even in infancy, must achieve his own health and strength of personality…. If [his habits] are wholesome, and if the child is stimulated by influences of encouragement and good cheer, he steadily acquires a trust in life and a confidence in himself, and escapes those corroding feelings of inferiority which lie at the basis of so many personality difficulties. (Gesell, 1925a, p. 86)

Although this was a familiar theme for Gesell, he could now include examples of developmental milestones to reassure parents that growth was proceeding. At 6 months, for example, the child begins to grasp objects, bang them, and manipulate them. "His numerous reactions are suffused and bound together by emotional attitudes. Personality is in the making" (Gesell, 1925b, p. 16).

GESELL'S MODEL OF DEVELOPMENT

While Gesell rejected recapitulation, he did rely on an embryological model of human maturation and growth. He was particularly influenced by the embryologist George Coghill (e.g., Gesell, 1933; Gesell & Armatruda, 1945). Coghill (1969) studied the development of the vertebrate nervous system, focusing on the relationship between neural growth and behavior in *Amblystoma*, a species of salamander. He found that the growth of neural structures precedes the development of the sensory neural pathways. Based on his interpretation of Coghill's work, Gesell concluded that motor behavior, such as swimming, depends on the maturation of the relevant neural structures and that behavioral functions do not play a major role in promoting that maturation. Gesell believed that there is a one-way relationship between structure and function; mind depends directly on and reflects the growth of the nervous system. This growth is inherent and lawful; it reflects maturational patterns that are the product of evolution (Gesell, 1933).

Not everyone agreed with Gesell's interpretation of Coghill's (1969) work. Myrtle McGraw, another prominent developmental researcher, for example, believed that Coghill's work was compatible with the idea that experience has a role in neural development and that the relationship between brain and behavior is reciprocal (Dalton, 1996, 2002). In contrast, Gesell believed that experience might influence but does not fundamentally shape or alter neural maturational process and that learning itself depends on the genetically controlled maturation of neural structures. (For a review of Coghill's work and its significance, see Oppenheim, 1978.) Gesell also incorporated Coghill's idea of *fore-reference*; that is, because of evolutionary selection, neural structures develop prior to the actual behaviors they govern. Congruent with this idea, Gesell believed that behavior is not rigid in its timing, and experience may determine when and to what extent given behaviors may occur. In addition, depending on the environment, behaviors and the corresponding neural structures develop for one set of adaptive purposes could be used for others; for example, the structures and behavioral patterns involved in swimming could be transferred to other kinds of motor behavior.

Following Coghill (1969), Gesell believed that it was the development of the organism as a whole that dominates; localized reflexes are a secondary development resulting from a process of neural differentiation. This view contrasted with the views of behaviorists who believed that reflexes are primary and that complicated behaviors result from the mechanical building up of these reflexes. Moreover, for Gesell the impact of environmental stimuli is not automatic but is mediated by and subordinate to existing neural structures, behavioral patterns, and the directionality inherent in the growth process. This fit with Gesell's belief that individuals have an "inborn tendency toward optimum development" (Gesell, 1928, p. 328), which serves as a buffer against deleterious environment influences. (Elsewhere, as noted already, Gesell had suggested that it is the parents who buffer the child from such influences.)

Another area that reflected Gesell's emphasis on maturation was his research on twins. Beginning in the early 1920s, Gesell started to investigate the resemblance between twins as a way of exploring problems of "heredity, development and education" (Gesell, 1922, cited in Ames, 1989, p. 91). In 1929, Gesell and his associates developed a method (Gesell, 1933; Gesell & Thompson, 1929) for teasing out the effects of teaching and added experience on development. One member of an identical twin pair would be given extra instruction in a motor skill (e.g., climbing stairs). The other twin received no such teaching. Generally speaking, while the extra instruction resulted in the temporary superiority of the trained twin in the relevant skills, this difference soon disappeared. These findings were taken to demonstrate that maturation mattered more than specific experiences in shaping development (Hilgard, 1998, pp. 552–555). Gesell & Thompson (1929) argued for the greater importance of maturation vis-à-vis training. There is no arguing with the emphasis on maturation in Gesell's theory. Although the infant has "great plasticity" and the ability to learn, even that ability is subject to "constitutional traits and tendencies, largely inborn," which "determine *how, what* and to some extent even *when* he will learn" (Gesell & Ilg, 1943, p. 40, italics in original). Gesell also emphasized the importance of individuality, noting that infants too are individuals and maintain their individuality as they grow even in the face of cultural forces pushing towards uniformity (Gesell & Ilg, 1943).

McGraw carried out a well-known study of twins (1935, 1939) similar to Gesell's, and her data were also widely interpreted as providing support for a maturational model. However, unlike Gesell, McGraw (Dalton, 1996, 2002; McGraw,

1935) did not believe that the early acquisition of motor skills could be explained by simple maturation. Nonetheless, she did not call attention to the differences between her interpretations and Gesell's at the time, and her differences with Gesell were ignored for many years (Dalton, 2002).

GESELL AS A CHILD CARE EXPERT

In 1925, Gesell published both an illustrative film record of his work, *The Mental Growth of the Pre-School Child,* and a book (discussed already) under the same title. It was this book that brought Gesell to a larger public audience. The American Library Association listed it as one of the 37 notable books of the year for the League of Nations Committee on International Intellectual Cooperation (Miles, 1964, p. 65). His films were also widely distributed, with showings sponsored by local groups and sometimes even shown in department stores (Hulbert, 2003, p. 158). His work attracted the attention of the Laura Spelman Rockefeller Memorial (LSRM—later absorbed by the larger Rockefeller Foundation), as well as other corporate and foundation supporters (for accounts, see, e.g., Harris, 1999; Hulbert, 2003, chapter 4; Miles, 1964). The LSRM, in large part influenced by Gesell's own laboratory at Yale, sponsored the establishment of a number of child development institutes, nurseries, and child guidance centers in the United States and Canada. It also provided a grant so that Gesell could move to and equip a much larger research facility at Yale. On the occasion of a major conference on childhood in New York City sponsored by the LSRM, the *New York Times* published (November 1, 1925) a feature article headlined *Rearing of Children Becoming a Science.* The article gave a prominent place to Gesell's work and to his institute at Yale but also highlighted the growing importance of scientific research on child-rearing practices, especially for the preschool child.

The article documented the increased influence that research on child development was having on parenting and linked these developments to broader social changes, such as increased urbanization and the emancipation of women. These changes increased societal interest in the welfare of individual children and, together with the advent of mass communication media, like radio and motion pictures, as well as magazines and newspapers, validated and amplified the role of the child-care expert.

From the 1920s on, Gesell was increasingly recognized as the preeminent expert in the field. Although the influence of behaviorism was growing, and Watson had published his book, the *Psychological Care of Infant and Child* in 1928, it was Gesell's book, *Infancy and Human Growth* (1928) that won the *Parents' Magazine* award "for outstanding contribution to child development published in 1928" (Hulbert, 2003, p. 120). Over the next decade-and-a-half Gesell published several books, including *Infant Behavior: Its Genesis and Growth* (Gesell & Thompson, 1934), and *An Atlas of Infant Behavior* (Gesell, Thompson, & Armatruda, 1934). He wrote numerous scientific and professional articles as well as many popular articles and columns for newspapers. He also appeared on the radio, broadcasting to national audiences.

In 1943, Gesell and Ilg published *Infant and Child in the Culture of Today,* the first of three books for parents. This was shortly followed by *The Child from*

Five from Ten (Gesell, 1977) and, a decade later, *Youth: The Years from Ten to Sixteen* (Gesell, Ilg, & Ames, 1956). It was the first two books, however, that gave Gesell his greatest popularity. As one commentator wrote (Smuts, 2008, p. 183), "Parents wanted to know what to expect of their children at different ages. Gesell told them." Gesell rejected both *laissez-faire* parenting and the kind of authoritarian parenting advocated by behaviorists like Watson and tried to find a middle ground between the two (Smuts, 2008, pp. 183–184).

In keeping with his emphasis on individuality, Gesell did warn parents (e.g., Gesell & Ilg, 1943, pp. 68–72) that children vary in their rates of development and that the norms were not to be taken as absolute. However, it is not surprising that while some parents may have been reassured by these norms, others were made anxious (Hulbert, 2003, p. 121; Smuts, 2008, Chapter 10). Long before the appearance of *Infant and Child in the Culture of Today*, the pediatrician Joseph Brennemann (1931) observed that in his experience with parents, infants were being "matched with Gesell with resulting gloom or elation" (Brennemann, 1931, p. 377). Even in Gesell's own writings, the "typical" tended to become the "desirable" and the abstraction a "biological reality" (Thelen & Adolph, 1992, p. 373).

In 1930, the Institute of Human Relations was founded at Yale under the aegis of the Rockefeller Foundation. The institute was interdisciplinary in nature; its membership consisted of a variety of social scientists, psychologists, and others from the human sciences and medicine. The aim of the institute was to discover and synthesize knowledge about human conduct and apply that knowledge to the solution of social problems and conflicts. Gesell's clinic, now renamed the Yale Clinic of Child Development, was moved into the institute, although it remained independently funded. The attempted collaborative model that the institute supported, however, never really succeeded, and for his part Gesell resisted any real integration (Morawski, 1986, p. 232) but continued his investigations into development independently of what was happening in the institute. Lawrence Frank, one of the major figures in the Rockefeller philanthropies and one of Gesell's major supporters, commented on his own disappointment that "Gesell refused to allow any others to participate and gave no encouragement for anyone to visit his nursery or to otherwise collaborate" (Frank, in Smuts, 2008, p. 320). (For more on the role of the Rockefeller Foundation focusing particularly on Frank's influence, see Bryson, 2002.)

In addition, Gesell was a strong critic of both psychoanalysis and learning theory, which were major influences on other researchers at the institute. Louise Bates Ames (1989, p. 292) later defended Gesell's role by quoting a reporter who noted that Gesell's Clinic was one of only two parts of the institute that had done work of real value. In fairness, the institute suffered from very basic problems in its conception and design (see Morawski, 1986), and Gesell's participation would not have solved these problems. Nonetheless, it does indicate Gesell's attitude toward those he considered outsiders.

By 1940, the institute's failure was acknowledged. It had lost much of its support and effectively went out of business. Gesell's clinic was then absorbed by the medical school. Gesell continued to direct the clinic for a few more years but was forced to step down in 1948 because of Yale's retirement policies. His successor, Milton

Senn, took the clinic in a new direction, much to the dismay of Gesell's remaining coworkers at Yale (and one assumes, Gesell himself; see Ames, 1989, chapter 26). Senn, a psychoanalytically trained pediatrician, thought the clinic's emphasis under Gesell was too narrowly focused on the maturation of the child from a biological perspective. Senn made the clinic into a broad, multidisciplinary, academically comprehensive institution, one that became an early center for the training of child psychiatrists. He also changed the name of the Yale Child Development Clinic to the Yale Child Study Center to reflect its expanded mandate. Some of Gesell's disgruntled colleagues then founded a new private institute, the Gesell Institute (Ames, 1989, Chapter 26), employing Gesell as a research consultant.

While Gesell continued to be active long after his retirement and remained an important figure, his fate at Yale reflected his larger loss of influence after World War II. In 1946, Benjamin Spock, who, like Senn was a psychoanalytically oriented pediatrician, published the first edition of *The Common Sense Book of Baby and Child Care* (for which Senn served as a consultant). Spock displaced Gesell as the reigning child care expert in the 1950s, and his book sold tens of millions of copies in multiple editions and translations over the years. There are ironies in Spock's success vis-à-vis Gesell. Spock himself relied on the stage model of growth popularized by Gesell, and he was influenced by Gesell's and Ilg's (1943) *Infant and Child in the Culture of Today*. While Spock became known for his advocacy of flexible parenting, it was actually Gesell among child-care experts who had first advocated flexible parenting. Spock continued in that tradition but placed it within a liberalized psychodynamic model. Although we cannot go into it more extensively here, part of the reason for Spock's success was due in part to the increasing popularity of psychoanalysis and to other deep cultural changes that took place during and after World War II. (For more on Spock, see Graebner, 1980; Hulbert, 2003, Chapter 2. For more on the history of psychoanalysis in America, see Hale, 1971, 1995).

GESELL'S AMBIGUOUS LEGACY

Gesell's major achievements include his pioneering investigations into early development, his advocacy of humane educational and social reforms to benefit children, his concern with children with disabilities, his advocacy of preventive mental health programs, and the dissemination of the findings of child-rearing research to a wide public audience. Gesell did more than any other figure, arguably including Jean Piaget, to root psychological development in biology in a painstaking, detailed, and concrete fashion. These and other achievements led Thelen and Adolph (1992, p. 368) to describe Gesell as a "giant in the field of developmental psychology."

Notwithstanding his achievements, his reputation in the field waned in the years following his retirement. Thelen and Adolph (1992) wrote that although Gesell's work continued to influence developmental psychology his influence was subtle and often unacknowledged. His approach seemed increasingly old-fashioned. Although the popularity of psychoanalysis began to decline and cognitive approaches encroached on the territory claimed by learning theory in the 1960s, Gesell continued to be unfashionable. He was out of step with the "cognitive revolution" and the new emphasis on cognitive development in children. In an important work that helped reintroduce Piaget's theorizing to North America and presented evidence for the role of early experience in cognitive development, J. McV. Hunt (1961), representing a widely held opinion, dismissed Gesell as a believer in predetermined development and compared Gesell's work unfavorably with what he considered Piaget's more interactional theory. Although Piaget can also be characterized as a maturationist, he provided a theory of cognitive development that incorporated a concrete and important role for experience.

Ironically, an important precursor for the compensatory education programs developed in the 1960s can be found in the kind of nursery school programs that Gesell himself had championed much earlier in the century. Despite his minimization of environmental contributions to development, it is easy to imagine that Gesell would have approved of the kind of supportive educational environment, concern for disadvantaged children, and search for effective educational techniques that characterized these efforts. This seeming contradiction between his concern about environmental supports for children and the neglect of environmental determinants in his views of development appears to exemplify the "unresolved tensions" that Thelen and Adolph (1992) argued can be found in his work. They suggested that these contradictions limited his influence among developmental psychologists. The central problem is that, while Gesell believed strongly in individuality and tacitly acknowledged the existence of multiple influences in development, he also viewed development as a gene driven universal maturational process. Perhaps the key to these contradictions may be Gesell's identification of individual differences and maturational processes with democratic and progressive values; he thought that young children's ability to resist environmental influences saves them "from being mere pawns to culture." It guaranteed their individuality and uniqueness. It was their way of saying to the world, "Lo, I too am here" (Gesell & Ilg, 1943, p. 41).

In the 1970s and 1980s there was a renewed emphasis on the role of biological and maturational factors in development. Although he never regained his former influence, his work began to be seen in a more positive light. As the psychologist and behavior-geneticist Sandra Scarr (1993) ruefully (if perhaps hyperbolically) exclaimed, "We traded Arnold Gesell for John Watson" (p. 1334). Yale even endowed a chair in his name at the Yale Study Center, and many developmental researchers now study maturational changes linked to biological processes.

When one looks beyond Gesell's explicit maturationism, one can also find evidence for interactional thinking in his writings. Cairns (1998) argued that Gesell did recognize the importance of the interrelationship between parent and child and at least implicitly acknowledged that maturation in the area of social development did involve interaction; there are certainly places (e.g., Gesell, 1928, p. 71) where Gesell does seem to recognize that growth comes about through interaction. As he wrote, "... We are led astray by an artificial dualism of heredity and environment, if it blinds us to the fact that growth is a continuous self-conditioning process, rather than a drama controlled, *ex machina*, by two forces" (Gesell, 1928, p. 357). Thelen and Adolph (1992) noted that at times Gesell's thinking and writing foreshadow current dynamic systems perspectives on development.

However, as Cairns (1998, p. 70) admitted, Gesell's potential psychobiological theory of social development was never developed and "remained in bare out-line form." While Gesell's was concerned with the environment of the child, his emphasis on maturation and on the boundaries that separate the child from his or her world are so strong that they obscure these other themes. As Thelen and Adolph (1992, p. 379) concluded:

> His devotion to maturation as the final cause was unwavering yet he acted as though the environment mattered, and his work contains threads of real pro-cess. He believed in the individuality of the child but chose the dictates of the genes over the whims of the environment.... He was committed to the welfare of children, but in his zeal to classify by age, children often come across as passive and lifeless. He left few acknowledged disciples, yet many today are working within his assumptions. What is not at issue, however, are Gesell's lasting contributions to the field of developmental psychology.

SUGGESTED READING

Gesell, A., & Ilg, F. (1943). *Infant and Child in the Culture of Today*. New York: Harper and Brothers.

This book was Gesell's most popular and best typifies his view of development and his writings for parents. *The Embryology of Behavior*, written with Catherine Amatruda and published in 1945, presents a more systematic and scholarly summary of his views of development. Louise Bates Ames's (1989) *Arnold Gesell: Themes of His Work* is a book-length account of Gesell's work. Ames was a close collaborator and a partisan defender of Gesell, which defines both the virtues and the limitations of the work.

REFERENCES

Ames, L. B. (1989). *Arnold Gesell: Themes of his work*. New York: Human Sciences Press.

Bergenn, V., Dalton, T. C., & Lipsitt, L. P. (1992). Myrtle McGraw: A growth scientist. *Developmental Psychology*, 28, 381–395. doi:10.1037/0012-1649.28.3.381

Brennemann, J. (1931). The menace of psychiatry. *American Journal of Diseases of Children*, 42, 376–402.

Brooks, J., & Weintraub, M. (1976). A history of infant intelligence testing. In M. Lewis (Ed.), *Origins of intelligence* (pp. 19–58). New York: Plenum.

Buckley, K. W. (1989). *Mechanical man: John Broadus Watson and the beginnings of behaviorism*. New York: Guilford.

Bryson, D. R. (2002). *Socializing the young: The role of foundations, 1923–1941*. Westport, CT: Bergin & Garvey.

Cairns, R. B. (1998). The making of developmental psychology. In R. M. Lerner (Ed.), *Handbook of child psychology. Vol. 1. Theoretical models of human development*, 5th ed. (pp. 25–106). New York: Wiley.

Coghill, G. E. (1969). *Anatomy and the problem of behavior*. New York: Macmillan. (Original work published in 1929.)

Dalton, T. C. (1996). Was McGraw a maturationist? *American Psychologist*, 51, 551–552. doi:10.1037/0003-066X.51.5.551

Dalton, T. C. (2002). Myrtle McGraw and the maturation controversy. In V. W. Bergenn & T. C. Dalton (Eds.), *The life cycle of psychological ideas*. Boulder, CO: Westview.

Darwin, C. (1860). Letter to Asa Gray, Sept. 10, 1860. In Francis Darwin (Ed.), *The life and letters of Charles Darwin*, Vol. II (p. 131). New York: Appleton, 1896.

Davidson, P. E. (1914). *The recapitulation theory and human infancy*. New York: Columbia University Teachers College.

Deater-Deckard K., & Cahill, K. (2006). Nature and nurture in early childhood. In K. McCartney & D. Phillips (Eds.), *Handbook of early childhood development* (pp. 106–125). Malden, MA: Blackwell. doi:10.1002/9780470757703.ch1

Dreyer, B. A. (1976). Adolf Meyer and mental hygiene: An ideal for public health. *American Journal of Public Health, 66*, 998–1003. doi:10.2105/AJPH.66.10.998

Gesell, A. L. (1898). John Brown, the Man. Arnold Gesell Papers, Box 149, folder "John Brown, 1898," Library of Congress, Washington, DC.

Gesell, A. L. (1899, April). The development of the spirit of truth. *Normal Pointer*, 75–77.

Gesell, A. L. (1906). Funeral Oration. Arnold Gesell Papers, Box 228, folder "Funeral Oration on Gerhard Gesell," Library of Congress, Washington, DC.

Gesell, A. (1906). Jealousy. *American Journal of Psychology*, 17, 437–496. doi:10.2307/1412347

Gesell, A. L. (circa 1909). Untitled talk to teachers at Los Angeles Normal School. Arnold Gesell Papers, Box 236, folder "Notebooks," Library of Congress, Washington, DC.

Gesell, A. L. (1910). A California bungalow treated in Japanese style. *Craftsman, 18*, 694–698.

Gesell, A. L. (1911, May). A baby traveler's outfit: If the baby must a journey go, make him comfortable. *Designer*, 56.

Gesell. A. (1921). Kindergarten control of school entrance. *School and Society*, 14, 559–561.

Gesell, A. (1924, May). Why children are afraid. *Delineator*, 16, 82.

Gesell, A. (1925a, April). Moulding your child's character. *Delineator*, 16, 86–87.

Gesell, A. (1925b). *The mental growth of the pre-school child: A psychological outline of normal development from birth to the sixth year, including a system of developmental diagnosis*. New York: Macmillan. doi:10.1037/11012-000

Gesell, A. (1928). *Infancy and human growth*. New York: Macmillan.

Gesell, A. (1933). Maturation and the patterning of behavior. In C. Murchiston (Ed.), *A handbook of child psychology* (2d ed. rev., pp. 209–235). Worcester, MA: Clark University Press. doi:10.1037/11552-004

Gesell, A. (1938). A half century of science and the American child. *Child Study*, 16, 35–37.

Gesell, A. (1948). *Studies in child development*. New York: Harper.

Gesell, A. (1952). Arnold Gesell. In E. C. Boring, *History of psychology in autobiography* (vol. 6, pp. 123–142). New York: Russell & Russell.

Gesell, A. (1977). *The child from five to ten* (rev. ed.) New York: Harper/Collins. (Original 1946 edition coauthored by Frances Ilg.)

Gesell, A., & Armatruda, C. S. (1941). *Developmental diagnosis: A manual of clinical methods and applications designed for the use of students and practitioners of medicine*. New York: Harper & Row.

Gesell, A., & Armatruda, C. S., (1945). *The embryology of behavior*. New York: Harper.

Gesell, A., & Gesell, B. C. (1912). *The normal child and primary education*. Boston: Ginn.

Gesell, A., & Ilg, F. L. (1943). *Infant and child in the culture of today*. New York: Harper.

Gesell, A., Ilg, F. L., & Ames, L. B. (1956). *Youth: The years from ten to thirteen*. New York: Harper.

Gesell, A., & Thompson, H. (1929). Learning and growth in identical twin infants. *Genetic Psychology Monographs*, 6, 1–124.

Gesell, A., & Thompson, H. (1934). *Infant behavior: Its genesis and growth*. New York: McGraw-Hill. doi:10.1037/11333-000

Gesell, A., Thompson, H., & Armatruda, C. S. (1934). *An atlas of infant behavior: Normative series*. New Haven, CT: Yale University Press.

Gould, S. J. (1977). *Ontogeny and phylogeny*. Cambridge, MA: Harvard University Press.

Graebner, W. (1980). The unstable world of Benjamin Spock: Social engineering in a democratic culture, 1917–1950. *Journal of American History, 67*, 612–629. doi:10.2307/1889870

Hale, N. G. (1971). *Freud and the Americans: The beginning of psychoanalysis in the United States, 1876–1971*. New York: Oxford University Press.

Hale, N. G. (1995). *The rise and crisis of psychoanalysis in the United States: Freud and the Americans*. New York: Oxford University Press.

Hall, G. S. (1883). The contents of children's minds on entering school. *Princeton Review*, 249–272.

Harris, B. (1984). "Give me a dozen healthy infants...": John B. Watson's popular advice on childrearing, women, and the family. In M. Lewin (Ed.), *In the shadow of the past: Psychology portrays the sexes* (pp. 126–154). New York: Columbia University Press.

Harris, B. (1985). The role of film in John B. Watson's developmental research program: Intellectual, disciplinary, and social influences. In G. Eckhardt, W. G. Bringmann, & L. Sprung (Eds.), *Contributions to a history of developmental psychology* (pp. 359–366). Berlin: Mouton.

Harris, B. (1999). Arnold Gesell. In J. A. Garraty & M. C. Carnes (Eds.), *American National Biography* (vol. 8, pp. 877–878). New York: Oxford University Press.

Horn, M. (1989). *Before it's too late: The child guidance movement in the United States, 1922–1945*. Philadelphia: Temple University Press.

Hulbert, A. (2003). *Raising America*. New York: Knopf.

Hunt, J. McV. (1961). *Intelligence and experience*. New York: Ronald Press.

Kaplan, R., & Saccuzzo, D. (1909). *Psychological testing: Principles, applications, and issues* (pp. 274–280). New York: Wadsworth.

Key, E. K. S., & Franzos, M. (1909/2010). *The century of the child*. Charleston, SC: Nabu.

Laubichler, M. D., & Maienschein, J. (2007). *From embryology to evo-devo: A history of developmental evolution*. Cambridge, MA: MIT Press.

Maynard, W. B. (1999). "An ideal life in the woods for boys." *Winterthur Portfolio, 34*, 1–29. doi:10.1086/496760

McGraw M. B. (1935). *Growth: A study of Johnny and Jimmy*. New York: Appleton-Century-Crofts.

McGraw, M. B. (1939). *The neuromuscular maturation of the human infant*. New York: Institute of Child Development.

Miles, W. R. (1964). *Arnold Lucius Gesell, 1880–1961: A biographical memoir*. Washington, DC: National Academy of Science, 55–96.

Morawski, J. G. (1986). Organizing knowledge and behavior at Yale's Institute of Human Relations. *Isis, 77*, 219–242.

Oppenheim, R. W. (1978). G. E. Coghill (1872–1941): Pioneer neuroembryologist and developmental psychobiologist. *Perspectives in Biology and Medicine, 22*, 45–64.

O'Shea, M. V. (1901, January 10). Highways of mental growth in childhood. *Independent*, 87–91.

O'Shea, M. V. (1903). *Education as adjustment; Educational theory viewed in the light of contemporary thought*. New York: Longmans, Green.

Our Oratory (1899). *Normal Pointer*, May–June, 115–120.

Program for Commencement. (1896). Arnold Gesell Papers, Box 1, folder "Arnold Gesell, 1896," Library of Congress, Washington, DC.

Rasmussen, N. (1991). The decline of recapitulationism in early twentieth century biology: Disciplinary conflict and consensus on the battleground of theory. *Journal of the History of Biology, 24*, 51–89. doi:10.1007/BF00130474

Richardson, R. (1989). *The century of the child: The mental hygiene movement and social policy in the United States and Canada*. Albany: State University of New York.

Scarr, S. (1993). Biological and cultural diversity: The legacy of Darwin for development. *Child Development*, 63, 1333–1353. doi:10.2307/1131538

Siegel, A. W., & White, S. H. (1982). The child study movement: Early growth and development of the symbolized child. In H. W. Reese (Ed.), *The child study movement. Advances in child development and behavior* (vol. 17, pp. 233–285). New York: Academic Press.

Smuts, A. B. (2006). *Science in the service of children: 1893–1935*. New Haven, CT: Yale University Press.

Skinner, B. F. (1945, October). Baby in a box. *Ladies Home Journal*, pp. 30–31, 135–138.

Spock, B. (1946). *The common sense book of baby and child care*. New York: Duell, Sloan and Pearce.

The Yale Psycho-Clinic (1923). Mimeographed statement of Dr. Gesell. Laura Spellman Rockefeller Memorial Fund Papers. Rockefeller Archive Center, Tarrytown, NY.

Thelen, E., & Adolph, K. E. (1992). Arnold L. Gesell: The paradox of nature and nurture. *Developmental Psychology*, 28, 368–380. doi:10.1037/0012-1649.28.3.368

Watson, J. B. (1919). *Psychology from the standpoint of a behaviorist*. Philadelphia: Lippinicott. doi:10.1037/10016-000

Watson, J. B. Writer/Director. (1923) *Experimental investigation of babies* [motion picture]. Chicago: C. H. Stoelting Company.

Watson, J. B. (1928a, December 22). It's your own fault. *Collier's*, pp. 29, 34.

Watson, J. B. (1928b). *Psychological care of infant and child*. New York: Norton.

Weizmann, F. (2010). From the "Village of a Thousand Souls" to "Race Crossing in Jamaica": Arnold Gesell, eugenics and child development. *Journal of the History of the Behavioral Sciences*, 46, 263–275. doi:10.1002/jhbs.20440

Williams, R. H. (2007). Film resources for a teacher education program. *Educational Technology Research and Development*. Boston: Springer. ISSN1042-1629 (Print) 1556-6501 (Online) Pages 147–224 Subject Collection Humanities, Social Sciences and Law Springer Link Date Thursday, October 4, 2007.

Zenderland, L. (1998). *Measuring minds: Henry Herbert Goddard and the origins of American intelligence testing*. New York: Cambridge University Press.

ENDNOTES

[1] Fifteen years later, Gesell's research on children would depend on the largess of the Laura Spellman Rockefeller Memorial Foundation, however. Although he never lost his sympathy for the underdog, Gesell would later join the academic and medical elite at Yale and in professional associations. In those environments, his goal became leading parents towards enlightenment and shaping public policy, not rabble rousing.

2

Florence L. Goodenough:
Developmental Pioneer,
Innovator, and Mentor

ANN JOHNSON
University of St. Thomas

In 1925 Florence Goodenough wrote from Minneapolis to her mentor, Lewis Terman, at Stanford: "I've been waiting until things became sufficiently shaped so that one could look at them before writing you about the new job, which, I must say in the beginning, promises to be mighty interesting" (Goodenough, 1925). The new job at the just-launched Minnesota Institute of Child Welfare proved to be both interesting and a perfect fit for Goodenough. As a teacher, researcher, and mentor at the Minnesota Institute,

she left a lasting imprint on the testing and child development fields, contributing multiple textbooks, innovative research methods, and a well-known intelligence test for children. She was one of the few women of her era to achieve the status of starred scientist in *American Men of Science,* an honor bestowed by professional peers. Her legacy is all the more impressive given the short span of her university career: She worked at the Institute for only 22 years, only 61 when forced to retire in 1947 due to illness.

Figure 2.1   Florence Goodenough. (Courtesy of the University of Minnesota Archives, University of Minnesota–Twin Cities. With permission.)

Born in 1886 in Honesdale, Pennsylvania, Goodenough was the youngest of eight children (Thompson, 1990; Wolf, 1980). According to her grandniece, Goodenough's parents encouraged all the children to pursue education or other endeavors (F. R. Webb, personal communication, August 6, 2010). She seemed to be unaffected by the "family claim" that limited professional mobility for so many early women professionals (Scarborough & Furumoto, 1987); her career would take her to New Jersey, New York, California, and Minnesota. Her early schooling was in Pennsylvania, where she completed a bachelor of pedagogy degree from the Millersville Normal School (what would now be called a teachers' college) in 1908. After a decade of teaching in Pennsylvania rural schools, she began teaching and conducting research in New Jersey public schools and at the well-known Vineland Training School (Wolf, 1980). Like so many psychologists of this era, she was drawn into the field at a time when psychology was extending its reach into educational areas, developing testing and diagnostic practices in clinics and schools, and engaging teachers in the work of research (see Zenderland, 1988). She served as director of research in the Rutherford and Perth Amboy, New Jersey, public schools (a position we would now call school psychologist) while completing advanced training at Columbia in 1920–21; she earned her master's degree there in 1921 with Leta Hollingworth as her official advisor. Goodenough's student and colleague Dale Harris would later recount about this period at Columbia: "She was a student of Thorndike, but an advisee of Leta Hollingworth. I remember her once saying that she saw Dr. Hollingworth just once during her entire year as a Master student and then for twenty minutes. This was when she submitted her thesis. This is independent study with a vengeance [sic]!" (Harris, 1961, p. 2). The two women stayed in contact, however, and Goodenough would confide in Hollingworth later, in 1939, while embroiled in a public controversy over IQ malleability (see Minton, 1984).

Goodenough praised Thorndike as a "great teacher": "'Look to the evidence' was his constant admonition. His courses were often strenuous but they were never dull" (Goodenough, 1950, p. 301). Edna Heidbreder overlapped with Goodenough; completing her PhD at Columbia in 1924, she described that program as "present[ing] a motley aspect" that combined "animal psychology, the psychology of tests and measurement, the various kinds of applied psychology, the orthodox and unorthodox varieties of experimental psychology, theoretical discussions of learning, of intelligence, of measurement" (Heidbreder, 1933, p. 298). Somehow, the disparate parts formed a workable coalition: "The different projects are not always harmonious; they jostle each other … but they all persist" (Heidbreder, 1933, p. 299). Goodenough would take away from her Columbia experience an appreciation for both the "orthodox and unorthodox varieties of experimental psychology" that would allow her to evolve into a major methodological innovator in the field of child psychology.

Goodenough's desire to pursue study of gifted children motivated her move to Stanford in 1921 to work with Lewis Terman (F. R. Webb, personal communication, August 6, 2010). Terman put her to work on his gifted children study; she served as chief field psychologist on the project for 1 year and chief research psychologist for 2 years, completing her PhD in 1924 (Thompson, 1990). Her thesis was not related to giftedness, however. During her years working in the New Jersey public schools she had begun collecting data on children's drawings, using them to develop a nonverbal test of intelligence for children.

THE DRAW-A-MAN TEST AND CONTRIBUTIONS TO TESTING

The result of her thesis work was the Goodenough Draw-a-Man Test, introduced in her 1926 book *Measurement of Intelligence by Drawings*. The test enjoyed significant popularity for many years and is still in use; intended for use with children aged 2 to 13, it was simple to administer—children were simply asked to produce a drawing of a man—and proved to possess strong reliability when correlated with standard IQ tests of the period (Thompson, 1990). "Drawing, to the child, is first of all a language, a form of expression," Goodenough noted; "he draws what he knows, rather than what he sees" (n.d., p. 1). Based on her own extensive data collection, Goodenough included numerous illustrations and detailed instructions for interpreting drawings. Never one to drop her guard when it came to issues of measurement, Goodenough continued to gather data investigating the test's validity and reliability and published an extensive report with Harris in 1950 (Goodenough & Harris, 1950). They worked together on a revision that included a drawing of a man, a woman, and self. Goodenough, who became almost entirely blind in the late 1940s, involved herself as much as possible in the work of modifying the scoring and analyzing of age trends for the revised test after her retirement but in the end insisted it should be published as Harris's own project (Harris, 1996). Harris completed and published this work after Goodenough's death (Harris, 1963).

Goodenough also made contributions to the construction of more traditional verbal measures of IQ for young children. While still new at the Minnesota Institute of Child Welfare, she took on a revision of the Kuhlman scale—a 1922 adaptation of the Binet-Simon scale for use with preschool children (Goodenough, 1928a). Confiding to Terman, "Just between us I am not altogether crazy about the Kuhlman revision" (Goodenough, 1925), she developed her own version of a preschool scale, adapting some of the Binet items (Goodenough, Foster, & Van Wagenen, 1932; Goodenough & Maurer, 1942). This combined work made her one of the major contributors to the intelligence testing movement of the 1930s and 1940s and secured her high standing in the field.

The early 1940s witnessed a surge of interest in projective tests for personality assessment and, while they were viewed with skepticism by most of her measurement-minded experimental colleagues, Goodenough defended their application – but with qualifications (Goodenough, 1949a). According to her student Theta Wolf, Goodenough overcame an initial aversion to projective techniques during World War II; serving in the Women's Army Corps, she developed a test for officer-selection purposes that incorporated projective elements (Wolf, 1980). It was this experience that led her to appreciate Alfred Binet's neglected contribution to projective methods as reported in his 1902 analysis of the personality characteristics of his two daughters (Goodenough, 1949a). Citing Binet's careful, rigorous cross-checking of findings and use of multiple measures, she argued that projective tests could be used in a way that conforms to high scientific standards. Goodenough's championing of Binet's qualitative work reveals a paradox in her approach to research. She was an insider in the mainstream world of scientific study of the child, which was becoming increasingly quantitative and experimental. She was faithful to her own hunches about methodology, however, and felt strongly that descriptive and qualitative methods could be both valid and useful. To make these approaches conform to the scientific norms of the time, Goodenough sometimes embedded her descriptions of them in acceptable, quantitative language. About Binet's qualitative study of his daughters' personalities, for example, she asserted with confidence: "All of the differences in the foregoing analyses would meet even the most rigid of modern requirements for 'statistical significance'" (1949b, p. 422). As Wolf (1973) noted, this remark was "undoubtedly a case of hyperbole" (p. 118). The contemporary reader may wonder about the infrequent appearance of critical perspective on experimental or statistical methods evident in Goodenough's writing, but professional norms shared by most mental testing experts of that era mandated robust faith in the efficacy of those methods to deliver purely objective results. Adherence to those norms was expected, and they were challenged only rarely (see Chapter 1 in this volume). In addition, the psychology and child welfare programs at the University of Minnesota—the home of dustbowl empiricism—were known for their emphasis on testing, measurement, and experimentation.

INNOVATIVE RESEARCH AT MINNESOTA'S INSTITUTE OF CHILD WELFARE

Goodenough's letter to Terman, quoted earlier, hints at the excitement surrounding the opening of the Minnesota Institute—one of five founded in the early 1920s with philanthropic funding. They were intended to be centers of research but also, importantly, sources of public guidance on child rearing; each was required to have an active parent education program (see Cravens, 1985; Schlossman, 1981). This dual mission was a good fit for the University of Minnesota, a land-grant university mandated to serve the state, but the psychology faculty members were tepid in their response to the parent education component; scientific work on childhood was still seen as generally unmanly at that time and parent education was women's work (Cahan, 1991; Hartup, Johnson, & Weinberg, 2001). John Anderson, a student of Robert Yerkes, was brought in to serve as institute director, and he recruited Goodenough to serve as chief research scientist. Having completed her PhD at age 38 in 1924 with Terman at Stanford, she took a job as chief psychologist at the Minneapolis Child Guidance Clinic. Accepting the Institute of Child Welfare (ICW) position of assistant professor in 1925, she initiated a remarkably productive set of research programs with graduate students, beginning more than 20 projects during the first year. Edna Heidbreder was a member of the psychology faculty at Minnesota from 1925 to 1934; she noted that women psychologists of that era were not generally thought to be productive researchers and then cited Goodenough as an exception: "When she came to Minnesota, she showed no signs whatsoever of abandoning her interests and activities in research. She calmly and cheerfully went on with it, quite as a matter of course, and she was so competent in it and so clearly engrossed in it, that others too took it as a matter of course, that her research was her central interest." She added, "I used to think that she and her job were made for each other" (Heidbreder, 1977, p. 35).

Heidbreder also commented on a quality that stands out in all of Goodenough's writing—untrammeled enthusiasm about the science of psychology: "She seemed to be quite untroubled by the doubts that assailed some psychologists about psychology. About whether the whole enterprise might not somehow have taken the wrong track. She seemed to believe wholeheartedly in the importance of her field" (Heidbreder, 1977, p. 35). Heidbreder continued, clarifying an approach to research that accounts for Goodenough's creativity as a methodological innovator: her belief "that for anyone interested in [psychology] the obvious course of action was to work in it with the best methods and techniques and instruments then available and to cope with their shortcomings by exercising one's ingenuity to the utmost" (1977, p. 35). Goodenough developed, for example, the data collection strategy that later became known as time sampling (Goodenough, 1928b) and was a pioneer in the use of event sampling in natural environments, which she employed in her landmark study, *Anger in Young Children* (1931).

This study is worth further attention. *Anger in Young Children* was the first published study of the emotional behaviors of young children using multiple subjects; previous work by Watson and Rayner (1920) and Mary Cover Jones (1924) focused on the training of emotional responses with single subjects in laboratory settings. Goodenough's goal was descriptive. To gather data on children's angry behaviors in natural settings, she trained mothers to fill out detailed observational record forms amounting to a qualitatively descriptive event sampling method. In addition to providing extensive demographic and personal family data, mothers used a standard form to record the time and place of a child's angry outburst, specifying its "immediate cause of provocation," classifying and describing the behaviors involved (e.g., motor vs. vocal), and finally documenting the maternal "methods of control" and outcome (Goodenough, 1931, pp. 8–9). With 45 child subjects ranging from infancy to age 7, Goodenough was able to document age trends in the expression of anger and identify typical situational causes of angry outbursts.

The study illustrates both Goodenough's commitment to parent education and her willingness to make risky choices as a scientist. Dale Harris (1961) noted, "She took the term 'child welfare' quite seriously. An impeccable scientist, she felt very strongly an obligation to return the results of scientific endeavor to the people [whose] efforts had contributed them – the parents and children who had served as subjects" (p. 2). She published regularly in *Parents' Magazine*, a major dissemination vehicle for the parent education movement and shared with other ICW staff members the task of delivering regular radio talks for parents on child-rearing topics. Scientific knowledge of childhood ought to be useful, in her view, and though she promoted experimental laboratory research enthusiastically (she coauthored *Experimental Child Study* with John Anderson in 1931), she never lost sight of the need for experimental data to be tethered to real-life experience. Toward that end she dedicated much of her energy to making home-based naturalistic study of the child feasible and rigorous.

Given this goal, employing mothers as observers and data collectors was a reasonable strategy and one that would have been endorsed by two of her mentors:

Terman used data from mothers in his longitudinal study on gifted children, and Thorndike was an early defender of collaborating scientifically with nonprofessionals (Clifford, 1968). Even so, this approach to research was becoming increasingly unpopular as the child development field became more professionalized. A telling exchange between Goodenough and Lawrence Frank, chief administrator of the national Parent Education program, shows that Goodenough had to defend her commitment to descriptive fieldwork. In a 1944 letter to Goodenough, Frank offered, "Some of us believe that it is questionable to undertake any more of the straight observational studies … since further observation of growth and development of children, suffering from all the sins of omission and commission of their parents, their teachers and others, doesn't seem to promise much of value" (Frank, 1944). Goodenough defended naturalistic studies, arguing that the facts gathered through observational research "are needed as reference points from which progress can be measured and the value or worthlessness of our attempts can be judged" (Goodenough, 1944c).

IQ Testing Controversy

Her views on methodology were sometimes unorthodox, but when it came to questions surrounding IQ debates she was firmly in the scientific mainstream, at least initially. It was her status as an intelligence testing expert and connection to Lewis Terman that drew Goodenough into a public controversy over the malleability of children's IQ scores in the late 1930s and early 1940s. When a research team from the Iowa Child Research Station headed by Beth Wellman and George Stoddard began reporting marked improvement in IQ outcomes for children exposed to enhanced preschool experience in the late 1930s, Terman was outraged. A strong proponent of the "nature" side of the nature–nurture controversy regarding IQ, he promoted the view that IQ scores gleaned early in life reflect inborn potential and so could accurately predict intellectual performance later. This view was widely shared in the 1920s and 1930s and was used to justify widespread use of testing for school tracking and vocational planning purposes (see Guthrie, 2004; Minton, 1984, 1988). Goodenough's early work on intelligence in children and her familiarity with Terman's research led her to adopt his conclusions about IQ immutability, so it was easy for Terman to recruit her as an ally in his efforts to refute the Iowa studies.

The Terman–Goodenough critique of the Iowa findings hinged on methodology and data analysis. They argued that the positive findings of the Iowa group had been purchased only through methodological sloppiness; Goodenough published a critique titled "Look to the Evidence!" (1939b), reviving the slogan of her old mentor, Thorndike. These were harsh charges and proved to be especially painful for Wellman. At that time, the professional testing establishment was mainly on the side of IQ constancy, so Terman and Goodenough played to a sympathetic audience. The battle between the two camps was enacted publicly in various publications and conference presentations, but also privately in correspondence, and the heated disagreements permanently damaged a previously friendly relationship between Goodenough and Wellman. Both privately and publicly, Goodenough was blunt in her repudiation of the Iowa claims. Yet in a letter to Leta Hollingworth she expressed

sincere concern for the impact of the controversy on Wellman: "I am really quite concerned about Beth Wellman…. Terman thinks that she has deliberately attempted to
present her data in a way calculated to deceive the reader. I cannot agree with him
in this. I have known Beth very intimately for a number of years, and I am personally
entirely convinced of her sincerity. What has happened is, I am confident, that she
has deceived herself. I have told Terman that I think the situation is entirely compa-
rable with that of a religious fanatic who hears the wings of angels in every rustle of
the dish towels on the family clothes line" (Goodenough, 1939a).

She was persistent in her criticism of the methods and interpretations of
data coming from the Iowa group, writing to Terman in 1940, "Next week I am
to go to Chicago for one more discussion on the sins of our neighbors at Iowa"
(Goodenough, 1940a), but she eventually revised her views of IQ immutability.
Examining data from the Minnesota Preschool Scale (Goodenough & Maurer,
1942), she concluded that preschool scores failed to predict with consistency later
IQ performance, conceding the likelihood of IQ changes and malleability.

As Thompson (1990) points out, she was equally open to changing her views
on the question of innate intelligence differences separating cultural and ethnic
groups. Many have documented how racial bias embedded in test construction and
application led to a variety of discriminatory practices affecting children of color
and limiting their access to educational opportunities during those early years of
IQ testing. As Guthrie (2004) summarized, "Sadly, in the United States, the los-
ers in the testing world were Black children who struggled to meet a[n] unreal-
istic standard. They were excluded—victims of poor schools and legalized racial
segregation" (p. 69). Native American and Hispanic children also were subject to
tracking systems and biased labeling practices. Lewis Terman was one of the chief
proponents of the belief in innate, race-based differences in IQ and educability
and Goodenough's training took place within that Zeitgeist. Yet she reversed herself in 1950, writing about her own Draw-a-Man test, "the naive assumption that
the mere freedom from verbal requirements renders a test equally suitable for all
groups is no longer tenable" (Goodenough & Harris, 1950, p. 399), and attached a
footnote that reads: "The early study by Goodenough … which reports the differences in standing on the Draw-a-Man Test by the children of immigrants to the
United States from various European countries is certainly no exception to this
rule. The writer hereby apologizes for it!" (p. 399).

The Best Mentor in the Country

Goodenough was known as a remarkable teacher and her students remember her
fondly. Recalled as enthusiastic and articulate in the classroom, she would sometimes hold seminar classes at her Minneapolis apartment, entertaining students
with her collection of Gilbert and Sullivan records (Templin, n.d.). According
to Dale Harris (1961), she tore up her lecture notes every 3 years to ensure that
they were fresh and timely. Harris landed at the Minnesota ICW because Lewis
Terman advised him to pursue graduate work there and, in particular, to seek out
Goodenough: "If I was interested in child psychology … [Terman advised] she was
the best mentor in the country!" (Harris, 1996, p. 89). Her students' recollections

are filled with admiration. Leona Tyler (1978) called her "one of psychology's great women" (p. 293), even while acknowledging her somewhat frightening reputation as an exacting research advisor. Harris (1961) recounted that, in the early years of the institute, "she was a terror to the graduate students! … She was exceedingly intolerant of laziness, carelessness, and lack of intellectual acuity," but in her later years she became "more mellow and gentle" (p. 3). Theta Wolf (n.d.) described her as "continuously supportive of serious students" (p. 4), and correspondence between the two of them while Wolf was completing her PhD thesis confirms Goodenough's application of stringent standards and sometimes blunt communication style.

Commenting on a section of Wolf's study that summarized case study data, Goodenough complained, for example, "To be frank, your accounts bore me almost to tears" (Goodenough, 1936a). After tearing apart her descriptions she offered, "This is the way I should do it" and laid out her suggestions for reorganization. Reviewing the subsequent draft, Goodenough (1936b) kept pushing for more changes: "I wish I could be more complimentary," she wrote. "Really I do not want to seem so critical but I have served on too many thesis committees not to know how material of this sort is likely to be received." Finally, Wolf (1936) sent her mentor a new version with a note that began, "Dear Miss Goodenough: I have revised everything." Goodenough's (1936d) response to this draft was finally positive: "Dear Theta: Now I like it. In my opinion you've done a corking job; one of the best, if not the best that has appeared." She could be scathing in her criticism, but Wolf (1980) also recalled her as "pixielike … a delightful companion who shared her fondness for music, nature study, and photography" (p. 286).

Correspondence with Wolf reveals another interesting aspect of Goodenough's mentoring influence. The newly emerging field of child study was an attractive destination for women who wanted to pursue psychology; the study of children was consistent with gender roles, and scholarship funds aimed at increasing access to graduate schooling for women made it possible for women to receive training at the various Institutes of Child Welfare around the country. The vast majority of Goodenough's advisees were women, and many of them went on to establish highly successful careers (e.g., Theta Wolf, Dorothea McCarthy, Marian Radke Yarrow). Goodenough never married, though she was very close to several nieces and nephews and two of them lived with her during their college years. But many of her students married and became working mothers—in an era when doing so still aroused suspicion and employers could legally discriminate against them. Goodenough supported her students' efforts to combine work and family and, in correspondence, encouraged them to persist toward their professional goals and to combine their parenting experiences with their training in ways that would benefit the field of child study. She clearly delighted in hearing about her students' offspring, her "professional grandchildren" (1940b), and encouraged students to bend the rigid gender roles of the time to equalize child care arrangements, permitting them to accomplish their goals. During the final phases of writing her thesis, Theta Wolf was pregnant with her son, whom Goodenough christened "the little Wolf." When Wolf expressed her concerns about trying to respond to all her domestic demands and complete the thesis before her child arrived, Goodenough counseled her: "Of course I understand the difficulties that you are having with the time limit that is so inexorably set by having a little Wolf on the door-step.... All that I suggest is that you take things as easily as you can, curtail other activities to the lowest possible minimum (it won't hurt your husband or your friends to be neglected a little for a time) and center your activities upon seeing this thing through" (Goodenough, 1936c). When another advisee, Russell Smart, announced his engagement to a fellow student and mentioned that she planned to continue her professional life after marriage, Goodenough (1940b) responded approvingly:

> You know so well what my ideas about what the intelligent woman should do after marriage are that I need not tell you how much I approve of your plans for a joint professional life. And you know as well as I that it may not be the easiest thing in the world for you to carry out your plans without some type of adjustment. Nevertheless, particularly since you are both in agreement as to what you want, you have unquestionably taken the first step toward getting it.

Counseling "adjustment" in gender roles to facilitate a "joint professional life" was quite progressive in 1940. To do so publicly would have exposed Goodenough to censure from her male peers. But Goodenough was practical and wanted to secure a place for women in the field. Though women were entering psychology in large numbers—constituting one-third of the membership of the American Psychological Association (APA) by 1950 (Mitchell, 1951)—employment options for women were still limited, particularly in academic jobs, and many women ended up leaving the field after earning the PhD. There was concern in some quarters about this trend; instead of examining structural or economic reasons for this phenomenon, the fault was placed on the women themselves: they were framed as wasting their training by electing to pursue marriage and motherhood. It must have been disheartening for Goodenough when male colleagues like John Anderson suggested that women graduate students be tracked into applied positions, since the job opportunities in academia were limited and should go to men, who were less likely to leave the field (Napoli, 1981).

Goodenough also showed concern about the dropout rate among women, but her remedy was to encourage her students to use their parenting experiences, to meld them with their scientific training and produce educational parenting books that would integrate the latest scientific knowledge of development. She made this proposal to Russell and Mollie Smart (who took her up on it and authored a series of books on parenting) and, according to Wolf, suggested the project to a number of her former students who were married and mothers: "Her words made the project an important undertaking to the young woman who felt that she was fulfilling the expectations of her specialized training in child development!" (Wolf, 1978). Both Wolf and Dorothea McCarthy, another student of Goodenough's, achieved full professor status while combining work and motherhood; it was rarely discussed publicly at the time, but these women opened doors for the next generation, quietly rewriting the gender code in academic psychology to admit married women and mothers into the professorial ranks. Goodenough's encouragement erased the either–or quality of the choices facing those early working mothers and undoubtedly helped to counter the censure they endured.

GOODENOUGH AND THE NATIONAL
COUNCIL OF WOMEN PSYCHOLOGISTS

Goodenough's support of her women students was unambiguous, but her relationship to organized feminism was complex. When a group of women psychologists organized in 1941 to form an organization to contribute to the war effort (a similar group had been formed earlier by prominent male psychologists who barred women from participating), they tapped her for the presidency (see Capshew & Laszlo, 1986; Carrington, 1952; Johnson & Johnston, 2010). It is likely that her status as one of the few women with a high-level university position, and her close alliances with several prominent men in the field made her an attractive candidate; they would be harder to dismiss with Goodenough at the helm.

Goodenough accepted the post reluctantly. She was 56 when she became National Center for Women and Policing (NCWP) president; coming of age professionally in the 1920s, she was shaped by the norms governing entry of women into the professions summarized by Cott (1987): to succeed as professionals, women were expected to "leave behind the sex loyalty that was a prerequisite for feminism" (p. 238) and to align themselves instead with their male peers. Goodenough's correspondence with her male colleagues bears this out, and she was critical of efforts to organize on the basis of gender, insisting, "I am a psychologist, not a *woman* psychologist" (Stevens & Gardner, 1982, p. 195). At the same time, Goodenough used her leadership position to think strategically about how best to secure successful careers for women during the volatile, postwar years when workplace gender roles and expectations were being renegotiated. Recognizing that women held a majority of the professional psychology positions in schools, clinics, and guidance centers, Goodenough capitalized on the still active doctrine of separate spheres in the 1940s, arguing that women could reasonably make use of their "assets" as women by claiming those jobs. "Logically it might be argued," she wrote to an NCWP colleague, "that if women's place is in the home, then women psychologists may be better suited than are men to solve problems related to the home" (Goodenough, 1944b).

Having benefited in her own career from the meritocracy norms endorsed by most women and men of her professional group, she freely imposed them on other women. In a 1944 article on postwar opportunities for women psychologists, she exhorted female colleagues to seek professional work strategically, avoiding positions that might be deemed socially as unfit for women (like counseling male war veterans) and focusing on producing original scientific work. At the same time she castigated those who cited gender discrimination as a reason for women's lower status in the field:

> If opportunities for women are to expand the impelling force must come from within. Women must train themselves to see beyond the little routine problem with which they have been preoccupied in the past and concern themselves with larger issues. And they must cease to use sex discrimination as an excuse for their failure to do this. There is not, and never has been, any sex barrier to thought. (Goodenough, 1944a, p. 708).

Goodenough's formulation was widely shared by many psychologists at the time, both women and men (see, e.g., Boring, 1951). It would be 20 years before structural critiques of professional gender discrimination gained a foothold in the culture and could be used by second-wave feminist psychologists to force change within psychology.

Goodenough served as president of NCWP for a year, helping the group navigate through a difficult beginning and all the time hoping that it would be "disbanded automatically on the day peace is signed" (Goodenough, 1942, p. 2). In spite of her efforts toward that end, the council persisted after the war. Some of the members had become interested in international issues, particularly the postwar status of women and children abroad, and in 1946 "it was decided to reorganize the group into the International Council of Women Psychologists [ICWP] in order 'to promote psychology as a science and as a profession, particularly with respect to the contribution of women throughout the world'" (Carrington, 1952, p. 100). Eventually members voted to drop the word *women* from the group's name and mission, and it became, in 1959, the International Council of Psychologists. Goodenough declined to participate during the ICWP years, but she was honored by the group in 1951 as part of a 10-year anniversary celebration. Publishing a short history, members dedicated it to Goodenough, citing her many contributions and outlining her legacy: "To her many of us owe our initiation into the excitement of research design and the solid satisfaction which comes from the arduous completion of the tasks. Her inspired exploration of many diverse fields and new problems will encourage others in the years ahead to follow up her trails and blaze new ones as these are needed. This is scientific immortality" (NCWP Tenth Anniversary Handbook, 1952). Though she would have resisted being cast as a role model for women psychologists, she enlarged opportunities for women in the field simply by her example—and by her many efforts to place women students in meaningful careers. In her behind-the-scenes promotion of altered gender roles to encourage women's scientific careers she was a pioneer, preparing the ground for the later, more revolutionary developments of the 1970s.

ILLNESS AND RETIREMENT

Goodenough became a full professor at the University of Minnesota in 1931 and earned her star in *American Men of Science* in 1936. But in the late 1930s she contracted an obscure illness that some believed initiated a premature aging process; photographs show her hair to be completely white while she was still in her 50s. Her hearing and vision deteriorated progressively; diabetes was likely part of the problem (Wolf, 1980). For someone so driven and committed to her work, losing her eyesight, in particular, must have been devastating. In addition, Goodenough was an enthusiastic photographer and had constructed a darkroom in the basement of her Minneapolis apartment building. During the early 1940s, Minnesota colleagues began noticing Goodenough's increasing difficulty in carrying out teaching activities. Trying to carry on, in 1946 she accepted the presidency of the Society for Research in Child Development; during the annual business meeting she had difficulty hearing and her friend's who were present grew concerned. In early 1947 she took a leave of absence and underwent more medical treatment.

Forced to retire in 1947, she moved to New Hampshire to live with her sister and learned Braille; she built a "magnificent study, the first she had ever possessed in her life" and moved her enormous collection of books and periodicals there (Harris, 1961). She maintained a high level of productivity for the next 10 years, continuing her work on the Draw-a-Man test with Harris and producing three of her most notable books: *Mental Testing* (1949b); *Exceptional Children* (1956) (assisted by her niece, Lois M. Rynkiewicz); and the third edition of her popular text, *Developmental Psychology* – co-authored by former student Leona Tyler (1959). In 1956, nearing 70, she made a round-the-world trip with her elderly sister, which included stops in Australia and Manila to visit friends and family (Moore, 1978). While visiting another sister in Florida, she suffered a stroke and died in 1959. Some of her library remained in Minneapolis and is now housed in the Florence L. Goodenough Library at the University of Minnesota Institute of Child Development.

Writing of psychology in 1945, Goodenough notes, "In the early stages of any science, a great deal of spadework has to be done in the way of describing, arranging, and classifying the material with which it deals" (1945, p. 20). Goodenough felt keenly the promises of mental testing: The observation and classification of children would usher in a new age of improved child rearing and enhanced developmental outcomes for children. The early child experts took up residence in the home and the school room; they would, Goodenough was confident, "discover the special aptitudes and weaknesses of the children in order that their training may be more wisely directed" (1934, p. 20). That dream has given way to a more tempered view of what scientific child study can offer, but Goodenough's quest continues into the present, importing both the positive potential embedded in scientific representation of the child and its inherent dangers. In this regard, Goodenough's work and life, her faith in science, and the stands she took and sometimes reversed make her an important and compelling historical figure.

SUGGESTED READINGS

Goodenough, F. L. (1949). *Mental testing: Its history, principles, and applications.* New York: Rinehart.

> Written at the end of Goodenough's career, *Mental Testing* is both a sustained tribute to Alfred Binet and a thorough history delineating the expansion and diversifying of testing practices in the United States from their advent and through the 1940s. Always practical, Goodenough explained her motive in writing the book was to assist those trained to make use of tests in clinical, school or institutional settings, to rectify "a basic defect in the scientific background of a large number of persons at present engaged in testing," that is, "their lack of understanding of the theoretical principles" grounding their practice (p. viii). There is thorough coverage of IQ testing, but she also describes developments in aptitude, developmental (motor skill), personality, and vocational tests and includes a chapter on projective tests. Goodenough's discussion

of IQ constancy and comparisons of ethnic and cultural groups reflects the shifting ideas on those topics in the 1940s, while her evaluation of research on sex differences remains firmly planted in uncontested midcentury gender norms.

Goodenough, F.L. (1931). *Anger in young children.* Minneapolis: University of Minnesota Press.

An overlooked classic in the history of developmental psychology, Goodenough's study represents the first large-scale empirical study of emotional behavior in young children. We would now call it a descriptive field study, but her approach generated plenty of quantitative data intended to "throw some light on the frequency, duration, causes, and methods of handling anger outbursts among children in the home" (p. 4). Goodenough trained mothers of 45 children between 7 months and 7 years of age to fill out detailed observation records allowing her to summarize age trends and gender differences and offer some conclusions regarding the efficacy of mothers' response strategies (or "methods of control"). Goodenough's defense of the adequacy of mothers as research participants in the introductory chapter hints at the scientific politics of the time: The trend in child psychology was toward controlled laboratory studies, and many scorned involvement of amateurs in the research process. Some reviewers raised questions about Goodenough's reliance on nonscientists to document observations, but she defended the practice, which allowed otherwise inaccessible data from home settings to be claimed for scientific purposes.

REFERENCES

Boring, E. G. (1951). The woman problem. *American Psychologist, 6,* 679–682. doi:10.1037/h0061181

Cahan, E. (1991). Science, practice, and gender roles in early American child psychology. In F. S. Kessel, M. H. Bornstein, & A. J. Sameroff (Eds.), *Contemporary constructions of the child: Essays in honor of William Kessen* (pp. 225 251). Hillsdale, NJ: Erlbaum.

Capshew, J. H., & Laszlo, A. C. (1986). "We would not take no for an answer": Women psychologists and gender politics during World War II. *Journal of Social Issues, 42,* 157–180. doi:10.1111/j.1540-4560.1986.tb00213.x

Carrington, E. M. (1952). History and purposes of the International Council of Women Psychologists. *American Psychologist, 7,* 100–101. doi:10.1037/h0058267

Clifford, G. J. (1968). *Edward L. Thorndike: The sane positivist.* Middletown, CT: Wesleyan University Press.

Cott, N. F. (1987). *The grounding of modern feminism.* New Haven, CT: Yale University Press.

Cravens, H. (1985). Child-saving in the age of professionalism, 1915–1930. In J. M. Hawes & N. R. Hiner (Eds.), *American childhood: A research guide and historical handbook* (pp. 415–488). Westport, CT: Greenwood Press.

Frank, L. K. (1944, May 5). Letter to Florence Goodenough. F. L. Goodenough Papers (Box 1, Correspondence, 1936-1947), University Archives, University of Minnesota Libraries.

Goodenough, F. L. (n.d.). Unpublished manuscript. Florence Goodenough papers, University Archives, University of Minnesota Libraries.

Goodenough, F. L. (1925, June 21). Letter to Lewis Terman. Lewis Terman papers, Box 14, Folders 13–14, Department of Special Collections, Stanford University Archives, Stanford, CA.

Goodenough, F. L. (1926). *Measurement of intelligence by drawings.* Yonkers-on-Hudson, NY: World.

Goodenough, F. L. (1928a). *The Kuhlman-Binet tests for children of preschool age: A critical study and evaluation.* Minneapolis: University of Minnesota Press. doi:10.1037/11328-000

Goodenough, F. L. (1928b). Measuring behavior traits by means of repeated short samples. *Journal of Juvenile Research, 12*, 230–235.

Goodenough, F. L. (1931). *Anger in young children*. Minneapolis: University of Minnesota Press.

Goodenough, F. L. (1934). *Developmental psychology: An introduction to the study of human behavior*. New York: Appleton-Century.

Goodenough, F. L. (1936a, January 28). Letter to Theta Wolf. Florence L. Goodenough papers (Box 1, Correspondence, 1936–1947), University of Minnesota Archives, Minneapolis.

Goodenough, F. L. (1936b, January 30). Letter to Theta Wolf. Florence L. Goodenough papers (Box 1, Correspondence, 1936-1947), University of Minnesota Archives, Minneapolis.

Goodenough, F. L. (1936c, March 7). Letter to Theta Wolf. Florence L. Goodenough papers (Box 1, Correspondence, 1936-1947), University of Minnesota Archives, Minneapolis.

Goodenough, F. L. (1936d, April 7). Letter to Theta Wolf. Florence L. Goodenough papers (Box 1, Correspondence, 1936-1947), University of Minnesota Archives, Minneapolis.

Goodenough, F. L. (1939a, April 5). Letter to Leta S. Hollingworth. Florence L. Goodenough papers (Box 1, Correspondence, 1936-1947), University of Minnesota Archives, Minneapolis.

Goodenough, F. L. (1939b). Look to the evidence! A critique of recent experiments on raising the I.Q. *Educational Methods, 19*, 73–79.

Goodenough, F. L. (1940a, November 19). Letter to Lewis Terman. Florence L. Goodenough papers, University of Minnesota Archives, Minneapolis.

Goodenough, F. L. (1940b, January 20). Letter to Russell Smart. F. L. Goodenough papers (Box 1, Correspondence, 1936-1947), University Archives, University of Minnesota Libraries.

Goodenough, F. L. (1942, June 21). Letter to Lewis Terman. Lewis Terman papers, Box 14, Folder 13, Department of Special Collections, Stanford University Archives, Stanford, CA.

Goodenough, F. L. (1944a). Expanding opportunities for women psychologists in the post-war period of civil and military reorganization. *Psychological Bulletin, 41*, 706–712. doi:10.1037/h0059004

Goodenough, F. L. (1944b, May 15). Letter to Gladys Schwesinger. Margaret Ives Papers, Box M474, Folder: NCWP. Archives of the History of American Psychology, Akron, OH.

Goodenough, F. L. (1944c, May 18). Letter to Lawrence K. Frank. F. L. Goodenough papers (Box 1, Correspondence, 1936–1947), University Archives, University of Minnesota Libraries.

Goodenough, F. L. (1945). *Developmental psychology: An introduction to the study of human behavior,* 2d ed. New York: Appleton-Century.

Goodenough, F. L. (1949a). The appraisal of child personality. *Psychological Review, 56*(3), 123–131. doi:10.1037/h0062894

Goodenough, F. L. (1949b). *Mental testing: Its history, principles, and applications*. New York: Rinehart.

Goodenough, F. L. (1950). Edward Lee Thorndike, 1874–1949. *American Journal of Psychology, 63*, 291–301.

Goodenough, F. L. (1956). *Exceptional children*. New York: Appleton-Century-Crofts.

Goodenough, F. L., & Anderson, J. E. (1931). *Experimental child study*. New York: Century. doi:10.1037/11015-000

Goodenough, F. L., Foster, J. C., & Van Wagenen, M. J. (1932). *The Minnesota preschool tests: Manual of instructions. Forms A and B*. Minneapolis, MN: Educational Testing Bureau.

Goodenough, F. L., & Harris, D. B. (1950). Studies in the psychology of children's drawings: II. 1928–1949. *Psychological Bulletin, 47*, 369–433. doi:10.1037/h0058368

Goodenough, F. L., & Maurer, K. (1942). *The mental growth of children from age two to fourteen years: A study of the predictive value of the Minnesota Preschool Scales.* Minneapolis: University of Minnesota Press.

Goodenough, F. L., & Tyler, L. E. (1959). *Developmental psychology*, 3d ed. New York: Appleton-Century-Crofts.

Guthrie, R. V. (2004). *Even the rat was white*, 2d ed. Boston: Pearson Education, Inc.

Harris, D. B. (1961, May 4). Letter to Virginia Lee Fisher. Florence L. Goodenough papers (Box 1, Theta Wolf correspondence), University of Minnesota Archives, Minneapolis.

Harris, D. B. (1963). *Children's drawings as measures of intellectual maturity: A revision and extension of the Goodenough Draw-a-Man test.* San Diego, CA: Harcourt Brace Jovanovich.

Harris, D. B. (1996). Dale B. Harris. In D. Thompson & J. Hogan (Eds.), *A history of developmental psychology in autobiography* (pp. 84–104). Boulder, CO: Westview Press.

Hartup, W. W., Johnson, A., & Weinberg, R. A. (2001). *The Institute of Child Development: Pioneering in science and application, 1925–2000.* Minneapolis: University of Minnesota Press.

Heidbreder, E. (1933). *Seven psychologies.* New York: Century.

Heidbreder, E. (1977). Oral history interview with Laurel Furumoto. Wellesley College Archives, Wellesley College, Wellesley, MA.

Johnson, A., & Johnston, E. (2010). Unfamiliar feminisms: Revisiting the National Council of Women Psychologists. *Psychology of Women Quarterly, 34,* 311–327. doi:10.1111/j.1471-6402.2010.01577.x

Jones, M. C. (1924). A laboratory study of fear: The case of Peter. *Pedagogical Seminary, 31,* 308–315. doi:10.1080/08856559.1924.9944851

Memorandum re the disability of Florence L. Goodenough (1946). Florence L. Goodenough papers, University of Minnesota Archives, Minneapolis.

Minton, H. L. (1984). The Iowa child welfare research station and the 1940 debate on intelligence: Carrying on the legacy of a concerned mother. *Journal of the History of the Behavioral Sciences, 20,* 160–176. doi:10.1002/1520-6696(198404)20:2<160::AID-JHBS2300200205>3.0.CO;2-X

Minton, H. L. (1988). *Lewis M. Terman: Pioneer in psychological testing.* New York: New York University Press.

Mitchell, M. (1951). Status of women in the American Psychological Association. *American Psychologist, 6,* 193–201. doi:10.1037/h0063616

Moore, L. (1978, July 31). Letter to Theta Wolf. Florence L. Goodenough papers (Box 1, Theta Wolf correspondence), University of Minnesota Archives, Minneapolis.

Napoli, D. S. (1981). *Architects of adjustment: A history of the psychological profession in the United States.* Port Washington, NY: Kennikat.

NCWP Tenth Anniversary Handbook. (1952). Margaret Ives Papers (Box M42, Folder 1). Archives of the History of American Psychology, University of Akron, Akron, OH.

Scarborough, E., & Furumoto, L. (1987). *Untold lives: The first generation of American women psychologists.* New York: Columbia University Press.

Schlossman, S. L. (1981). Philanthropy and the gospel of child development. *History of Education Quarterly, 21,* 275–299. doi:10.2307/367699

Stevens, G., & Gardner, S. (Eds.). (1982). *The women of psychology (Vol. 1: Pioneers and innovators).* Cambridge, MA: Schenkman.

Templin, M. (n.d.). Florence Goodenough—A memoir. Unpublished paper, Florence Goodenough papers (Box 1, Theta Wolf correspondence), University Archives, University of Minnesota Libraries.

Thompson, D. N. (1990). Florence Laura Goodenough (1886–1959). In N. O'Connell & N. F. Russo (Eds.), *Women in psychology: A bio-bibliographic sourcebook* (pp. 125–133). Westport, CT: Greenwood Press.

Tyler, L. E. (1978). My life as a psychologist. In T. S. Krawiec (Ed.), *The psychologists: Autobiographies of distinguished living psychologists* (vol. 3, pp. 289–302). Brandon, VT: Clinical Psychology Publishing.

Watson, J. B., & Rayner, R. (1920). Conditioned emotional reactions. *Journal of Experimental Psychology, 3*(1), 1–14. doi:10.1037/h0069608

Wolf, T. H. (n.d.). [Draft of biography of Florence Goodenough for *Notable American women*]. Florence Goodenough papers (Box 1, Theta Wolf correspondence), University Archives, University of Minnesota Libraries.

Wolf, T. H. (1936, April 2). Letter to Florence Goodenough. Florence L. Goodenough papers (Box 1, Correspondence, 1936–1947), University of Minnesota Archives, Minneapolis.

Wolf, T. H. (1973). *Alfred Binet*. Chicago: University of Chicago Press.

Wolf, T. H. (1978, August 9). Letter to Willard Hartup. Florence L. Goodenough papers (Box 1, Theta Wolf correspondence), University of Minnesota Archives, Minneapolis.

Wolf, T. H. (1980). Florence Laura Goodenough, August 6, 1886–April 4, 1959. In B. Sicherman & C. Green (Eds.), *Notable American women: The modern period* (pp. 284–286). Cambridge, MA: Belknap Press of Harvard University Press.

Zenderland, L. (1988). Education, evangelism, and the origins of clinical psychology: The child-study legacy. *Journal of the History of the Behavioral Sciences, 24*, 152–165. doi:10.1002/1520-6696(198804)24:2<152::AID-JHBS2300240203>3.0.CO;2-6

3

Heinz Werner:
A Differentiation Theory of Development

JAAN VALSINER
Clark University

Heinz Werner (1890–1964) was Viennese—and remained so all of his life. Vienna is a town of special significance in European cultural history. A long-time capital of the Austro-Hungarian Empire, it was a city of political power and culture, literature, and music. The musical nature of life in Vienna was a constant company for Werner's work in psychology throughout his years in academia—in Germany and later in the United States. In general, psychology in its late 19th-century version developed on the basis of music—and Werner's developmental psychology was a good example of this. A pattern of sounds that we recognize as *music* is a whole. So is a human being. Every person acts in that person's social context—as a whole person, and not a sum of different composite properties.

Figure 3.1   Heinz Werner, 1962. (Courtesy of Clark University Archives. With permission.)

Werner was a developmental scientist° who united different key ideas of European sciences and literature in his developmental theory. These were the ideas of the *Naturphilosophie* traditions that were the result of the thinking of Friedrich

---

° Developmental science is the general science of processes of development—in any kind of system that develops (e.g., embryo, society, psyche, galaxies). Developmental psychology is one of the sub-fields of developmental science.

Schelling, Georg Hegel, and Friedrich Hölderlin in the 1790s and early 1800s. The voice of Johann Wolfgang von Goethe is also present in Werner's work. He was closely related with the philosophy of Ernst Cassirer and with the personology of William Stern; both were his colleagues in Hamburg. He became influenced by the ecological theoretical biology of Jakob von Uexküll. The result was a coherent theory of development as a process of constant *differentiation* that involves *articulation, hierarchical integration*, and *de-differentiation*.

BASIC CONCEPTS: DIFFERENTIATION, ARTICULATION, AND INTEGRATION

Werner's notion of differentiation entailed a holistic (all developmental phenomena are wholes, not accumulations of elements) view that is also dynamic. The view entails recognition that all psychological phenomena change under specifiable conditions. Some of these changes lead to development—emergence of new, higher level, qualities. A child who starts to speak has developed to a higher level of psychological organization than a preverbal child. Speaking radically reorganizes the whole psychological life of the child. In a similar vein, a young psychology student who discovers that mere gathering of data does not guarantee better understanding—and starts to ask theoretical questions—has developed into a new qualitative state. If the student also comes to realize that each theoretical perspective in psychology has its own history of ideas we see even further development.

Differentiation

In general terms, differentiation is a process of emergence of parts within the previously unstructured whole (Figure 3.2). This is a basic chemical and biological process—the synthesis of a new quality that cannot be reduced to its constituent elements. In biology it is best illustrated by examples from embryology. A fertilized ovum develops into a multicellular organism through differentiation of its neuronal structure into organs. In psychology, the making of any distinction (e.g., "this is not me") is the starting point for psychological differentiation. All human language use involves such differentiation; with the help of language we can create highly sophisticated texts of poetry and write novels. In a similar vein we can also use language in ways that eliminate the complex structure of thought and feeling, as we can see in public signs ("stop") or advertisements ("good buy").

Articulation

Differentiation of the parts of the whole—yet without subordinating any part to any other—is called *articulation*. As one can see from Figure 3.2, articulation of the parts of the whole is a result of the differentiation processes.

If articulation, making parts of the whole observable in terms that allow category assignment (coding), were all there is to psychological phenomena, our present-day psychology should have reached solutions to our pressing problems in

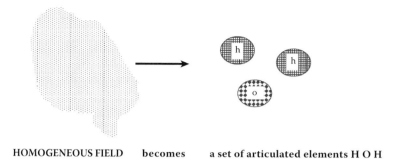

HOMOGENEOUS FIELD   becomes   **a set of articulated elements H O H**

Figure 3.2   The process of differentiation: articulation.

society and in human minds. Most of our statistical inference in psychology builds its knowledge construction on discovering and accumulating the articulated parts of the whole and losing the character of the whole in that operation. The articulated parts are considered to be equivalent to the whole, either individually or (more often) in some aggregated version. Psychology is dominated by "standardized scales" in which responses to items of approximately similar content are counted, added up, and treated as if these are "measures" of the supposed quality "behind" them. Yet that quality is of a different kind than the accumulated "indices." In sum, contemporary psychology treats the articulated states of affairs in psychological issues as if these could be reassembled into quantified "indices" that reveal the "hidden" (usually considered "causal") guiding forces in the mind (or society). It overlooks the intricate processes of hierarchical integration. This gap in psychology led another developmental scientist, James Mark Baldwin (1930), to claim appropriately:

> The … quantitative method, brought over into psychology from the exact sciences, physics and chemistry, must be discarded; for its ideal consisted in reducing the more complex to the more simple, the whole into its parts, the later-evolved to the earlier-existent, thus denying or eliminating just the factor which constituted or revealed what was truly genetic [developmental—JV]. Newer modes of manifestation cannot be stated in atomic terms without doing violence to the more synthetic modes which observation reveals. (p. 7).

Hierarchical Integration

In Werner's view, it is precisely the synthesis of novelty that psychology needs to study. This is characterized by the concept of hierarchical integration, the process of establishment of hierarchical—fluid or relatively stable—relationships between the articulated parts (Figure 3.3). Hierarchical integration guarantees the possibility of innovation. Werner's theoretical credo, emphasizing the role of cultural means in human development, was a close parallel to that of Lev Vygotsky (see Chapter 7 in this volume). These two highly creative scholars shared the same cultural-historical roots in the continental European philosophies of the 18th and 19th centuries. Psychology, then and now, cannot survive as science without answering basic questions that philosophers raise. How development is possible is one of those questions.

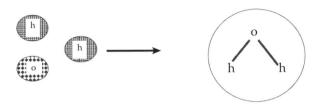

ARTICULATED ELEMENTS   become   A SYSTEM OF FUNCTIONING STRUCTURE

H – O – H (or known also as H$_2$O)

Figure 3.3   The process of differentiation: hierarchical integration.

These terms, articulation and integration, need to be taken seriously. Werner's differentiation theory is similar in its generality to Albert Einstein's relativity theory. Werner's perspective specifies what kinds of phenomena are developmental and sets up clear prescriptions for how to study them. Our contemporary psychology may be unused to the level of generalization and abstraction that was characteristic of Werner (and his era), a feature that may make a serious reconsideration of Werner's work all the more productive.

HEINZ WERNER'S LIFE AND INTERESTS

Werner's development is closely intertwined with the history of the German-speaking part of Europe in the 20th century (Valsiner, 2005)—the flourishing of psychology until 1933, followed by forced emigration. As a youngster of 18, Werner attended an engineering school (Technische Hochschule) in Vienna. Dissatisfaction with the idea of becoming an engineer led to his shift to the University of Vienna and to the topic of history of music. From there he then moved to philosophy, psychology, biology, and Germanic languages. In 1914, at age 24, he defended his doctoral dissertation, *Psychology of Aesthetic Experience* (*Zur Psychologie des ästhetischen Genusses*), published in 1916. Music and aesthetics, two central themes for the Viennese, were Werner's guiding arenas for his development. Yet he also was schooled in physiological psychology: In 1915–16 he worked in the Physiological Laboratory (under Sigmund Exner). As for his musical theme, he also worked at the Phonogram Archive of the Imperial Academy in Vienna where he studied musical abilities of children.

Werner's primary focus on human psychology made him close to the traditions of *Ganzheitspsychologie* (Diriwächter, 2008; Krueger, 1915) and to the introspective psychology of the Würzburg school of Oswald Külpe and Karl Bühler. Werner served as an assistant to Bühler at the University of Munich in 1915–1917.

The Hamburg Years (1917–1933): Era of Innovations

In 1917 he moved to Hamburg as assistant to William Stern and then took a professorship at Hamburg University in 1926. The years 1926–1933 were the most fertile for Werner's ideas; it was in the context of Hamburg where his basic theoretical system matured and the key empirical work was accomplished. There he finished his *Habilitationschrift* [a specific German tradition of a second doctoral thesis after the PhD that links the person to the given university]: *Grundfragen der Intensitätspsychologie (Foundations of Intensity Psychology)*, in 1922. He published *Die Ursprünge der Lyrik (Roots of lyric)* in 1924. The year 1926 was important in that the first German edition of *Introduction to Developmental Psychology (Einführung in die Entwicklungspsychologie)*, which became the basis for his later English foundational monographs of 1940 and 1948, was published. In 1932 he published his crucial analysis of how the human act of speaking is built upon all bodily activity—*Basic Questions of Speech Physiognomy (Grundfragen der Sprachphysiognomik,* Werner, 1932).

In Hamburg, Werner lectured widely—and much—on general and experimental psychology, developmental psychology, psychology of character, psychology of art, ethnopsychology, and psychology of language. His erudition was profound. Werner's intellectual circle at the University of Hamburg included the best minds of philosophy and biology of the 1920s and 1930s—Ernst Cassirer, Jakob von Uexküll, and William Stern (Müller, 2005; van der Veer, 2005). It is in conjunction with Stern's personology that Werner's ideas of differentiation and integration developed. Yet the crucial focus of genetic (i.e., developmental) analysis was his own: the goal of finding the process mechanisms that lead to developmental outcomes (Werner, 1937). Each psychological function—feeling, thinking, or acting—can be viewed as either an ongoing process or as an outcome. Thus, if a person is given a task to solve, the efforts toward finding a solution unfold in time; they are a process of problem solving. Once the problem is solved—that is, an outcome is reached— the process through which the outcome was achieved may be forgotten. This has happened in psychology, as the focus on processes has been largely lost (Cairns, 1998). Such loss is a major detriment to the effort to make sense of human psychological functions. For example, the right (or wrong) answers to multiple-choice test items fail to inform psychology about the processes through which they were obtained.

Years in Exile

After the Nazi party came to power in 1933 and began to persecute all liberal thinkers in academia, Werner was forced to leave his position (Kreppner, 2005). He emigrated to the United States where his future, during the years following the Great Depression, was not easy. He managed to find temporary research and teaching appointments for about a decade, until Clark University in 1947 offered him a permanent position as head of the newly reestablished psychology department.

While an accomplished and widely recognized scholar in the German-speaking psychological community, which until 1933 was the central arena for psychology, Werner became known in the English-speaking world only slowly. His classic book, *Comparative Psychology of Mental Development*, appeared in English during his time of adaptation to the conditions of the United States (Werner, 1940). Werner's orientation is best outlined in this classic monograph.

From 1947 to his death in 1964, Werner enjoyed a productive life at Clark University in Worcester, Massachusetts, surrounded by two faithful collaborators, Seymour Wapner and Bernard Kaplan, and guiding a very large number of mostly empirical master's and doctoral dissertations on various aspects of his differentiation theory. The second English edition of *Comparative Psychology of Mental Development* appeared in 1948. This version, and its later editions, has remained the summary of the "Werner Project" in his terms. It provides an empirical elaboration of Werner's ideas that developed in his Hamburg years but does not add further theoretical articulation (Valsiner, 2005), with the exception of a joint effort with Bernard Kaplan on issues of symbolic reflection of the world.

WERNER'S PHILOSOPHICAL ORIGINS: GOETHE AND NATURAL PHILOSOPHY

All ideas in psychology are deeply rooted in philosophy. Werner carried forth the *Naturphilosophie* traditions of Johann Wolfgang Goethe in his notion of the orthogenetic principle (see Kaplan, Bhatia, & Josephs, 2005; Werner, 1926, p. 32; Werner, 1940, p. 40). Werner's work systematized the basic ideas of developmental thought over the past two centuries while offering new modes for encounters with reality. Werner's perspective in psychology clearly prioritized field-theoretical constructs, in contrast to the use of categories:

> The position that seems to me most fertile … requires the abandoning of the widespread notion of a duality between person and field, irrespective of whether "field" pertains to a domain of objects or people. If one attempts to study the functioning of the individual in regard to his social climate or objective environment it seems to me that even the often used formulation of this relationship in terms of an "interaction" of two somehow "given" entities may be questioned; I deem it to be so much more fruitful to think here rather in terms of a growing polarization within a primary entity entailing the molding of not-yet-formed raw material into a self versus a field of objects and of "others." (Werner, 1962, p. 14)

Werner's ideas were linked with Hegel's notion of superseding previous levels of development (van der Veer, 2005, p. 76).

The Orthogenetic Principle

The idea of the orthogenetic principle, a principle central to differentiation theory, was built upon the ideas of Goethe. This was clear in Werner's first edition of his main book in German (Werner, 1926, p. 32), yet it surfaced in English only in the mid-1950s (Werner & Kaplan, 1956). In developmental psychology it is usually known through its presentation at the First Minnesota Symposium on Child Development:

> Developmental psychology postulates one regulative principle of development; it is an orthogenetic principle which states that wherever development occurs it proceeds from a state of relative globality and lack of differentiation to a state of increasing differentiation, articulation, and hierarchical integration. (Werner, 1957, p. 126)

The roots of Werner's thinking in *Ganzheitspsychologie* (see Diriwächter, 2008) are clear here—the direction of development from "state of relative globality" to that of "differentiation and hierarchical integration." This happens in the relation of the person and the environment:

> … Increasing subject–object differentiation involves the corollary that the organism becomes increasingly less dominated by the immediate concrete situation; the person is less stimulus-bound and less impelled by his own alternative states. A consequence of this freedom is the clearer understanding of goals, the possibility of employing substitutive means and alternative ends. There is hence a greater capacity for delay and planned action. The person is better able to exercise choice and willfully rearrange a situation. In short, he can manipulate the environment rather than passively respond to the environment. This freedom from the domination of the immediate situation also permits a more accurate assessment of others. (Werner, 1957, p. 127)

One General Principle, Many Specific Versions

While the general direction of development is specified by the orthogenetic principle, the specific pathways of development are highly variable. Werner recognized the multilinearity of developmental trajectories (Werner, 1957, p. 137). Such multilinearity is a result of pressures of opposite forces acting within the field. Differentiation was viewed by Werner as including its opposite process—de-differentiation—as its complementary part. The process of hierarchical integration involves qualitative reorganization of the lower (i.e., previously established) levels of organization, when the higher levels emerge in their specificity:

> … Development … tends towards stabilization. Once a certain stable level of integration is reached, the possibility of further development must depend on whether or not the behavioral patterns have become so automatized that they cannot take part in reorganization…. The individual, for instance, builds up sensorimotor schemata…. These are the goal of early learning at first, but later on become instruments or apparatuses for handling the environment. Since no two situations in which an organism finds itself are alike, the usefulness of these schemata in adaptive behavior will depend on their stability as well as on their pliability (a paradoxical "stable flexibility").… If one assumes that the emergence of higher levels of operations involves hierarchic integration, it follows that lower-level operations will have to be reorganized in terms of their functional nature so that they become subservient to higher functioning. A clear example of this is the change of the functional nature of imagery from a stage where images serve only memory, fantasy, and concrete conceptualization, to a stage where images have been transformed to schematic symbols of abstract concepts and thought. (Werner, 1957, pp. 139–140)

Werner's perspective on subject–object differentiation consistently led to the notion of psychological mediating devices emerging as human-made organizers of the mental and affective processes.

WERNER'S METHODOLOGICAL CREDO

Werner was primarily an experimentalist who wove empirical evidence from any applicable source into a general developmental theoretical scheme. The targets of science, developmental science in particular, are the general laws. These laws become known to us through episodic and particular encounters with psychological phenomena. Yet the issues at stake are those of basic universal science, not those of getting to know the particular context in some postmodern incarnation.

The Centrality of the Differentiating Whole

Largely in line with the ideas of the Second Leipzig School of Felix Krueger (1915) and his colleagues (see Diriwächter, 2008), Werner focused on the emergence of structure out of the quasi-differentiated field (see Figures 3.2 and 3.3). Hence, he added his countervoice to Wilhelm Wundt's focus on creative synthesis (*schöpferische Synthese*—emergence of new forms from recombination of elementary constituents) by giving primacy to the analysis of differentiating wholes:

> Psychology, including ethnopsychology, must proceed from larger living unities and arrive by analysis at unities of a lower order. It is not the concept of "creative synthesis" but that of "creative analysis" which leads to fruitful results. The component members of a mass are dependent parts of this mass, which represents the real, living unity. The single man as a member of a generic unity possesses characteristics which are his because of his integration within a totality, and are intelligible only in terms of this totality. The problem of generic unity can be solved only by conceiving this unity to be a non-derivative whole governed by special laws which affect the human bearers of this unity in their role of dependent members. (Werner, 1940, p. 9)

The primacy of the whole is reinstated as a methodological starting point. From here follows the central focus of Werner's methodology—the study of individuals in terms of their holistic organization:

> The individual thinks, speaks a certain language, and acts in a characteristic way because of his participation, his integration, in the whole; and his thinking, talking, and acting are primarily understandable only in so far as he is identified with this totality. (Werner, 1940, p. 9)

Developmental Experiments: Testing the Upward and Downward Movements

Werner was a cofounder—with Friedrich Sander, Erich Wohlfart, and Günter Ipsen—of the microgenetic experimental tradition in psychology (Abbey & Diriwächter, 2008; Valsiner & van der Veer, 2000, chapter 7). Werner considered two types of developmental (in his terms, genetic) experiments as the core for methodology.

First, it is possible to follow the formation of ordinary psychological functions, either in a laboratory under artificial conditions or in natural settings. This is made possible by the axiomatic focus on psychological events as unfolding processes (Werner, 1940, p. 37). The time frame of such processes may vary, from percept formation within a fraction of a second to the emergence of intellectual events over days, months, or years. Yet their basic pattern, that of becoming new organizational forms, is similar across domains. Second, it is possible to study developmental processes through experiments on primitivation—looking at the processes of breakdown of psychological functions. Such experiments can be made due to the vertical heterogeneity of the already established organizational forms—hierarchical system of layers:

> … [The] normal adult, even at our own cultural level, does not always act on the higher levels of behavior. His mental structure is marked by not one but many functional patterns, one lying above the other. Because of this the isolated individual … must occasionally exhibit in his varying behavior different phases of development. (Werner, 1940, p. 38)

It is obvious that the two methodological schemes—looking at the "upwardly emerging" forms of organization and at "downwardly occasional" functioning at lower levels—follow from the general notion of development as differentiation and hierarchization. The investigator can observe naturally occurring movements in either of these directions or can evoke either of them through experimental intervention.

FROM PHYSIOGNOMIC PERCEPTION TO MICROGENESIS OF SYMBOL FORMATION

Werner introduced the notion of the physiognomic nature of human functioning in 1926 at the eighth International Congress of Psychology in Groningen (Werner, 1927). It grew out of his basic roots in the *Ganzheitspsychologie* tradition and developed into two basic research streams—on perceptual processes (Wapner, 2005) and symbol formation (Kaplan et al., 2005).

The sensori-tonic field theory of perception (Werner & Wapner, 1956—see overview of the empirical projects in Wapner, 2005) was the framework for the majority of experimental studies conducted by Werner's disciples at Clark from the 1950s onward. The sensori-tonic theory provided an alternative to psychological explanations promoted by psychoanalysis—by conceptualizing the notion of energy transformation without any link with a posited substrate (libido). It also provided a rich ground for a set of clever experimental studies that demonstrated how the person's bodily system is in a relation of equilibrium with the surrounding sensory environment.

Symbol Formation

The symbol formation direction in Werner's thought was exemplified by the classic book on that topic, *Symbol Formation* (Werner & Kaplan, 1963). This book could be considered a presentation of the work done in the 1950s on issues of semiotic (in Werner's terms, symbolic) distancing of the psychological functions from their immediate, here-and-now contexts. The work on symbol formation continued the person-centered focus that Werner carried with him from his Hamburg times (see Kreppner, 2005; Langer, 1970; Müller, 2005; van der Veer, 2005). Human beings—in their ontogeny—are involved in constant overcoming of the immediacy of their situated activity contexts through semiotic construction. Werner's focus was on the formation of psychological functions, either in a laboratory under artificial conditions or in natural settings. Kaplan added to this an astute analysis of everyday symbol construction—that we do it instantly, under any circumstances.

The work on symbol formation continued the person-centered focus that Werner carried with him from his Hamburg times yet with the addition of new connections with post World War II linguistics (Kaplan et al., 2005). He pointed to the limitations of the reduction of psychology to the investigation of products and called for the primacy of the study of processes (in contrast to outcomes) as central for all psychology.

DISTANCING AS THE KEY PROCESS IN DEVELOPMENT

Development means distancing from the previous states of being. Human beings, in their ontogeny, are involved in constant overcoming of the immediacy of their situated activity contexts. His focus was on the act of speaking as the place where symbolic vehicles are constructed. Thus, in the course of human development:

> There is a progressive distancing or polarization between person and object of reference, between person and symbolic vehicle, between symbolic vehicle and object, and between the persons in the communicative situation, that is, the addressor and the addressee. (Werner & Kaplan, 1963, p. 42)

This focus on distancing is clearly developed by 1963 beyond the shape it took in the 1940s. *Symbol Formation* (Werner & Kaplan, 1963) moves the coverage to the structure of the organization of the activity of speaking. In some sense there may be a formal parallel between the focus on construction of signification in human speech in its many forms and Werner's early interest in children's construction of melodies.

WERNER'S IDEAS FOR THE FUTURE OF PSYCHOLOGY

Werner's contributions serve as a fruitful catalyst for developmental science in the 21st century. He raised key issues and attempted to provide fitting answers to questions that developmental science started to (re)consider in the 1990s (Cairns, 1998; Carolina Consortium of Human Development, 1996; Valsiner & Connolly, 2003). In his deeply interdisciplinary ways, Werner provides us with a model of how knowledge from different disciplines—psychology, anthropology, linguistics, to name a few—can be creatively combined in our knowledge construction.

Study of the formation of psychological functions can happen only if psychology's methodology is changed from detecting static entities to looking at the ongoing construction (and destruction) processes. Werner was a pioneer of consistently developmental methodology that focuses on psychological events as they are unfolding, through the use of the *microgenetic methods* (Abbey & Diriwächter, 2008). The psychology of today is in need of serious redirection of its main orientation, toward quantified transformations of the realities of the phenomena into the irrealities of the data. Werner's efforts in the 1920s in Hamburg and the 1950s at Clark provide examples of how a theoretical system that is well grounded in phenomena can be built to generate a rich empirical evidence base.

Werner's orthogenetic principle—his perspective of differentiation and de-differentiation through hierarchical integration—is a valuable arena for further theory construction in developmental psychology and in contemporary neurosciences. The latter, largely due to technological innovations, are rediscovering the hierarchical nature of the functional organization of the brain. At the same time, psychology, which has been dominated by nondevelopmental thinking over the past 60 years (Toomela & Valsiner, 2010), continues to avoid the notion of hierarchical organization of psychological functions. Werner's perspective, of course, makes the notion of *dynamic* hierarchical organization the center point of its theoretical generativity. It is not surprising that Werner's ideas have failed to proliferate in the North American psychological mindscape after their heyday at Clark in the 1950s. However, as globalization is leading to worldwide equality in the perspectives that lead the development of different scientific disciplines and as the North American traditions of rigid behaviorism and its equally rigid sequel—cognitivism—are losing their social dominance, the notion of dynamic hierarchization of biological, psychological, and social processes is likely to return to science. The reemergence of the focus on gene regulation in research on protein genetics since the 1960s is a first example of the kind—some areas of the DNA sequence establish hierarchical regulatory roles over other areas.

The focus on dynamic hierarchies in psychological functioning that constitutes the core of Werner's legacy leads to innovation in the methodology of psychology. The microgenetic study of processes of emergence of new phenomena, the quintessence of any developmental perspective, needs to become the central feature of empirical work. This may benefit from a careful new look at the past efforts to develop microgenetic methods (Abbey & Diriwächter, 2008) as well as from a theoretical consideration of how the dialectical perspective could be constructively reintroduced to psychology's methodology. The rigidity of the empire of chance (Gigerenzer, Swijtink, Porter, Daston, Beatty, & Krüger, 1989) in psychology needs to be replaced by a reunification of the data, phenomena, and theoretical breakthroughs. This process of liberation is already going on through the movement toward idiographic science (Molenaar, 2004) and the efforts to elaborate qualitative methods.

Werner's legacy helps psychology of the 21st century to restore its interest in higher mental functions. This focus, shared by Werner and Vygotsky, is predicated upon the hierarchical and dynamic premises on which Werner's perspective was built. Our everyday life brings us ever new examples of the need for a person to make sense of and selectively relate with the extensive and escalating flow of communicative messages from the media. In the middle of such overstimulation from the social worlds, the person's own role in making sense and acting in accordance with one's will emerge as ways of coping with this twittering kaleidoscope of everyday events. Werner's integrative perspective—if developed further—can make it possible to explain how seemingly rational and independent minds that seem to be increasingly informed about the world can convert to ever new identification ideologies and follow them with remarkable zeal. The conceptual system that Werner painstakingly built between Europe and North America has a future as a theoretical unifier of the social sciences of our time.

SUGGESTED READINGS

Werner, H. (1948). *Comparative psychology of mental development*, 2d ed. Chicago: Follett.
    This is the central source where the synthesis of Werner's pre-1933 work in Germany and his first period of research in the United States were brought together. To understand Werner's theoretical contribution this thick book is best read together with his developmental manifesto (Werner, 1957).
Werner, H., & Kaplan, B. (1963). *Symbol formation*. New York: Wiley.
    This is a rich overview of the work on semiotic organization of human lives based on the large number of master's and doctoral theses done at Clark in the 1950s. It represents the cultural-psychological direction in Werner's work after taking his position at Clark and building up the second Clark tradition in the 1950s and beyond (the first tradition of note was that by G. Stanley Hall, in the 1890s to the 1910s, mostly dedicated to the study of psychology of religion and education).

REFERENCES

Abbey, E. A., & Diriwächter, R. (Eds.). (2008). *Innovating genesis: Microgenesis and the constructive mind in action*. Charlotte, NC: Information Age.
Baldwin, J. M. (1930). James Mark Baldwin. In C. Murchison (Ed.), *A history of psychology in autobiography* (vol. 1, pp. 1–30). New York: Russell & Russell. doi:10.1037/11401-001
Cairns, R. B. (1998). The making of developmental psychology. In W. Damon & R. Lerner (Eds.), *Handbook of child psychology: Theoretical models of human development* (vol. 1, 5th ed., pp. 25–105). New York: Wiley.
Carolina Consortium on Human Development. (1996). Developmental science: A collaborative statement. In R. B. Cairns, G. H. Elder, & E. J. Costello (Eds.), *Developmental science* (pp. 1–6). New York: Cambridge University Press.
Diriwächter, R. (2008). Genetic Ganzheitspsychologie. In R. Diriwächter & J. Valsiner (Eds.), *Striving for the whole: Creating theoretical syntheses* (pp. 21–45) New Brunswick, NJ: Transaction.
Gigerenzer, G., Swijtink, Z., Porter, T., Daston, L., Beatty, J., & Krüger, L. (1989). *The empire of chance*. Cambridge, UK: Cambridge University Press.
Kaplan, B., Bhatia, S., & Josephs, I. J. (2005). Re-thinking development. In J. Valsiner (Ed.), *Heinz Werner and developmental science* (pp. 121–154). New York: Kluwer/Academic/Plenum. doi:10.1007/0-306-48677-6_7
Kreppner, K. (2005). Heinz Werner and the Psychological Institute in Hamburg. In J. Valsiner (Ed.), *Heinz Werner and developmental science* (pp. 55–74). New York: Kluwer Academic/Plenum. doi:10.1007/0-306-48677-6_4

Krueger, F. (1915). Über Entwicklungspsychologie. [On developmental psychology]. *Arbeiten zur Entwicklungspsychologie, 1*, 1 (pp. 1–232). Leipzig: Wilhelm Engelmann.

Langer, J. (1970). Werner's comparative organismic theory. In W. Kessen (Ed.), *Handbook of child psychology: History, theory, and methods* (vol. 1, 4th ed., pp. 733–771). New York: Wiley.

Molenaar, P. C. M. (2004). A manifesto on psychology as idiographic science: Bringing the person back into scientific psychology, this time forever. *Measurement: Interdisciplinary Research and Perspectives, 2*, 201–218. doi:10.1207/s15366359mea0204_1

Müller, U. (2005). The context of the formation of Heinz Werner's ideas. In J. Valsiner (Ed.), *Heinz Werner and developmental science* (pp. 25–53). New York: Kluwer Academic/Plenum. doi:10.1007/0-306-48677-6_3

Toomela, A., & Valsiner, J. (Eds.). (2010). *Methodological thinking in psychology: 60 years gone astray?* Charlotte, NC: Information Age.

Valsiner, J. (Ed.). (2005). *Heinz Werner and developmental science*. New York: Kluwer Academic/Plenum Publishers.

Valsiner, J., & Connolly, K. J. (2003). The nature of development: The continuing dialogue of processes and outcomes. In J. Valsiner & K. J. Connolly (Eds.), *Handbook of developmental psychology* (pp. ix–xviii). London: Sage.

Valsiner, J., & van der Veer, R. (2000). *The social mind: Construction of the idea*. New York: Cambridge University Press.

Van der Veer, R. (2005). The making of a developmental psychologist. In J. Valsiner (Ed.), *Heinz Werner and developmental science* (pp. 75–103). New York: Kluwer Academic/Plenum Publishers. doi:10.1007/0-306-48677-6_5

Wapner, S. (2005). The sensory-tonic field theory of perception. In J. Valsiner (Ed.), *Heinz Werner and developmental science* (pp. 155–177). New York: Kluwer Academic/Plenum. doi:10.1007/0-306-48677-6_8

Werner, H. (1926). *Einführung in die Entwicklungspsychologie*. [Introduction to developmental psychology]. Leipzig: Johann Ambrosius Barth.

Werner, H. (1927). Ueber physiognomische Wahrnehmungsweisen und ihre experimentelle Prüfung [On physiognomic modes of perception and their experimental test]. *Proceedings and papers of the 8th International Conference of Psychology* (pp. 443–446). Groningen: P. Noordhoff.

Werner, H., (1932). *Grundfragen der Sprachphysiognomik*. Leipzig: J. A. Barth.

Werner, H. (1937). Process and achievement: A basic problem of education and developmental psychology. *Harvard Educational Review, 7*, 353–368.

Werner, H. (1940). *Comparative psychology of mental development*. New York: Harper & Brothers.

Werner, H. (1948). *Comparative psychology of mental development*, 2d ed. Chicago: Follett.

Werner, H. (1957).The concept of development from a comparative and organismic point of view. In D. B. Harris (Ed.), *The concept of development* (pp. 125–147). Minneapolis: University of Minnesota Press.

Werner, H. (1962). Significance of general experimental psychology for the understanding of abnormal behavior and its correction or prevention. In *The relationship between rehabilitation and psychology* (pp. 1–19). Washington, DC: Office of Vocational Rehabilitation.

Werner, H., & Kaplan, B. (1956). The developmental approach to cognition: Its relevance to the psychological interpretation of anthropological and ethnolinguistic data. *American Anthropologist, 58*, 866–880.

Werner, H., & Kaplan, B. (1963). *Symbol formation*. New York: Wiley.

Werner, H., & Wapner, S. (1956). Sensory-tonic field theory of perception: Basic concepts and experiments. *Rivista di Psicologia, 50*(4), 315–337.

4

Helena Antipoff:
A Quest for Democracy and Human Rights With the Help of Psychological Science

REGINA HELENA DE FREITAS CAMPOS

Universidade Federal de Minas Gerais, Brazil

Helena Antipoff, a Russian-born psychologist and educator who migrated to Brazil in 1929, played an important role in the establishment of the areas of developmental and educational psychology in Brazil. Drawing on her previous training in Paris, Geneva, and Petrograd, she assumed at that time the directorship of one of the first laboratories of psychology established in the country, linked to the Belo Horizonte Teachers College, in the state of Minas Gerais. In this position, she participated actively in the movement of school renewal in Brazilian public schools during the 1930s, as a teacher, as a researcher, and as an institution builder.

Figure 4.1   Helena Antipoff, 1925.
(Courtesy of the Center of Research
and Documentation Helena Antipoff,
Archives of the History of Brazilian Psychology,
Universidade Federal de Minas Gerais.
With permission.)

The research done in the laboratory aimed at describing psychological and psychosocial characteristics of the school population—children's ideals, interests and cognitive development—inspired by Jean-Jacques Rousseau's idea that knowledge of the child is necessary for a better education. The institutions she initiated aimed at providing special care for exceptional children, particularly those who present deficiencies and mental health problems; these were at-risk children who were deserving of treatment and education.

From 1940 onward, she assumed the chair of psychology that was established with the founding of the School of Philosophy, Humanities and Sciences of the University of Minas Gerais. In this role and others, she contributed to the education of the first generations of Brazilian psychologists and helped initiate the movement aimed at the legal regulation of the profession. She also continued to expand the applications of psychology to education, both as a psychologist and through her students who came from all over the country to learn new methods in the education of exceptional children. In 1972, she became professor emeritus at the School of Education of the University of Minas Gerais for her contribution in the theory and practice of psychology and education.

Her work was characterized by a sound theoretical foundation, stemming from her European training, and by a deep concern with practical applications of psychological knowledge to the specific situation faced by Brazilian educational and mental health systems. Her sensitivity to local culture helped her to cross social boundaries and promote the development of institutions directed to the poor and aimed at the empowerment of grassroots populations, and for this she became an important leader in popular and rural education in Brazil.

EDUCATION IN EUROPE

Helena Antipoff (1892–1974) was born in Grodno, Russia. Her father was a colonel in the Russian army and her mother the descendant of a Russian aristocratic family. She lived in Saint Petersburg until 1909, where she was educated in the traditional aristocratic style, learning to play the piano and to speak German, English, and French. While attending the normal school, she was influenced by the increasing valuation of scientific activities in Russian society, intensified with the Nobel award in physiology to Ivan Pavlov in 1904 and the foundation of the Saint Petersburg Institute of Psychoneurology in 1907. At the same time, the burgeoning cultural and political life of the city—the seat of the Russian empire—led her to develop an interest in music, literature, and politics and to witness the social unrest that traversed Russian society during the first decade of the twentieth century. In an autobiographical manuscript, she remembers the piano played by her mother, the folk songs sung by street vendors, and the popular folk tales of different cultural environments told by the house employees. Her reports suggest an attitude of curiosity regarding something forbidden (Russian folk culture) in a young girl educated in an environment of formalism.

An atmosphere of insecurity and the signs that a revolutionary movement was about to occur in Russia led the Antipoff family to move to Paris in 1909, following a trend observed in most Russian families in the period looking for better opportunities of study for their offspring in Western Europe. The colonel stayed in St. Petersburg, while Sofia Antipova, the mother, took their three daughters to France. While her mother taught Russian to small groups of French students at home, Helena decided to pursue her studies at the University of Paris (the famous Sorbonne), where she chose psychology as her focus.

FROM PARIS TO GENEVA—STUDIES IN PSYCHOLOGY AND EDUCATION (1909–1915)

Antipoff acknowledged the influence the Collège de France seminars had on her line of thought. Among the French philosophers and psychologists, she particularly admired Henri Bergson (1859–1941) for his phenomenological approach to human consciousness and Pierre Janet (1859–1947) for his functional approach to human behavior. Bergson was one of the founders of phenomenology as a school of thought in philosophy and psychology. Janet was a psychopathologist who had studied with Charcot at La Salpêtrière. Like Sigmund Freud (1856–1939), Janet interpreted mental diseases as disorders in consciousness generated at an unconscious level (Zusne, 1975).

Other strong influences on Antipoff's education in France stemmed from the work of Alfred Binet (1857–1911) and Théodore Simon (1873–1961) on intelligence tests, made at the Sorbonne Laboratory of Psychology. Till 1900, the laboratory carried out experiments on human perception in the German tradition. After publishing *The Experimental Study of Intelligence* (Binet, 1902), Binet was appointed by the French Ministry of Public Instruction to a committee whose task was to study the problem and make recommendations concerning the education of retarded children in Paris. For this purpose, the first Binet-Simon Intelligence Scale was constructed in 1905. The scale was revised in 1908, and the tests were arranged according to the different ages at which they were to be passed by normal children. In 1911, Binet's last revision, in which the concept of mental age was included for the first time, was published (Binet, 1920).

At the laboratory, Antipoff participated in the studies of the mental development of children enrolled in Paris public schools, aimed at verifying the accuracy of the Binet-Simon intelligence scale in measuring the mental development of primary school children. During her apprenticeship, she became acquainted with the techniques used to validate mental tests, the analysis of different items of the scale, and the study of the relationship between verbal development and motor skills.

The Sorbonne Laboratory attracted researchers from several parts of the world interested in studies on intelligence. There Antipoff was introduced to Édouard Claparède (1873–1940), professor at the University of Geneva, who was organizing in Switzerland the *Institut des Sciences de l'Éducation* (Institut Jean-Jacques Rousseau) for the purpose of "introducing students to scientific methods required for the advancement of child psychology and instructional techniques" (Claparède, 1931, p. 267). Since 1899, Geneva had been the headquarters of the Bureau International des Écoles Nouvelles, organized by the Swiss educator Adolphe Ferrière (1879–1960) to gather information regarding the movement of school renewal in Europe. Ferrière became one of the main disseminators of the doctrine of the "École Active"—the school whose purpose was to develop children's auton- omy and whose teaching methods relied upon children's interests (Claparède, 1931, p. 195; Hameline, Jornod, & Belkaïd, 1995).

Claparède went to Paris to recruit students to attend the Rousseau Institute, and Antipoff was invited to join the Swiss group. The contact with Claparède was crucial for the development of Antipoff's scientific view on intelligence and education. At the institute, she acquired a more complete knowledge of the functional approach to the psychology of intelligence and of the "Active School" methods. Claparède approached the study of intelligence as an active process, in the tradition of func- tional studies already being developed by John Dewey (1859–1952) and William James (1842–1910) in the United States. This approach was opposed both to the aprioristic concept of intelligence, as a "system of faculties of the mind that considers intelligence as a primordial faculty, unique and impossible to analyze," and to the associationist assumption that considered intelligence as a "game of acquired asso- ciations" (Claparède, 1931, pp. 138–139). The author, on the contrary, emphasized intelligence as an active instrument of adaptation to new situations. This approach— known as interactionist or, more recently, constructivist—assumes that the develop- ment of intelligence results from the subject's active exploration of possible solutions to a new problem. Therefore, intelligence derives from the subject's action upon the environment, and it is the structure of the action that, once internalized, constitutes the structure of intelligent thought. This position was fully stated in 1933 in the paper "The Genesis of the Hypothesis," published in the *Archives de Psychologie*° and dedicated to Antipoff, who had collaborated in the data collection and analysis while working as the author's assistant in Geneva (Claparède, 1933). This article had a direct influence on the work of Jean Piaget (1896–1980), who was Claparède's assis- tant at the Rousseau Institute during the 1920s.

The principles of functional education adopted by Antipoff stated that the edu- cational process might rely upon children's interests as the basis for their activities at school. In this approach, the purpose of education became the development of intelligence. It was assumed that intelligence would be developed to the extent that students were given opportunities to manipulate their environment and to search actively for solutions to problems posed to them at school. In this approach, educa- tion, rather than depending on children's given mental abilities, was the process of enhancing these abilities. For this reason it is called a constructivist approach.

Functional education was supposed to provide the basis for the planning of "Active School" methods that were developed at the Maison des Petits, an experi- mental school linked to the Rousseau Institute for the purposes of experimenting with new methods of education (Audemars & Lafendel, 1950, p. 10). The Maison des Petits was founded in November 1913 and incorporated by the Swiss public school system in 1922. Antipoff did her apprenticeship as a researcher in education between 1912 and 1916 at the Rousseau Institute, where she attended classes and seminars and worked as the first school teacher at the Maison des Petits, under Claparède's supervision (Hameline, 1996).

° The *Archives de Psychologie*, one of the first periodicals in psychology in the French language, was founded in 1901 by E. Claparède. He was the editor until his death in 1940.

These first experiences, in Paris and Geneva, contributed to Antipoff's development of a sound interest in scientific activities, both as a way to pursue her intellectual advancement and to solve practical problems. The Binet-Simon Laboratory and the Rousseau Institute were, at the time, institutions involved in the movement of school renewal in Europe. The extension of access to education and the universalization of public education systems posed new questions for educators: how to educate many children together? How to attain the ideals regarding the right to education and at the same time managing individual differences and sorting individuals for different occupations? These tensions traversed mass education systems, built under contradictory demands: the quest for expanding educational opportunities for workers' offspring, and elites' pressures on schools for the training of workers in modern industrial societies. The large educational systems were producing continuing evidence of individual differences in intelligence and performance, leading to inefficiency in mass education. These were the questions posed to psychologists of intelligence at the time.

Alfred Binet answered them with the development of the metric intelligence scale, aiming at contributing to evaluate children's cognitive capacities and to plan their education in different levels. Claparède proposed the "school made to measure" to attend to individual differences. This was the context of scientific work applied to social issues, in an atmosphere of great confidence in science, in which Antipoff was educated. The way she dealt with the movement from czarist Russia, turbulent and contradictory, to the democratic experience of Western Europe was the commitment to scientific work associated with social concerns.

In 1916, however, she had to leave Geneva and go back to Russia to take care of her father, severely wounded in the 1914–1918 war.

IN RUSSIA (1916–1924): HOW SCIENCE COULD HELP THE RECONSTRUCTION OF SOCIETY

From 1916 till 1924, Antipoff stayed in Russia. During the years 1916–1917, while looking after her father, she witnessed the effects of war and revolution. Her father, a colonel of the czar's army, had been wounded in a battle at Smolensk. As an official of the regime, he could not be treated in a public hospital, where the rebels could still try to kill him. She arranged for him to be treated by distant relatives in Crimea, and returned to St. Petersburg, where she worked in a shelter for abandoned children just after the Russian Revolution.

These children, she reported, had lost their families in the process of disorganization of the country, and lived in the city streets, frightening the population. The government organized several centers for the purpose of sheltering these children, arranging for their medical and psychological examinations, and planning their education in institutions providing further support (Antipoff, 1924, 1937). At the Petersburg medical-pedagogical station, her task was to examine children sheltered at the orphanage and to plan their reeducation. The examination was made through psychological tests she was already familiar with, such as the Binet–Simon intelligence scale, and also Lazurski's technique for studying children's personality. Alexander Lazurski was one of the first Russian specialists in mental testing, having worked at the Psychoneurological Institute of St. Petersburg, directed by Vladimir Bekhterev. Lazurski's technique, called "natural experimentation," included the observation of children in their natural environment, with the purpose of avoiding the artificial situation of the laboratory or of tests (Antipoff, 1992a).

After the revolution, scientific studies were highly valued in Russia. Revolutionary leaders believed that science should help solve the social and economic problems of the country. They expected, as well, that the concepts of dialectical materialism would be better developed and explored by social scientists. This agenda was embraced by a group of Soviet psychologists dedicated to research on educational psychology and mental retardation—the area of pedology, well developed after the revolution and enhanced by the educational experiments promoted by the new government, aimed at expanding educational opportunities and shaping human nature for socialist purposes. It was in this cultural and intellectual environment that the historical-cultural theory was developed, which considered that higher mental processes in human beings are determined by their sociocultural experiences and suggested the mechanisms through which cultural experiences help shape human cognitive abilities. As a consequence of this approach, schooling, rather than relying on the individual's already given mental capacities, was considered a means to develop these capacities (Vygotski, 1991; van der Veer & Valsiner, 1996).

Antipoff's work with street children in Russia seems to have been influenced by the historical-cultural approach. While submitting the children to psychological examinations, she observed that their performance on the Binet-Simon scale was poor but that they could not be considered feeble-minded. On the contrary, they would reveal "an amazing ability to deal with concrete problems of life" (Antipoff, 1937, p. 133). Their troubles could be better explained by their lack of a regular family life and schooling, that is, by their sociocultural background. In 1924, Antipoff published two papers in Leningrad—"Plan and Techniques for the Psychological Examination of Children" and "The Mental Development of Pre-school Children" in the *Journal Trondovaia Schkola* and in the *Journal of Pedology*, respectively (see Murchison, 1929)—on the results of the investigation of children's mental capacities. These articles were criticized by Soviet authorities, since they seemed to demonstrate that upper-class children did better in standardized tests than working-class ones, although Antipoff's interpretation of these results aimed at showing that the test's scope was limited to the cultural universe of the upper classes. Probably due to these problems and also to her husband's exile in Berlin,° she left Russia at the end of the year, with an authorization signed by Nechaev, professor of pedagogical psychology at the University of St. Petersburg.

° While in Petrograd (formerly Saint Petersburg), Antipoff met the journalist and writer Viktor Iretzky, whom she married in 1918. Their son, Daniel, was born in 1919, when Iretzky was imprisoned by the political policy (then called Cheka, later KGB). As a writer, Iretzky defended the right of the artist to freedom of expression, a position not accepted by the communists, who wanted all professionals to apply their efforts in the development of historical materialism; in the arts, this position meant to be a realist, to describe the common people's life and the success of the revolution. After being prosecuted, Iretsky was exiled to Berlin, where he wrote his most famous novel ("She"), dedicated to his homeland, Russia (see Antipoff, 1975).

Upon leaving Russia, she also lost her Soviet citizenship. However, during the troubled years of the revolution, she added to her intellectual training that unique experience with a sociocultural approach to psychology that would profoundly influence her work in Brazil, as will be elaborated next.

FROM EXILE IN GENEVA TO ADVENTURE IN BRAZIL (1925–1929)

Back in Europe, Antipoff lived for a year in Berlin but in January 1926 decided to return to Geneva when Claparède invited her to work as his assistant at the Rousseau Institute. During her stay in Geneva, from 1926 till 1929, her research was centered on the development of intelligence, the relationship between higher mental processes and motor skills, and the development of moral judgment in children. At that time, her papers, published in the *Archives de Psychologie* and in the *Intermédiaire des Éducateurs,* were devoted to a concern for the study of children in their natural environment and directed at the study of children's process of knowing and of reacting to their environment. One of the papers dealt with the application of Lazurski's natural experimentation method in schools. The technique consisted of allowing children freely to explore different activities at school. It was supposed that children would stop exploring when they found the activity most attuned to their natural interests. During the exploratory period, the children were observed and several dimensions of their personalities evaluated. In the same year, Antipoff published a paper on the development of motor aptitudes (Antipoff, 1926, 1927, 1928a, 1928b, 1992b).*

By the end of the 1920s, the Institut Jean Jacques Rousseau attracted educators from all over the world. Claparède's work had been translated into several languages, and Geneva was established as a widely known center of studies on child psychology and "Active School" methods.† For this reason, when the Minas Gerais state government decided to establish a Teachers Training College designed for the training of educational specialists and managers in Belo Horizonte, capital of the state, a mission was sent to Geneva as well as to Paris and to Columbia University in New York to invite foreign specialists to prepare Brazilian teachers

---

* A complete list of Antipoff's published works, until 1929, as well as her academic biography, are found in Murchison (1929). The Register lists around 1300 psychologists active at the time, all over the world. It includes all full members of the APA, those with PhDs in psychology, and nominees from other countries selected by the editorial board (F. Bartlett, England; Karl Buhler, Austria; H. Piéron, France; S. De Sanctis, Italy; and four other members, representing Poland, Sweden, Japan, and USSR). The nominees represent probably the large majority of researchers in psychology around the world at the time.

† The Rousseau Institute received nearly 200 foreign students in 1926. Claparède's Psychologie de l'enfant et pédagogie expérimentale had been translated into Rumanian (1911), Italian (1912), English (1911), Hungarian (1915), Polish (1918), Czech (1925); L'école et la psychologie expérimentale (Lausanne: Payot, 1916) was translated into German, Spanish, Armenian, Polish, and Portuguese, L'orientation professionnelle (Geneva: Bureau International du Travail, 1922) into English, Spanish, Polish, Rumanian, and Russian. Comment diagnostiquer les aptitudes chez les écoliers (Paris: Flammarion, 1924) into Spanish and Russian (Claparède, 1926).

at the newly established institution. Helena Antipoff accepted the offer of a 2-year contract in 1929 and left Geneva once again. After several renewals, she decided to stay in Brazil for good and in 1952 became a Brazilian citizen.

WORK AS A PSYCHOLOGIST AND EDUCATOR IN BRAZIL

During the 1920s, several educational reforms were promoted in Brazilian states. Under the influence of a group of progressive educators, the founders of the Brazilian Education Association in 1924 aimed both to expand the number of available opportunities for schooling and to rationalize school administration. The contribution of psychologists to these reforms was highly valued. Having had access to the literature on the progressive education movement in Europe and in the United States, the early leaders of the "Escola Nova" movement recommended the introduction of IQ tests for the purpose of evaluating the potentials of the many children looking for a place within the system. Besides this, they reinforced the importance of the training of the new generation in the academic and civic skills required for a society in a process of modernization and urbanization (O'Neill, 1975; Wirth, 1977).

In Minas Gerais, the 1927 school reform, among other initiatives, proposed the establishment of a Teachers' Training College, where educators would be prepared to apply the new methods proposed by the "escolanovistas." Educational psychology was introduced as a regular course at normal schools, and at the Teachers' College the study of educational psychology aimed at further developing knowledge of local children through research and standardization of IQ tests (Peixoto, 1981).

In August 1929, Helena Antipoff began teaching at the Belo Horizonte Teachers Training College. Her students were, for the most part, normal school graduates already working as school principals or supervisors in the public school system. A few students came from other states to attend the full-time 2-year program. At the Teachers Training College Laboratory of Psychology, she started a program of research for the purpose of studying the mental development, ideals, and interests of local children.

In 1930, the first report was published, with the results of an inquiry into fourth graders' ideals and interests. Antipoff's purpose in this study was to "orient myself, as soon as possible, as to the psychology of small Brazilians, and to understand their general psychic character" (Antipoff, 1930, p. 5). The influence of the Geneva "Active school," as well as of the Soviet historical-cultural approach, can be observed in this research: Antipoff aimed at investigating the kind of children to which Brazilian schools should be adapted. A questionnaire was designed, to be answered by a sample of fourth graders, dealing with preferred tasks at home and at school, preferred toys and books, adult models, and plans for the future. The results were compared with those obtained in other countries and revealed the action of social environment in shaping children's inner trends.

Brazilian children's ideals and interests seemed more limited and less diversified than those of their foreign counterparts. Antipoff interpreted these results in light of their coming, for the most part, from a modest social milieu, in which family life was still the predominant experience in children's lives. She also observed the influence of schooling in these results: Brazilian children had fewer daily hours of classes than Europeans or North Americans. How would school enrich and diversify students' experiences? In her view, children's inner nature could develop adequately only in a sufficiently diversified environment, in which "several kinds of children will find an adequate destiny for their nature" (Antipoff, 1930, p. 42). These basic assumptions would guide her later work in Brazil: on one hand the concern over the impact of social environment in shaping human cognitive features, and on the other the idea that schools could successfully help to develop children's capacities.

Continuing the research on local children, Antipoff studied the mental development of schoolchildren using adaptations of IQ tests such as the Binet-Simon scale and the Goodenough *Draw-a-Man* test. The purposes of the studies were (1) to investigate the mental development of local schoolchildren by age group; (2) to compare their mental development with that of school-age children in other countries; and (3) to investigate how mental development varies according to social background. In these researches, Antipoff provided a deeper examination of the impact of society and culture on the development of cognitive skills, a theme that increasingly influenced her work in Brazil. Based on Claparède's and Binet's definitions of intelligence as a "capacity for solving, through thought, new problems" (Claparède, 1933, p. 3), Antipoff observed that intelligence tests only imperfectly rely on abilities of comprehension and invention implied in such a definition. In her view, mental tests' results should be considered more modestly as an evaluation of what could be called the level of mental development of a given population. This would include, rather than a pure capacity for invention, the abilities for concentrating attention, for observation, logical reasoning, and a general "fluidity of thought." But this was only part of the problem. The other important question that should be asked was whether intelligence could be considered natural, that is, depending only on children's innate disposition and age for its development. For Antipoff, intelligence was a combination of innate intellectual dispositions and biological growth, character, and social environment—including life conditions and culture, influenced also by the experience of the child at school.

Following this reasoning, Antipoff provided her own definition for the capacities measured by intelligence tests—the mental abilities polished by the action of society and culture, which she called *civilized intelligence.* In this definition she recalled her experience with Soviet street children as well as the observation of street children in Brazil. Those children, although presenting lower scores when subjected to intelligence scales, were not feeble-minded. They lacked a certain capacity to concentrate voluntary attention on one hand and to attain a certain abstraction leading to conceptual thought on the other hand. But in the concrete domain, stimulated by instinct, interest, or spontaneous attention, they would certainly succeed.

The investigation of the mental development of Belo Horizonte schoolchildren verified empirically the accuracy of Antipoff's concept of civilized intelligence. Test results showed, on average, an inferior performance by local children compared with European or North American ones. The results suggested also an association between socioeconomic status and test scores. To confirm this correlation, the mean IQ scores for each school were compared, leading to the conclusion that "the ranking of each school corresponds roughly to the level of economic and social welfare of the neighborhood where each school is located" (Antipoff, 1937, p. 191). As a conclusion, she observed that IQ tests should be used carefully in the evaluation of children's general level of mental development but that they could be considered a reasonable instrument to assess the level of social and economic welfare of the social group.

EXCEPTIONAL CHILDREN

Starting in 1932, Antipoff became involved in initiatives aimed at helping to solve the problems of intellectually retarded or poorly adapted children, which she proposed to name *exceptionals* to avoid the negative meaning associated with the word *abnormal*. Together with a group of Catholic priests, intellectuals, teachers, and philanthropists, she founded the Belo Horizonte Pestalozzi Society, an organization named after the famous Swiss educator, designed to help exceptional and socially disadvantaged children. In 1933, the Pestalozzi Society established a medical-pedagogical station for the examination and guidance of those children. Soon after, the station became the Pestalozzi Institute, receiving children "bearing any mental deficiency or disorder such as feeblemindedness, mental retardation, nervousness, language or writing disorders, deaf-mutes, enuretics, or bearers of defects of a social or moral character" (Sociedade Pestalozzi, 1934, p. 129).

The treatment of children's troubles was to be performed in the special classes established at the institute, where they would be divided into groups according to their IQs. The definition of the concept of exceptionality adopted by Antipoff included, in addition to organic troubles found in a minority of school-age children, also the abnormality socially produced by a school system the requirements of which were beyond common children's possibilities. Above all, Antipoff did not consider abnormality a definitive, irremediable defect. For her, the majority of children presenting some mental abnormality was educable and could be helped to succeed (Antipoff, 1992b).

Moreover, for Antipoff the concept of mental exceptionality included disorders other than limited intelligence. Children presenting lower results in IQ tests could also present personality troubles due to their primary socialization. She was aware that families living below the poverty line were far from offering the ideal conditions for their children's healthy development. Pestalozzi Society researchers found a high incidence of alcoholism, violence, and other problems in lower-class families, the children of which were examined at their Medical-Pedagogical Station. In most cases, IQ test results could be considered a symptom of an entire complex of social and family problems experienced by "exceptional" children. Her proposals at the Pestalozzi Society aimed at providing support for children bearing a variety of social, domestic, and psychological troubles—from physical disabilities to tendencies toward early delinquency. For this reason, her concept of exceptionality included several types of disorders.

By the end of the 1930s, and having decided to stay in Brazil, Antipoff promoted the establishment of a model school for retarded and abandoned children, sponsored by the Pestalozzi Society, in the countryside next to Ibirité, a small town near Belo Horizonte. In her view, this school would be the site for the demonstration of practical ways of dealing with exceptional children. Following guidelines issued by the Bureau International des Écoles Nouvelles in 1919, the Fazenda do Rosário Farm School was created for the purpose of applying "Active School" methods for the education of exceptional children in an appropriate rural environment (Antipoff, 1946, 1952, 1956, 1966).

The Farm School can be considered Antipoff's major creation. At Rosário she attempted to provide the ideal environment for the education of all exceptional children. The school became a living experiment during the 1950s and 1960s, including among its activities those related to the education of teachers for rural schools. In Antipoff's view, since the majority of Brazilians lived in the countryside (from where came most of the exceptional children who failed in urban schools), the civilization provided by educational institutions should be taken to rural areas. This would enable the common people to make their living out of the earth, contributing to eliminating poverty from urban squatters. For these reasons, Antipoff saw the education of common people as an end in itself, considering schooling as a source of democratization. Her reactions to children's poor living conditions stemmed mostly from her concern with their rights, quoting the Genevan Declaration of Children's Rights issued by the League of Nations in 1924. In her view, schools are not supposed to provide a limited consciousness of citizenship. On the contrary, citizenship was seen as the consequence of a steady support for the development of children's capacities (Antipoff & Rezende, 1934).

Dissatisfied with her experience with war and revolution in Europe, Antipoff strove for harmony, not for struggle. In her view, social harmony would be attained if all individuals were given the opportunity to develop their own calling. In this development, education had a central role. Believing in education as a scientifically based process, Antipoff followed her master Claparède: the science of education would little by little accumulate knowledge to help children's development in a harmonious, free, and cooperative environment. All her life, Antipoff kept this faith in science as well as the view that individuals become useful to society to the extent that they are allowed and helped to develop their vocations. In this sense, a school system would be democratic to the extent that students are supported and encouraged to develop their capacities. Mental tests could be useful instruments to be employed when a deeper knowledge of children's possibilities is required. But they are just a beginning, a first step for schools in the planning of their development. Children's success in education is, therefore, the responsibility of schools and not of individuals alone. A variety of methods of instruction, stemming from "Active School" proposals, should be put into practice to allow schools to accomplish their civilizing role.

Helena Antipoff died on August 9, 1974. She is considered a pioneer in developmental and educational psychology in Brazil for her work as a researcher, a university professor of psychology, and as an institution builder. As a researcher, she established one of the first laboratories of psychology in the country, leading a consistent program of investigations about Brazilian children's psychological and psychosocial characteristics, a unique experience in the country at the time. In this laboratory, she contributed to the scientific training of a generation of school teachers and educational specialists with a lasting influence on Brazilian education in general and special education in particular. As a professor, she initiated the training of psychologists at the university level in the State of Minas Gerais and contributed substantially to the movement leading to the regulation of the profession in Brazil in 1962. As an institution builder, she designed a model for the first child guidance clinics and for a wide-ranging system of institutions dedicated to the education of individuals with special needs now represented by the several Pestalozzi Societies and Associations of Parents and Friends of Exceptionals distributed throughout the country. The model and methodology adopted in all these institutions, based on tolerance and respect for differences, was initiated at the small Pestalozzi Society created in Belo Horizonte in 1932, under her leadership and care.

Her main legacy is considered to be in the hands and heads of the many students and disciples spread throughout institutions of education and higher learning in Brazil. A modest and unpretentious person, she received the many honors bestowed on her works with detachment, transferring her prestige to her followers and collaborators. The money she received in 1973 as a prize for her work as an educator of children with special needs, granted by an association of Brazilian industrialists,° was invested in a new institution, designed for the education of the gifted. Regarding the many prizes and accolades she received during her extended and productive life, she commented that this was purely a demonstration of kindness from the part of the people who promoted them.

As a psychologist, she combined two attitudes that many may consider irreconcilable: the scientific rigor of a researcher along with the richness and sensibility of a clinical approach. This blend led her to value science as a guide for well-informed action for the benefit of mankind. Having lost her native homeland, Russia, and having learned deep respect for human rights during her education in Geneva, she adopted many Brazilian students and children as her family, dedicating to them her energy, dynamism, knowledge, and professional competence. Her dedication to the ideals of democracy was expressed in her belief that education should be a right for every human being and that helping others is a way to attain human understanding and happiness.

In the education of exceptional children she recommended:

> To highlight truly democratic attitudes, in which personal responsibilities are together with consciousness of collective responsibilities, so that work is the product of everyone and everybody at the same time…. To prove that every human being has his/her own value and that all people must contribute, with their talents, to the progress of humanity. To show also that human value is not limited to intellectual abilities, but that other characteristics, such as moral aptitudes, effort, humility, altruistic feelings, virtues found so often in exceptional individuals, are a relevant social treasury in those

---

° The 1973 Boilesen Prize was awarded to Antipoff by the Associação Brasileira de Produtores de Gás (Brazilian Association of Gas Producers) for her work in the education of exceptional children in Brazil (Antipoff, 1975).

times in which selfishness, greedness and the exploitation of the weak by the strong prevail. Our Pestalozzian works thus appear as a work of justice and of compensation for the evils pervading present social life. (Antipoff, 1992a, p. 307)

SUGGESTED READINGS

Antipoff, H. (1992). *Coletânea das Obras Escritas de Helena Antipoff* (vol. 1—Psicologia experimental; vol. 2 – Fundamentos da educação; vol. 3—Educação do excepcional; vol. 4—Educação rural; vol. 5—A educação do bem dotado). Belo Horizonte: Imprensa Oficial.

The five volumes of Antipoff's collected works present her most important contributions in the areas of experimental psychology, foundations of education, education of exceptionals, rural education, and education of the gifted. Her most relevant research findings in psychology are presented in the first and third volumes, where the concepts of intelligence as the product of cultural experiences and of exceptionality as difference are explained. The second, fourth, and fifth volumes present her ideas and suggestions concerning education from the standpoint of the socioconstructivist approach she adopted.

Ruchat, M. (Ed.). (2010). *Édouard Claparède—Hélène Antipoff—Correspondance* (1914–1940). Firenzi: Leo S. Olschki Editore.

A careful organization of the correspondence between two important leaders of psychology in the twentieth century, Édouard Claparède, psychiatrist and psychologist in Geneva, and his student and later collaborator Helena Antipoff, a pioneer psychologist in Brazil. Nearly 160 letters found in Claparède's and Antipoff's archives are organized chronologically and include 333 footnotes with data about the several persons and events referred in the letters. The volume is an outstanding contribution to the history of psychology in the twentieth century, including an important testimony regarding the relationship between science and politics, since both authors were engaged in the defense of democracy and human rights in an era of great social transformations, crisis, and violence (the two World Wars, the Russian Revolution, the Brazilian education reforms, and the 1930 Revolution, among other events). The correspondence also highlights their collaboration in the building of the field of developmental and educational psychology.

REFERENCES

Antipoff, D. (1975). *Helena Antipoff, Sua Vida, Sua Obra* (Helena Antipoff, her life and work). Rio de Janeiro: José Olympio Editora.

Antipoff, H. (1924). L'expérience russe. L'éducation sociale des enfants. (Russian experience. Social education of children) *Semaine Littéraire*, Geneva, *32*(1615), 592–594.

Antipoff, H. (1926). L'étude de la personnalité par la méthode de Lasoursky. (Personality study by the Lasoursky method). *L'Éducateur, 62*, 285–292.

Antipoff, H. (1927). Contribution à l'étude de la constance des sujets (Contribution to the study of constancy in subjects). *Archives de Psychologie, 20*(79), 177–90.

Antipoff, H. (1928a). L'évolution et la variabilité des fonctions motrices (Evolution and variability of motor functions). *Archives de Psychologie, 21*(81), 1–54.

Antipoff, H. (1928b). Observations sur la compassion et le sentiment de justice chez l'enfant (Observations about compassion and the feeling of justice in the child). *Archives de Psychologie, 21*(82), 209–215.

Antipoff, H. (1930). *Ideais e interesses das crianças de Belo Horizonte e algumas sugestões pedagógicas* (Ideals and interests of Belo Horizonte schoolchildren and some pedagogical suggestions). *Boletim* 6, Belo Horizonte, Secretaria do Interior do Estado de Minas Gerais, 46 pp.

Antipoff, H. (1937, January–March). O desenvolvimento mental das crianças de Belo Horizonte (The mental development of Belo Horizonte schoolchildren). *Revista do Ensino, 134*(6), 127–204.

Antipoff, H. (1946, December). A função social da assistência aos excepcionais (Assistance to exceptionals as a social work). *Neurobiologia*, Recife, 9(4).

Antipoff, H. (1952). *Missão rural para a Fazenda do Rosário* (A rural mission for the Rosário Farm-School). Ibirité, MG: Centro de Documentação e Pesquisa Helena Antipoff, unpublished.

Antipoff, H. (1956, January–March). Educação dos excepcionais (Education of exceptionals). *Revista Brasileira de Estudos Pedagógicos*, Rio de Janeiro, 25(31), 222–227.

Antipoff, H. (1966). Educação dos excepcionais e sua integração na comunidade rural (The education of exceptionals and their integration into the rural community). *Boletim da Sociedade Pestalozzi do Brasil*, Rio de Janeiro, *31*, 7–18.

Antipoff, H. (1992a). *Coletânea das Obras Escritas de Helena Antipoff* (Vol. 1—Psicologia Experimental). (Helena Antipoff's Collected works, Vol. 1—Experimental psychology). Belo Horizonte: Centro de Documentação e Pesquisa Helena Antipoff.

Antipoff, H. (1992b). *Coletânea das Obras Escritas de Helena Antipoff* (Vol. 3—Educação do Excepcional), (Collected Works of Helena Antipoff, Vol. 3—Education of exceptionals). Belo Horizonte: Centro de Documentação e Pesquisa Helena Antipoff.

Antipoff, H., & Rezende, N. (1934). Ortopedia mental nas classes especiais (Mental orthopedics in special classes). *Boletim* 14, Belo Horizonte, Secretaria de Educação e Saúde Pública (State Secretary of Education and Public Health).

Audemars, M., & Lafendel, L. (1950). *La maison des Petits de l'Institut Jean-Jacques Russeau*. Neuchâtel: Delachaux et Niestlé.

Binet, A. (1902). *L'étude expérimentale de l'intelligence* (The experimental study of intelligence). Paris: Alfred Costes.

Binet, A. (1920). *Les idées modernes sur les enfants* (Modern ideas about children). Paris: Flammarion.

Claparède, E. (1926). *Psychologie de l'enfant et pédagogie expérimentale* (Child psychology and experimental pedagogy). Genève: Librairie Kundig.

Claparède, E. (1931). *L'Éducation fonctionnelle* (Functional education). Neuchâtel: Délachaux et Niestlé.

Claparède, E. (1933). Génèse de l'hypothèse (The genesis of the hypothesis). *Archives de Psychologie, 24*, 1–155.

Hameline, D., Jornod, A., & Belkaïd, M. (1995). *L'école active—textes fondateurs* (Active school —foundational texts). Paris: Presses Universitaires de France.

Hameline, D. (1996). Aux origines de la Maison des Petits (The origins of the House of Children). In C. Perregaux, F. Rieben, & C. Magnin (Eds.), *"Une école où les enfants veulent ce qu'ils font"—La Maison des Petits hier et aujourd'hui* (A school where children want what they do—the House of Children yesterday and today) (pp. 17–62). Lausanne: LEP—Loisirs et Pédagogie.

Murchison, C. (Ed.). (1929). *The psychological register* II. Worcester, MA: Clark University Press.

O'Neill, C. F. (1975). *The search for order and progress: Brazilian mass education 1915–1935*. PhD dissertation, University of Texas at Austin.

Peixoto, A. M. C. (1981). *A reforma educacional Francisco Campos* (The Francisco Campos School Reform). Belo Horizonte: Faculdade de Educação da UFMG.

Sociedade Pestalozzi. (1934). *Ata da Assembléia Geral de Março de 1934* (Minutes of the General Assembly of March 1934). *Boletim* 16, Belo Horizonte, Secretaria de Educação e Saúde Pública.

van der Veer, R., & Valsiner, J. (1996). *Vygotski: uma síntese* (Vygotski, a synthesis). São Paulo: Ed. Loyola.

Vygotski, L. S. (1991). *Obras escogidas*, Vol. 1. (*Problemas teóricos y metodológicos de la psicología*) (Collected works—Theoretical and methodological problems in psychology). Madrid: Centro de Publicaciones del M.E.C. / Visor Distribuciones S.A.

Wirth, J. D. (1977). *Minas Gerais in the Brazilian federation*. Stanford: Stanford University Press.

Zusne, L. (1975). *Names in the history of psychology*. New York: Wiley.

5

Charlotte Bühler:
Scientific Entrepreneur in Developmental, Clinical, and Humanistic Psychology

WILLIAM R. WOODWARD

University of New Hampshire

This chapter will situate Charlotte Bühler (1893–1974) as a professional woman in developmental psychology and humanistic psychology. I will give special attention to *The First Year of Life* (Bühler, 1930), "The Human Life Course as Psychological Problem" (Bühler, 1933), *From Birth to Maturity* (Bühler, 1935), *The Child and His Family* (Bühler, 1939) and *The Course of Human Life* (Bühler & Massarik, 1968). Bühler belongs to the late first generation of women in psychology. Bühler's case is exceptional in that she had two children, did not take time off from her career, and secured family and extracurricular funding to support herself, her husband, and dozens of students in Austria up to 1938. In the United States as an émigré from 1940 to her death in 1974, she shifted to private practice to provide increasing support for a retired husband. She stood out as a creative scientific manager, writer, clinician, and theoretician in developmental psychology across the life span.

Figure 5.1   Charlotte Bühler.
(Courtesy of Verlag Hans Huber in Berne, Switzerland. With permission.)

FAMILY BACKGROUND AND EARLY YEARS, 1893–1912

Charlotte Malachowski was born the first child of Hermann Malachowski (1853–1934) and his wife, Rose Kristeller Malachowski (1873–1942?), in Berlin, Germany. She wrote, "Although descended from a largely Jewish family, I was confirmed and raised Protestant, as was the custom in the assimilation period then. Personal as well as metaphysical needs led me early to pursue the question of the existence of God" (Bühler, 1972, p. 9). Her father was an architect who designed numerous government buildings and worked with Alfred Messel (1853–1909) on the construction and expansion of the first German department store. Her mother was frustrated by the educational advantages of her brother, the art historian Paul Kristeller (1863–1931). She entertained lavishly and dressed in expensive outfits but regretted not having more education and opportunity, which her daughter sought to rectify in her own life (Bürmann & Herwartz-Emden, 1993). "Our travels belong to the most significant cultural influences that I owe to my parents.… I still cherish the unusually deep impression that the museums of Belgium and Holland made on me as a 9 to 12 year old" (Bühler, 1972, pp. 12–13). Charlotte wrote that her mother wanted her to become a singer, and that she took lessons in Greek and Latin while auditing courses at Berlin University (1972, p. 12). In the end, however, both parents allowed her to develop as she wished.

UNIVERSITY STUDIES, 1913–1916

Studying at a succession of universities, like many German students in that time, she sampled life in Freiburg in the Black Forest and Kiel on the North Sea, ending up in Prussian Berlin and Bavarian Munich during 1913 to 1916. "For me it was certain that I wanted to study psychology as a major in order to get clarity about human life, if not about God and the universe" (C. Bühler, 1972, p. 14). She ranged far and wide in her courses, taking philosophy in Freiburg with Heinrich Rickert (1863–1936) and Edmund Husserl (1859–1938), though she was unimpressed by Jonas Cohn (1869–1947) in a psychology class. In any case, philosophy and psychology were not yet separate disciplines. Returning to Berlin, she attended the lectures of Benno Erdmann (1851–1921) and Georg Simmel (1858–1918), and took philosophy of religion from Adolf von Harnack (1851–1930), and some medical courses. The decision for liberal arts over medicine became "a huge problem," but her subsequent courses confirmed her choice: She sampled national liberal historian Friedrich Meinecke (1862–1954) and Swiss art historian Heinrich Wölfflin (1864–1945), who drew from Wundt for his stylistic analysis and held that art resembled the human body, such as house façades as faces.

In spring and summer 1914 she attended both the Psychological Institute and Women Teacher's College in Kiel. Worried about her father's gambling habit, she wanted to have a teaching degree to fall back on. She was also concerned about Prussian attitudes toward women. She returned to Berlin for the winter semester and took the teacher's examination at Easter 1915 (Birren, 1971; Bühring, 2007, pp. 32–33, 193).

She also fell in love and became engaged: "for the first time I experienced love paired with sexual needs, which had developed very slowly in me" (Bühler, 1972, p. 16). Then war broke out; Heinz Horstman was sent to the Russian front and returned in an unstable mental condition. He broke off their engagement, saying he needed a wife "oriented to care and attention." Evidently he recognized her ambition. She remarked in retrospect, "I felt not only the loss of my first love but a rejection as the woman that I was" (1972, p. 16).

Obtaining an endorsement from the Kiel Psychology Institute director, Goetz Martius (1853–1927), she took her dissertation idea on "psychological thought processes" to Carl Stumpf (1848–1936; Chapter 4, *Pioneers IV*) in Berlin. With typical strong will, she declined his suggestion to write about "feeling sensations" for a prize competition "because his ideas did not persuade me and my own research plans were closely connected with my personal train of thought" (Bühler, 1972, p. 17). Recognizing her unusual self-direction, and perhaps impressed by her family background, Stumpf wrote a warm letter of recommendation to Oswald Külpe (1862–1915) in Munich. Her mother brought her to Munich and installed her in a rooming house in fall 1915. Stumpf's unmarried sister hosted her socially. Professor Külpe impressed her with his kind interest in her experiments and his personality. But he died suddenly of an infection contracted in a military hospital during the Christmas break in 1915. He was only 53 years old, and his death came as a "thunderbolt."

Würzburg School Experimental Roots

By the time of Külpe's death, Charlotte had read the work of the Würzburg School on imageless thought and seen its promise. Experimenting psychologists, including Stumpf in Berlin and Külpe in Würzburg, had begun to challenge positivism in psychology and philosophy (Ash, 1995; Kusch, 1995). Positivism meant treating sensations, cognitions, and feelings as elements of consciousness and association as the law of their combinations. Inspiration for this challenge came from Alexius Meinong in Graz, Austria, and William James in Cambridge, Massachusetts. James called attention to the Psychologist's Fallacy of saying, for example, that we do not retain the perception of one eye when we combine it with the perception of the other eye. Rather, we fuse the sensations into one. Wilhelm Dilthey in Berlin called for the study of "lived experience" and recommended the study of lives, but he lacked empirical methods. Edmund Husserl (1859–1938) advanced phenomenology as descriptive psychology, the theoretical claim that experiences have primacy over complexes of sensations. Charlotte had listened to his lectures in Freiburg.

These revolutionary currents in psychology and philosophy came together in the work of Karl Bühler (1879–1963). He had a reputation for challenging Wundt: "Bühler's investigation was much more ambitious than his colleagues.' His stimulus materials were complex questions requiring extensive thought processes.... Perhaps the success of the Würzburger attack can be measured by the virulence of the reply" (Mandler, 2007, pp. 85, 88). He was well known for his work on thought processes (Bühler, 1907), and the topic became central to Charlotte's dissertation. Thought psychology (*Denkpsychologie*) represented a bold challenge to the psychology of Wilhelm Wundt and Hermann Helmholtz. In choosing Külpe's laboratory over Stumpf's, Bühler thus affiliated with the Würzburg experimental program in psychology. The model of cognition involved "mental set" and "directed thought" rather than conscious cognitions. She recalled that she was surprised to find Bühler visiting her laboratory daily, yet her experiments were "not dissimilar" to his (Bühler, 1972, p. 18). In claiming that he pursued her, she was being disingenuous, as archival materials suggest that she was actively courting him and that he had a long-standing girlfriend at the time (Eschbach, September 27, 2010, personal communication; Bürmann & Herwartz-Emden, 1993, p. 207; Bühring, 2007, p. 194). They married in April 1916 in Berlin in the presence of Kurt Koffka and his wife and Johannes Lindworsky, a Jesuit father who had studied with Külpe and Bühler.

CHILDREN AND STUDIES OF THOUGHT PROCESS, 1916–1922

Her first year of marriage was difficult due to pregnancy interfering with the continuation of her studies. She also felt rejection among Bavarian professors' wives as "a student married to a professor" and a North German. In addition, Karl suffered stress from serving as military doctor in the mornings and lecturer on logic in the afternoons. Meanwhile, she gave birth to a daughter, Ingeborg, on February 23, 1917. She also completed a dissertation on "Thought and Sentence Construction" in fall 1917 under Erich Becher (1882–1929) and Clemens Baeumker (1853–1924), at a time when Becher gained Külpe's chair (Bühring, 2002, p. 186). She published "on thought processes" (Bühler, 1918a) and "sentence formation" (Bühler, 1919), and her later work on life span development drew upon Karl's thought psychology indirectly, in that she emphasized "goal orientation" and self-direction. At Karl's urging, she also published her first book (Bühler, 1918b) on the conviction that fairy tales exercise the child's mental functions of thought, empathy, and desire. This book went through seven editions. Child psychologist William Stern (1871–1938) commented approvingly about Bühler's little book in later editions of his textbook (1987).

Karl, meanwhile, published *The Intellectual Development of the Child* (1918), which became a leading text in the field. It was based on his own brand of thought psychology and the psychology of language. As a result of his promise as a scientist, he gained a professorship in Dresden in October 1918. Charlotte gave birth to a son, Rolf Dietrich, on June 2, 1919. She later completed a *Habilitationschrift* on the psychology of literature (1920) under Oskar Walzel (1884–1944) at Dresden, and she immediately became a *Privatdozentin* with the right to teach (Bühler, 1972, p. 21).

She made two more detours before turning to life span work. The first involved the psychology of youth, stemming from a contract with the state to study youth criminality statistically. The Prussian State government invited Karl to take on the project. He, in turn, recommended Charlotte to continue his work on perception and language. Her second detour grew out of her own diary along with three others given to her, which she compiled into a small book, *The Mental Life of Young People* (Bühler, 1922). The book became a huge success, complementing the contemporary work of philosopher and educationist Eduard Spranger (1882–1963). She expanded the project to 79 diaries in 1929 (5th ed.), and by 1934 the

Vienna Institute had received 93 donated diaries (Bühring, 2007). This work thus stretched over a decade. We see here how Bühler combined literary talent with psychology as she pursued her question "how a person ought to live human life appropriately" (Bühring, 1972, pp. 22–23). "My success was unexpectedly large but I was not satisfied with myself because I felt that this book did not reach the theoretical level I was striving for" (p. 23).

She claimed that she was happy in Dresden, but her husband complained of limited opportunities because psychology remained a marginal discipline at the technical university, and he gladly accepted a call to Vienna after placing second on the list for Berlin when Wolfgang Köhler was called there.

THE EARLY VIENNA YEARS: EARLY CHILD DEVELOPMENT INSTITUTE AND U.S. FUNDING, 1922–1928

When Karl then received a prestigious appointment to Vienna in 1922, he nego-tiated a psychological laboratory. The conditions of acceptance in Vienna were propitious with the Vienna city government under Social Democratic control (Ash, 1987, p. 146). The city provided laboratory space in the School Board building and later hired both Karl and Charlotte to teach at the Paedagogical Academy, while the Ministry of Education paid salaries to an assistant and a maintenance worker. A recently passed school reform law endorsed a "unified school" that superseded a class-based one (Benetka, 1995; Weinzierl, 1981).

Soon after they arrived in Vienna, a colleague from another discipline rec-ommended her for a 10-month stay in the United States. The historian Alfred Francis Pribram (1859–1942) was in charge of recruiting applications to the Laura Spellman Rockefeller Fund. He was known for a book in English on the causes of the First World War. She recalled that "the honor was too great to turn down, despite the enormous personal sacrifice of a 10-month separation from my husband and children. In addition I feared this foreign land unknown to any European" (Bühler, 1972, p. 25). During her stay in 1924–1925 she made the acquaintance of leading figures in psychology. She visited Edward Lee Thorndike (1874–1949) at Columbia and Arnold Gesell (1880–1961) at Yale, sending home much American psychological literature. Her critiques of these and other leading psychologists, which I will examine next, reveal a scientific mind of great originality.

In her autobiography (Bühler, 1972), she wrote that she recoiled from studying reflexes like the American behaviorists John B. Watson and Arnold Gesell. Instead, she took up the study of "the entire behavior of the child," especially social behav-ior (Bühler, 1931). She said she adapted the method of studying chicks employed by Thorlief Schjelderup-Ebbe and David Katz. Thus, her initial inspiration seemed to be the study of animal behavior. She did not credit her husband for her scien-tific methods, though she was otherwise generous in acknowledging his theoretical ideas. Both were syncretic thinkers who integrated the work of others (Ash, per-sonal communication, October 3, 2010). Karl earned a reputation as a strong critic of behaviorism in his *The Crisis in Psychology* (1927) (Wellek, 1964).

She, on the other hand, seems to have welcomed behaviorism's approach in general, though not the emphasis on reflexes and conditioning (Bühler & Hetzer, 1929). For example, she replaced the "behavior items" of Gesell and Vladimir Bechterev (1857-1927) with the term "performances, which proves to be the much more successful and productive viewpoint" (Bühler, 1930, p. 14). Attentive to her own priority, she claimed that Gesell did not acknowledge her idea of development as a sequence and of a development quotient, akin to the intelligence quotient (Bühler, 1972, p. 26). She did credit her husband for the conception of motor and inhibitor, which he called the hedonalgic reaction. She gave the example of a boy who smokes. He may react negatively to smoke, but he does it anyway (Bühler, 1930, p. 17).

Her early interest in the lives of infants may have stemmed from her own child rearing, albeit with the help of a governess. Her decision to study infants at this time is noteworthy too in that the conditions of her Rockefeller support were to study school children. She and Hetzer later admitted that they may have strayed from the Vienna School Board's plans for pedagogical reform (Ash, 1987, p. 151). "I thought that if I studied humans at the beginning of their lives, I would learn to understand the goal directions of life" (Bühler, 1972, p. 26).

She sharpened her observations and her theoretical framework through discussion with Edward Lee Thorndike at Columbia University. She saw a problem in his "quantitatively defined behavioral units," that is, the learning curves of which he was so enamored. "Even today I find that the selection of various units into numbers is a fundamental problem" (Bühler, 1972, p. 26). She corresponded with Thorndike for years: "there was a certain rivalry" (Hetzer, 1982, p. 193).

She may have overstated her financial prowess when she reported that they received a 10-year fellowship of monthly funds beginning in 1926 (Bühler, 1972, p. 26). Mitchell Ash found documents in the Rockefeller archives only for support of $4,000 per year beginning in 1931 (LSRM, Box 57, Folder 51; Ash, 1987, pp. 153, 162, n. 37). After the Nazis took over in Austria and a conservative city government was installed, this sum was cut in half for 1936 and 1937 and then dropped altogether (Ash, 1987, p. 155). The funds, in any case, found valuable use in supporting graduate student assistants. The Bühlers were hardly alone in receiving aid. The Laura Spellman Rockefeller child study program led to the funding of many institutes in the United States and Europe, including Jean Piaget's institute in Geneva (Samelson, 1985). Her role in securing this prestigious funding cannot be overestimated, however. It was an extraordinary accomplishment for a woman in that era.

In the first 3 years from 1923 to 1926, the Bühlers had one assistant, Helmut Boeksch. When Charlotte returned to Vienna in 1925, now 32 with children aged 6 and 8, Karl had gotten the institute rolling with three divisions: (1) experimental psychology directed by himself and assisted by Helmut Boksch until 1929, then by Egon Brunswik; (2) economic and social psychology, headed by Paul Lazarsfeld, then by Herta Herzog and Marie Jahoda-Lazarsfeld; and (3) child and youth psychology, which he assigned to her to direct.

In 1926 Charlotte convinced the Child Reception Center to assign a teacher, Hildegard Hetzer, to assist her in child development research. Lotte Schenk-Danzinger joined them in 1927. Paul Lazarsfeld, at the time a high school teacher on leave, reported that Karl left the administration to his "full professor assistant"

Charlotte, who had "an almost Prussian ability to organize the activity of many people in various places" (Bühring, p. 54, quoted in Lazarsfeld, 1969, p. 161).

Charlotte's opportunity to build a research and teaching institution came with a personal cost (Bühler, 1972, p. 22). Her children told her as adults that she did not give them enough time. She admitted that this remains "certainly one of the greatest problems of the career woman." Whereas many émigré women denied the importance of gender in their professional careers, Bühler did acknowledge it (Chodorow, 1989, p. 200, cited in Ash, 1995, p. 239). She did hire a governess, thanks to financial help from her parents. And they did own an expensive Packard.

Unique in the German-speaking countries and perhaps in the world, her team began literally dozens of fruitful collaborations with young doctoral students as well as guests from abroad. They directed a laboratory for round-the-clock observation of the child, including full body measurements and "the observer separated … by a glass wall" (Bühler, 1930, p. 4), comprising "an apparatus for total observation of the child" (Benetka, 1995). This was high-level science directed to technocratic reform. None of the other child study centers that the Laura Spelman Rockefeller Memorial funded had such resources, including human resources. At the Wednesday Colloquia, students, professors, and postdoctoral graduates would come together to discuss the latest research (Benetka, 1995; Bühring, 2007, pp. 94–96). Karl Bühler never reacted sharply to those who sometime dominated the discussion but turned the discussion to a new topic (Kardos, 1984). One imagines that he conducted himself in the marriage with equal grace.

FRUITS OF HER LABORATORY: COLLABORATIVE EMPIRICAL STYLE AND THEORETICAL MASTERY

Her book *The First Year of Life* (Bühler, 1930) represented a team effort, originally published under several coauthorships in German. Curiously, it appeared in English only under Charlotte's name. Two more women, Pearl Greenberg and Rowena Ripin, did the English translations. Clearly she had an administrative talent in building a team effort, while she functioned as scientific manager and theoretician.

Charlotte and her team took aim at several leading psychologists as she advanced Karl Bühler's pleasure theory against psychoanalytic pleasure theory. Drawing upon his child psychology book (1918, section vii), she argued that Freud's claim for the pleasure of sucking (*Befriedigungslust*) ignores the "function pleasure" (*Funktionslust*) of nourishment (Bühler, 1930, p. 45).

She also embraced her husband's developmental critique of the Gestalt school. She wrote that Koffka, in *The Growth of the Mind* (1921), implies that the child has the mind of an adult, "well established in all directions" (Bühler, 1930, p. 50). By contrast, he does not even consider the possibility that the newborn makes a forward-turning reaction independent of a stimulus.

Criticizing Bechterev's "defense movements," she argued that infants have both flight movements, like turning their head away when their nose is cleaned and movements toward objects, such as seeing and grasping a rattle (Bühler, 1930, pp. 22, 54). She found the presence of both positive and negative activities in the organism's repertoire from the very onset of life. She also improved on Arnold Gesell's 24-hour observations by doing a 9-day observation (pp. 129–135). She explained how her husband's approach differed: He was interested in perceptual and cognitive structures, especially language. His theory of speech acts in 1934 served as a precursor to that of Wittgenstein after World War II (Eschbach, 1989, p. 400).

Still, she was dissatisfied because she wanted to write a more theoretical work. "Only with my book 'Childhood and Youth' [*Kindheit und Jugend*] (1928) was I convinced that I could theorize adequately" (Bühler, 1972, p. 24). In it she introduced a five-phase scheme for the life course (*Lebenslauf*): (1) a functional phase of childhood; (2) youths begin to assert themselves by setting goals; (3) acting more maturely with productive work; (4) new tensions and intellectual connections sought and result (*Ergebnisse*); and (5) new personal relations as persons reach their conclusion and look backward. She was only 35 when she postulated this scheme, and it would continue to evolve into a humanistic theory of human development that is based on relatively healthy individuals. It is worth noting that Piaget in Switzerland and Oswald Kroh in Germany also proposed stage theories of child development at around this time. But she viewed life as a project and self as a structure that protects "the whole person" from being deconstructed by neurosis (Derobertis, 2006, p. 54).

Scientific Couples

A book on scientific couples (Abir-Am & Outram, 1987) found three instances (including Marie Curie) where the wives "succeeded in maintaining an independent scientific credit rather than being assimilated into the husband's reputation," due to the wives' "great talent and determination" as well as their "husbands' progressive, liberal, or unconventional beliefs and attitudes" (p. 11). This fits Bühler, who wrote retrospectively about complementary research interests: "The fact that Karl and I worked in such diverse fields came as a benefit to our students though of course there was only one full professor for psychology" (Bühler, 1972, p. 27). In Europe at the time a single full professor often directed the assistant and associate professors of an institute, who were paid only from student fees:

> I myself was at least promoted to Associate Professor in 1929, though without salary. Fortunately, I had a sufficient income from my books and lecture tours to cover our child care and household help. (Bühler, 1972, p. 27)

Note the sex role assumption that her income covered domestic expenses. Surely it benefited their scientific partnership that she worked in a related area that qualified them to receive external funding for school-related projects. Karl was also "stepping outside of the conventional marriage patterns" while benefitting from the "emotional and sexual assets" of an attractive wife (Abir-Am & Outram, 1987, p. 12). A Dutch interviewer reported "an unusually good looking, confident self-conscious woman, arriving now—slender, sporty, average size, in bright sand-colored summer dress, shining hair.... She is accustomed to awaken notice and become the focus of attention.... She speaks meanwhile in flowing English" (Ammers-Küller, 1935, pp. 276–277). Socially, she outshone her husband, who was "more restrained," coming from modest circumstances, though he "was an extremely charming, entertaining, and inspiring man" (Kardos, 1984, pp. 31–39, quoted in Bürmann & Herwartz-Emden, 1993, p. 209). Intellectually, she was clearly his match. Her scientific output of books and articles, as reviewed here only in part, equaled or even surpassed his. She wrote as a scientific entrepreneur for many and varied audiences.

Both Karl and Charlotte gave lectures in many European countries, and each enjoyed extended stays in the United States. In 1929 they attended the International Congress of Psychology in New Haven, and she remained for the winter at Barnard College. In 1930, he lectured at Johns Hopkins, Stanford, and Harvard and received a call to Harvard. He was inclined to settle there, but as Charlotte later wrote, "I loved Vienna and my circle of co-workers and found America at the time culturally unattractive. If I had guessed how America would develop and change culturally in the 1940's, I would not have approved that fatal decision of Karl to decline" (Bühler, 1972, p. 27). This was not the only time that she decided their fate. It happened again under threatening political circumstances. Her husband declined an offer from Fordham University in 1937, and then she persuaded him to accept it only to have it withdrawn early in 1938. "The reason was the intervention of a cleric colleague who notified the Curia in Rome that the Catholic Karl Bühler entered a Protestant marriage and raised his children Protestant" (Bühler, 1965, p. 188). The betrayal came, she surmised, from Johannes Lindworsky, who attended their wedding and taught psychology in Rome (Bühring, 2007, p.124). In March 1938, he was arrested by the Nazis and released months later.

"THE LIFE COURSE": MULTIPLE METHODS IN RESEARCH, 1929–1938

During the later 1920s, Bühler had a testing program on children up to the sixth year of life. She completed another book with Hildegard Hetzer in 1932, and it appeared in English in 1935: *Testing Children's Development from Birth to School Age*. They tried to improve on Binet, Stern, Thorndike, the National Army Tests in the United States, and Gesell by testing the child's "total level of development" (Bühler, 1935, p. 30): "a good test should have the same function as a good diagnosis," to be followed up with "proper treatment" through education and child guidance (p. 19). "We never spoke about what it cost in effort for Charlotte Bühler to gain the agreement of the municipal authorities and to maintain their good will" (Hetzer, 1987, p. 19). Hetzer, who lived with the Bühlers, also provided child care for their two children (Bürmann & Herwartz-Emden, 1993).

More or less concurrently, Charlotte spent several years working with colleagues to assemble a detailed theory of the life course (Bühler, 1933). She acknowledged the help of studies of technicians and actors (Grete Mahrer), sports and life stages (Frieda Sack), dangerous moments in the lives of athletes and mountain climbers (Klaus Mohrmann), the lives of Liszt and Bruckner (Rudolf Schramek), works on life psychology reviewed (Ruth Weiß), achievements of workers and women's lives (Maria Schalit), philosophers and business lives (Paula Klein), politicians and journalists (Hedwig Kramer), the life of Bismarck (Erich Kollmann), the life of Casanova (Else Freistadt), the lives of farmers (Martha Fischer), and Vienna nursing homes (Marie Lazarsfeld, Margarete Andics). She singled out Miss Else Frenkel, "who led the younger colleagues in their research," acknowledging her "deep understanding and indefatigable cooperation" (p. ix). Frenkel later married Egon Brunswik, Karl's most famous student, who gained a professorship at the University of California–Berkeley.

The resulting book in German, *The Human Life Course as Psychological Problem* (Bühler, 1933), contained six chapters: (1) Behavior and Objective Data, (2) Experience and Subjective Data, (3) Work or Results, (4) The Phase Problem, (5) Basic Structure of Life Courses, and (6) Entire Structure and Partial Structure of Life Course. She reported that 250 lives support this work, including 50 from rest homes and 200 life stories from the literature, reworked by Egon Brunswik and Else Frenkel. Bühler explained that their team was not interested in individuals or individual types or with their development. Rather, they sought "developmental rules" and "a formal structure of this phenomenon" (Bühler, 1933, pp. 6–7). Then they applied this science to individual cases. The human being is not steered by instincts, as in psychoanalysis. Humans can be selective and "may even go against their own 'nature' and still believe that they are fulfilling themselves," as in Father Paul Ginhac, "who confessed that every minute of his life he condemned himself to death, in the name of his faith" (Bühler, 1959, p. 562, note 6). The book received some 48 reviews, for the most part praising the structural approach to life span as a whole (Bühring, 2007, pp. 90–91).

Only a few members of the psychoanalytic community secretly participated in their colloquia at the Institute, among them Siegfried Bernfeld, Ernst Kris, Friedrich Hacker, Paul Schilder, and Rudolf Ekstein (Bühring, 2007, p. 106; Ash, personal communication, October 3, 2010). Benetka (1995) refers to "the double life" of many Institute participants who dared not mention psychoanalysis in front of the Bühlers but who obtained analyses anyway. One such future analyst sensed significance in this book as well as a shortcoming. Paul Schilder (1933) reported that "C.B. has the tendency to overestimate the work, the objective mind, over the mental process that is undocumented. One has again and again the feeling that moral evaluations come into play for the author unconsciously" (p. 569). She may have taken this to heart, judging from her effort to get training in clinical psychology in the next phase of her life.

A New Education Fellowship took Charlotte to England in 1935, where she began a practice at the Parents' Association (Ash, 1995, p. 246). Lectures there led to a translation of a popular book, *From Birth to Maturity*, in 1935. She showed that the child maintains its balance in the face of external stimuli, drawing on her own institute's researches and others. In a hostile review, psychoanalyst Susan Isaacs noted that "the somewhat arrogant need to lay claim to her own method leads the author to confusion of judgment and leads her to minimize the researches of others" (Isaacs, 1937, p. 383).

MEASURING PARENT–CHILD RELATIONSHIPS, 1931–1939

The large role that family has in the social development of a child became the basis for her next collaborative project, *The Child and His Family* (1939). The data collection had occurred in 1931–1933. She and coworkers examined both parent–child relationships and sibling relations in 17 middle-class families. Bühler developed a system for measuring the interactions between parents and children that were evaluated by the purpose and situation under which the reaction took place (Bühler, 1939). Bühler's team measured relationships between siblings by "contacts;" they could be verbal or nonverbal, two-phased (93.83%) or multiphased (6.17%), including phases of "approach [has taken the initiative] and response [to another's advances]" (Bühler, 1939, p. 18). She called particular attention to the attitude of the interaction, classifying statements as neutral, for, or against another person. She conjectured that if interactions between siblings or between parents and children failed to express attitudes overtly, either positive or negative, "relations in their true colors" may not emerge and there is a dilemma that must be resolved (p. 20). The interactions reflect their views of love, affection, and romance, which in turn help to predetermine relationships the children will have. This includes romantic relationships as well as platonic and future parental relationships. Recall that she had not yet received training in clinical psychology, and she carried the torch for a soft behavioral approach to human social interaction emphasizing "behavioral tendencies." Her book bristled with bar graphs of "intentions": social, pedagogical, organizational, charitable, and economic (Bühler, 1939, p. 19), in addition to "intended purposes" of affection, instruction, guidance, consideration, giving help, asking help, and taking care (p. 85).

The Vienna research style became the model for later empirical research institutes, such as the Bureau of Social Research at Columbia under Paul Lazarsfeld (1969) and the Cologne Institute of Sociology under René König. The director would guide projects under a common theme, such as the aforementioned books demonstrate. Students received considerable freedom to construct their own research project (Benetka, 1995, pp. 64–67). Karl was averse to any kind of "representing" of the institute, recruiting students, or showing visitors around (Hetzer, 1987, p. 19). Yet students came from around the world. If this testimony is accurate, Charlotte must have served as the entrepreneur who marketed the shop.

ESCAPE FROM NAZI AUSTRIA, 1938–1939

The political situation had been changing since the late 1920s in Vienna. The conflict between the Social Democrats and the clerical-conservative Christian Social movement became increasingly violent. The signature of Karl Bühler, Alfred Adler, and Sigmund Freud on a petition in 1927 testifies to this (Ash, 1987, note 162). Engelbert Dollfuss instituted a dictatorship in 1934, and the cooperation of city and national officials gradually came apart. Her work for the socialist city government exposed her to criticism from the Right when the Dollfuss dictatorship took over.

Traveling again to the United States, France, and England as a Rockefeller Fellow in 1935, Charlotte did not listen to the warnings of emigrated German colleagues. Meanwhile, a change had occurred at the Rockefeller Foundation. The Medical Division instead of the Social Sciences Division now administered the Rockefeller funding of the Vienna Institute. A 1934 report mentioned "too large a percentage of students of inferior quality" coming from foreign countries (Ash, 1987, p. 155). In 1936, the Bühlers petitioned the Ministry for money, receiving a fifth of what they had received from the foundation. They gathered private support from a patrons' group. On November 17, 1936, police raided the Research Center for Economic Psychology and arrested five staff members for using the center's rooms as a secret mail drop for the Social Revolutionary underground.

In 1937, the Bühlers received joint calls to Fordham University; however, this time Charlotte wanted to accept, and Karl did not. Finally he gave in and they accepted for fall 1938, but it was too late. The Nazis annexed Austria on March 12 while she was in England. The Nazis arrested Karl and released him in May. He had the choice of early retirement or forced emigration (DAÖW, 1938, cited in Ash, 1987, pp. 158, 164n). In the meantime, Charlotte Bühler had received a visiting appointment in Oslo.

RETRAINING IN CLINICAL PSYCHOLOGY AND FINDING A FOOTING IN THE UNITED STATES, 1938–1950

Charlotte had a benefactor in Oslo who provided housing, and the university invited her and Karl to give lectures. In 1939 she was appointed professor at Trondheim Teacher's Academy, and in 1940 she was called to a professorship at the University of Oslo, as successor to Helga Eng. Karl landed a professorship at Scholastica College in Duluth in 1940 and then St. Thomas College in St. Paul, Minnesota, with the assistance of the American Psychological Association's Emergency Committee in Aid of Foreign Psychologists (Ash, 1995). She left Oslo on March 29 on the last free flight out of Norway; the Nazis took over April 10. Later she wrote, "I knew that my life would be ended if I fell into the hands of the Nazis" (Bühler, 1972, p. 32). She paid for her flight with a summer position at Berkeley, thanks to their friend Edward Tolman. She was hired at St. Catherine College in St. Paul. Tragically, her widowed mother was deported to a concentration camp and murdered, presumably, in 1942.

Lacking graduate students, they tried to gain positions in the East, and she taught for 2 years at Clark University in Worcester, Massachusetts. She also founded a child guidance center and commuted to teach at City College of New York by invitation of Gardner Murphy. Now 47, she tired of living separately from Karl, who was teaching back in St. Paul. She had gotten to know Bruno Klopfer in New York, who interpreted her Rorschach test himself, and she next took up a position in clinical psychology at the Minneapolis General Hospital. She became interested in diagnosis and psychotherapy. Suffering "inner collapse," she worried that "without studying the motivational process at a deeper *niveau* [level] and penetrating psychoanalysis theoretically and practically, I could no longer suitably lead my own search for full understanding of the life course" (Bühler, 1972, p. 35).

This decade was more fruitful professionally than her slowed publication rate showed. Her manual for the administration, scoring, interpretation, and statistical treatment of Rorschach scores established her as a leader in this clinical field (Bühler, Bühler, & Lefever, 1949). She included her husband as coauthor, and, indeed, he seems to have helped her to interpret the cognitive and emotional content of the protocols. A wartime committee and a general editor, Gardner Murphy, asked her to reflect on "the problem of Germany" (Bühler, 1945): "Is German war-mindedness due to personality maladjustment in the clinical sense?" (p. 93). She studied 12 families from Germany, Austria, Norway, Holland, and England, plus 24 from the United States. She recommended re-education in Germany, compulsory nursery school, child-guidance clinics, and political education. Germans would be "unresponsive to the casual and empirical ideology that Anglo-Saxons handle so successfully" (p. 107). One wonders what her findings would be today.

In 1945 they moved again, to Pasadena, California, where their son had started work on his doctorate and married an American. Charlotte was hired by the Los Angeles County General Hospital, an offer of professorships in psychology at the University of Southern California fell through, and Karl took a clinical position at Cedars of Lebanon Hospital. This therapeutic turn "meant ... a new beginning in the direction that I had recognized already in Europe as urgently necessary for my further development. For Karl, however, there was unfortunately no corresponding renewal" (Bühler, 1965, p. 189). Lewis Coser (1984) may have missed the mark in claiming that "stimulating exchanges with students and colleagues" were "denied her in America, and her work suffered as a result" (p. 41).

In 1951, at age 58, 11 years after immigrating, she finally began to publish research articles again, this time with her newfound clinical orientation (Bühler, 1954, 1959). She also built up a private practice in child psychology and then increasingly with adults. She and colleagues developed psychodrama with children and youths. She also began group therapy with adults and became active in the Group Psychotherapy Association of Southern California, becoming its president in 1957–58.

COLLABORATION ON A BOOK FOR TEACHERS AND COUNSELORS, 1952

There are important needs families meet for children. It is when these needs are not met that emotional disturbances can develop. The needs Bühler found most influential in the stability of the individual were emotional security, the home as "a refuge and guide," and behavior that does not exhibit the idea that affection must be earned by children (Bühler, 1952).

In *Childhood Problems and the Teacher* (Bühler, Smitter, & Richardson, 1952), published at age 59, she established her reputation in school psychology, contributing to the professionalization of educational psychologists and school counselors. In this book, once again, she assembled a network of collaborators: Faith Smitter, a director of child guidance in Santa Barbara, composed chapters on "the role of home and school" and on "the teacher's approach to problems." Sibyl Richardson, coordinator of research and guidance in the Los Angeles County Superintendent of Schools Office, presented "situational difficulties" and "work with parents." In a chapter on "the teacher's study of individual children," Richardson presented methods of observation records, the personal interview, standardized tests, sociometric analysis, reaction stories, art expression, interviews with adults, and cumulative records in folders (Bühler et al., 1952, pp. 143–154). Franklyn Bradshaw wrote on "remedial work in school." In her own opening chapter, she cited Lawrence K. Frank's (1949) book on projective techniques, Erik Erikson (1940) on play therapy, and Florence Goodenough on children's drawings (Goodenough & Harris, 1950). Her syncretic style worked well to legitimate a range of techniques to mostly female primary and secondary school teachers.

HUMANISTIC PSYCHOLOGY, 1959–1974

In the late 1950s, Bühler worked with Abraham Maslow to promote a third force in psychology based on the primary role of values in life. In 1961 they founded the *Journal of Humanistic Psychology*. In 1970 Charlotte lectured in Amsterdam at the First International Congress on Humanistic Psychology (Baumgartner, 2010). Their group included Kurt Goldstein, H. L. Ansbacher, J. F. T. Bugenthal, Rollo May, Henry Murray, David Riesman, Carl Rogers, Ernest Schachtel, Adrian van Kaam, and Anthony Sutich. She announced this in *Psychologie im Leben unserer Zeit* (1962), translated as *Psychology for Contemporary Living* (1970), which sold 170,000 copies and was translated into Dutch, Italian, Finnish, Spanish, Hebrew, English, Portuguese, and Swedish.

She had a gift for publicizing her research. She published *An Introduction to Humanistic Psychology* with Melanie Allen in 1972. She was now 79. As Samantha Ragsdale (n.d.) remarked, citing Bugental (1975), "she seems never to quit." Her crowning collaborative project, *The Course of Human Life* (Bühler & Massarik, 1968), featured the chapters of eighteen colleagues, both clinicians and academicians. She theorized about determinants of goal setting. She acknowledged Abraham H. Maslow, who "encouraged the senior editor to bring her earlier studies on the course of human life into the frame of present-day American psychology" (p. vi).

In one of her six chapters, she questioned "How does the emotional impact of adequate or inadequate maternal love and care affect a child's goal setting? (Bühler, 1968, p. 174, citing Murphy, 1962; Spitz & Wolf, 1964; Bowlby, 1944). We recall her worries about her own child rearing. "My children, with whom I am thankfully close friends, told me as adults that I had not given them enough time. They had the benefit of an excellent governess for years with whom I discussed many problems as they came up … [H]ere lies one of the greatest problems of the wife who is active in a career" (1972, p. 22). Her leading concepts for the lifespan remained "self fulfillment" and "self-determination," and she certainly lived them.

CONCLUDING THOUGHTS ON AN ENTREPRENEURIAL WOMAN PSYCHOLOGIST

It is a shame that Charlotte Bühler has not taken her rightful place in developmental psychology textbooks. As a valuable step in this direction, one developmental and philosophical psychologist has not only analyzed her originality *vis à vis* Freudian theory and ego psychology but also has laid out her stage theory of self-development. Although she comes close to other humanistic models, such as Karen Horney, Carl Rogers, and Abe Maslow, none of them had an articulated stage theory as she did. Yet "Bühler felt that there was potential insight to be gained by leaving intact alternate conceptual frameworks…. She was able to profess a more dialogal [sic] developmental theory than most developmental psychologists" (Derobertis, 2006, p. 71). Even in her major collaborative work (1968), she repeatedly showed where her contributors agreed and disagreed with her, all in a positive spirit of advancing developmental knowledge. In an interview between her husband and John Burnham (2006) in the 1960s, she interrupted to suggest that she also be interviewed (p. 22). She was not shy about promoting herself. Yet she graciously promoted others in countless edited chapters and co-authored works. She excelled in scientific collaboration and leadership. Her colleague James Bugental at the Cedars of Lebanon Hospital in Los Angeles wrote:

> Charlotte Bühler was a very real and at times formidable person who knew her own mind and set about doing things the way she believed they should be done. She could be imperious, humble, tough, gentle, petty, generous, formal, companionable, creative, curiously blind, and a whole array of other ways. In short, … a fully rounded human being. Yet not all of her attributes were as balanced as that list suggests. Charlotte was seldom boring, often courageous. She was usually on the move, active, doing, involved. She never seemed to have less than four important projects going at the same time. When she was in a room, you knew it; and when she was a part of a task group—be it a committee, a board of some kind, a group of authors—she was an influential part. (Bugental, 1975, pp. 48–49)

Looking back at her entire life course, two women scholar-biographers note that Bühler "barely mentioned the fact that she was one of the first women to penetrate the domain of psychology" (Bürmann & Herwartz-Emden, 1993, p. 219). Others have observed that it was typical of women to downplay the significance of gender in their professional work (Ash, 1995; Chodorow, 1989; Johnston & Johnson, 2008). Yet the idea of a woman attaining a full professorship was unlikely in German-speaking and English-speaking countries (outside of women's colleges). She began her studies during World War I in a decade when women were first allowed in Prussian universities. She must have had to struggle like other women against the social attitude that a married woman's place was in the home. She generally acknowledged the positive side, for example, that it was an honor to be offered an assistant position by Carl Stumpf. She did note that "I found unacceptable the prevailing view in Germany that women could never be creative, whereas

I knew that I would be able to be creative if the opportunity was given to me and if I had an appropriate education" (Bühler, 1972, p. 15). She became the *de facto* administrator of an institute of international acclaim, while her husband "towered above Freud in social respect and scientific recognition" in Vienna at the time (Lebzelten, 1969, p. 38ff). She shared in his glory, but her reputation grew in the United States while his declined. She never achieved a full professorship, despite earning eminence. Instead, she capitalized on the post-World War II boom in clinical psychology through skillful networking with numerous leading male figures, such as Bruno Klopfer and Abraham Maslow.

Certainly she was an exception to the pattern of the first U.S. generation of women psychologists who earned a PhD before World War I (Scarborough & Furumoto, 1987). That first generation had to choose between career and marriage, and they did not have children. She married and had children as well as a career. The first U.S. generation was limited to employment in women's colleges; we have no data on German women in that generation. The second U.S. generation moved on to "women's work" in academia, chiefly in developmental and clinical psychology. This fits Bühler, who in Vienna achieved associate professor without pay in 1929. Her work in U.S. academia also belonged to the margins in clinical settings, with temporary academic teaching positions. She displayed "a quieter, more sporadic, and less organized form of feminism," like women of the second generation (Johnston & Johnson, 2008, pp. 63–64).

Charlotte Bühler was a highly determined individual who also juggled multiple roles. She was a woman who seemed to have the energy to do it all. She was also a mother and continued her education through her pregnancy and continued her career throughout the lives of her two children. She made the fulfillment of a human life more and more her major focus. Emphasizing technique, she sought a "less scholastic and broader frame of reference" than the Allport-Vernon test, coming up with the Life Goal Inventory in 1964 (Bühler, 1968, p. 99). This consisted of 86 questions, an empirical approach. Acknowledging Lois Murphy's use of psychoanalytic explanations (1962), Bühler wrote that she herself "sees the id, ego, and superego triad as an incomplete conceptualization of creativity and of those aspects of conscience which are the result of self-realization" (1968, p. 99). She maintained that early cultural goals are key, citing Anne Roe's (1953) finding that scientists come from homes with cultural interests (p. 181). Cultural deprivation may paralyze a person. She was attentive to class differences, an unusual feature among U.S. psychologists. In Vienna, she studied upper middle-class families "to avoid extreme situations at the outset of our work" (Bühler, 1939, p. 3). Yet she maintained a keen eye for class differences in all her writings.

Not every psychologist can achieve a best seller at the age of 76. Her popular book in 1969 bore the poetic German title, "If life is to succeed." The English translation in 1971 carried the more mundane title *The Way to Fulfillment: Psychological Techniques*. She presented case after case of persons seeking meaning in life. Her chapter "Love and Sex" noted that Freud conflated the two concepts. A working-class woman told of having sex in cemeteries without romantic attachment. Her middle-class women spoke in generalities, unable to grapple with sex. Fulfillment, she concluded, comes from joining the physical and the psychological.

Why is Bühler unknown outside of German-speaking countries? I can think of several reasons. Her major life span book in 1968 was an edited one, whereas Carl Rogers and Viktor Frankl wrote single-authored books. In addition, she could have been overlooked because she was a woman and a foreigner. Moreover, life span psychology emerged as a field after she died, with Daniel Levinson and Gail Sheehy in the United States and Ursula Lehr, K. Werner Schaie, and Paul Baltes in Germany. I found little secondary literature on her reception in life span psychology. She was so broad—spanning developmental, clinical, humanistic, life span—that it is hard to peg her. She was a remarkable woman.

She returned to her native land in 1972 so that her son could care for her after a hip operation. Then she expressed misgivings about missing her community in southern California. However, she was grateful for a life well lived, and she expressed appreciation for the opportunity to become involved with her son's children when they were growing up in California. She missed being more involved with her daughter's children in Norway. Charlotte died on February 3, 1974, at the age of 80. She left us with this parting question and answer:

> But how does a person know that he has made the "right" decision, or that he has lived "right?" Curiously enough, people do know this, and need no one to explain it to them. Their innermost self tells them. They know whether they ought to be praised or condemned for the way they have lived and for the decisions they have made—provided that they are capable of being honest about themselves and are not neurotically blinded. (Bühler, 1971, p. 208).

SUGGESTED READINGS

Bühler, C. M. (1930). *The first year of life.* New York: John Day.
> This multiauthored book offered qualitative and quantitative measurements of very young children in an adoption center and in private homes in Vienna. Numerous observers observed 69 children for 24 hours a day in 8 hour shifts during 1926. The women researchers defended larger units of behavior than observed in behaviorism and Gestalt psychology.

Bühler, C. M. (1935). *From birth to maturity. An outline of the psychological development of the child.* London: Kegan Paul, Trench, Trubner. Further editions 1937, 1945, 1951. Translated by E. W. Menaker.
> This little book, derived from lectures given in England, concerns the "normal average child" but discusses personality deviations as well. It raised eyebrows among British psychoanalysts and mental testers, yet it put the Vienna Institute on the map with similar ones at Yale, Columbia, Iowa, California, and elsewhere.

Bühler, C., & Massarik, F. (Eds.) (1968). *The course of human life. A study of goals in the humanistic perspective.* New York: Springer.
> Bühler brought humanistic psychology into the mainstream of child development and life span psychology with this edited volume. She proposed that there are different degrees to which humans experience their lives as a whole. For example, they often fail to develop the right sex–love relationship and to accomplish what they could have. The book offered new ideas for psychotherapists and educators.

Bühler, C., & Allen, M. (1972). *Introduction to humanistic psychology.* Belmont, CA: Brooks/Cole.

> This was her signature book. She noted a crisis in Western Civilization involving discontent and abuses of relationships. She proposed encounter groups for people to fill this emptiness. A humanistic psychology can help to define what people think is a healthy and meaningful life.

REFERENCES

Abir-Am, P., & Outram, D. (Eds.) (1987). *Uneasy careers and intimate lives. Women in science, 1789–1979.* New Brunswick, NJ: Rutgers University Press.

Allen, M. (1980). Bühler, Charlotte. In B. Sicherman & C. H. Green (Eds.), *Notable American women. The modern period* (pp. 119–121). Cambridge, MA: Belknap Press of Harvard University Press.

Ammers-Küller, J. van (1935), Charlotte Bühler. In J. Ammers-Küller, *Bedeutende Frauen der Gegenwart. Zehn Frauenbildnisse* [Significant women of the present: Ten portraits of women] (pp. 269–300). Bremen: Schünemann.

Ash, M. G. (1987). Psychology and politics in interwar Vienna: The Vienna Psychological Institute, 1922–1942. In M. G. Ash & W. R. Woodward (Eds.), *Psychology in twentieth-century thought and society* (pp. 143–164). New York: Cambridge University Press.

Ash, M. G. (1995). Women émigré psychologists and psychoanalysts in the United States. In S. Quack (Ed.), *Between sorrow and strength. Women refugees of the Nazi period* (pp. 239–264). New York: Cambridge University Press.

Ash, M. G. (1998a). Bühler, Charlotte. In J. A. Garraty (General Ed.), *American National Biography online.* New York: Oxford University Press.

Ash, M. G. (1998b). Bühler, Karl. In J. A. Garraty (General Ed.), *American National Biography online.* New York: Oxford University Press, 1998.

Baumgartner, E. (2010). Charlotte Bühler. In H. Gundlach (Ed.), *European pioneer women in psychology* (pp. 75–88). Milan, Italy: F. Angelli.

Benetka, G. (1995). *Psychologie in Wien: Sozial- und Theoriegeschichte des Wiener Psychologischen Instituts, 1922–1938* [Psychology in Vienna: Social and theoretical history of the Vienna Psychological Institute, 1922–1938]. Vienna: WUV-Universitätsverlag.

Birren, J. (1971). Four interviews for a biography of Charlotte Bühler (1967–1968). In conjunction with the American Psychiatric Association. Unpublished manuscript, Washington, DC.

Bowlby, J. (1944). Forty-four juvenile thieves. *International Journal of Psychoanalysis, 25,* 1–57.

Bühler, C. (1918a). Über Gedankenentstehung. Experimentelle Untersuchungen zur Denkpsychologie. Inaugural-Dissertation [On the origin of thoughts: Experimental research on thought psychology]. Leipzig: J. A. Barth. Published in *Zeitschrift für Psychologie, 80,* 129–200.

Bühler, C. (1918b). Das Märchen und die Phantasie des Kindes [Fairy tales and fantasy in the child]. *Zeitschrift für angewandte Psychologie,* Beiheft 17. Republished with J. Bilz, Munich: Barth, 1968, introduced by H. Hetzer (4th ed., 1958, 5th ed., 1961, 6th ed., 1971, 7th ed., Berlin: Springer).

Bühler, C. (1919). Über die Vorgänge bei der Satzbildung [On the processes of sentence formation]. *Zeitschrift für Psychologie, 81,* 181–206.

Bühler, C. (1920). Entdeckung und Erfindung. Zwei Grundbegriffe der Literaturpsychologie [Discovery and invention. Two basic concepts in the psychology of literature]. *Zeitschrift für Ästhetik und Allgemeine Kunstwissenschaft, 15,* 43–87.

Bühler, C. (1922). *Das Seelenleben des Jugendlichen* [The mental life of young people]. Jena: Fischer. 6th ed. Stuttgart: Fischer, 1967. Translated into Hungarian, Swedish, Spanish, Dutch, Japanese.

Bühler, C. (1929, 1931, 1967). *Kindheit und Jugend* [Childhood and youth]. Leipzig: S. Hirzel, 4th ed. Göttingen. Translated into Polish, Swedish, Icelandic, Spanish.

Bühler, C. (1930). *The first year of life*. New York: John Day. Translated by P. Greenberg & R. Ripin. [Published in German with 3 co-authors, H. Hetzer, K.Wolf, and L. Koller.] doi:10.1037/11625-000.

Bühler, C. (1931). The social behavior of children. In C. Murchison (ed.), *Handbook of child psychology* (2nd ed., pp. 374–416). Worcester, MA: Clark University Press.

Bühler, C. (1933). *Der menschliche Lebenslauf als psychologisches Problem* [The human life course as a psychological problem]. Leipzig: Hirzel. 2nd ed., Göttingen: Hogrefe, 1959.

Bühler, C. (1935). *From birth to maturity. An outline of the psychological development of the child*. London: Kegan Paul, Trench, Trubner. Further editions 1937, 1945, 1951. Translated by E. W. Menaker.

Bühler, C. (1939). *The child and his family*. With the collaboration of E. Baar and others. Translated by H. Beaumont. New York: Harper. German: *Kind und Familie*. Jena: Gustav Fischer, 1937.

Bühler, C. (1945). The problem of Germany. Dr. Bühler's reply. In G. Murphy (Ed.), *Human nature and enduring peace* (pp. 93–107). Boston, MA: Houghton Mifflin.

Bühler, C. (1954). The reality principle. Theories and facts. *American Journal of Psychotherapy, 8*, 626–647.

Bühler, C. (1959). Theoretical observations about life's basic tendencies. *American Journal of Psychotherapy, 13*, 561–581.

Bühler, C. (1962a). Goals of life and therapy. *American Journal of Psychoanalysis, 22*, 153–175. doi:10.1007/BF01873506.

Bühler, C. (1962b). *Psychologie im Leben unserer Zeit* [Psychology in the life of our time]. Munich: Droemer Knauer.

Bühler, C. (1962c). *Values in psychotherapy*. New York: Free Press of Glencoe.

Bühler, C. (1965). Die Wiener Psychologische Schule in der Emigration [The Vienna Psychological School in emigration]. *Psychologische Rundschau, 16*, 187–196.

Bühler, C. (1968). Psychotherapy and the image of man. *Psychotherapy, 5*, 89–94. doi:10.1037/h0088673

Bühler, C. (1969). *Wenn das Leben gelingen soll. Psychologische Studien über Lebenserwartungen und Lebensergebnisse* [If life is to succeed: Psychological studies of life expectations and results]. Munich: Droemer Knaur.

Bühler, C. (1970). *Psychology for contemporary living*. New York: Delta.

Bühler, C. (1971). *The way to fulfillment. Psychological techniques*, translated by David J. Baker. New York: Hawthorne (English translation of *Wenn das Leben gelingen soll*).

Bühler, C. (1972). Charlotte Bühler. In L. Pongratz, W. Traxel, & E. G. Wehner (Eds.), *Psychologie in Selbstdarstellungen* [Psychology in self-portrayals] (pp. 9–42). Berne: Hans Huber. English translation in progress by K. Weihs, York University, under the direction of A. Rutherford.

Bühler, C., & Allen, M. (1972). *Introduction to humanistic psychology*. Belmont, CA: Brooks/Cole.

Bühler, C., Bühler, K., & Lefever, D. W. (Eds.). (1949). *Development of the basic Rorschach score, with manual of directions*. Beverly Hills, CA: Western Psychological Services.

Bühler, C., & Hetzer, H. (1927). *Inventar der Verhaltungsweisen des ersten Lebensjahres* [Inventory of modes of behavior in the first year of life]. Jena: Gustav Fischer.

Bühler, C. & Hetzer, H. (1929). Zur Geschichte der Kinderpsychologie. In E. Brunswick et al. (Eds.) *Beiträge zur Problemgeschichte der psychologie* (pp. 1–77). Jena: Fischer.

Bühler, C., & Hetzer, H. (1935). *Testing children's development from birth to the school age*. Translated from 1st ed. (1932) by H. Beaumont. New York: Farrar & Reinhart.

Bühler, C., & Massarik, F. (1968). *The course of human life. A study of goals in the humanistic perspective*. New York: Springer.

Bühler, C., Smitter, F., & Richardson, S. (1952). *Childhood problems and the teacher*, with a chapter on remedial work by F. Bradshaw. New York: Holt.

Bühler, K. (1907). Tatsachen und Probleme zu einer Psychologie der Denkvorgänge, I. Über Gedanken [Facts and problems for a psychology of the thought processes. I. On thoughts]. *Archiv für die gesamte Psychologie, 9*, 346ff.

Bühler, K. (1918). *Die geistige Entwicklung des Kindes* [The intellectual development of the child]. Jena: Fischer. 6th ed., 1930.

Bühler, K. (1927). *Die Krise der Psychologie* [The crisis in psychology]. Jena: Fischer.

Bühler, K. (1930). *The mental development of the child: A summary of modern psychological theory*. New York: Harcourt Brace.

Bühring, G. (2002). Charlotte Bühler: Der menschliche Lebenslauf als psychologisches Problem [The course of human life course as a psychological problem]. *Bedeutende Psychologinnen. Biographien und Schriften* [Significant female psychologists: Biographies and writings] (pp. 183–198). Weinheim & Basel: Beltz.

Bühring, G. (2007). *Charlotte Bühler oder Der Lebenslauf als psychologisches Problem* [Charlotte Bühler or the life course as a psychological problem]. Frankfurt am Main: Peter Lang.

Bürmann, I., & Herwartz-Emden, L. (1993). Charlotte Bühler: Leben und Werk einer selbstbewußten Wissenschaftlerin des 20. Jahrhunderts [Life and work of a self-conscious female scientist of the 20th century]. *Psychologische Rundschau, 44*, 205–225.

Bugental, J. F. T. (1975). Toward a subjective psychology: Tribute to Charlotte Bühler. *Interpersonal Development. 6*, 48–61.

Burnham, J. C. (2006). Interviewing as a tool of the trade: A not-very-satisfying bottom line. In D. B. Baker, (Ed.), *Thick description and fine texture: Studies in the history of psychology* (pp. 19–37). Akron, OH: University of Akron Press.

Chodorow, N. J. (1989). *Feminism and psychoanalysis*. New Haven, CT: Yale University Press.

Coser, L. A. (1984). *Refugee scholars in America*. New Haven, CT: Yale University Press.

DeRobertis, E. M. (2006). Charlotte Bühler's existential-humanistic contributions to child and adolescent psychology. *Journal of Humanistic Psychology, 46*, 48–76. doi:10.1177/0022167805277116

Erikson, E. H. (1940). Studies in the interpretation of play. *Genetic Psychology Monographs, 22*, 557–671.

Eschbach, A. (1989). Karl Bühler und Ludwig Wittgenstein. In A. Eschbach (Ed.). *Karl Bühler's theory of language* (pp. 385–406). Amsterdam: John Benjamins Publishing Co.

Frank, L. K. (1949). *Projective methods. American Lecture series Monograph 10*. Springfield, IL: Charles C. Thomas.

Gavin, E. A. (1990). Charlotte M. Bühler (1893–1974). In A. N. O'Connell & N. F. Russo (Eds.), *Women in psychology: A bio-bibliographic sourcebook* (pp. 49–56). New York: Greenwood.

Goodenough, F. L., & Harris, D. B. (1950). Studies in the psychology of children's drawings. *Psychological Bulletin, 47*, 349–433.

Hetzer, H. (1982). Kinder- und jugendpsychologische Forschung im Wiener Psychologischen Institut von 1922–1938 [Child and adolescent psychological research in the Vienna Psychological Institute from 1922 to1938]. *Zeitschrift für Entwicklungspsychologie und Pädagogische Psychologie, 14*, 175–244.

Hetzer, H. (1987). Karl Bühlers Anteil an der kinder- und jugendpsychologischen Forschung im Wiener Institut [Karl Bühler's part in the child and adolescent psychological research at the Vienna Institute]. In A. Eschbach (Ed.), *Karl Bühler's theory of language* (pp. 17–32). Amsterdam: John Benjamins.

Isaacs, S. (1937). Review of *From birth to maturity*, by C. Bühler. London: Kegan Paul. (1935). *International Journal of Psycho-Analysis, 18*, 326–327.

Johnston, E., & Johnson, A. (2008). Searching for the second generation of American women psychologists. *History of Psychology, 11*, 40–72. doi:10.1037/1093-4510.11.1.40

Kardos, L. (1984). Erinnerungen an Karl Bühler [Reminiscences of Karl Bühler]. In A. Eschbach (Ed.), *Bühler-Studien*. Frankfurt: Suhrkamp, Vol. 1, pp. 31–39.

Koffka, K. (1921). *Die Grundlagen der psychischen Entwicklung; Eine Einführung in die Kinderpsychologie*. Osterwiek am Harz: Zickfeldt. Translated as *The growth of the mind: An introduction to child psychology*. London: Paul, Trench, 1924.

Kurz, E. M., & Velichkovsky, B. M. (2006). Charlotte and Karl Bühler in Dresden: A chapter in the history of German and international psychology. Technische Universität Dresden, Fachrichtung Psychologie. http://tu-dresden.de

Kusch, M. (1995). *Psychologism: A case study in the sociology of philosophical knowledge*. London: Routledge.

Lazarsfeld, P. (1969). An episode in the history of empirical social research. In D. Fleming & B. Bailyn (Eds.), *The intellectual migration. Europe and America, 1930–1960* (pp. 250–367). Cambridge, MA: Harvard University Press.

Lebzelten, G. (1969). Karl Bühler—Leben und Werk [Karl Bühler—life and work]. In G. Lebzelten (Ed.), *Karl Bühler: Die Uhren der Lebewesen und Fragmente aus dem Nachlaß* [Karl Bühler: The clocks of living things and fragments from the archive] (pp. 7–70). Vienna: Böhlaus.

Mandler, G. (2007). *A history of modern experimental psychology*. Cambridge, MA: MIT Press.

Murphy, L. B. (1962). *The widening world of childhood*. New York: Basic Books.

Ragsdale, S. (n.d.). *Charlotte Malachowski Bühler, Ph.D. (1893–1974)*. Retrieved from http://www.webster.edu/~woolflm/charlottebuhler.html 4/18/2010

Roe, A. (1953). *The making of a scientist*. New York: Dodd, Mead.

Samelson, F. (1985). Organizing for the kingdom of behavior: Academic battles and organizational policies in the twenties. *Journal of the History of the Behavioral Sciences, 21*, 204–224. doi:10.1002/1520-6696(198501)21:1<33::AID-JHBS2300210104>3.0.CO;2-F

Scarborough, E., & Furumoto, L. (1987). *Untold lives: The first generation of American women psychologists*. New York: Columbia University Press.

Schilder, P. (1933). Charlotte Bühler: *Der menschliche Lebenslauf als psychologisches Problem* [The human life course as a psychological problem]. *Psychologische Monographien*, ed. Karl Bühler. Vol. 4, Leipzig: S. Hirzel, 1933.

Spitz, R. A., & Wolf, K. (1946). Analytic depression. *Psychoanalytic Study of the Child, 2*, 313–342.

Sprung, H., & Sprung, L. (2002). Carl Stumpf: Experimenter, theoretician, musicologist, and promoter. In G. A. Kimble & M. Wertheimer (Eds.), *Portraits of pioneers in psychology* (pp. 51–69). Washington, DC: APA; Mahweh, NJ: Erlbaum.

Stern, W. (1987). *Psychologie der frühen Kindheit bis zum sechsten Lebensjahr* [Psychology of early childhood to the sixth year of life] (12th ed.) Darmstadt: Wissenschaftliche Buchgesellschaft. First edition 1914.

Weinzierl, E. (1981). Sozialdemokratische Schulpolitik und 'Einheitsschule' in der Ersten Republik [Social democratic school politics and the idea of a general public school in the First Republic]. In R. Olechnowski & E. Weinzierl (Eds.), *Neue Mittelstufe. Skizze eines Modells für die Sekundarstufe I* [A new middle stage: Sketch of a model for teaching classes 7–10]. Vienna: Herder.

Wellek, A. (1964). Karl Buehler. *Archiv für die gesamte Psychologie, 116*, 3–8.

6

Jean Piaget:
Theorist of the Child's Mind

BERNARD C. BEINS
Ithaca College

Jean Piaget (b. August 9, 1896, d. September 16, 1980) has had more influence on the study of cognitive development than any other psychologist. As

soon as his first books appeared, psychologists recognized the fertility of his ideas, even though those ideas had to make a linguistic journey from French to English, a translatlantic journey from Switzerland to the United States, and a methodological journey from more philosophical to more psychological. Piaget's theory of cognitive development continues to dominate developmental psychology over 80 years after its introduction.

Figure 6.1   Jean Piaget.
(Courtesy of the Jean Piaget Society. With permission.)

Piaget's background mirrored that of the earliest generation of psychologists in his combined focus on the natural sciences and philosophy. Piaget credited his early work in the natural sciences with keeping his focus scientific, but he also maintained a European flavor to his ideas with a greater attachment to philosophy and logic than was common among psychologists in English-speaking countries at the time.

Even with the shared background, however, Piaget developed his ideas largely independently of mainstream experimental psychology of the 1920s, which was already being led by English-speaking, behaviorally oriented psychologists in the

United States. Piaget's empirical approach was called "clinical," relying on small samples and attention to children's verbal statements to provide insights into cognitive processes. This approach was at variance with American psychology in that the latter had moved away from the study of mental processes that featured so prominently in Piaget's work. In addition, whereas Piaget tended to study small numbers of children, American psychology had moved toward studying groups, averaging out the effect of unusual behaviors that might have been of great interest to Piaget. The few structuralists of Edward Bradford Titchener's bent who remained active in psychology in Piaget's early years would not have studied children because of the children's relatively limited verbal skills. Their inability to report their introspections would have ruled them out as experimental participants.

In spite of the differences between Piaget's approach and that of American behaviorists, Piaget gained quick recognition among developmentalists. One particularly salutary effect of Piaget's work, at least according to a recent, more cognitively oriented psychologist, was that Piaget was instrumental in removing "the behaviorists' long stranglehold on the study of cognition" (Beilin, 1992, p. 202).

Over the course of his career, Piaget authored some 60 books and numerous articles. The power of his ideas is apparent in that they have dominated developmental psychology even though Piaget published much of his work alone. He is the sole author of most of his books and journal articles, and he did not oversee a large cadre of graduate students who would have promoted his theory and methodology.

His theory of the stages of intellectual development has been the fundament of developmental psychology for decades, although even from the start, other researchers probed his ideas critically and reported limitations to the data. Many of Piaget's basic concepts have withstood experimental scrutiny, although with some modification. According to Beilin (1992), there is no rival to Piagetian theory in its scope and depth, nor has any other theory generated as much research. With Piaget's influence in psychology as obvious as it is, however, Beilin speculated that it has passed its peak in popularity. Nonetheless, Beilin stressed that the theory is in no danger of disappearing from psychology.

PIAGET'S LIFE

Piaget grew up in Neuchâtel, a French-speaking region of Switzerland, where his father was a professor of medieval history at the university. His home life when growing up might charitably be described as interesting. His father appears to have been something of a taskmaster. When Piaget was about 10 years of age, he wrote a book that he titled *Our Birds*, whereupon his father pointed out that it was a "mere" compilation of the ideas of others. Even in Piaget's first decade of life, his father seemed to expect originality. Such influence taught him "the value of systematic work even in small matters" (Piaget, 1952/1968, p. 237).

Piaget's description of his mother reveals what seems to have been a difficult home life. He noted that she was intelligent and kind but displayed a neurotic personality. At one point, she insisted that he take religious instruction. At that time, he appears to have had little patience with religious dogma, a trait he shared with his father. Nonetheless, he complied with his mother's wishes, successfully completed the course, and was later involved in the Swiss Christian Students' Association (Vidal, 1994). This combination of a father with high expectations and a mother who posed some problems in the family life shaped Piaget's childhood in ways that remained with him throughout his academic career. As he noted, before the age of 10, he decided to forego play and to become serious in his work.

Fortunately, Piaget was a highly gifted student. When he gravitated to the natural sciences as a child, he spent considerable time in the Neuchâtel Museum of Natural History, where the director, Paul Godet, guided Piaget's work on mollusks. Piaget was competent enough to write treatises that appeared in the *Revue Suisse de Zoologie*. This era predated easy travel and the instant communication taken for granted today, so the curator of the natural history museum in Geneva knew of Piaget only through his manuscripts. The curator thus offered Piaget the position of curator of mollusks at age 15, which, naturally, he declined. He maintained his interest in natural history throughout his life and noted that the scientific approach saved him from the "demon" of philosophy. In fact, he characterized himself as a genetic epistemologist, not a psychologist, because he viewed psychology as only a vehicle for integrating his two main loves, philosophy and biology (Boden, 2006).

Piaget's interest in psychology arose initially as a result of his mother's psychological problems. As such, he developed an interest in psychoanalysis. He discovered, though, that he was not particularly drawn to psychopathology; rather, his interests lay in normal psychological processes. Before his inroads into developmental psychology, he produced a novel, *Recherche*, that like B. F. Skinner's early attempts at fiction, was less than spectacularly successful. To a 21st century reader, Piaget's prose would be fairly opaque:

> Now there can be no awareness of these qualities, hence these qualities can not [sic] exist, if there are no relationships among them, if they are not, consequently, blended into a total quality which contains them while keeping them distinct. For example, I would not be aware either of the whiteness of this paper or of the blackness of this ink if the two qualities were not combined in my consciousness into a certain unit, and if, in spite of this unity, they did not remain respectively one white and the other black…. (Piaget, 1952/1968, p. 243)

According to Piaget, he wrote his fiction to avoid compromising his scientific status. The work was intended for the general public. Current psychologists might be happy that Piaget forwent a career as a novelist in favor of psychology.

He attended the University of Neuchâtel, where he received his PhD in science in 1918. Interestingly, in his autobiographical sketch (Piaget, 1952/1968), he did not highlight his relationship with Arnold Reymond, with whom he completed his doctoral work, and gave much more attention to the guidance that Godet provided when he was 10 years old than to any subsequent scientist. Not long after earning his doctorate, he worked with Théodore Simon, which exposed him to psychological ideas that he would later pursue (Bryant, 1995).

In 1929, while developing his ideas at the University of Neuchâtel, he accepted an offer from the University of Geneva to be professor of the history of scientific thought and to direct research at the Institut Jean-Jacques Rousseau, which became part of the university while he was there. Before leaving Neuchâtel, however, he decided that he needed to conclude the research on mollusks that had fascinated him since childhood. The problem he addressed involved whether learning or heredity led the creatures to attach themselves to rocks in the turbulent lake, thereby attaining their rounded shape. After observing more than 80,000 individual mollusks, he concluded that the effect was due to development: Not all behavior results merely from maturation and learning.

In the 1920s, his theory began to emerge from his systematic research, but during the 1930s administrative responsibilities reduced the amount of psychological research that he conducted. However, it did lead to collaborations with a number of other psychologists, including Bärbel Inhelder, who later headed the institute, and Alina Szeminska. Much of Piaget's earlier work was solitary, so this collaboration was a departure from his typical pattern. Interestingly, he noted that he also engaged in intense study of the history of mathematics, physics, and biology during this period. It was also during this period that he solidified his ideas on the developmental stage of concrete operations.

During the years of World War II, Piaget was able to maintain his research without undue disruption because of Switzerland's neutrality. So while the work of many psychologists in other parts of Europe faltered, he maintained a program of research. After the war, he became active internationally in UNESCO, while pursuing collaborative work with Inhelder and others. In the postwar era, Piaget continued to generate new ideas based on his older work, although at least one psychologist has described the final theoretical development as constituting a new theory (Beilin, 1992). In the final years of Piaget's career (and life), he paid renewed attention to the functional aspects of children's thoughts, including a renewed attention to notions of causality, intentional logic, and the theory of meaning.

The systematic collaboration that he undertook with other psychologists when he started his administrative and culturally oriented work persisted to the end of his career. As Piaget (1976) noted in one autobiographical sketch, others' evaluation of his early work on children's language and their representation of reality "showed in general a more or less total lack of understanding of the problem" (p. 139) on the part of his critics. So he generally ignored those criticisms. In the late stages of his career, however, he was more amenable to exchanging ideas with other scholars and modifying his thoughts based on such interchanges. His final hope was to see the development of a neurological model of development that would mirror the functional aspects of cognition.

Piaget (1952/1968) was generally not forthcoming about the details of his personal life in his autobiographical sketches. In fact, he maintained that "an autobiography has scientific interest only if it succeeds in furnishing the elements of an explanation of the author's work" (p. 237). Consistent with that logic, he limited himself to a description of his professional life. Consequently, current psychologists have access to much less information about the details of his life compared with those of many other prominent historical figures in the discipline. Consider, for instance, Cyril Burt, a psychologist contemporary with Piaget who set the stage for Piaget's methodologies. In stark contrast to Piaget's spartan autobiographical sketch, Burt's (1952/1968) is rife with the highlights not only of his own life but also even of his genealogy. Nonetheless, Piaget's relative personal obscurity does not seem to have hampered the prominence of his ideas throughout the psychological world.

Over the course of his career, he was affiliated with the University of Geneva, the Institut Jean-Jacques Rosseau, the University of Lausanne, and the Sorbonne. Administratively, he was director of the International Bureau of Education, the Institute of Educational Sciences at the University of Geneva, and the International Centre for Genetic Epistemology (Jean Piaget Society, 2007). Piaget's widespread recognition led to his receipt of honorary doctorates from institutions across the world, including Belgium, Brazil, Canada, England, France, Norway, Poland, and the United States.

THE FOUNDATIONS OF PIAGETIAN THEORY

Piaget did not receive his training with prominent psychologists, as was true of many well-known historical figures in German- and English-speaking countries. It is not always easy to identify the thinkers who influenced Piaget's ideas, although he was very much a product of his times (Elkind, 1996) and was aware particularly of biological models of development. At various points in his early writing, he referred to James Mark Baldwin, Simon (and, derivatively, Alfred Binet), Cyril Burt, Reymond, Sigmund Freud (and other psychoanalysts), and Pierre Janet.

Baldwin's influence seems to have been significant (Shuttleworth, 2010), although not until after Piaget had conducted his own empirical research (Morss, 1990). Baldwin (1906) used the terms *accommodation* and *assimilation* in describing developmental processes. He wrote, "Accommodation is the principle by which an organism comes to adapt itself to more complex conditions of stimulation by performing more complex functions" (p. 455), which is highly consonant with Piaget's conceptualization. He is the only American psychologist who seems to have influenced Piaget greatly, perhaps because Baldwin relocated to France after his resignation from The Johns Hopkins University.

Additional examination of writings before Piaget's also reveals that scientists were referring to "sensori-motor" activity, involving the same meaning as that used by Piaget. For example, Maudsley (1886) wrote that "the first movements of the child are reflex; but sensorial perceptions with motor reactions thereto follow these early movements so soon that we can make only an ideal boundary between reflex and sensori-motor acts. The aimless thrusting out of a limb brings it in contact with some external object, whereupon it is probable that a sensation is excited … and one of the first steps in the process of mental formation accomplished" (p. 256).

It became clear quite early to Piaget that children went through different stages of intellectual development. He was fascinated not so much by the measurement of intelligence, which was Burt's focus, but rather by the errors that children made in trying to solve problems (Bryant, 1995). His initial discovery involved the inordinate difficulty that young children experienced with transitive relations like *A is bigger than B, B is bigger than C. Is C smaller or bigger than A?* However, because his training reflected a more philosophical than an experimental approach, he noted that he first developed a theoretical system that he later subjected to empirical tests (Piaget 1952/1968, pp. 240–243). Further, he began studying mental rather than behavioral development. As such, both his background and his theory were at variance with American behavioral psychologists who dominated the landscape at the time.

His early ideas involved a focus on animistic beliefs of children, that is, the thought that objects are alive and have mental characteristics. He was certainly not the first to recognize children's animism or to depict it clearly. The idea that people view the world from their own perspective, that is, egocentrically, has a long tradition. According to Dennis (1938), writers recognized animism in the classical era: Zenophanes is thought to have written that if "horses and oxen thought in the human manner they would imagine gods in the forms of horses and oxen" (p. 258). Dennis opined that Piaget may have believed that only children display animism. Philosophers like Zenopanes, David Hume, and Auguste Comte, however, described it as characteristic of human thought, not simply childish thought. Empirical work on animism appeared in G. Stanley Hall's research, although Piaget did not seem aware of it. In fact, Piaget cited only the English philosopher James Sully and psychologist V. Rasmussen as influences on his thinking (Dennis, 1938).

Similarly, although Piaget identified stages of development that have received ubiquitous acceptance, he was not the first person to posit discrete stages through which a child would pass. In the realm of philosophy, Comte's work presaged Piaget's in the former's identification of stages of cognitive development. Within psychology, Hall is well known as the originator of the stage of adolescence as a distinct period in one's life. In addition, Piaget would have been aware of Freud's developmental stages, although Freud was clearly operating in a different realm of human development. Abel (1932) pointed out that Piaget identified a connection between Freud's mechanisms of displacement and condensation and the generalizations permitted by synthetic thought. This link is the so-called syncretism of children in which they take in general patterns of information without attending to details.

As noted already, Piaget relied on small samples and subjective reports that had been relatively common in the first decades of psychology in America but that had been abandoned (Goodwin, 2010). Lynd (1927) foretold the type of criticism Piaget would face in this regard, a prediction that proved accurate. Even with the novelty of his approach to American psychologists, though, the environment in the United States was surprisingly receptive to Piaget's ideas.

THE SPREAD OF PIAGET'S IDEAS

Piaget developed his ideas in an era in which rapid communication was not as easy as it is in the 21st century. Nonetheless, psychologists in the United States were quick to appreciate the power of his model. His five initial books on child development appeared between 1924 and 1932, all written in French, but American psychologists were already discussing his ideas by the end of the 1920s. At that point, many well-educated American psychologists would have spoken or read French to some degree. But it is still somewhat surprising that responses to his work and empirical tests of his tenets began to appear in English-language journals as quickly as they did.

Lynd (1927) reviewed Piaget's *The Language and Thought of the Child* (1926) in the *Journal of Educational Psychology* very positively and recognized the importance of the questions that Piaget was asking. Stone (1930) was similarly positive regarding Piaget's theory in a review of Piaget's volume *The Child's Conception of the World* (1929). Not only did Stone praise the theory, but he also lauded the ingenuity of the methodology that Piaget developed. Prior to Piaget's systematic investigations of children, investigations of children's cognition often took the form of questionnaires of the kind that Hall pioneered. With Piaget, for the first time, investigations took on a more systematic, observational approach. Stone wrote that "Piaget's writings are not merely splendid examples of ingenuity and cautiousness of method; they are vital revelations of the nature of the child mind. Happily the author has been most generous in interspersing samples of children's conversations. Such material not only furnishes necessary illustration; it makes Piaget's volumes valuable documentary contributions to genetic and social psychology" (p. 94).

In current expositions of his ideas, it is easy to take for granted the methodologies associated with demonstrating a child's level of cognitive development. Descriptions of ideas of conservation of volume, for instance, appear universally in textbooks, and it is common to hear anecdotes about instructors who bring young children to the classroom so that students can see the cognitive errors that the children exhibit. When a paradigm dominates a discipline, it is altogether too easy to forget that some researcher had to invent its methodology. Piaget's creation of novel tasks to assess cognitive level and the quick and widespread adoption of his methods and ideas are remarkable for a number of reasons.

First, Piaget did not study with a prominent mentor whose ideas he would develop and modify. Piaget was exposed to Cyril Burt's reasoning tests that piqued his curiosity, but he developed a new set of creative assessments quite different in scope from the tasks that Burt created. On his own, Piaget developed a system unlike any previous one. Piaget's ideas seem to have arisen as a product of his own creativity and took hold in psychology by subsequent generations of psychologists who were more attached to the ideas than to the man himself.

Second, for Piaget's ideas to spread, his writings required translation into English. By the time he began to establish himself, psychology in the United States had largely jettisoned work written in languages other than English. This stands in contrast to the early years of psychology. For example, the *Psychological Review*, then later the *Psychological Bulletin* (starting in 1904), published summaries and evaluations of works written in several languages, mostly German and French. In the 6-year period of 1900 to 1905, *Psychological Review* and *Psychological Bulletin* published an average of 24 reviews of German and 14 French titles each year. One might assume that many readers would have been conversant in those languages because the journals reviewed work that actually appeared in German or French. However, by the end of the 1920s, this pattern had changed. In the 6-year period of 1925 to 1930, when Piaget was writing his first volumes, *Psychological Bulletin* reviewed an annual average of fewer than four German and two French titles.

English-speaking psychologists had to rely on translations, which may have slowed the spread of Piaget's ideas somewhat, but another problem arose in connection with the translations into English. According to Isaacs (1929), problems in translation sometimes led to an emphasis that was not present in Piaget's original writing and to some outright errors in translations of Piaget's *The Language and Thought of the Child* (1926) and *Judgment and Reasoning in the Child* (1924). Isaacs asserted that the translations of these books "are full not only of clumsiness and confusions…, but also of actual errors, sometimes being the exact opposite of what Piaget says" (p. 607).

The surprising speed with which Piaget's ideas gained popularity is reflected in a 1929 book review by Meltzer in which he criticized the authors for failing to cite Piaget's 1926 book in their chapter titled "The Relation of Sensori-motor Development to the Growth of Intelligence." So even if Piaget had critics in the early years, it was quite clear that his ideas had a currency that developmental psychologists recognized. Isaacs (1929) specifically commented on the richness of the data that Piaget had provided and recognized the importance of the methodology that Piaget had developed.

In addition, in a review of Goodenough's *Developmental Psychology*, Cantril (1935) lamented the lack of reference to psychologists outside of the United States and to the absence of any treatment of mental development. He pointed out that the names of Piaget and other Europeans did not merit an appearance in the book's index. Cantril suggested that if the book had been titled *Development of Behavior*, Goodenough could have justified omission of Piaget. This tension between American psychologists' focus on behavior, reductionism, and strictly controlled experimental procedures and Piaget's focus on mental processes would remain into the 1960s, with Piaget more often serving "as a target than a guide" (McKee & Honzik, 1962, p. 604).

Another piece of evidence about the rapid and long-lasting impact of Piaget's work is apparent in a brief review of the ninth International Congress of Psychology in 1929 (Impressions of the International Congress, 1930). The reviewer mentioned the "truly brilliant and crucial investigations" (p. 417) described at the meeting. The psychologists associated with that brilliance included Edward Thorndike, Karl Lashley, Albert Michotte, George Coghill, William McDougall, Ivan Pavlov, and Piaget (with Bühler). The list includes figures whose historical work is still recognized, but some of the psychologists have passed into obscurity. It may be that Piaget and Pavlov are the only figures on that list whose ideas still constitute a vital component of current psychology.

In *The Language and Thought of the Child* (Piaget, 1926), Piaget relied extensively on observations of the language use of two children, Pie and Lev. Piaget noted in this book that he was more interested at that point in compiling facts than in creating theory (pp. xix–xx). As such, relying on two children would suffice at this point. One reason for the fact-based approach, he explained, was that by entertaining theory *a priori*, one can fall prey to drawing conclusions supporting that theory alone. Piaget's statements in this regard are somewhat at variance with his earlier statement that he developed a system before he had the methodological wherewithal to collect systematic data (Piaget, 1952/1968).

Isaacs (1929) described the tension between American and European psychology well, noting that Piaget approached his research and theory more as a philosopher and logician than a psychologist. As such, Piaget was more interested in the syllogistic reasoning of a child than in how the child developed its knowledge. She suggested that he viewed the children's thoughts as a logician and a writer of text books, not in the same way as the "ordinary grown-up-in-the-street" (p. 604). Further, Isaacs predicted that, if one were to place adults in a context beyond their ken, they would likely revert to more childlike explanations, which is just what Abel (1932) discovered: that a "grown-up-in-the-street" showed the same tendencies in causal explanations as children did when the adult confronted a situation beyond his or her grasp. Somewhat later, Nass (1956) also showed limitations in Piagetian notions of causality. (Piaget later revised his theory of causal thought.)

Another source of criticism included that children would be responding to questions at an intellectual level that they normally would not encounter, so the research setting would not be an appropriate test of the child's understanding. Still, the strength of Piaget's approach led Lynd (1927) to suggest that "that there can be no adequate interpretation of children's verbalizations without a patient unravelling of the genesis of these thought patterns" (p. 278), which Piaget provided.

Not long after the positive critique by Lynd, her predictions about the emergence of criticisms of the developmental theory were validated. The early empirical tests of Piaget's ideas were not entirely supportive; nonetheless, Piaget's influence continued to grow, even if he served more as the target to which McKee and Honzik (1962) alluded.

THE EMERGENCE OF PIAGETIAN THEORY

Piaget was extremely prolific in presenting his ideas to the psychological world, writing his first five books between 1924 and 1932. His work described an emerging theory of cognitive development that he documented through children's use of language. Based on his research, he developed the idea that children's cognitions are fundamentally different from those of adults; that is, the difference between thought processes and logic of children and adults is qualitative, not simply quantitative. Specifically, he saw a child's perspective as initially being egocentric, with the world being an extension of the child. Adult language and thought, on the other hand, are more socially oriented. Psychologists today still recognize the importance of these ideas.

Piaget theorized that children slowly adopt adultlike thought processes through a constant interplay between existing mental schemes and new information that upsets the equilibrium of those schemes. In this regard, he became fascinated early in his career by cognitive relations of the part to the whole and, reciprocally, the whole to the parts. He suggested that there are no isolated mental "elements" in one's construction of reality. Instead, he theorized that the whole of one's reality depends on changes in the part, that the individual parts depend on the whole, and ultimately that the parts and the whole could exist in a reciprocal relationship. Generally, only the latter case, he argued, leads to a stable conceptualization of reality. This interplay of part and whole has a clear connection to Baldwin's ideas of assimilation and accommodation and still figure predominantly in developmental psychology. (Piaget noted that had he been aware of the work of the Gestalt psychologists Max Wertheimer and Wolfgang Köhler on the part–whole relationship, he would probably have become a Gestaltist, but his scholarly knowledge was limited largely to work written in French.)

Piaget pointed out in his first book, *The Language and Thought of the Child* (1926), that it was clear to him that children develop a sense of the whole of a perception before they were able to differentiate the parts. He argued that the same pattern occurs with language; by extension, cognition could be seen as emerging the same way. These ideas differ notably from the psychology that was developing in the English-speaking world. Even though he started developing his system at a time when Titchener's elemental style of structuralism still held some sway in America, it is clear that Piaget would have rejected the elemental, structuralist approach as being inappropriate for an understanding of cognitive processes.

Similarly, he dismissed the associationist approach to language that behaviorists favored. He cited Henri Bergson's assertion that people learn language not by associating disparate elements but rather by dissociating them. That is, sentences for children take precedence over individual words; similarly, whole words take precedence over the individual sounds or letters that constitute them. Piaget also cited research by M. O. F. Cook that described a group of preliterate Liberians whose unit of linguistic consciousness was the sentence rather than the word.

This pattern of consciousness, which Piaget classified as syncretism, can be seen as a foundation for his later work on egocentrism, in which the infant's world is characterized by a unified whole in which infants do not differentiate between themselves and the world around them. Only with the development of more sophisticated thought do individual elements become recognized, much less important to infants (Piaget, 1926, pp. 132–134).

Piaget's work on egocentrism appeared early in *The Language and Thought of the Child* (1926). He identified three different types of egocentric language: enumerated repetition, monologue, and collective monologue. All three have in common that the child is not speaking to anybody in particular and the child expects no response. The child's perspective is entirely internal. Piaget (1926) noted that young children do verbalize their thoughts, although the purpose is not social. Rather, he suggested that it is simply the case that the child "has no verbal continence" (p. 38).

He postulated that children under the age of 7 or 8 are incapable of social interaction that adults take for granted. Furthermore, according to Piaget, the language of children at play comprises a constellation of gestures and movement in addition to verbalizations. Just as movement is open to viewing, so is language; neither is fundamentally private for the child.

This conceptualization of egocentrism has become one of the fundamental tenets of current developmental psychology. The idea has changed over time, becoming more detailed and nuanced, but the basic idea took hold early and has remained an important element in explaining children's thought processes and how they slowly move from internal and intuitive (*syncretic* in Piaget's terminology) to external and logical.

As egocentrism diminishes, so does another important aspect of preadult thought, animism, with which Piaget concerned himself. Young children see the world from the vantage point of their own behaviors. If they have the capability of self-directed movement, then so would inanimate objects. If a desire motivates their behaviors, then other objects in the world must be influenced by their own desires. This animistic perspective was not entirely new to him, but he was the first to apply it systematically to children and develop a model of how this mental model gradually evolves toward the adult conceptualization of the world.

In this early work, he was influenced by Freudian psychology, which Piaget specifically mentioned as he drew the connection between psychoanalytic theory and his own. He saw children's thoughts as having commonality with unconscious thought, in contrast with directed, conscious thoughts of adults. The child's hidden thoughts are intuitive rather than logical, and the conclusion is more important than the reasoning process. As the child moves toward adult thinking, it goes through several well-documented stages. According to the theory, the child progresses from the sensorimotor stage and then to preoperational, concrete operational and finally into formal operational. What is less well known to casual readers is that Piaget subdivided these main stages into substages that, on the whole, the psychological community has not abandoned.

Sensorimotor Stage

Psychologists generally agree that children are in the sensorimotor stage during the first 2 years of life. In the first of the six sensorimotor substages, the child's response to the world involves simple reflexes. Cognition is primitive and not oriented toward the external world. Then, in the second substage, the child attempts to coordinate habits (behaviors initially associated with reflexes but that have become separated from the initial releasing stimulus) and primary circular reactions (repetitive behaviors that initially occurred through random movements).

The next sensorimotor substage involves secondary circular reactions in which infants become attentive to objects in their environment. Thus, their sole focus is no longer on their own movements. Once they learn that they have an effect on their environment, infants attempt to coordinate different senses, such as seeing an object and reaching for it, which constitutes a fourth substage. They begin to coordinate their schemes with intentionality and may try to manipulate those objects (including people). According to Piaget, at this point, the child's reality is beginning to consist of more discrete elements rather than undifferentiated wholes, although only at a very general level of awareness.

In the fifth substage, children develop tertiary circular reactions in which they actively manipulate objects to explore new ways to interact with those objects. According to Piaget, this is the point at which children recognize novelty and at which curiosity emerges. In the final sensorimotor substage, children internalize schemes. This means that they begin to use primitive symbols and are no longer completely dependent on direct contact or perception of an object to think about it.

Preoperational Stage

In the second, preoperational stage, children begin to develop the ability to use abstractions, that is, symbols and words, to represent objects in their world. This stage is typically reported as persisting from about age 2 to 7. The term *preoperational* refers to Piaget's recognition that children in this stage of development do not have the ability to engage in reversible mental operations, such as addition and subtraction; thus, they are preoperational.

Two substages characterize preoperational thought. The first is the symbolic substage. Although it represents a cognitive advance in children's conceptualizations of the world relative to the sensorimotor stage, this stage is limiting in that children are egocentric, unable to take another's perspective. In addition, children show animism, the belief that inanimate objects have thoughts and can engage in willful action. Children will describe an object as acting in the same frame of reference as they themselves.

The second preoperational period is the intuitive thought substage. In this period, children develop mental models of the world around them. As such, they believe that they understand their world. At the same time, their ability to provide rational explanations is limited. Rather, they rely on a global, intuitive understanding without focusing on details.

One characteristic of thought at this substage is centration, the focusing on one dimension of a task or problem to the exclusion of others. Centration, according to Piaget, is responsible for young children's inability to recognize that a change in the appearance of an object does not necessarily change the nature of the object, an ability called conservation. This inability reveals that a child is in the preoperational stage; when the child is able to conserve, it signals the child's movement into the next stage of development.

Concrete Operations

According to Piaget, when children develop the ability to engage in reversible mental operations, they enter the stage of concrete operations. This stage lasts from about age 7 to 11. At this point, they can mentally represent a behavior (e.g., adding elements in two sets of concrete objects) and also reverse the behavior (e.g., subtracting elements that have been combined). At this point, children gain the ability to perform seriation, that is, to order stimuli on some dimension, such as placing the stimuli in a series from small to large. In the preoperational stage, children have difficulty with such systematic ordering.

Formal Operations

The final stage is formal operations, which involves rational, adultlike thought. In the previous stage of concrete operations, children can mentally manipulate concrete objects but cannot deal with abstractions. In the stage of formal operations, abstract logic is possible. Children can now develop hypotheses and can articulate the logic that underlies their predictions.

This stage, which Piaget argued begins around age 11, represents the culmination of the development of thought processes. In formal operations, a child (or adult) can appreciate philosophical arguments and can develop logical plans for the future. These stages of development have emerged as the canon in psychology. Piaget's ideas are ubiquitous in any discussion of cognitive development and constitute a major component of any developmental psychology text. As with any theoretical model, though, continual refinement takes place. Piaget's basic tenets remain viable, but psychologists have pointed out flaws in the theory and limitations to its generality.

EMPIRICAL TESTS OF PIAGETIAN THEORY

As noted already, reviews of Piaget's books in the 1920s and 1930s were generally quite positive (e.g., Cantril, 1935; Isaacs, 1929; Stone, 1930), and psychologists embraced many aspects of his theory. However, empirical tests of Piagetian theory did not produce universal support for his ideas.

Any theory this comprehensive will have difficulties, so it is not surprising that there were numerous reports of divergence of empirical data and theoretical postulates. Interestingly, the researchers who probed the theory seemed inclined to criticize some aspects of the theory while leaving others alone. For example, psychologists were quite critical of the ages at which Piaget specified that the transitions across stages occurred and the role of culture in cognitive development. But those researchers appeared to accept the nature of the phenomena that Piaget described.

In many cases, reports of children's cognition showed that they were advanced in their thinking at an earlier age than Piaget had suggested. For example, Hazlitt (1930) reported that children as young as 3 could overcome egocentrism in ways that Piaget claimed they should not be able to do. She also asserted that Piaget's focus on verbalizations overestimated the logic of adult thought. Hazlitt's assessment of the lack of universality of adult logic received further empirical support when Abel (1932) presented college students with a difficult memory task. The question was whether the students would show the same logical lapses that children do. With a difficult task, the students' comprehension resembled the cognitive processes of children. Huang (1931) attributed such a difference between children's and adults' cognitions to the increased level of knowledge of adults, not to the nature of their thought processes.

According to Abel (1932), the differences between adults and children with respect to the nature of the logical processes "hold true only under limited conditions; where the material presented is not difficult for the adult to comprehend, where one child is inferior in chronological age, in ability, or in cultural heritage to another" (p. 132). In addition, Johnson and Josey (1931) reported that few of Piaget's claims were substantiated with their population of North Dakota children. Six-year olds showed little animism, artificialism, or finalism; furthermore, the children that they studied were not particularly egocentric at ages when Piaget said they should be. The Johnson and Josey sample contained young children who were socially minded, could take the perspective of others, and could formulate hypotheses. In addition, the children showed success in 33 tests on which Piaget's sample could solve only one.

Johnson and Josey (1931) noted that their North Dakota and Piaget's Swiss samples may have differed with respect to IQ; most of their children were slightly above average, but it is not clear how the Swiss samples would have tested had Piaget been inclined to test them. As a second hypothesis for the differential performance of the samples, Johnson and Josey suggested somewhat parochially that "perhaps the English language is superior to the French as an instrument for logical thinking" (p. 339). Furthermore, although Piaget maintained that children's cognitive development is more dependent on their interaction with adults than with other children, Harrower (1934) found no generalized support for this contention with respect to an emerging sense of justice, nor did MacRae (1954) support Piaget's hypotheses about moral judgments 2 decades later. Cognitive change occurs, according to this research, only in conjunction with children's interactions with other children. In addition, students in a school similar to that of Piaget's child participants performed as Piaget's did but not a control group, which seemed more advanced and which did not appear to go through the same developmental process that Piaget theorized.

Another specific element associated with the impact of environment in development is the role of culture. The data were not favorable to Piaget's ideas. For example, Dennis (1943, 1957) reported that the Hopi Indian children showed higher levels of animism than children of European descent, a difference most probably attributable to cultural factors. The role of culture was also identified early in the emergence of Piagetian ideas (e.g., Morgan's, 1932, report on causation in relation to the dreams of Navaho Indians) and is still being felt (e.g., Goodnow, 1969, comments on varying degrees of attainment of conservation across African cultures). The cross-cultural generality of Piaget's postulates is still a matter of controversy.

His ideas continue to receive scrutiny. For example, Pramling (2006) repeated one of Piaget's early studies on animism, generating results that required a reinterpretation that differed from that of Piaget. This is another instance of theory-driving research that fits within a Piagetian framework but that requires modification of his initial conclusions.

THE IMPACT OF JEAN PIAGET

It may not be an exaggeration to claim that no theorist has had more impact on the discipline of psychology than Jean Piaget. And there is no question that his impact has far surpassed that of any other developmental psychologist. Sigmund Freud may have a greater level of popular recognition, but the contribution of psychodynamic theory to the research enterprise in psychology is not all that remarkable (Robins, Gosling, & Craik, 1999). On the other hand, after over 80 years, Piagetian theory still appears to be the driving theoretical force among developmental psychologists.

One interesting facet of the acceptance of the theory is that, although Piaget has been the dominant theoretical force in developmental psychology for decades, the number of citations of his work in peer-reviewed journals was relatively small until the early 1960s, some 40 years after psychologists began to recognize the importance of his ideas (and to criticize them). For example, in each year of the 1950s, the number of articles listed in PsycINFO® that cited him failed to reach double digits. In contrast, in the 1950s, researchers cited Clark Hull more in each year than had cited Piaget in total in that 10-year period. However, from the early 1960s to the late 1970s, citations of Piaget rose exponentially (Kessen, 1996). Piaget has achieved legendary status even though relatively few people initially cited his research compared with Hull's, whose ideas have almost disappeared from psychology entirely.

Ironically, many 21st-century citations of Piaget's work are of his work from the 1950s rather than of his theoretical revisions that appeared in the 1960s and later. One reason for this gap may be that a number of his later books were slow to be translated into English or not translated at all (Beilin, 1992). Thus, current psychologists may be less familiar with changes in Piagetian thought. In addition, if his popularity has passed its peak, as Beilin suggested, today's psychologists may be less inclined to read his work to begin with.

This gap is important in understanding Piaget's contributions because his work was far from static through his career. He changed focus at times and emphasized different aspects of children's thought at various points. According to Beilin (1992), Piaget first concentrated on the child's conception of reality as mediated through language then on children's action related to objects in the sensorimotor stage. A third period involved more detailed work on concrete and formal operations. Finally, Piaget returned to the preoperational stage and the logic that accompanies it.

The widespread acceptance of Piaget's ideas today and the way they appear in textbooks do not reflect the empirical research beginning in the 1930s that found fault with specific aspects of Piagetian theory. Psychologists were obviously influenced by the theory and recognized its importance, but the data called into question some of Piaget's conclusions. McGranahan (1936) commented that nobody had yet reconciled the discrepancies between Piaget's findings and those of his critics but that the differences were probably due to methodological issues. However, American psychologists continued to amass a significant amount of discrepant data, enough that in a review of Jean Marquis Deutsche's *The Development of Children's Concepts of Causal Relations*, McCarty (1938) concluded, "Thus is added to the American child psychology literature one more well-executed experimental study, which was stimulated by Piaget's work, but which resulted in conclusions directly opposed to his claims" (p. 476). By the 1950s, systematic tests of Piagetian theory with sound methodology produced results that were no more favorable, as reviewed by Vinacke (1951).

These patterns of results appear to have been the norm in the early research and have persisted (e.g., Pramling, 2006; Sophian, 1985). Nonetheless, psychologists have accepted the reality of psychological processes associated with qualitatively different stages, including children's egocentricity, animism, and perceived causation, even though the data are at considerable variance with specific mechanisms that Piaget postulated. Within the past few decades, some of his adherents have downplayed the idea of discrete stages as important to the theory although, as Beilin (1992) noted, he maintained the centrality of the stages to his theory until the end of his life.

Regarding the status of Piagetian theory now, Gardner (1985) speculated that Piaget's most enduring legacy would be his "brilliant experimental paradigms and riveting demonstrations" (p. 117) but that his grand theory would hold less sway. Gopnik (1996) echoed these sentiments: "The field of cognitive development had a coherent, interesting, testable, and widely accepted theory. Now, alas, we are back in the preparadigmatic boat with our colleagues in the rest of psychology" (p. 221). Just as major systems like structuralism and functionalism have disappeared as meaning-ful entities, Piaget's broad-ranging conceptualizations of stages may no longer be tenable. Instead, cognitive development is better regarded within specific domains.

Gardner (1985) and Gopnik (1996) also spoke with one voice regarding the influ-ence of Piaget on psychology. Gardner commented that he provided a viable cog-nitive approach during the reign of behaviorism and provided a mode of research that continues in psychology. The signal contribution of Piaget, Gopnik noted, was to have shown that we can learn about the process of development through the systematic study of the small details of children's behavior. Furthermore, accord-ing to Gardner, although Piaget's formalisms are under attack, the specific stages are not as he observed, and his speculations on underlying biological processes have not received support, "even disproofs of his specific claims are a tribute to his general influence" (p. 118).

In addition, one important facet of Piagetian dominance is that the study of childhood that he engendered was far from predetermined. As Siegler and Ellis (1996) noted, current investigations of adult cognition study mental architecture; there is no reason that the study of children might not have followed that path. Furthermore, before Piaget's ideas took hold, the processes of discrimination and generalization as they mediate children's learning took center stage.

Flavell (1996) summarized Piaget's effect on psychology: His ideas are so uni-versal in psychology that they have become invisible. It would be virtually impos-sible to understand the state of developmental psychology except from within a Piagetian context. To appreciate the unfolding of theories of development, one can examine the state of the field in the 1950s, which would reflect a less coherent and sophisticated perspective on development.

Piaget had hoped to see the emergence of a biological model that would capture the functional changes in children's cognition. With the rise in models of cognitive neuroscience, psychologists should be able to generate further tests of Piagetian theory, whose impact will persist until a new, comprehensive model of cognitive development appears. As of now, there is no sign of such a model.

SUGGESTED READINGS

Brainerd, C. J. (Ed.). (1996). Piaget: A centennial celebration. [Special section]. *Psychological Science, 7*, 191–225.

>This special section of *Psychological Science* provides commentary on Piaget's ideas on development from infancy through adolescence. It also illustrates the overwhelm-ing effect that Piaget had on transforming the study and theory of cognitive develop-ment over the past half century. It also gives some insight into the post-Piagetian era that we have entered.

Beilin, H. (1992). Piaget's enduring contribution to developmental psychology. *Develop-mental Psychology, 28*, 191–204. doi:10.1037/0012-1649.28.2.191

>This article recounts the development of Piaget's theory through the stages of his career. Piaget's theory was anything but static during the course of his life. He incorporated aspects of both structuralism and functionalism (not in the sense of the American schools of thought) in producing a powerful model of cognitive develop-ment that motivates ongoing research.

Piaget, J. (1952/1968). Jean Piaget. In E. G. Boring, H. Werner, H. S. Langfeld, & R. M. Yerkes (Eds.), *A history of psychology in autobiography* (vol. 4, pp. 237–256). New York: Russell & Russell.

The brief autobiographical sketch in Piaget's own words gives an interesting depiction of the line of thought that led to his theory and the research that generated and supported the theory. Although he was not terribly forthcoming about personal details of his life, the autobiographical sketch traces the logical unfolding of his ideas.

REFERENCES

Abel, T. M. (1932). Unsynthetic modes of thinking among adults: A discussion of Piaget's concepts. *American Journal of Psychology, 44*, 123–132. doi:10.2307/1414959

Baldwin, J. M. (1906). *Mental development in the child and the race: Mental processes*, 3d ed. New York: Macmillan. Retrieved from http://www.archive.org/stream/mentaldevelopmen00baldiala#page/n5/mode/2up

Beilin, H. (1992). Piaget's enduring contribution to developmental psychology. *Developmental Psychology, 28*, 191–204. doi:10.1037/0012-1649.28.2.191

Boden, M. A. (2006). *Mind as machine: A history of cognitive science*, vol. 1. Oxford: Clarendon.

Bryant, P. E. (1995). Jean Piaget (1896–1990). In R. Fuller (Ed.), *Seven pioneers of psychology: Behavior and mind* (pp. 130–154). New York: Routledge.

Burt, C. (1952/1968). Cyril Burt. In E. G. Boring, H. Werner, H. S. Langfeld, & R. M. Yerkes (Eds.), *A history of psychology in autobiography* (vol. 4, pp. 53–73). New York: Russell & Russell.

Cantril, H. (1935). Review of *Developmental psychology. Journal of Abnormal and Social Psychology, 30*, 272–273. doi:10.1037/h0052189

Dennis, W. (1938). Historical notes on child animism. *Psychological Review, 45*, 257–266. doi:10.1037/h0060375

Dennis, W. (1943). Animism and related tendencies in Hopi children. *Journal of Abnormal and Social Psychology, 38*, 21–36. doi:10.1037/h0059037

Dennis, W. (1957). Animistic thinking among college and high school students in the near east. *Journal of Educational Psychology, 48*, 193–198. doi:10.1037/h0045658

Elkind, D. (1996). Inhelder and Piaget on adolescence and adulthood: A postmodern appraisal. *Psychological Science, 7*, 216–220. doi:10.1111/j.1467-9280.1996.tb00362.x

Flavell, J. H. (1996). Piaget's legacy. *Psychological Science, 7*, 200–203. doi:10.1111/j.1467-9280.1996.tb00359.x

Gardner, H. (1985). *The mind's new science: A history of the cognitive revolution*. New York: Basic Books.

Goodnow, J. J. (1969). Problems in research on culture and thought. In D. Elkind & J. H. Flavell (Eds.), *Studies in cognitive development: Essays in honor of Jean Piaget* (pp. 439–462). New York: Oxford University Press.

Goodwin, C. J. (2010). Using history to strengthen a research methods course. *History of Psychology, 13*, 196–200.

Gopnik, A. (1996). The post-Piaget era. *Psychological Science, 7*, 221–225. doi:10.1111/j.1467-9280.1996.tb00363.x

Harrower, M. R. (1934). Social status and the moral development of the child. *British Journal of Educational Psychology, 4*, 75–95.

Hazlitt, V. (1930). Children's thinking. *British Journal of Psychology, 20*, 354–361.

Huang, I. (1931). Children's explanations of strange phenomena. *Psychologische Forschung, 14*, 63–182.

Impressions of the International Congress. (1930). *Journal of Abnormal and Social Psychology, 24,* 415–417. doi:10.1037/h0064812

Isaacs, S. (1929). The language and thought of the child; Judgment and reasoning in the child; The child's conception of the world. [Book reviews]. *Pedagogical Seminary and Journal of Genetic Psychology, 36,* 597–607.

Jean Piaget Society. (2007). Retrieved April 15, 2010 from http://www.piaget.org/aboutPiaget.html

Johnson, E. C., & Josey, C. C. (1931). A note on the development of the thought forms of children as described by Piaget. *Journal of Abnormal and Social Psychology, 26,* 338–339. doi:10.1037/h0075301

Kessen, W. (1996). American psychology just before Piaget. *Psychological Science, 7,* 196–199. doi:10.1111/j.1467-9280.1996.tb00358.x

Lynd, H. M. (1927). An empirical study of child logic. *Journal of Educational Psychology, 18,* 277–278. doi:10.1037

MacRae, D., Jr. (1954). A test of Piaget's theories of moral development. *Journal of Abnormal and Social Psychology, 49,* 14–18. doi:10.1037/h0061606

Maudsley, H. (1886). *The pathology of mind.* New York: Appleton.

McCarty, D. (1938). The development of children's concepts of causal relations. *Journal of Educational Psychology, 29,* 474–476. doi:10.1037/h0049853

McGranahan, D. V. (1936). The psychology of language. *Psychological Bulletin, 33,* 178–216. doi:10.1037/h0056934

McKee, J. P., & Honzik, M. P. (1962). The sucking behavior of mammals: An illustration of the nature-nurture question. In L. Postman (Ed.), *Psychology in the making: Histories of selected research problems* (pp. 585–661). New York: Knopf.

Meltzer, H. (1929). Review of *The process of human behavior. Journal of Educational Psychology, 20,* 717–718. doi:10.1037/h0066738

Morgan, W. (1932). Navaho dreams. *American Anthropologist, 34,* 390–405. doi:10.1525/aa.1932.34.3.02a00030

Morss, J. (1990). *The biologising of childhood.* Hillsdale, NJ: Erlbaum.

Nass, M. L. (1956). The effects of three variables on children's concepts of physical causality. *Journal of Abnormal and Social Psychology, 53,* 191–196. doi:10.1037/h0044090

Piaget, J. (1918). *Recherche.* [Research]. Lausanne: La Concorde.

Piaget, J. (1924). *Judgment and reasoning in the child.* London: Kegan Paul.

Piaget, J. (1926). *The language and thought of the child.* New York: Harcourt, Brace.

Piaget, J. (1929). *The child's conception of the world.* London: Routledge and Kegan Paul.

Piaget, J. (1952/1968). Jean Piaget. In E. G. Boring, H. Werner, H. S. Langfeld, & R. M. Yerkes (Eds.), *A history of psychology in autobiography* (vol. 4, pp. 237–256). New York: Russell & Russell.

Piaget, J. (1976). A history of psychology in autobiography. In S. F. Campbell (Ed.), *Piaget sampler: An introduction to Jean Piaget through his own words* (pp. 115–147). New York: Wiley.

Pramling, N. (2006). "The clouds are alive because they fly in the air as if they were birds": A re-analysis of what children say and mean in clinical interviews in the work of Jean Piaget. *European Journal of Psychology of Education, 21,* 453–466.

Robins, R. W., Gosling, S. D., & Craik, K. H. (1999). An empirical analysis of trends in psychology. *American Psychologist, 54,* 117–128. doi:10.1037/0003-066X.54.2.117

Shuttleworth, A. (2010). *The mind of the child: Child development in literature, science, and medicine, 1840–1900.* Oxford: Oxford University Press.

Siegler, R. S., & Ellis, S. (1996). Piaget on childhood. *Psychological Science, 7,* 211–215. doi:10.1111/j.1467-9280.1996.tb00361.x

Sophian, C. (1985). Perseveration and infants' search: A comparison of two- and three-location tasks. *Developmental Psychology, 21,* 187–194. doi:10.1037/0012-1649.21.1.187

Stone, C. L. (1930). Review of *The child's conception of the world*. *Journal of Abnormal and Social Psychology, 25*, 93–94. doi:10.1037/h0065677

Vidal, F. (1994). *Piaget before Piaget*. Cambridge, MA: Harvard University Press.

Vinacke, W. E. (1951). The investigation of concept formation. *Psychological Bulletin, 48*, 1–31. doi:10.1037/h0054378

7

Lev Vygotsky:
Philologist and Defectologist, A Sociointellectual Biography[1]

ANTON YASNITSKY

York University

Among the pioneers of psychology, Lev Vygotsky (1896–1934) may be the best known of those who are least understood. This is not just a problem of historical scholarship: The misunderstanding of Vygotsky started with his

own students and collaborators—during his lifetime—and continued after his death. It is, in other words, integrated into the literature. And that literature, as a result, appears fractured and inconsistent. Indeed, the largest and the best intellectual biography of Vygotsky is titled *Understanding Vygotsky: A Quest for Synthesis* (van der Veer & Valsiner, 1991). Yet even this excellent book is far from providing a full and complete story. The discovery of the real Vygotsky is still to come.

Figure 7.1   Lev Vygotsky, 1925.

There are many reasons for systematic misunderstanding—even misrepresentation. Among them we can include Vygotsky's changes in theoretical outlook; his premature death at the age of 37, when he was in the middle of the most prolific period of his career; the lack of public access to manuscripts and documents in the Vygotsky archives; problems of posthumous editing; and the censorship of his works published in the Soviet Union, the effects of which were in turn multiplied by mistakes that accumulated in Western translations (Yasnitsky, 2010; van der Veer & Yasnitsky, in press). These confusions, and many others, have resulted in an image of Vygotsky that can be described charitably as having been constructed by his students, followers, and admirers.

The beginning of the cult of Vygotsky dates back to 1978. This was the start of the present Vygotsky boom (Cole, 2004; Garai & Kocski, 1995). Two inaugural events took place in this year: First, the book *Mind in Society* came out under Vygotsky's name (Vygotsky, 1978); and second, the well-known British and American philosopher Stephen Toulmin published his programmatic book review titled *The Mozart of Psychology* (Toulmin, 1978). There, Toulmin compared Lev Vygotsky to Wolfgang Mozart and his right-hand man and coworker, Alexander Romanovich Luria (1902–1977), to Ludwig van Beethoven. Whereas the second part of this comparison has since been largely forgotten, the association of Mozart with Vygotsky as the quintessential creative genius of psychology has survived and prospered.

After the publication of *Mind in Society*, the celebrated notion of the "zone of proximal development" became synonymous with Vygotsky's name. Interestingly enough, however, Vygotsky never actually wrote this book: It is a compilation and juxtaposition of fragments taken from different works written during different periods of his career. This is made clear in the preface: The editors—Michael Cole, Vera John-Steiner, Sylvia Scribner, and Ellen Souberman (1978)—confess that they "constructed" some chapters, whereas others are summarized or "based on" Vygotsky's actual writings: "We realize that in tampering with the original we may have distorted history; however, we hope that by stating our procedures and by adhering as closely as possible to the principles and content of the work, we have not distorted Vygotsky's meaning" (Cole et al., 1978, p. x).

The multitude and, even more importantly, the diversity of contemporary interpretations of Vygotsky's theory lead some authors to discuss the "multiple readings" (van der Veer, 2008) or even "versions of Vygotsky" (Gillen, 2000). Some even question, pessimistically, if anybody ever actually reads Vygotsky's own words these days (Gredler & Schields, 2004). This chapter is therefore an attempt to do just that: to return to the source and to trace the genesis and development of Vygotsky's works, while providing the means to contextualize new readings.

The novelty of the story presented here is due, in part, to recent research in Vygotsky's personal archives (Zavershneva, 2010a, 2010b, 2010c). It also considers the international and interdisciplinary nature of Vygotsky's project. However, our story is also distinct in yet another sense. One of the main achievements of the last decade is the realization that the gigantic and ambitious project of Vygotskian psychology cannot be understood if treated as the "single-handed" effort of a "solitary genius." Instead, when one looks behind the constructed facade, there is a noticeable shift from *Vygotsky as such* to *Vygotsky as corporate author*: the leading representative, like Jean Piaget or Kurt Lewin, of a dense personal network of scholars who shared the same research agenda, similar views on methods , and a common understanding of the development of scientific theory.

The scholars of this "Vygotsky Circle" worked in parallel in several cities of the Soviet Union in Belarus, Russia, Ukraine, and Georgia—chiefly in Moscow, Kharkov, and Leningrad—and traveled frequently to take part in "internal conferences" to coordinate their research. This network was instrumental in the development and dissemination of Vygotskian thought during his lifetime, although especially after his death, both in the Soviet Union and internationally. This huge network centers on Lev Vygotsky but includes several dozen associates and collaborators. Virtually all these individuals were instrumental in the development of his scientific thought, the progress of his career, and the later dissemination, and—for good or bad—the global popularization of Vygotskian ideas after his death (Yasnitsky, in press).

THE CONTOURS OF THE PORTRAIT: THE TWO PASSIONS OF VYGOTSKY

Only two lines are really needed to draw a contour of the portrait of Vygotsky the scholar. These lines span Vygotsky's entire life and career and can be detected in virtually anything he wrote, said, and did. Both lines begin in his early life as a provincial Jewish boy living with his family in the town of Gomel, in Belarus, where Vygotsky spent more than half his short life. The first, *philological,*° line is formed by Vygotsky's affection for "the Word," an affection he developed through his childhood reading and early studies in the humanities. Set within the broad Zeitgeist of German Romanticism—specifically, the works of the great German scholar Wilhelm von Humboldt (1767–1835) and his Russian-Ukrainian follower Alexander Potebnya (1835–1891)—Vygotsky considered the Word (i.e., human speech and language) as the highest manifestation of a dialectic unity of human culture and its products. He also considered it an instrument for shaping human thought and spirit. This understanding of human culture is clearly in line with Vygotsky's Romanticist predecessors. In his last book, *Thinking and Speech* (1934), Vygotsky unambiguously refers to and continues Potebnya's earlier work, *Thought and Language* (1892), as well as his later works on the cultural influence of art and poetry, myth, cultural symbols, verbal understanding, and language. Despite the critical attitude that he often expressed toward the legacy of arguably the greatest Russian Humboldtian—for instance, in his *Psychology of Art* (1926/1971)—Vygotsky seems to be in total agreement with Potebnya's most essential views about the nature of language.

In 1913–1917, Vygotsky's pursued full-time studies at Moscow State University in the Law Department and was simultaneously auditing courses in the Historical-Philosophical Department at Shaniavsky Open University. Little is known about the law degree that Vygotsky obtained from Moscow State University in 1917. In contrast, Vygotsky's philological treatise on Shakespeare's *Hamlet*, which he completed in 1916 at the age of 20, received international acclaim. Vygotsky's admiration for the beauty of the Word—including the problems of understanding art and masterpieces of world literature, the complexities of language in its historical development, the intricacies of speech production and their interplay

---

° Here, by philology we understand, following Russian scholarly tradition and according to Merriam-Webster Dictionary, the study of literature and of disciplines relevant to literature or to language as used in literature.

with thinking, emotions, personality, and culture—remained at the center of his interests throughout his life.

The second line tracing the contour of Vygotsky's portrait is *defectological* and it is formed by Vygotsky's concern with freedom and liberation. Social injustice became obvious fairly early in Vygotsky's life, when, in 1913, the quota system for accepting Jews to Russian universities was changed from achievement based to mere vote casting. Exceptionally well prepared for entrance exams, Vygotsky was obviously frustrated to learn about this policy change, but, to his great surprise, he won the ballot and was accepted at Moscow University. It is difficult—perhaps impossible—to trace the source of Vygotsky's sentiment for freedom, and his ideas on human liberation are scattered throughout the entire corpus of his preserved written works: from his early literary reviews and essays on art and the "Jewish question" to his later works on the interrelations between affect and intellect, human will and freedom of choice, and language and consciousness. The perceived imperfection of the world motivated Vygotsky's activism toward changing this imperfect world. This "progressivist" stance was quite in line with the prosocialist sentiments of the Russian intelligentsia after the October 1917 Revolution and the call for creating a "New Man," capable of overthrowing the social constraints of the capitalist "Old World" of violence, inequity, and oppression, equally capable of overcoming the limits of his own biological nature. At the end of his doctoral dissertation, *Psychology of Art* (Vygotsky, 1926/1971), Vygotsky enthusiastically quoted Leon Trotsky (1924/2005), specifically his views on "reshaping of man" in his *Literature and Revolution*. For political reasons the following quote from Trotsky was later removed by the editor of the Soviet edition of the mid-1960s and was first restored only in the most recent Russian edition of the book (Vygotskii, 1926/2008):

> [Man] will try to master first the semiconscious and then the subconscious processes in his own organism, such as breathing, the circulation of the blood, digestion, reproduction, and, within necessary limits, he will try to subordinate them to the control of reason and will. Even purely physiologic life will become subject to collective experiments. The human species, the coagulated *Homo sapiens*, will once more enter into a state of radical transformation, and, in his own hands, will become an object of the most complicated methods of artificial selection and psycho-physical training. This is entirely in accord with evolution. ... Man will make it his purpose to master his own feelings, to raise his instincts to the heights of consciousness, to make them transparent, to extend the wires of his will into hidden recesses, and thereby to raise himself to a new plane, to create a higher social biologic type, or, if you please, a superman. (Trotsky, 1924/2005, pp. 206–207)

Yet then, quite characteristically (as if to undermine his fascination with Marxism and underline the diversity of various philosophical influences on his thought), Vygotsky complemented this Marxist quote with another one that actually concludes his dissertation work. The concluding quote comes from a philosophical idol of Vygotsky's youth, Baruch Spinoza: "That of which the body is capable has not yet been determined" (Vygotskii, 1926/2008, p. 283).

It is clear that Vygotsky was no traditional ivory-tower academic but was a profound thinker driven to participate in an ever-changing world and to contribute to the improvement of man and society, and overcoming various defects of human social, cultural, and biological development. This applied, pragmatic orientation of Vygotsky's theorizing is highly reminiscent of the famous saying that "there is nothing more practical than a good theory," the motto of yet another luminary of psychological theory and practice, Kurt Lewin. The similarity between the views of the two is no mere coincidence and was based on personal acquaintance, familiarity with each other's works, and intensive intellectual exchange (either direct or mediated by their numerous collaborators and associates such as Alexander Luria, Sergei Eisenstein, Tamara Dembo, Gita Birenbaum, Bluma Zeigarnik, and Nina Kaulina) and, reportedly, heated discussions during several meetings that they had (Yasnitsky, in press).

In sum, these two lines—philology as "passion for word (*logos*)" and striving for freedom—evolved and transformed into Vygotsky's interest in the problems of children's "defects" (i.e., physical disability, retardation, and regression) and into his psychological research on the genesis and evolution of distinctly human *higher mental functions* in their cultural development. Indeed, the connection between these two seemingly unrelated research programs cannot be adequately understood except as driven by Vygotsky's efforts to find a theory of human development that would inform pedagogical and rehabilitation practice and overcome developmental defects in impaired and abnormal children, consequently improving human nature. Vygotsky's two passions materialized around 1917 upon his return from Moscow to Gomel, specifically through his subsequent work at the educational and research establishments in this provincial Belarus town.

During the early period of the new economic policy (NEP) of the Bolshevik state, which allowed for the reintroduction of small private businesses into the national economy in 1921, Vygotsky enthusiastically worked in Gomel with homeless children—the legacy of the years of revolution and civil war— and in education of children with normal and retarded development. He also lectured in a range of humanities and social sciences at a number of local educational establishments and professional organizations. Vygotsky even cofounded a publishing house and, appointed by the new Soviet government as a theatrical entrepreneur of the Gomel region, had to travel frequently across the country in search of new engagements. In 1923 Vygotsky also founded a psychological laboratory under the auspices of the local Pedagogical College: There he collected experimental data and completed and wrote what became his book, *Educational Psychology* (1926). Most of his dissertation on the *Psychology of Art* (1926/1971) was also completed in Gomel and summarized half a decade of experimental studies and theoretical generalizations.

Vygotsky's Gomel period (1917–1924) was instrumental in his later career as an experimental and developmental psychologist. The Gomel postrevolutionary years were significant and formative for Vygotsky on an existential and personal level, too. It was here that tuberculosis took the life of Vygotsky's younger brother— the same disease would later kill Vygotsky himself—and, within a year, his other brother died of typhus. During this period Vygotsky passed through a temporary crisis that was possibly caused by these untimely deaths and the aggravation of his own tuberculosis. For some reason, in the early 1920s—perhaps as an act of Marxist transformation of himself into a "New Soviet Man"—the young scholar slightly changed his distinctly Jewish name Lev Simkhovich Vygodsky (with "d" in the middle) into a somewhat Russified Lev Semenovich Vygotsky under which name we know him now (Mescheryakov, 2007). Finally, it was also in Gomel that Vygotsky met a young woman, Roza Noevna Smekhova, who later became his wife and the mother of his two daughters, Gita (born in Gomel in 1925) and Asya (born in Moscow in 1930).

THE EARLY MOSCOW YEARS (1924–1929) AND THE BIRTH OF A NEW PSYCHOLOGY

Vygotsky left Gomel for Moscow in early 1924. As for many provincial scholars and artists who left the outskirts of the country for urban centres like Moscow, Leningrad or Kharkov in the early 1920s, the move to Moscow marked the beginning of an entirely new period for Vygotsky's research, and it opened up new and unprecedented career opportunities for him. His personal network of informal contacts and connections included both his older Gomel and his newer Moscow acquaintances who were instrumental in getting him established as a professional. For example, he was hired as a psychologist through the recommendation of Kazan-born new Muscovite Alexander Luria and became an educational administrator and defectologist by invitation of his former Gomel colleague Izrail' Danyushevskii. From 1924 onward, Vygotsky was affiliated with the Institute of Psychology as junior researcher and the Ministry of Education (*Narkompros*) as the head of the Section of the Upbringing of Physically and Mentally Handicapped Children; he also taught psychology at a number of different educational establishments in Moscow. The move to Moscow also laid the foundation of a lifelong alliance, collaboration, and friendship between Lev Vygotsky and Alexander Luria.

Due to his extensive scientific, educational, and administrative activism, Vygotsky became one of the recognized leaders of Soviet defectology within just a year or so after his arrival and was even sent on a *Narkompros* funded trip to Europe to represent the Soviet Union at a conference on the education of the deaf and blind in London in summer 1925 (van der Veer & Zavershneva, in press). This turned out to be his only trip abroad. Upon his return from the trip, in fall 1925, Vygotsky was hospitalized after an outbreak of tuberculosis and stayed in the hospital for almost half a year until late spring 1926. Due to his severe illness, Vygotsky could not even attend the public defense of his own dissertation on the *Psychology of Art*, and the degree of doctor of sciences was awarded to him in absentia in October–November 1925. Undoubtedly, otherwise great news for Vygotsky, the degree was not much consolation to him at that time: In winter 1925–1926, in an overcrowded and noisy hospital room that accommodated five other terminally ill patients, Vygotsky was literally struggling for life. Miraculously, Vygotsky survived and was released from the hospital in May 1926. The disease took its toll: Unable to move independently and with a lingering disability as evidenced by his medical and employment records, for medical reasons Vygotsky was qualified as legally incapacitated, as an invalid, and remained out of work for the entire year of 1926. Yet the year turned out to be a very productive one.

Crisis in Psychology

In 1926, Vygotsky reflected on his earlier engagement with the variety of psychological systems and theoretical frameworks proposed by his contemporaries (e.g., Pavlov and Bekhterev's notion of reflex, Kornilov's concept of reaction, Alfred Adler's ideas on overcompensation). He came to the conclusion that a radically new, distinctly innovative, and revolutionary way of psychological theorizing was needed. According to Luria, Vygotsky accomplished historical and theoretical work, enormous in its scope, reading basically all of Russian and Western psychologies of the time, and reflecting on the methodological foundations of psychology as a discipline: "Our aim, overambitious in the manner characteristic of the times, was to create a new, comprehensive approach to human psychological process" (Luria, 1979, p. 40). Indeed, very much in the spirit of the "prophet armed" Leon Trotsky's announcement of the new man of communism, Vygotsky prophesied the advent of the new psychology of the future:

> Such a system has not yet been created. We can say with confidence that it will not arise out of the ruins of empirical psychology or in the laboratories of reflexologists. It will come as a broad biosocial synthesis of the theory of animal behavior and societal man. This new psychology will be a branch of general biology and at the same time the basis of all sociological sciences. It will be the knot that ties the science of nature and the science of man together. It will therefore, indeed, be most intimately connected with philosophy, but with a strictly scientific philosophy which represents the combined theory of scientific knowledge and not with the speculative philosophy that preceded scientific generalizations. (Vygotsky, 1925/1997, p. 61).

Vygotsky framed his theoretical and methodological work in terms of a "crisis" in psychology, a theme that seems to have been there since the very beginning of the discipline (see, e.g., the treatises on "psychological crisis" by Karl Bühler, Hans Driesch, Kurt Koffka, William Stern, Nikolai Kostyleff, Mary Whiton Calkins, N. N. Lange, S. L. Frank, Edmund Husserl, Kurt Lewin). Vygotsky's contribution to this discussion of the methodological crisis in psychology was a now famous theoretical and methodological study, "The Historical Meaning of the Crisis in Psychology" (written in 1926–1927). Judging from the manuscript of the treatise on the *Crisis* and, especially, the marginal handwritten notes and anonymous reviewer's comments on it, Vygotsky apparently realized numerous flaws and methodological problems with his argument, and it appears that he did not intend to publish it as such. Instead, a series of journal articles came out in the second half of the 1920s (e.g., Vygotskii, 1928), in which Vygotsky exposed his views on the historical crisis in psychology and succinctly formulated his methodological credo (Zavershneva, 2009).

In these works Vygotsky discussed the crisis in psychology in terms of a perceived need in general psychological theory. The whole multitude of contemporary psychological theories, argued Vygotsky, could be reduced to two principal worldviews and theoretical positions. Vygotsky refers to these two worldviews as two psychologies that reflect the split between the world of the physical and that of the mental. To prevent such a split, Vygotsky suggested three requirements for the unified psychological science of the future that, as a matter of fact, have not lost their importance for contemporary theoretical and empirical antireductionistic psychology (Clegg, 2009): (1) a unified *theoretical basis*; (2) a sound *methodology* of empirical research; and (3) a strong *connection between theory and practice* in contemporary psychological theories and practices of industrial, child, and clinical psychology. Vygotsky argued that, rather than reducing theoretical psychology to either the physical and physiological or the mental and cognitive, a third, radically different way was needed. Thus, one of the most principal topics of Vygotsky's theorizing became the interrelation between mind and body, the physiological and the psychological, which he referred to as the "psychophysical problem" throughout his writings over the last and the most productive decade of his life. A nonreductionist solution to this problem needed to be found somewhere—but where? The answer is as simple as it is confusing and vague: in human culture.

Cultural Mediation

Like many thinkers before him, for instance, Pierre Janet, James Mark Baldwin, George Herbert Mead, Karl Marx, and his associate Friedrich Engels, Vygotsky cherished the idea of the social and cultural origin of human mind and consciousness, also referred to as "sociogenesis" (Valsiner & Van der Veer, 2000). Furthermore, the idea of centrality of labor, tools, and instruments in human culture and practice of humankind is not unique to Vygotsky's thought and can be found elsewhere in the writings of his predecessors, perhaps most notably in the works of Marx and Engels. Yet Vygotsky's scientific contribution is highly original. He was the first to come up with the idea of the leading role of signs as *psychological* tools in human *psychological* development and, even more importantly, to productively apply it in *experimental psychological studies*. This innovative intellectual synthesis is currently widely known as Vygotsky's pioneering idea of *cultural mediation of psychological processes*. Thus, by the beginning of 1927 Vygotsky understood human development as intrinsically cultural—mediated by human artefacts created through people's social practice and used as psychological self-directed tools to overcome the constraints of humanity's biological nature, thus creating a uniquely biocultural entity, pretty much in the spirit of Trotsky's utopian call for the creation of a "higher social biologic type." For Vygotsky, cultural artefacts included a wide range of "psychological instruments," from the alphabet, the Braille system, mnemonics, charts, visual learning aids, and systems of counting to language, literature, and art. All are cultural mediators that preexist any individual human mind and shape its development through the individuals' conscious and active participation in cultural practices, and all, on the other hand, are shaped and continuously altered by cultural innovations of humankind. Vygotsky's private notes from 1926–1927 show that these ideas were developed by the beginning of 1927 but were first formulated and published only a year later, after a series of experimental studies on cultural mediation were completed (Zavershneva, 2010a).

The phenomenon of cultural mediation was empirically studied by Vygotsky and his associates, who modified a wide range of classical research methods borrowed from a great many Western studies, including those of Wolfgang Köhler, Jean Piaget, and Narziss Ach. Vygotsky and his team believed that the only way to investigate distinctly human psychological phenomena is through their development—that is, as a process rather than a result—and conducted research on *higher mental functions* in their development in ontogenesis. The studies of Vygotsky, Luria, and their collaborators of 1920–1930s, based on the postulate that "behavior can only be understood as the history of behavior" (Blonsky, quoted by Vygotsky, 1929/1994, p. 70) were described as *historical-genetic research* in Vygotsky's terminology of the late 1920s. Interestingly, a recently published book presented this as a new approach under the name of *microdevelopmental research* (Granott & Parziale, 2002).

Instrumental Psychology: Experimental Research on Microdevelopment

The first cultural-historical publications specifically discussed the original microgenetic method of *double stimulation*, designed to investigate the development of cultural forms in a child's behavior (see, e.g., Luria, 1928/1994; Vygotsky, 1929/1994). The method places emphasis on the creation and the strategies of the use of *mediators, psychological tools*, or *instruments*, which is why the author of arguably the first presentation of these studies ever published in English referred to it as "the method of instrumentally psychological research" (Luria, 1928/1994, p. 48). In these experimental studies of cultural development, a child was placed in problem-solving situations and assigned a task so difficult that it could not be solved without the application of some special technical means, either invented by the child herself or ready-made and suggested to the child by adult researchers. Thus, in many experimental studies on cultural mediation using the *method of double stimulation* two sets of stimuli were given to the participants: The first set of stimuli was used as an object of a specific goal-driven action, and the second, auxiliary set of stimuli was used as an instrument, or cultural tool, to achieve the goal and to facilitate certain psychological functions, such as perception, attention, or, more typically, memory. The results of this series of experimental studies were not published until 1928–1929 at the earliest, quite often under the names of Vygotsky's collaborators (Sakharov, Zankov, Leontiev).

Perhaps the most illustrative of these—at least one of the most well known worldwide—is the study of concept formation by Vygotsky's collaborator, Leonid Sakharov (1900–1928). In Sakharov's study of concept formation, participants aimed to understand artificial concepts denoting certain, unknown to the participants, combinations of the characteristics of three-dimensional geometrical figures of varying size, shape, and color—the figures themselves being the first set of stimuli—with the help of the second set of stimuli (i.e., the artificially created words denoting these concepts that were written on the bottom of the figures; Sakharov, 1930/1994). In the same spirit, Vygotsky's and Luria's students worked on a study using pictograms in which the participants were required to draw pictures—that is, to create the auxiliary means—that would help them memorize specific given words. This study, reportedly conducted by a large group of young student researchers, continued throughout the entire academic year of 1929, and, although it did not result in any formal academic publication, it seems to have been a very educational experience for both the supervisors of this research project (Vygotsky, Luria, Leontiev) and the young scholars involved (A. V. Zaporozhets, L. I. Bozhovich, L. I. Slavina, N. G. Morozova, and R. E. Levina) alike. In another series of studies by Vygotsky's collaborators, Zankov and Leontiev, two sets of pictures were assigned to normal and mentally retarded participants, and the first set was to be remembered with the help of the other set. For instance, Leontiev's famous cross sectional study was done with three age groups: (1) preschoolers and elementary schoolchildren, (2) middle schoolchildren, and (3) adults. In the first series of experiments the participants were asked to remember as many as possible of the 15 pictures that were given to them. In the second series, the same task was accompanied with an instruction to use an additional set of similar—but not identical—pictures that might help the subjects to remember those in the first set. The results of this study are often presented as a figure with two curves indicating recall rate in the three age groups in the situations of "direct" and "mediated" remembering. Quite predictably, both curves on the chart show considerable growth of recall rate with age. However, interestingly enough, while younger children and adults remembered the items virtually equally well (rather, equally bad, in case of the younger children) in both experimental conditions of mediated and non-mediated remembering, the middle school children demonstrated a tremendous difference in their remembering abilities in the situation of facilitated and aided (i.e., mediated) remembering approaching that of the adult subjects. The figure formed by the two curves on the chart—starting and ending virtually in the same points and diverging in the middle—is somewhat reminiscent of a parallelogram and famously described by Vygotsky, Luria, and Leontiev as the parallelogram of development (Figure 7.2).

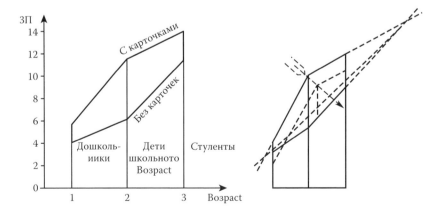

Figure 7.2   Parallelogram of development. (From A. N. Leontiev, Moscow, Uchpedgiz, 1931. With permission.)

The parallelogram of development was used to illustrate the instrumental role of "psychological tools" in the development of "lower-level" human memory in early childhood into "higher mental function" of logical and culturally mediated remembering of the adults (Leontiev, 1931). Another important outcome of this research was a clear, fairly visual illustration of the notion of *internalization*, also variously referred to as *ingrowing* (in Russian, *vrashchivanie*, Vygotsky) and *appropriation* (Leontiev): psychological tools that initially constitute an interrelation between a physical object, meaningful situation, and a goal-directed activity become *internalized* psychological skills in adults, who, according to Leontiev's study, demonstrate virtually equal mastery of remembering quite a few objects with and without mnemonic aids. According to the logic of these earlier studies, internalization is possible due to the use of a *sign* that facilitates achieving the goal of meaningful activity (e.g., the activity of memorizing) but either does not have a meaning of its own or whose own meaning is irrelevant to the task. Thus, the cycle of experimental studies done by Vygotsky and his associates in the 1920s can be described as cross-sectional or microgenetic (microdevelopmental) research on cultural, sign-mediated development of higher mental functions.

All these experimental studies on the cultural development of psychological functions along with considerable theoretical work done by Vygotsky and his group, resulted in a fairly substantial corpus of publications in the second half of the 1920s and contributed to a comprehensive theory of human development. Thus, Vygotskian theory of development needs to be understood as an ambitious tripartite enterprise that deals with three main lines in the development of behavior: (1) development of humans as a biological species *Homo sapiens* (phylogenesis); (2) cultural development of a community or a nation (culturogenesis); and (3) individual development throughout the life span (ontogenesis). Vygotsky and his associates argued that all three of these kinds of development are interrelated and have effects on each and every person. In their coauthored book, *Studies in the History of Behaviour: Ape, Primitive, and Child*. Vygotsky and Luria describe their work as three psychological essays united by one idea, that is, the idea of development, and point out that "the behavior of a cultural man … may be understood and explained scientifically only by analyzing *the three different paths that make up the history of human behavior*" (Vygotsky & Luria, 1930/1993, p. 36, emphasis in original).

Overall, the second half of the 1920s was the formative period for Vygotsky's new program of psychological research, referred to variously as an instrumental or cultural-historical developmental psychology of higher mental functions.

VYGOTSKY'S CRISIS (1929–1930)

However, by the end of this decade Vygotsky had already realized numerous flaws, imperfections, and inconsistencies of this nascent system of thought. Vygotsky was not very satisfied with their book, *Studies in the History of Human Behavior: Ape, Primitive, and Child*, begun in 1927 and published in 1930 (Vygotsky & Luria, 1930/1993). By the end of summer 1929, Vygotsky's coauthor, Alexander Luria, left for the United States to attend the Ninth International Congress of Psychology, held at Yale University in early September, while Vygotsky stayed in Russia to edit the manuscript in preparation for publication. Vygotsky showed his disappointment with their collaborative work in a letter he sent that summer to another active participant of the Vygotsky–Luria group, Aleksei Leontiev:

> I am revising the s[econd] part of "monkey"[i.e., the book *Ape, primitive, and child*]. Alas! The f[irst] chapter is written wholly according to the Freudianists [...]; then the impenetrable Piaget is turned into an absolute beyond all measure; instrument and sign are mixed together even more, and so on and so forth.[°] This is not the fault of A.R. [Luria] personally, but of the entire "epoch" of our thinking. We need to put a stop to this unrelentingly. [...] Let there be the most rigorous, monastic regime of thought; ideological seclusion, if necessary. And let us demand the same of others. Let us explain that studying cultural psychology is no joke, not something to do at odd moments or among other things, and not grounds for every new person's own conjectures. (Vygotsky, 2007, p. 26)

What was so wrong, for Vygotsky, about their effort at presenting an instrumental theory of cultural development that seemed to have so far convincingly explained the role of culture and sign mediators in human development? Leontiev referred to this episode in his memoirs of mid-1970s as the "unique turn" and as "the study objectively turned around" (Leontiev, 1976/1989, p. 30). This "discovery of meaning" ultimately provoked a new and productive series of experimental studies of meaning and sense-making processes that later considerably changed the entire landscape of Vygotskian psychology of the 1920s. Second, an occasional and almost incidental observation made during the experiments using the instrumental method essentially exploded the whole construction of the theory as it was built by 1929. This was the observation that children in experimental situations not only act to achieve their goal, but at the same time also speak. This discovery was made in preliminary observations of children solving subjectively difficult problems. Vygotsky and Luria suggested that "these observations lead us to the conclusion that *the child solves a practical task with the help of not only eyes and hands, but also speech*" (Vygotsky & Luria, 1930/1994, p. 109; italics in original).

This seemingly occasional observation and incidental discovery might have been missed by another group of researchers. However, for Vygotsky and his team, this phenomenon was no serendipitous discovery. It was predetermined by their interest in the evolution of cultural forms of children's behavior and of children's inventing and using cultural methods and instruments of behavior to solve challenging problems (cf. Luria, 1928/1994) and by Vygotsky's lifelong passion about the issues of the interrelations among consciousness, language, and thinking. Therefore, not surprisingly having discovered this phenomenon, the group turned it into an object of their research. Vygotsky and Luria presented the first results of this very important study at the Ninth International Psychological Congress

---

[°] The first two sections of the book were written by Vygotsky; the third one was authored by Luria. Thus, the reference to the first chapter of the second part seems to be to the beginning of Luria's section on child development.

in 1929 under the title *The Function and Fate of Egocentric Speech* (Vygotsky & Luria, 1929/1930). In their 1929 presentation, Vygotsky and Luria challenged Piaget's views on children's "private" egocentric speech and argued that the traditional schema of the evolution of explicit speech needs to be dramatically revised. On the basis of their experimental research Vygotsky and Luria suggested that egocentric speech does not simply disappear, being replaced by a socialized form of verbal behavior, but is gradually substituted for by inner speech that assumes the instrumental function of the former.

The investigation of the phenomenon of egocentric speech in the context of problem solving was continued by Vygotsky and Luria's student Roza Levina, whose findings were briefly reported in various Vygotsky texts. Perhaps the most remarkable discovery made in these investigations was the evolution of children's speech that is typically addressed to an adult (e.g., an experimenter) by the children of an earlier age and is thus dialogic and social. However, this social and dialogic speech later transforms into egocentric, planning speech that in the absence of a participating experimenter reenacts dialogue between the child and the knowledgeable other in older children. Then, egocentric speech gradually disappears or, in terminology of cultural-historical scholars, gets internalized in children of early school age (see Levina, 1968/1998). In this sense, in contrast to Piaget, Vygotsky and his team discovered the genetically dialogic nature of human thinking.

These studies on egocentric speech provided a concrete illustration of consciousness as an introspective system of social relationships (the idea of Karl Marx) and consciousness as an internal dialogue (Vygotsky cited noted Russian linguist Lev Shcherba for whom "speech is always a dialogue"). (See Vygotsky's notes in Zavershneva, 2010a, p. 26.) Vygotsky cherished this idea as early as the mid-1920s, as is evident from his private notebooks where he reflected on the idea of consciousness as a dialogue with oneself that apparently predated and anticipated these studies of the 1930s. Yet, it was only in the beginning of the 1930s—when Vygotsky and his associates found a concrete empirical instantiation of these ideas—that they arrived at the possibility of conducting psychological research *proper* on the complicated issues of the interrelations between consciousness, language and speech, thinking, volition, and emotion. These ideas in their more refined formulations of the early 1930s are exemplified by Vygotsky's famous yet still poorly understood statement on the general law of human development (the origin of which Vygotsky attributed to French scholar and clinician Pierre Janet):

> In general we might say that the relations between higher mental functions once were genuine relations between people. I relate to myself like people relate to me.... Every function in the cultural behavior of the child appears on the stage twice, in two planes, first, the social, then the psychological, first between people as interpsychological category, then within the child as an intrapsychological category. (translated by Valsiner & van der Veer, 2000, p. 370)

On the verge of new theoretical breakthroughs, Vygotsky was desperately struggling to name his theory and was reflecting on a number of options to give his psychological theory a distinctive name but "because of the internal lack of clarity" not fully satisfied with any of the options such as "instrumental," "cultural," "significative," "structural," or "historical" psychology, or "psychology of higher functions." Around 1930, Vygotsky dwelled on a most awkward option for the theory's designation of "historical theory of the development of higher psychological functions" (Vygotsky, quoted in Zavershneva, 2010a, p. 30). However, a year later the notion of *higher psychological function* had considerably lost its appeal as the central theoretical concept, although it still remained in the conceptual framework of the theory. Vygotsky's dissatisfaction with the accomplishments of the "instrumental," "cultural-historical" theory by the end of the 1920s, and his perceived need for a revision of the entire theoretical system resulted in a major breakthrough for Vygotsky at the beginning of the 1930s. This theoretical and experimental breakthrough, however, coincided with yet another significant break—famously referred to as Stalin's Great Break.

SOCIAL AND THEORETICAL EXPLOSION (1930–1934): TOWARD A NEW THEORY OF CONSCIOUSNESS AND PERSONALITY

The end of the 1920s and the beginning of the 1930s represent a significant change in the entire design and structure of the Soviet Union's national culture and economy. The Great Break that was announced by Joseph Stalin at the end of 1929 brought about the collectivization (deprivatization of large and middle-size farms, and agricultural households transformed into collective and state farms, *kolkhozy* and *sovkhozy*), forced industrialization, and renationalization of the private sector of the economy and the introduction of central planning, which marked the end of the New Economic Policy (NEP) of the 1920s. Historians and Sovietologists interpret these events as the beginning of an era of systematic political repressions leading to Stalin's Great Purges and an unprecedented period of modernization of the country's entire social system. Clearly, for science as a social institution in the USSR the Great Break began a period of increasing involvement of state power in science and a growing control over scientific research that culminated in rigid patron–client relations between the ruling Bolshevik bureaucracy and the scientific establishment and, ultimately, in the creation of a gigantic Soviet hybrid of party-state-Big Science topped by the behemoth Academy of Sciences of the Soviet Union. In practice, the Great Break and the beginning of centralization in scientific research in the early 1930s in the Soviet Union marked the launch of numerous public discussions in philosophy and, somewhat later, in the humanities and social and natural sciences—representatives of which aimed to define the politically and philosophically correct ways of conducting scientific research according to the principles of Marxist–Leninist dialectical materialism, which was the only philosophical, theoretical, and methodological position allowed in the USSR in the 1930s. Simultaneously, the many new psychoneurological disciplines like psychology, paedology, psychotechnics, reflexology, psychotherapy, and psychohygiene that had flourished and proliferated in the Soviet Union in the decade of 1920s—lavishly supported by the Bolsheviks in their attempt to rapidly modernize a technology-driven economy—dwindled to a few administratively controlled and planned disciplines unified within only a few highly hierarchical organizational structures (Krementsov, 1997).

Vicissitudes of Vygotskian Psychology in the Early 1930s

Vygotsky and his group were both active and enthusiastic participants in and, simultaneously, victims of theoretical discussions in the early 1930s: Although never officially banned, as were some other psychoneurological disciplines (e.g., Kornilov's *reactology* and Bekhterev's *reflexology* or, later, the discipline of paedology), Vygotsky and Luria's theory of cultural development of higher mental functions was severely criticized in the Soviet newspeak parlance of the time for its "idealism" and "right[wing] deviation" (cf. van der Veer, 2000). The Vygotsky and Luria project fell out of favor with the domestic patrons of science, and most members of their group suffered from two notable processes: the "truncation of collaboration" and the decline of their publications in the early 1930s.

A group of Vygotsky's students known as the *pyaterka* (i.e., "the five")—Zaporozhets, Bozhovich, Slavina, Levina, and Morozova—graduated in 1930, and thereafter the group was dispersed due to the lack of an organizational structure and funding to hold the group together in a research center in Moscow and also due to the requirement of graduates' mandatory employment. Another loss for Vygotsky was the departure of a group of his students and associates (Luria, Leontiev, Zaporozhets, and Bozhovich) from Moscow to Kharkov in the end of 1931. In 1932, this group began to establish a sector of psychology at the newly founded Ukrainian Psychoneurological Academy and to lead psychological research in the capital of Soviet Ukraine (Yasnitsky & Ferrari, 2008a, 2008b).

In an attempt to compensate for the shortage of collaborative research opportunities, Vygotsky and Luria initiated an unprecedented study on how rapid social changes in the traditional society of Central Asia during its modernization after the Bolshevik revolution affected the cognitive development of its population. They organized and undertook two psychological expeditions to Central Asia in summer 1931 and 1932. Vygotsky, who in spring 1929 made a trip to lecture at the Middle-Asian State University (SAGU) in Tashkent, initially had planned to participate too, but for reasons that remain unclear he did not actually make the trips with Luria and his research team. Perhaps seeking to establish an improved national profile and looking for some international acclaim and recognition for this project, Luria advertised in both German and English in a number of publications in such Western academic journals as *Zeitschrift für angewandte Psychologie, Journal of Genetic Psychology, Character and Personality*, and *Science*. In addition, a number of Western scholars, including Wolfgang Köhler, Kurt Koffka, and Kurt Lewin were personally invited to join; only Koffka took part in the second trip of 1932. These expeditions did, however, provoke a great deal of rage among the Soviet militant materialist critics of the Vygotsky–Luria project in 1932–33, and the results of these studies were not published until the mid-1970s (Luria, 1976).

Worse yet, Vygotsky's archives contain a wealth of extremely interesting materials written by him in the 1930s—some still, in fact, unpublished—but after their collaborative *Studies in the History of Human Behaviour* (Vygotsky &

Luria, 1930/1993) Vygotsky's publication rate dropped dramatically and, with the exception of several textbooks and curriculum materials, neither his major works written around 1929–1931 (e.g., *History of the development of higher mental functions, Tool and symbol in child development*) nor most of his smaller papers were published during his lifetime. Even his most famous book, *Thinking and Speech* (Vygotsky, 1934/1987), the last major *oeuvre* and swan song scheduled to appear in 1932 was indeterminately delayed. Vygotsky and Luria made numerous attempts to publish their work in foreign languages through their connections abroad. However, only some of their attempts were successful (e.g., Jacob Kasanin's translation of Vygotsky's 1932 paper on schizophrenia that came out in 1934; Vygotsky, 1934), and in large part most of their attempts failed.

From the early 1930s Vygotsky seemed to be strained financially, accepting numerous temporary arrangements with publishing houses and contracts for part-time editorial work that apparently provided an important source of extra income in the Vygotsky family; therefore, the shortage of publication projects meant financial losses for Vygotsky. Then a number of Vygotsky's jobs were cut in the early 1930s, when organizations where he was employed closed down or were restructured. In search of extra wages to support his family, and to compensate for these losses he had to take a teaching position at the Leningrad State Pedagogical Institute, commuting between Moscow and Leningrad—staying in each of the two cities for a couple of weeks each month—and making occasional trips to Kharkov from 1931 until his final days. At a certain point, Vygotsky was even considering a move to Sukhumi, Georgia, lured by an invitation to take a job at the local Center for the Study of Primates—but these plans never materialized.

Yet these last years of Vygotsky's life were particularly important for him: He worked on a comprehensive cross-disciplinary theory of consciousness, personality, and cultural development. Let us have a look at the contours of this emergent theory as it was presented in various rare Vygotsky publications and numerous yet mostly unpublished archival documents of the time.

The Interdependence of Clinical and Developmental Research: Psychological Systems

From the beginning of the 1930s two lines of Vygotsky's psychological research— the genetic (i.e., research on normal development) and the pathological (i.e. defectological, clinical studies on psychological regression understood as "disintegration" of complex psychological systems, developmental and speech pathology, and rehabilitation)—represent the two interrelated sides of the new integrated Vygotskian research program: "Pathology is the key to understanding development and development is the key to understanding pathological changes" (Vygotsky, 1931/1998, p. 152). This new research program—toward cultural-historical psychology of consciousness and personality—was articulated in a landmark talk on *psychological systems* presented at the Clinic of Nervous Diseases of the I Moscow State University in October of 1930. This novel idea of psychological systems—that Vygotsky confessed to have "nourished during a number of years but hesitated to express fully" (Vygotsky, 1930/1997, p. 107)—"surpasses in complexity the system of concepts with which we have operated thus far" (p. 91). In his presentation to his colleagues and collaborators, Vygotsky critically reviewed their studies on isolated psychological functions (e.g., memory, attention, perception) and proposed a new object of research, *psychological systems*:

> In the process of development, and in historical development in particular, it is not so much the functions which change (these we mistakenly studied before). Their structure and the system of their development remain the same. What is changed and modified are rather the relationships, the links between the functions. New constellations emerge which were unknown in the preceding stage. (Vygotsky, 1930/1997, p. 92)

This conclusion made Vygotsky revise the notion of *higher psychological functions* that he previously understood as cultural, sign-mediated, yet isolated higher-order psychological functions. In 1930s, Vygotsky revised his earlier ideas of hierarchical relations between the higher ("cultural") and the lower ("natural," "elementary") psychological functions and postulated that "the higher psychological functions are not superimposed as a second storey over the elementary processes, but represent new psychological systems which include a complex knot of elementary functions" (Vygotsky & Luria, 1930/1994, p. 140). To illustrate what he meant by *psychological systems*, Vygotsky discussed "sensorimotor unity" (the unity of intertwined perception and motion) in apes, very young children, or, in case of psychological regression, "adults in whom these processes are closest to the affective ones" (Vygotsky, 1930/1997, p. 93). In older children, the unity of perception and motor functions dissolves, giving place to the interconnection of perception and thinking, a psychological system of "visual thinking." Then, at the next stage of the child's development, Vygotsky argued, the unity of thinking and perception is overtaken by a unity of thinking and memory, or the psychological system of "logical memory" that forms in children around the end of primary school. The discovery of psychological systems was essential for Vygotsky and laid solid foundation for all his subsequent work of the 1930s.

Toward the Biosocial Synthesis: Person Within Social Environment

In the 1930s, Vygotsky, founder of the cultural-historical theory and professor of developmental and child psychology, turned to the study of biological aspects of child development and, along with Luria, became an extramural student at the Medical Department of the Ukrainian Psychoneurological Academy in Kharkov. In this period, many studies were completed under Vygotsky's supervision by his associates (most notably, Luria, Lebedinskii, Zankov, R. Levina, Boskis, Pevzner, Morozova, Birenbaum, and Zeigarnik) in Moscow, Leningrad, and Kharkov. These studies were typically published under the students' names. The studies reveal the magnitude of Vygotsky's project of the theory of sociobiological development and cover an impressive list of topics, such as oligophrenia, aphasia and speech pathology, hysteria, schizophrenia and other psychiatric disorders, and the problem of the interrelation between biogenetic and environmental factors as evidenced by the research on identical twins.

On the other hand, their earlier research on social and private (egocentric) speech of the child, experimental research on concept formation, and many other studies on sign-mediated cultural development significantly contributed to discovery of the leading role of interpersonal communication, human activity, and, generally, environmental factors in child development. For Vygotsky—for instance, for his great contemporary, friend, and correspondent German-American psychologist Kurt Lewin—"in the investigation of the fundamental dynamic relations between the individual and the environment, it is essential to keep constantly in mind the actual total situation in its concrete individuality" (Lewin, 1935, p. 68). However, to distinguish between the larger social and the immediate environment of an individual and, thus, environmental settings of macro- and microdevelopment (i.e., life span development as opposed to the change in abilities, knowledge, and understanding during short time spans), Vygotsky introduced the notions of an age-specific *social situation of development* and the *zone of proximal development* of the child.

Thus, the *social situation of development* that emerges by the beginning of each specific age period denotes "a completely original, exclusive, single, and unique relation, specific to the given age, between the child and reality, mainly the social reality that surrounds him" (Vygotsky, 1934/1998, p. 198; see also Bozhovich, 1968/2009). Reflections on the social situation of development and observations of children's involvement in various activities led Vygotsky to his hypothesis of *leading activity*, that is, to the specific activity that boosts and leads development of the child, like, for instance, *play activity* for preschoolers or properly organized *learning activity* for the children of early school age (Vygotsky, 1933/1967). The notion of the *social situation of development* figures prominently in Vygotsky's "pedological" writings of the 1930s on age periods and crises in child development that laid the foundation for Vygotskian developmental *stage theory*. Vygotskyan stage theory, unlike the celebrated stage theory of his contemporary Jean Piaget, accounted for the wide range of cultural, social, behavioral, and biological factors as well as cognitive, emotional, and volitional aspects of personality development. Most prominently this theory was later developed by Vygotsky's former students and collaborators Daniil Elkonin and Lidiya Bozhovich and their associates (Bozhovich, 1968/2009, 1978/2004, 1979/2004a, 1979/2004b; Elkonin, 1971/1999; Slobodchikov & Tsukerman, 2003).

In comparison with Vygotsky's notion of the *social situation of development* and his macrodevelopmental works, the notion of the *zone of proximal development* is considerably better known and far more often discussed (Valsiner & van der Veer, 1993). Ever since the publication of the book *Mind in Society*, the zone of proximal development has been understood as "the distance between the actual developmental level as determined by independent problem solving and the level of potential development as determined through problem solving under adult guidance, or in collaboration with more capable peers" (Vygotsky, 1978, p. 86). Several remarkable illustrations of Vygotsky's notion of the "zone of proximal development" can be found in his presentations and unpublished writings of 1932–34 (Chaiklin, 2003). Thus, according to Vygotsky:

> In child development that which it is possible to achieve at the end as the result of the developmental process, is already available in the environment from the very beginning. And it is not simply present in the environment from the very start, but it exerts an influence on the very first steps in the child's development. (Vygotsky, 1933/1994, pp. 347–348)

Elsewhere, Vygotsky discusses what he refers to as the driving force of development and, at the same time, the principal contradiction of child development: the distinction between the actual development of a child and an *ideal form*, a notion that is extremely important for understanding what Vygotsky meant by "zone of proximal development." A perfect example of such an ideal form is, for Vygotsky, human language: Indeed, language exists before the child is born, the child is exposed to it from the very first days of her life, and it definitely interferes with her development, typically through dialogue with the mother, being a major instrument of transformation of psychological processes of infants into the distinctly human higher order psychological systems of older children. Thus, an ideal form interacts with the actually developing one; for instance, the child's one-word sentence is part of a dialogue with her mother's "ideal speech" (i.e., the child's speech in potential) (Vygotsky's unpublished notes of 1932–33, quoted by Zavershneva, 2010b, p. 50).

Units of Analysis: Word Meaning and Perezhivanie

In his continuous quest for a nonreductionist cultural psychology that would equally well account for physiological and environmental aspects of human development, Vygotsky was particularly sensitive to the issue of identifying a *unit of analysis* that would preserve all qualities of the inseparable whole, like a molecule of water still remains water, and cannot be reduced to a simple combination of hydrogen and oxygen. Vygotsky argued that each specific research problem requires a specific unit of analysis. Thus, for instance, to investigate the interrelation between speech and thinking in their indivisible unity, Vygotsky proposed *word meaning* as such a unit: On one hand, "meaning of a word is a part of the word, a speech formation, because a word without meaning is not a word," and, on the other hand, "since all meaning of a word is a generalization, it is a product of the intellectual activity of the child" (Vygotsky, 1933/1998, p. 294).

Yet, in 1933 and early 1934, Vygotsky was primarily focused on his ultimate goal—the emergent theory of consciousness and it is from this perspective that Vygotsky conceived the research on the interrelations between environment and personality, the problem that became of primary importance for him. Vygotsky struggled to find a unit for the analysis of such interrelations so that neither the complexity of the interconnections of intellect, affect, and will nor the agency of an individual in the environment is lost. Around mid-1933, he finally identified such a unit: *perezhivanie*, a Russian word with its mixed meaning of either "emotional experience" or "emotional sense-making" that literally translates as "living through."[*] For Vygotsky, *perezhivanie* is "a unity of the personality and the environment as it is represented in development" that needs to be understood as the internal[†] relation of the child as a person to one aspect or another of reality. It a biosocial phenomenon; that is, "it is what lies between personality and the environment," does not exist in itself but is always *perezhivanie* of something, and shows what a given event or a situation of the environment means for the person. In sum, according to Vygotsky, environment affects development of the child through *perezhivanie* of the environment (Vygotsky, 1933/1998, p. 294). *Perezhivanie* as a unit of analysis of person in the environment requires from research that it "*ought to be able to find the relationship which exists between the child and its environment, the child's emotional experience [perezhivanie]*, in other words how a child becomes aware of, interprets, [and] emotionally relates to a certain event" (Vygotsky, 1933/1994, p. 341, italics in original).

The writings of 1932–34 of Vygotsky and some of his associates (e.g., Luria, Birenbaum, Zeigarnik, Lebedinskii, Zaporozhets, Asnin) reveal their rapidly growing interest in the issues of *awareness*, *interpretation*, *meaning*, and *sense-making*, and abound with such somewhat cryptic expressions as "dynamic semantic systems" that represent the "unity of affective and intellectual processes," "affective-dynamic systems" and "affective-volitional sphere," "semantic perception," "ideal form," "visual" versus "semantic fields," "imaginary situation," "zone of proximal development," "*semic* (i.e., semantic, or semiotic) analysis," "systemic and semantic structure of consciousness."

However, much of Vygotsky's theoretical work of the 1930s was never finished, nor was it properly operationalized or rigorously experimentally tested during Vygotsky's lifetime. Gravely ill, Vygotsky spent the last 3 years of his life intensely working against all odds on his nascent developmental theory of personality and consciousness. His major book on the psychology of emotions, dedicated to Spinoza, was never completed. The famous volume of collected papers of 1929–1934 that had previously been partially published and eventually came out posthumously under the title *Thinking and Speech* (1934/1987), according to Vygotsky, presented only an introduction to a larger not yet completed theory of consciousness. Indeed, in the conclusion of this book Vygotsky refers to future prospects for his research, stating that their investigation had brought them to the threshold of a problem of consciousness that is broader, more profound, and still more extraordinary than the problem of thinking (Vygotsky, 1934/1987, p. 285). Regrettably, the theory of consciousness in its cultural and biosocial development

---

[*] To avoid the "loss in translation," van der Veer and Valsiner (1994) in *Vygotsky Reader* preserved the transliterated Russian word in brackets throughout the text and provided the following explanatory note: "The Russian term serves to express the idea that one and the same objective situation may be interpreted, perceived, experienced or lived through by different children in different ways. Neither 'emotional experience' (which is used here and which only covers the affective aspect of the meaning of *perezhivanie*), nor 'interpretation' (which is too exclusively rational) are fully adequate translations of the noun. Its meaning is closely linked to that of the German verb '*erleben*' (cf. '*Erlebnis*', '*erlebte Wirklichkeit*')" (van der Veer & Valsiner, 1994, p. 354).

[†] There is a grave error in the 1998 translation of the text: the Russian word *vnutrennij* (internal) of the original was rendered as external. This mistake of translation is corrected here.

was not completed, and to date there is no book—neither by Vygotsky nor by any of his students or followers—that summarizes and explicitly unifies these diverse yet intrinsically interrelated ideas, and presents a nonreductionist psychological project of such enormous breadth and ambition. Without a doubt, future publication of such an important work may well be one of the most long-awaited, inspiring, and groundbreaking contributions to contemporary psychology of the 21st century.

VYGOTSKY AFTER VYGOTSKY

By the end of 1933 Vygotsky was a prolific author, a devoted lecturer, and an enthusiastic researcher, yet he was stressed and frustrated by the campaigns of public criticism and continuous interrogations. However, the outlook was to change significantly after November 1933. On November 26, 1933, Vygotsky was officially hired as head of the Department of Clinical Psychology at the Moscow branch of the newly reorganized All-Union Institute of Experimental Medicine (VIEM). This new appointment was followed by a surge in Vygotsky's publications starting at the beginning of 1934 as evidenced by his books, *Thinking and Speech* (Vygotsky, 1934/1987), *Foundations of Paedology* (Moscow, 1934 and Leningrad, 1935), and a collection of Vygotsky's papers, *Mental Development of Children in the Process of Education* (1935), not to mention smaller works.

Full of plans, at the beginning of 1934 Vygotsky was working intensely: He was organizing the new research unit, teaching, doing research, and writing papers. However, many of these plans were not realized. Due to the aggravation of his medical condition caused by a chronic tuberculosis outbreak, Vygotsky was brought home from his new workplace, prescribed bed rest on May 9, and was later hospitalized on June 2. Vygotsky stayed in the hospital until his sudden yet predictable death on June 11, 1934.

Recognized at his death as one of the leading Marxist thinkers of the time—ironically, just half a year after he had been ostracized, largely neglected, and an almost forgotten scholar with a dubious reputation of an "idealist" in the Bolshevik state at the time of Stalinism on the rise—Vygotsky was buried on June 13, 1934, at Novodevich'e Cemetery, a prestigious national cemetery for the most coveted politicians, military leaders, artists, and scientists. As a burial site, it is second in prestige only to the Kremlin Wall Necropolis. Furthermore, Vygotsky's brain was stored in the Moscow Brain Research Institute's "Pantheon of Brains": a collection of "elite brains" of the most prominent figures in Soviet culture, science, and government, including the brain of the Head of the Soviet state, Vladimir Lenin. Given such impressive posthumous recognition, it seems safe to assume that by the middle of 1934, Vygotsky was poised as a leader of the Soviet "historical" truly Marxist psychology.

After his death, Vygotsky's former collaborators and associates published quite a number of Vygotsky's as well as their own works under the banner of the continuation of Vygotsky's research. Thus, the period of 1934 to the first half of 1936 can be referred to as the "Golden Age" of Vygotskian psychology in the pre-WWII period. However, this did not last long: On July 4, 1936, the Central Committee of the Communist Party issued a special decree prohibiting the discipline of paedology in the country. Because of his notable involvement with paedology, Vygotsky's legacy, yet again, was put on trial: It was semiofficially outlawed or, perhaps more precisely, muffled. A full 20 years later the publication of one of Vygotsky's book, amid the cold war, became one of the first signs of a relative liberation in the country, known as the Thaw, and marked the post-Stalinist period of revival of psychology as a discipline in the Soviet Union. It also marked the beginning of the Vygotsky boom, evident by the countless posthumous attempts to construct, deconstruct, and reconstruct "the real Vygotsky" from the second half of the 20th century onward. However, this is an entirely different story, the most recent and exciting developments of which we are witnessing today, right now.

SUGGESTED READINGS

Van der Veer, R., & Valsiner, J. (1991). *Understanding Vygotsky. A quest for synthesis*. Oxford: Basil Blackwell.

> This is a classic social and intellectual history of Vygotsky and his scientific legacy that remains the best book about Vygotsky to date. Vygotsky's life from his earlier years in Gomel until his last days is discussed against social background of the Soviet Union of the 1920s and 1930s. The book presents the life story of Vygotsky chronologically and thematically, covering such topics as Vygotsky's "Psychology of Art" and "Pedagogical Psychology" of the mid-1920s and educational psychology of the early 1930s, his involvement with psychoanalysis, reactology, Gestalt psychology, cross-cultural research, cultural-historical psychology, defectology, and paedology. It is mandatory reading for anybody interested in Vygotsky's theory and its historical development.

Rieber, R. W., & Wollock, J. (Eds.). (1997). *The collected works of L. S. Vygotsky. Vol. 3. Problems of the theory and history of psychology*. New York: Plenum Press.

> This book belongs to a six-volume collection of Vygotsky's works published in Russian in the early 1980s in Soviet Union and later published in English by Plenum Press in the 1980s–1990s. The translation of the first volume of the original Russian edition presents a collection of a range of Vygotsky's theoretical and methodological works written throughout his lifetime. Virtually impeccable translation and excellent meticulous comments by Van der Veer make this the best volume of the six-volume collection.

Van der Veer, R., & Valsiner, J. (1994). *The Vygotsky reader*. Cambridge, MA: Blackwell.

> This book presents most of his works published (or planned for publication) in English during 1925–1934. This is a well-balanced set of papers representative of the development of Vygotsky's thought from his earlier somewhat radical and "reformist" papers until the last days of his life. The *Vygotsky Reader* can be used as the main source book for any course on Vygotskian or cultural-historical psychology of biosocial human development.

ENDNOTE

1. The author would like to express his gratitude to and acknowledge most valuable feedback from Ekaterina Zavershneva, René van der Veer, Jeremy T. Burman, Manissa E. Barn, and Michael Ferrari, who participated in discussion of the manuscript or assisted with the editing of the text at different stages of this project development.

REFERENCES

Bozhovich, L. I. (1968/2009). The social situation of child development. *Journal of Russian and East European Psychology, 47*, 59–86. doi:10.2753/RPO1061-0405470403.

Bozhovich, L. I. (1978/2004). Developmental phases of personality formation in childhood (I). *Journal of Russian and East European Psychology, 42*(4), 35–54.

Bozhovich, L. I. (1979/2004a). Developmental phases of personality formation in childhood (II). *Journal of Russian and East European Psychology, 42*(4), 55–70.

Bozhovich, L. I. (1979/2004b). Developmental phases of personality formation in childhood (III). *Journal of Russian and East European Psychology, 42*(4), 71–88.

Chaiklin, S. (2003). The zone of proximal development in Vygotsky's analysis of learning and instruction. In A. Kozulin, V. S. Ageyev, S. M. Miller, & B. Gindis (Eds.), *Vygotsky's educational theory in cultural context* (pp. 39–64). Cambridge, MA: Cambridge University Press.

Clegg, J. W. (Ed.). (2009). *The observation of human systems. Lessons from the history of anti-reductionistic empirical psychology*. New Brunswick, NJ: Transaction.

Cole, M. (2004). Prologue: Reading Vygotsky. In R. W. Rieber & D. K. Robinson (Eds.), *The essential Vygotsky* (pp. vii–xii). New York: Kluwer Academic/Plenum.

Cole, M., John-Steiner, V., Scribner, S., & Souberman, E. (1978). Editors' preface. In L. S. Vygotsky (Ed.), *Mind in society: The development of higher psychological processes* (pp. ix–xi). Cambridge, MA: Harvard University Press.

Elkonin, D. B. (1971/1999). Toward the problem of stages in the mental development of children. *Journal of Russian and East European Psychology, 37*(6), 11–30.

Garai, L., & Kocski, M. (1995). Another crisis in the psychology: A possible motive for the Vygotsky-boom. *Journal of Russian and East European Psychology, 33*(1), 82–94.

Gillen, J. (2000). Versions of Vygotsky. *British Journal of Educational Studies, 48*, 183–198. doi:10.1111/1467-8527.t01-1-00141.

Granott, N., & Parziale, J. (Eds.). (2002). *Microdevelopment: Transition processes in development and learning*. New York: Cambridge University Press.

Gredler, M., & Schields, C. (2004). Does no one read Vygotsky's words? Commentary on Glassman. *Educational Researcher, 33*(2), 21–25. doi:10.3102/0013189X033002021.

Krementsov, N. L. (1997) *Stalinist Science*. Princeton: Princeton University Press.

Leontiev, A. N. (1931). *Razvitie pamyati [Development of memory]*. Moscow: Uchpedgiz.

Leontiev, A. N. (1976/1989). The problem of activity in the history of Soviet psychology. *Soviet Psychology, 27*(2), 22–39.

Levina, R. E. (1968/1981). L. S. Vygotsky's ideas about the planning function of speech in children. In J. V. Wertsch (Ed.), *The concept of activity in Soviet psychology* (pp. 281–299). Armonk, NY: M.E. Sharpe.

Lewin, K. (1935). *Dynamic theory of personality*. New York: McGraw-Hill.

Luria, A. R. (1928/1994). The problem of the cultural behavior of the child. In R. v. d. Veer & J. Valsiner (Eds.), *The Vygotsky reader* (pp. 46–56). Oxford, UK: Blackwell.

Luria, A. R. (1976). *Cognitive development: Its cultural and social foundations*. Cambridge, MA: Harvard University Press.

Luria, A. R. (1979). *The making of mind: A personal account of Soviet psychology*. Cambridge, MA: Harvard University Press.

Mescheryakov, B. G. (2007). L.S. Vygotskii i ego imya [L.S. Vygotsky and his name]. *Kul'turno-istoricheskaya psikhologiya* (3), 90–95.

Potebnya, A. A. (1892). *Mysl' i yazk [Thought and language]*, 2nd ed. Kharkov: Tipografiya Adol'fa Darre.

Sakharov, L. (1930/1994). Methods for investigating concepts. In R. v. d. Veer & J. Valsiner (Eds.), *The Vygotsky reader* (pp. 73–98). Oxford: Blackwell.

Slobodchikov, V. I., & Tsukerman, G. A. (2003). Integral periodization of general psycho-
logical development. *Journal of Russian and East European Psychology, 41*(6), 52–66.
Trotsky, L. (1924/2005). *Literature and revolution*. Chicago: Haymarket Books.
Toulmin, S. (1978, September 28). The Mozart of psychology. *New York Review of Books,
14,* 51–57.
Valsiner, J., & Van der Veer, R. (1993). The encoding of distance: The concept of the zone
of proximal development and its interpretations. In R. R. Cocking & K. A. Renninger
(Eds.), *The development and meaning of psychological distance* (pp. 35–62). Hillsdale,
NJ: Erlbaum.
Valsiner, J., & Van der Veer, R. (2000). *The social mind: Construction of the idea*. Cambridge,
UK: Cambridge University Press.
van der Veer, R. (2000). Editor's introduction. Criticizing Vygotsky. *Journal of Russian and
East European Psychology, 38*(6), 3–9.
van der Veer, R. (2008). Multiple readings of Vygotsky. In B. Oers, W. van, Wardekker,
E. Elbers, & R. Van der Veer (Eds.), *The transformation of learning: Advances
in cultural-historical activity theory* (pp. 20–37). Cambridge, UK: Cambridge
University Press.
van der Veer, R., & Valsiner, J. (1991). *Understanding Vygotsky: A quest for synthesis.*
Blackwell.
van der Veer, R., & Valsiner, J. (1994). *The Vygotsky reader*. Cambridge, MA: Blackwell.
van der Veer, R., & Zavershneva, E. (in press). To Moscow with love: Partial reconstruction
of Vygotsky's trip to London. *Integrative Psychological and Behavioral Science.*
van der Veer, R. & Yasnitsky, A. (in press). Vygotsky in English: What still needs to be done.
Integrative Psychological and Behavioral Science. Oxford, UK.
Vygotskii, L. S. (1926/2008). *Psikhologiia iskusstva [Psychology of art]*. Moskva: Labirint.
Vygotskii, L. S. (1926) *Pedagogicheskaia psikhologiia [Educational Psychology].* Moscow:
Rabotnik prosveshcheniia.
Vygotskii, L. S. (1928). Psikhologicheskaia nauka [Psychological science]. In V. P. Volgin, G.
O. Gordon, & I. K. Luppol (Eds.), *Obshchestvennye nauki v SSSR [Social sciences in
the USSR]* (pp. 25–46). Moscow: Rabotnik prosveshcheniia.
Vygotskii, L. S. (1934). *Myshlenie i rech [Thinking and speech].* Moscow-Leningrad:
Gosudarstvennoe sotsial'no-ekono-micheskoe izdatel'stvo.
Vygotskii, L. S. (1934). *Osnovy pedologii [Foundations of Paedology].* Moscow: Izdatel'stvo
2-go Meditsinskogo instituta.
Vygotskii, L. S. (1935). *Umsvennoe razvitie detei v. protsesse obucheniia [Mental develop-
ment of children in the process of education].* Moscow: Uchpedgiz.
Vygotsky, L. S. (1925/1997). Preface to Lazursky. In R. W. Rieber & J. Wollock (Eds.), *The
collected works of L. S. Vygotsky* (Vol. 3., pp. 51–62). New York: Plenum.
Vygotsky, L. S. (1926/1971). *The psychology of art*. Cambridge, MA: MIT Press.
Vygotsky, L. S. (1929/1994). The problem of the cultural development of the child. In R. van der
Veer & J. Valsiner (Eds.), *The Vygotsky reader* (pp. 57–72). Cambridge, MA: Blackwell.
Vygotsky, L. S. (1930/1997). On psychological systems. In R. W. Rieber & J. Wollock (Eds.),
*The collected works of L. S. Vygotsky: Problems of the theory and history of psychol-
ogy* (vol. 3, pp. 91–108). New York: Plenum.
Vygotsky, L. S. (1931/1997). The history of the development of higher mental functions. In R.
W. Rieber (Ed.), *The collected works of L. S. Vygotsky* (Vol. 4). New York: Plenum.
Vygotsky, L. S. (1931/1998). Pedology of adolescence. In R. W. Rieber (Ed.), *The collected
works of L. S. Vygotsky* (Vol. 4, pp. 3–184). New York: Plenum.
Vygotsky, L. S. (1933/1967). Play and its role in the mental development of the child. *Soviet
Psychology, 5*(3), 6–18.
Vygotsky, L. S. (1933/1994). The problem of the environment. In R. van der Veer & J.
Valsiner (Eds.), *The Vygotsky reader* (pp. 338–354). Cambridge, MA: Blackwell.

Vygotsky, L. S. (1933/1998). The crisis at age seven. In R. W. Rieber (Ed.), *The collected works of L. S. Vygotsky* (Vol. 4, pp. 289–296). New York: Plenum.

Vygotsky, L. S. (1934). Thought in schizophrenia. *Archives of Neurology and Psychiatry, 31*, 1062–1077.

Vygotsky, L. S. (1934/1987). Thinking and speech (N. Minick, Trans.). In R. Rieber & A. Carton (Eds.), *The collected works of L.S. Vygotsky* (pp. 39–285). New York: Plenum.

Vygotsky, L. S. (1934/1998). The problem of age. In R. W. Rieber (Ed.), *The collected works of L. S. Vygotsky* (Vol. 4., pp. 187–205). New York: Plenum.

Vygotsky, L. S. (1978). *Mind in society: The development of higher psychological processes.* Cambridge, MA: Harvard University Press.

Vygotsky, L. S., & Luria, A. R. (1929/1930). The function and fate of egocentric speech. In J. M. Cattell (Ed.), *Ninth International Congress of Psychology held at Yale University, New Haven, Connecticut September 1st to 7th, 1929* (pp. 464–465). Princeton, NJ: Psychological Review Company.

Vygotsky, L. S., & Luria, A. R. (1930/1993). *Studies in the history of human behavior: Ape, primitive, and child.* Hillsdale, NJ: Erlbaum.

Vygotsky, L. S., & Luria, A. R. (1930/1994). Tool and symbol in child development. In R. van der Veer & J. Valsiner (Eds.), *The Vygotsky reader* (pp. 99–174). Oxford, UK: Blackwell.

Vygotsky, L. S. (2007). Letters to students and colleagues. *Journal of Russian and East European Psychology, 45*, 11–60. doi:10.2753/RPO1061-0405450201.

Yasnitsky, A. (in press). Vygotsky Circle as a personal network of scholars: Restoring connections between people and ideas. *Integrative Psychological and Behavioral Science.*

Yasnitsky, A. (in press). Izolyatsionizm sovetskoi psikhologii? Nauka kak deyatel'nost', sotsial'nyi institut i migratsiya znaniya [Isolation of Soviet psychology? Science as activity, social institute, and migration of knowledge] (in three parts). *Voprosy psikhologii.*

Yasnitsky, A. (2010). "Archival revolution" in Vygotskian studies? Uncovering Vygotsky's archives. *Journal of Russian and East European Psychology, 48*, 3–13. doi:10.2753/RPO1061-0405480100.

Yasnitsky, A., & Ferrari, M. (2008a). From Vygotsky to Vygotskian psychology: Introduction to the history of the Kharkov school. *Journal of the History of the Behavioral Sciences, 44*, 119–145. doi:10.1002/jhbs.20303.

Yasnitsky, A., & Ferrari, M. (2008b). Rethinking the early history of post-Vygotskian psychology: The case of the Kharkov school. *History of Psychology, 11*, 101–121. doi:10.1037/1093-4510.11.2.101.

Zavershneva, E. (2009). Issledovanie rukopisi L.S. Vygotskogo "Istoricheskij smysl psikhologicheskogo krizisa" [An investigation of the manuscript of L.S. Vygotsky's "Historical meaning of psychological crisis"]. *Voprosy psikhologii* (6), 119–137.

Zavershneva, E. (2010a). The Vygotsky Family Archive (1912–1934). New findings. *Journal of Russian and East European Psychology, 48*, 14–33. doi:10.2753/RPO1061-0405480101.

Zavershneva, E. (2010b). The Vygotsky family archive: New findings. notebooks, notes, and scientific journals of L.S. Vygotsky (1912–1934). *Journal of Russian and East European Psychology, 48*, 34–60. doi:10.2753/RPO1061-0405480102.

Zavershneva, E. (2010c). "The way to freedom" (On the publication of documents from the family archive of Lev Vygotsky). *Journal of Russian and East European Psychology, 48*, 61–90. doi:10.2753/RPO1061-0405480103.

8

Lois Barclay Murphy:
A Pioneer of Positivity

ELIZABETH JOHNSTON
Sarah Lawrence College

I was taught very, very young that as a Barclay with pioneer forebears, I was born to be a pioneer. (Lois Barclay Murphy, quoted in Squires, 1989)

I think that it would have pleased Lois Barclay Murphy to be included in this series because she did aptly think of herself as a pioneer. She pioneered in at least three important and interrelated ways: first, as a progressive educator of young women; second, as a member of the second generation of American women psychologists who were able to combine marriage and a family with a substantial career in academic psychology, a life choice that was not available to the first generation of women; and third, as a developmental psychologist who helped initiate the study of positive aspects of normal children's development and alter prevailing views of children.

Figure 8.1   Lois Barclay Murphy.
(Courtesy of Sarah Lawrence College Archives. With permission.)

135

IOWA FARM ROOTS OF BARCLAY MURPHY'S POSITIVE FOCUS

Barclay Murphy characterized herself as having sensitivity to the gap, strong convictions about what hadn't yet been done that urgently needed study, and the confidence to pioneer new means of investigation. In her autobiographical writings (Murphy, 1978, 1983a) she traced the roots of this confidence to her paternal family: her father, a Methodist minister and pioneer in religious education, and his parents, Iowa farmers. Her lifelong use of the middle name Barclay on all publications is one representation of the enduring importance of this connection.

Lois Barclay was born in Lisbon, Iowa, in 1902. Her family position as the oldest of five children meant that she spent a substantial amount of time at her grandparents' farm while her mother was busy with her younger siblings. She considered the farm paradise and claimed that she "learned more from her visits to the farm than she ever did in school" (Murphy, 1978, p. 168). This experiential learning involved helping with tasks such as plucking chickens and collecting eggs from small spaces that the grown-ups could not access, work that made her feel valued and competent. She thought of her grandparents' Iowa farm as her home base:

> I think of myself as essentially the granddaughter of an Iowa cattle breeder. Erik Erikson talks about himself as an immigrant. I told him, "Erik, I'm an immigrant too, in the sense of I'm a country girl immigrant to the city." That was the place that had meaning to me, where I got my foundation, where I had the freedom, the autonomy and where I learned so much from my grandmother's versatile skills. That's where I got my, whatever you want to call it, arrogance, or whatever. (Murphy, 1979)

Recognizing the importance of Barclay Murphy's rural experience as a young child and her deep identification with her grandparents' way of life helps to contextualize the cultural critique embedded in her view of how to study children and her advice to parents. She was alert to the tensions produced by industrialization and the rapid growth of technology that contrasted with the agrarian-based family order that was meaningful to her. The progressive child-centered stance that fueled her innovations in developmental psychology grew from her childhood experiences with feeling competent and understood by her grandmother. Barclay Murphy was instrumental in changing psychological views of children, helping to shift the field away from a rigid scientific and pathologizing approach that she found abhorrent. The following later statement of her views captures her push toward a psychology based on an empathic and positive view of children:

> It is something of a paradox that a nation which has exulted in its rapid expansion and its scientific-technological achievements should have developed in its studies of childhood so vast a "problem" literature.... There are thousands of studies of maladjustment for each one that deals directly with the ways of managing life's problems with personal strength and adequacy.... It has taken nearly two hundred years for the psychological sciences to be able to identify with the young child enough to try to understand his efforts to deal with the world in terms of his childish experience of it. (Murphy, 1962, pp. 2–3)

Barclay Murphy pioneered the study of prosocial behavior,° the social development of empathy, caring, and ethics. She was at the forefront of a change of direction in studies of early development that shifted the focus of the field away from an exclusive concern with the development of psychopathologies to refocus on the ongoing adjustment of all children (Magai & McFadden, 1995). In an era when the goal of psychology was formulated as "the prediction and control of behavior" (Watson, 1913, p. 158), Barclay Murphy emphasized the child's need for autonomy and freedom. She was aware that she was often going against the grain but seemed to enjoy the conflict when she was sure of her own position. Yet she was not an outsider; rather, she enjoyed tremendous support for her views as a result of the many close personal and professional relationships she built with fellow psychologists and progressive educators. In her extended study of three interconnected social psychologists, Gordon Allport, Gardner Murphy, and Lois Barclay Murphy, historian Katherine Pandora (1997) aptly labels them "rebels within the ranks," a phrase that captures their almost paradoxical attitude toward psychology: They simultaneously embraced and departed from disciplinary identity. Barclay Murphy's early experiences and college education prepared her to adopt such a stance. Her innovative and pioneering approach was nurtured by the institution where she spent the first 24 years of her research and teaching career, Sarah Lawrence College. The influence was mutual: Barclay Murphy had a profound effect on the unique form of progressive education for young women developed at Sarah Lawrence.

PIONEERING PROGRESSIVE EDUCATION

Lois Barclay Murphy was a founding member of the faculty when Sarah Lawrence opened as a 2-year women's college in 1928. An article in the *New York Times* announced that the college benefactor, William Lawrence, the first president, Marion Coats, and their advisor, Vassar College president Henry Noble MacCracken, had in mind a college that would better prepare young women for their role as wives and mothers (Lawrence College to Fit Girls to Wed, 1926, p. 8). Lois Barclay Murphy had other, more progressive, ideas. She was a key member of a group of young faculty, including the well-known social philosopher Helen Merrell Lynd, who made Sarah Lawrence into a more serious intellectual venture than the founder intended. In an oral history housed in the Sarah Lawrence archives Barclay Murphy (1969) recounts the following story that illustrates her powder-keg role. During the opening year of the college, President Coats took a leave of absence due to illness. She instructed the faculty in an authoritarian headmistress-like manner that they must suspend their pedagogical discussions while she was absent. Upon her return Coats discovered that the discussions had proceeded apace and decided that Barclay Murphy was a focal point of these subversive activities. She declared that Barclay Murphy was not a good teacher and fired her. Coats herself was fired the next year due to financial ineptitude. The next president, Constance Warren, came across a group of students meeting

---

° Barclay Murphy personally disliked the term prosocial; she preferred positive aspects of child development (Murphy, 1978, p. 175).

after hours and found out that they had been so intellectually stimulated by Barclay's class that they decided to continue meeting to further their discussions. On the strength of this demonstration of Barclay Murphy's pedagogical effectiveness, Warren invited her to return to the college where she remained as a vital and innovative member of the faculty for the next 22 years. Where did Barclay Murphy acquire the confidence, or you could even say hubris, to stand up to the college president in this way? What made her think that Sarah Lawrence could be much more than a school for wives?

PSYCHOLOGICAL BEGINNINGS AT VASSAR COLLEGE

One clear strand of influence was Barclay's experience at Vassar College. She entered Vassar in 1920, the year that American women finally obtained the right to vote, and studied psychology with a formidable early woman psychologist, Margaret Floy Washburn, who was at that time president of the American Psychological Association (Scarborough & Furumoto, 1987). Washburn was one of the many Vassar faculty who resisted President MacCracken's efforts to introduce a curriculum of euthenics, a term for home economics or domestic science that never took hold. Washburn refused to move her psychology laboratory into the newly constructed Euthenics building. Not all of the Vassar faculty members were as encouraging of Barclay's intellectual aspirations as Washburn. In an oral history interview Barclay Murphy recalled:

> …Many of the other faculty, I'm sorry to say, would tease us and say, "Oh well, you're so intellectual now, but you'll forget all these exciting ideas and settle down and get married and this will all be a part of the past." That infuriated me, and I developed out of that the commitment to show them that it wouldn't be true of me, that I would be able to carry on intellectual interests, marriage, and family at the same time. (1978, p. 173)

Barclay was able to realize this ambition; she balanced the potentially competing demands of scholarly work, college teaching, marriage, and raising children in the context of a strong work–life partnership with the social psychologist Gardner Murphy.

PARTNERSHIP WITH SOCIAL PSYCHOLOGIST GARDNER MURPHY

Ruth Munroe,° a close friend of Barclay's who was studying the history of psychology with Gardner Murphy at Columbia in 1924–25, was the conduit between them. Gardner Murphy describes their meeting in his contribution to the series *A History of Psychology in Autobiography*:

° Munroe (1903–1963) became a psychologist, obtaining a PhD from Columbia. She wrote a well-received book about psychoanalytic theory, *Schools of Psychoanalytic Thought* (1955). She worked on the Sarah Lawrence College Studies in the early 1940s.

When Ruth Munroe invited me over, I met her roommate, Lois Barclay, a student at Union Seminary, with whom a new kind of world began…. We began a sharing of intellectual, esthetic, philosophical and other concerns like music, mountains, and travel, which has never diminished…. Her interest in psychical research, as a challenging pioneer field was a primary factor in maintaining my own morale. (1967, p. 259)

Gardner Murphy reciprocated this support to a degree that was unusual for the time. Barclay Murphy later went so far as to describe Murphy as a feminist:

[Gardner] was really dedicated to supporting the productivity of a wife. He was, without thinking of himself that way, a pioneer feminist. He was very intense about his feeling. "I want my wife (this was before we got married) to use her brain, I don't want her picking up bits off the carpet." (1988, p. 9)

Not only did Murphy encourage his wife's scholarly use of her brain, but he was also a catalyst in the redirection of her intellectual interests to psychology after her first period of graduate training in comparative religion. Barclay had minored in psychology at Vassar, but she graduated with "mixed feelings" about the subject (Murphy, 1983a, p. 95). Although Washburn was a striking role model and a powerful undergraduate teacher, Barclay found herself departing from Washburn's ideas about the proper subject matter for psychology. She was intrigued by the psychologists Washburn ruled out of consideration: Washburn explicitly told her students not to read Sigmund Freud and warned them not to confuse the scientist Morton Prince with the fool Walter Prince. Barclay's own investigations of these forbidden writers led to her discovery of a book by F. W. H. Myers, *Human Personality and the Survival of Bodily Death*, where she came across the exciting phrase "subliminal uprush"* that resonated with her personal experience (Murphy, 1983a, p. 95). Although this interest in parapsychology initially led Barclay away from Washburn's teachings and the discipline of psychology it later provided a key point of connection with her future husband.

After a brief period working at the Psychological Laboratory of the Vocation Bureau of the Board of Education in Cincinnati as the assistant to the director Mabel Fernald, Barclay pursued graduate study at Union Theological Seminary with the goal of helping young people address religious questions through college teaching. She was originally hired by Sarah Lawrence College to teach comparative religion, not psychology. Meanwhile, her intense shared intellectual life with Murphy began to draw Barclay back to the study of psychology. Murphy's expansive approach to the subject matter of psychology was much closer to the progressive strain of psychological thinking that Barclay had grown up with: Her father often talked of his graduate study with John Dewey at the University of Chicago, and her parents met on the debate team at the University of Iowa where her mother studied with two students of William James, Carl Seashore and G. W. H. Patrick

---

* F. W. H. Myers defined subliminal uprush as "an emergence of hidden faculty, of nerve co-ordinations potential in his organism, but till now unused, which takes command of the man and guides his action at the moment when his being is deeply stirred." (1903, p. 308)

(Murphy, 1983a, p. 90). Murphy's new conceptions of the form that social psychology ought to take, "passing beyond the behaviorist emphasis and emphasizing a wide variety of research undertaken in the field of the cultural molding of individuality" (Murphy, 1968, p. 6), dovetailed with Barclay's interests in the growth of personality and individual adjustment. Lois and Gardner were married in 1926.

In the evenings the newlywed Murphys read aloud to each other from books about child development (Murphy, 1968, p. 6), and together with Margaret Mead they participated in Ruth Benedict's anthropology course (Murphy, 1983a, p. 97). Their shared interests in social development led to a collaboration on an advanced text surveying the field of experimental social psychology (Murphy & Murphy, 1931). Barclay Murphy was primarily responsible for the middle section on the social behavior of children. Her forced leave from Sarah Lawrence due to President Coats's disapproval gave her time to work on the text, cementing her burgeoning interest in social development. With characteristic directness she described her response to her dismissal by Coats as follows: "So I stayed home next year, got pregnant, produced a baby, and wrote a book" (Murphy, 1969, p. 2). The baby was their son Alpen, born in 1930; 2 years later they completed their family by adopting a German baby, Margaret. Rather than diverting Barclay Murphy from a career in psychology, her children stimulated her deepening interest in children's social development. In addition, furthering her study of religion required field work that would have taken her away from her young family, so she successfully redirected her teaching and research interests to developmental psychology.

DEVELOPMENT OF DOCTORAL STUDIES ON SYMPATHY IN YOUNG CHILDREN

In forming her research interests, Barclay Murphy reacted against the influence of behaviorist John B. Watson on the field of developmental psychology. She was convinced that Watson completely failed to understand children and grouped him with other "rigid hardnosed psychologists" who gave her "the feeling that psychologists were not really interested in people and human life" (Murphy, 1983a, p. 95). In contrast, Gardner Murphy's humanistic approach was a source of inspiration for her emphasis on positive aspects of normal development. One of the books that the Murphys read aloud in the evenings was a 1909 study of compassion in children, *Das Mitleid bei Kindern*, by W. Boeck, a text that charmed and impressed them because of the contrast with the widespread studies of aggression, conflict, and hostility that were engaging so much attention at that time (Murphy, 1968, p. 6). When Ludwig Kast, president of the Josiah Macy Foundation, asked the Murphys what kind of research would be useful in medical and paramedical practice, Barclay Murphy mentioned the relatively unexplored field of sympathy in young children. Kast was delighted by the possibilities opened up by this new line of inquiry and funded a research project that Barclay Murphy carried out at the Speyer School of Teachers College at Columbia. This groundbreaking work became the basis of Barclay Murphy's PhD in psychology, earned from Teachers College in 1937.° The

---

° Lois Meek (later Stoltz) was the chair of her research committee.

early sympathy work is a prime instance of Barclay Murphy's trend-bucking style of psychological research. Her observation that the field was emphasizing studies of aggression and conflict post World War I led to her perception of a need for studies on positive aspects of social development. She was met with skepticism, notably from the Director of the Speyer School, who thought that children had to be socialized over time to cultivate sympathetic behavior and that the nursery school children were too young to respond sympathetically to others. Barclay Murphy recalled that the director said to her, "You're crazy. Everybody knows that you can't expect three-year-olds to be sympathetic. You won't get any data. You'll waste your time" (1980, p. 5). In the face of this opposition, her husband's support bolstered her confidence in her own convictions: "Gardner was the major part, supporting with characteristic enthusiasm each new undertaking, regardless of the ridicule I encountered, for instance, in studying sympathy in three-year-olds" (Murphy, 1978, p. 175).

In her sympathy studies, Barclay Murphy employed an eclectic mixture of data collection techniques, composed of observational records from the playground, cumulative behavior records from the nursery school, samples from other investigators' studies of different aspect of development of the same children, parent interviews, detailed parent records, and framed situations with animals and children as sympathy stimuli. By casting the net wide Barclay Murphy was able to demonstrate convincingly that sympathetic behavior arises spontaneously in preschool children. Her papers and book on the subject (Murphy, 1936, 1937, 1942) catalog and classify numerous instances of sympathetic behavior and are packed with specific examples that attest to the ubiquity of young children's sympathetic behaviors. Many of the illustrations she gives would now be seen as evidence of the child's developing theory of mind (Astington, Harris, & Olson, 1990): They are full of young children's early realizations of other people's feelings.

Barclay Murphy did recognize that one of the reasons that sympathetic behaviors had not been noted by those who taught and studied preschool children was that they were far less frequently expressed than aggressive behaviors. A. T. Jersild was studying aggression in the same group of children; while he noted a conflict of some sort every 4 minutes, Barclay Murphy's sympathetic behaviors occurred only once an hour on average. This led her to develop multifaceted methodologies that spanned any sources of data generation that she could devise.

FOUNDING OF AN EXPERIMENTAL PRESCHOOL AND NEW METHODS OF STUDYING CHILDREN

In conversations with Lawrence Frank, a close friend and foundation executive who was instrumental in the funding and direction of many early to mid-20th-century child development studies, Barclay Murphy realized that many of the techniques that she had been using to study the neglected subject of sympathy fell into the category of projective tests. Together with another friend and fellow developmental psychologist Ruth Horowitz (later Hartley),[*] Barclay Murphy coauthored

---

[*] Ruth and Eugene Horowitz legally changed their family name to Hartley in the 1940s to avoid discrimination on the basis of their Jewish origin (personal communication with Wendy Hartley, 2006).

the first article on projective tests (Horowitz & Murphy, 1938) outlining the potentially wide application of open-ended toy and picture methods for the study of children's conscious and unconscious motivations, personality, attitudes, and needs. As Pandora (1997) explicates in *Rebels Within the Ranks*, Horowitz and Murphy's paper was radical in demonstrating that new "analytical tools of social psychology could be used to critique the status quo" (p. 104).

With the help of a research grant from the Macy Foundation, where Frank was in charge of funding, Barclay Murphy was able to initiate a laboratory preschool at Sarah Lawrence and to gather an innovative team of young researchers to pursue this new means of studying children's personality. Barclay Murphy had to struggle with the college treasurer to obtain the necessary resources to realize her vision, but with characteristic vigor she insisted to the administration that the nursery school was as essential to her college students' education as the physics laboratory and art studio. She was able to stand her ground so staunchly because of the productivity and support of her research group. Gardner Murphy recommended some new PhDs from Columbia, L. Joseph Stone and Eugene Lerner; Barclay Murphy found Evelyn Beyer, an innovative teacher, to direct the school, and Lawrence Frank suggested Dr. Benjamin Spock, fresh from his psychoanalytic training, as the consulting pediatrician. In collaboration with these enthusiastic young researchers, Barclay Murphy fused several strands of influence to form an approach to the study of child development that manifested her commitment to understanding the child's world on his or her own terms. The Gestalt social psychologist Kurt Lewin's concept of life space was a primary stimulus, along with Freudian notions of the unconscious and the concept of conflict, especially as they were interpreted by child analysts such as Anna Freud, Susan Issacs, and Erik Erikson (Murphy, 1956). Further inspiration was provided by the Murphys' joint visits to Henry Murray's Harvard Clinic where they learned about the Thematic Apperception Test and their nighttime reading of Hermann Rorschach's *Psychodiagnostik*. Barclay Murphy first read *Psychodiagnostik* in German in the early 1930s before it was available in English and was so enthralled that she felt that she had to read it aloud to Murphy; he was not interested at first but soon became as engaged as Barclay Murphy. She credits it as a major influence on his later "New Look" style studies of the influence of needs on perception (Murphy, 1979). From this array of influences Barclay Murphy drew the elements of her positive approach to normal personality development and embarked upon a long series of studies of personality reported in detail in a Society for Research in Child Development monograph and a later two-volume set (Lerner & Murphy, 1941; Murphy, 1956).

Their tasks and materials were created in contrast to structured psychological tests that created anxiety and frustration in the child and skewed the picture of the child's competencies and strengths. Instead, Barclay Murphy and her group developed more open-ended tasks that would allow the children to engage in spontaneous natural behavior. In addition to the classic projective task of the Rorschach inkblots administered by clinician Anna Hartoch, miniature life toys, paints, dough, and cold cream were some of the materials offered to the children for exploration. The experimental setup was free-flowing; in many of the tasks the children were basically instructed by the experimenter to play with the materials however they wanted, and all facets of their responses to the total situation were noted.

Barclay Murphy's use of dough and cold cream may have been inspired by her own daughter's behavior: Both children went to their rooms at 8 p.m. so that their parents could have grown-up time for talking, reading, and planning, and one of her daughter's inventive solutions for the period when she did not yet feel sleepy was to draw pictures on the window with toothpaste (Murphy, 1990, p. 191). It is telling that Barclay Murphy relates this story approvingly in her biography of Gardner Murphy: She cast the toothpaste drawing as a creative solution to the situation her daughter found herself in rather than as misbehavior. As Steven Mintz (2004) notes in his history of American childhood, Barclay Murphy's approach heralded a new attitude to children in the 1920s and 1930s that recognized their emotional needs to a much greater extent. He cites another story that Barclay Murphy liked to relate about her daughter. When the Murphys were driving across the United States in 1938, their daughter balked at entering Kansas because she did not want to be blown away by a tornado like Dorothy in *The Wizard of Oz*. Rather than using their parental authority to overrule her, they switched course and drove through Nebraska. Barclay Murphy explained that this "seemed a minor concession to make to a strong-minded child whom we respected" (Murphy, quoted in Mintz, 2004, p. 219). Barclay Murphy brought this same respect for children's emotional experiences to her work at the Sarah Lawrence Early Childhood Center, and it motivated her to find novel means of measuring spontaneous expressions of children's emotional life and personality.

A major aim of the group's use of such freewheeling sensory methods was to gain access to the deep feelings of very young children who were not yet able to communicate those feelings in language. The texts that report upon the series of exploratory studies in personality are full of detailed cases illustrating a range of responses to the expressive materials. A complimentary contemporary review of the work described it as a "riot of concreteness," commenting on the richness of the observations and the exceptional plasticity, complexity, and textured nature of the researchers' approach (Barron, 1957, p. 70). Yet even this sympathetic reviewer could not refrain from critiquing the scientific standing of the work, "its fascinating techniques and often brilliant speculations are not always accompanied by sufficient self-criticism concerning evidence and the grounds for belief" (Barron, 1957, p. 70). He cast it as "more intraceptive than extraceptive, and perhaps more tender-minded than tough-minded" (Barron, 1957, p. 69). Barclay Murphy would have agreed with this characterization of her work as tender-minded; her concern was to investigate children's emotional life under optimally gratifying conditions for the individual children she studied. The tough-minded conception of science was too limiting in her opinion; the series of studies that she and her Sarah Lawrence collaborators conducted in the later 1930s and the 1940s were a sustained attempt to enlarge the purview of the science of child development. In a later autobiographical piece Barclay Murphy reflects:

> I think child development is an embryonic science. My restlessness with it is not around the question of whether or not it is a science, but around the narrowness of the concept of science…. I want psychology to be more flexible and to be willing to consider using some of the other methods that are available. (1978, p. 175–176)

Her exploratory, projective studies of children's emotions pushed the boundaries of the expanding science of child development, even as they sometimes fell over those disciplinary edges.

Barclay Murphy had the confidence to pursue her own revisionist research agenda. As Pandora (1997) aptly notes, she could afford to take an unconventional attitude to the discipline because of her secure base in the progressive education environment of Sarah Lawrence (Pandora, 1997, p. 55). Yet Barclay Murphy had one lasting regret about her lack of disciplinary involvement: her failure to support Harold Skeels and Marie Skodak when their studies illustrating the changeability of the intelligence test scores of orphanage children were vigorously criticized on statistical grounds. Barclay Murphy knew from her experience with children at the Sarah Lawrence Early Childhood Center that large shifts in IQ scores could result from changes in the environment, but felt unable to speak out in the 1930s because she did not think that she had the necessary authority within psychological organizations (Murphy, 1980, pp. 7–8). Rather than being active in the psychological community through organizations such as the American Psychological Association, Barclay Murphy was focused on progressive education at the college level as well as at the preschool level.

FEMINISM AND WOMEN'S EDUCATION

In the 1930s Sarah Lawrence professors were actively researching their pedagogy, with the aid of a grant from the General Education Board. Barclay Murphy was a key figure in the development of this work: She was a coauthor on two self-study publications (Raushenbush, Murphy, Lerner, Judge, & Grant, 1942; Murphy & Ladd, 1944). The research methodology that she employed paralleled her work at the Early Childhood Center: The texts are packed with detailed case studies of individuals; they too can be aptly characterized as a riot of concreteness. The consistency in Barclay Murphy's focus also extends to the subject matter; her book coauthored with Sarah Lawrence professor of literature Henry Ladd explored "emotional factors in learning." I do not mean to suggest here that the college-aged students were encouraged to engage in free play with sensory materials; rather, their individual needs, interests, and emotional responses to their studies were considered vitally relevant to their intellectual development and open to study. Further, the educational approach pursued by Barclay Murphy and her socially progressive colleagues aimed to open up the life space of privileged young women. In a 1983 letter to Alice Ilchman, then the new president of Sarah Lawrence, Murphy mentioned "the problems involved when we cracked the 'protective shell' around the minds of overprotected well-to-do students by the encounters with reality we arranged" (Murphy, 1983b, p. 3).

I have pondered whether Barclay Murphy was promoting feminist views to her students. She certainly did not identify with the more radical feminisms that came before and after her time at Sarah Lawrence. For example, in a 1938 *Parents* magazine article she decried the denial of emotional mothering brought about by the feminist movement (Murphy, 1938, p. 5). It does seem, however, that she advanced a type of feminism characteristic of the time that emphasized individual development. Perhaps it is more apt to say that she was a progressive first and a feminist to the extent that the aims of progressivism and feminism coincided. Her energies were invested in her teaching and research in progressive education and in her family life. She did not join the first organized group of American women psychologists, the National Council of Women Psychologists, despite the fact that it was initially organized in New York in the early 1940s (Capshew & Laszlo, 1986; Johnson & Johnston, 2010; Walsh, 1985).

COPING AT THE MENNINGER FOUNDATION

Although Barclay Murphy was deeply involved in her teaching in the mid-1940s, her research productivity declined during this period. She felt paralyzed by the consecutive deaths of three of her closest colleagues and friends, Henry Ladd, Eugene Lerner, and Anna Hartoch (Murphy, 1969, p. 11). A sabbatical in 1949–50 gave Barclay Murphy the opportunity to further her early cross-cultural interests. She traveled to India with Gardner° and helped to plan an Institute of Child Development and Mental Health in Ahmadabad, for which she consulted in subsequent years. In the early 1950s an opportunity arose for Gardner. He was courted by the Menninger Foundation, a psychiatric clinic in Topeka, Kansas, which invited him to become their director of research. Murphy stated unequivocally that he would consider the position only if there was a worthwhile position for his wife. Karl Menninger invited Barclay Murphy to set up any research program she desired, a freedom that appealed to Barclay Murphy's exploratory personality. In addition, Sybille Escalona, the person Gardner would replace as director of research, bequeathed her extensive longitudinal data on infants to Barclay Murphy, so she had a foundational database on which to build her studies.

It was during this period that Barclay Murphy extended her interests in positive social development by initiating the study of coping. At that time the term was not in the *Psychological Abstracts Index*, and her first grant proposal to the National Institute of Mental Health (NIMH) initially evoked skepticism:

> I'm sure I told you about my first site visit with John Benjamin. He said, "What is this coping stuff? What makes you think you should get money from the NIMH to study coping in children and so forth?" And he really grilled me and I was angry. I liked John Benjamin and I didn't want to be treated that way by John Benjamin, and I thought he was stupid not to get the point of it. And I finally said, "Look I know this needs to be done and if you and NIMH don't want to support it I'll get support someplace else." (Murphy, 1979)

° They later collaborated on a volume on Asian Psychology (Murphy & Murphy, 1968).

Barclay Murphy's confidence in her project was rewarded; the NIMH did decide to fund it from 1953 to 1969, for the duration of Barclay Murphy's Menninger period. This longitudinal work, conducted with a new set of like-minded collaborators, proved deeply satisfying to Barclay Murphy. She was able to further her studies of emotional adjustment through the years between preschool and college, tracking individuals and their life worlds in the kind of depth that was rewarding to her. In 1976 she published a volume titled *Vulnerability, Coping and Growth* that presented the findings of this long-term developmental study; the whole span from infancy to adolescence was investigated through a high-focus observational lens and presented in her usual riot of concreteness style (Murphy & Moriarty, 1976).

Other investigations and their rewards compensated for the sense of loss that Barclay Murphy felt at leaving the progressive educational environment of Sarah Lawrence. She took the opportunity afforded by the Menninger Clinic to undergo a training analysis with Ishak Ramzy, a former student and colleague of Anna Freud (Lambert, 1992). Close to the end of her time at Menninger in the mid-to-late 1960s, Barclay Murphy was an active participant in designing the Head Start educational program, part of President Lyndon Johnson's War on Poverty that aimed to develop compensatory early education programs for low-income children. She felt that the concept of Head Start "touched all her deepest interests in the needs of children" (Murphy, 1983a, p. 101). She participated at many levels, helping with the national planning, including a presentation at a congressional committee hearing in 1969, the preparation of a series of 10 training booklets, Caring for Children, planning and reporting on the Parent–Child Centers, and hands-on work one morning a week for 3 years at the local Head Start Center in Topeka.

A story that Barclay Murphy told about her Head Start parent education work illustrates the consistency of her progressive approach to education at all levels. In response to the mothers' flat-out rejection of the idea of parent education, Barclay Murphy asked them what they would like to learn about instead and then organized sessions on those topics. She led them herself when it was something she knew about, like stretching the family budget, and brought in other speakers when they wanted to investigate subjects she did not feel competent to discuss, such as cosmetics. After 6 months the mothers said, "We want to know how you help the children to grow so good" (Murphy, 1980, p. 10). Only then was Barclay Murphy able to give them the kind of parent education that she had originally hoped for: a discussion of how to open up possibilities for their children and ways of supporting their healthy emotional development. She recognized that it could not be forced on the mothers; they had to develop the need for the knowledge and trust in her before her expertise could be helpful to them.

BARCLAY MURPHY'S LEGACY

There was a unity and coherence to Barclay Murphy's long career in psychology. The support of her husband, Gardner, was crucial in the realization of her goals, and their level of intellectual mutuality, what their friends called their twoness, was unusual. After Gardner's death, Barclay Murphy reflected that she would not have achieved a fraction of what she had if she had not married the person she did

(Murphy, 1979). It would be a mistake, however, to view her as simply following Murphy's lead and benefiting from his insights and connections. She described him as 7 years older and 7 inches taller, with a quicker, more critical mind, but Barclay Murphy was her own person, a strong, focused researcher who had a clear vision of the developmental psychology that she wanted to create. Close to the end of his life Gardner Murphy confided to a friend that initially he had a Pygmalion fantasy about Barclay Murphy but in a few years realized that she was simply going to be herself (Murphy, 1990, p. 179). He later came to think of her as the original one in the family.

In one of her autobiographical sketches Barclay Murphy commented, "I hope that insofar as I am remembered, it would be as a person who tried to conceptualize and communicate positive aspects of children's development in integrated terms" (Murphy, 1978, p. 175). She pioneered a more inclusive and positive developmental psychology that had room for the complexity and emotionality of children's messy and changeable lives. In looking back over the course of her long career in psychology a quality that stands out is her prescience. Her tender-minded studies of positive social emotions in young children anticipated and fueled a new view of childhood that continues to have resonance in current work in developmental psychology, positive psychology, and affective neuroscience. After a life rich with the riot of concreteness, Lois Barclay Murphy died on December 24, 2003, in Washington, DC.

SUGGESTED READINGS

Murphy, L. B. (1956). *Personality in young children*. Volume 1: Methods for the study of personality in young children. Volume 2: Colin—A Normal Child. New York: Basic Books.

    This two-volume set reports on the studies that Barclay Murphy and her collaborators, Evelyn Beyer, Anna Hartoch, Eugene Lerner, L. Joseph Stone, and Trude Schmidl Waehner, conducted in the late 1930s and 1940s at the Sarah Lawrence Nursery School. The first coauthored volume describes their innovative free expressive techniques with plastic materials such as dough and cold cream and their development of active games as a means of exploring personality development. The second volume is an in-depth case study of one normally developing child who was carefully observed from age 2 years 9 months until the time of his graduation from the nursery 3 years later. It is a sympathetic portrait that reveals Barclay Murphy's deep understanding of his life space. Both volumes provide ample illustrations of Barclay Murphy's progressive riot of concreteness approach.

Murphy, L. B., & Moriarty, A. E. (1976). *Vulnerability, coping, and growth: From infancy to adolescence*. New Haven, CT: Yale University Press.

    This coauthored text presents the findings of the rich longitudinal study conducted by Barclay Murphy and her collaborators at the Menninger Clinic in the 1950s and 1960s. They describe the spectrum of normal viscissitudes of a group of children in the heartland of America adjusting to and coping with the usual stresses and challenges of growing up. Their focus is on the resilience and variety of the coping mechanisms exhibited by the children. In keeping with the clinical context of the Menninger clinic the writing often has a psychoanalytic flavor with a heavy emphasis on the development of ego strength. The text is replete with concrete examples and individual stories.

REFERENCES

Astington, J., Harris, P., & Olson, D. (1990). *Developing theories of mind*. New York: Cambridge University Press.

Barron, F. (1957). Dignity for unquantified children. *Contemporary Psychology, 2*, 69–70.

Capshew, J. H., & Laszlo, A. C. (1986). "We would not take no for an answer": Women psychologists and gender politics during World War II. *Journal of Social Issues, 42*, 157–180. doi:10.1111/j.1540-4560.1986.tb00213.x

Daniels, E. (1994). *Bridges to the world: Henry Noble MacCracken and Vassar College*. Clinton Corners, NY: College Avenue Press.

Horowitz, R., & Murphy, L.B. (1938). Projective methods in the psychological study of children. *Journal of Experimental Education, 7*, 133–140.

Johnson, A., & Johnston, E. (2010). Unfamiliar feminisms: Revisiting the National Council of Women Psychologists. *Psychology of Women Quarterly, 34*, 311–327. doi:10.1111/j.1471-6402.2010.01577.x

Lambert, B. (1992, February 10). Ishak Ramzy, 80, pioneer in the field of child psychology. *New York Times*.

Lawrence College to fit girls to wed. (1926, December 14). *New York Times*, p. 8.

Lerner, E., & Murphy, L. B. (1941). Methods for the study of personality in young children. *Monographs for the Society for Research in Child Development, 6*, no. 4. doi:10.2307/1165455

Magai, C., & McFadden, S. H. (1995). *The role of emotions in social and personality development: History, theory & research*. New York: Springer.

Mintz, S. (2004). *Huck's raft: A history of American childhood*. Cambridge, MA: Belknap Press of Harvard University Press.

Munroe, R. L. (1955). *Schools of psychoanalytic thought*. New York: Dryden Press.

Murphy, G. (1967). Gardner Murphy. In E. G. Boring & G. Lindzey (Eds.), *A history of psychology in autobiography* (vol. 5, pp. 255–282). New York: Appleton-Century-Crofts.

Murphy, G. (1968). A story of dyadic thought and work with Gardner and Lois Murphy as written by Gardner. Archives of the History of American Psychology, Akron, Ohio. Murphy Papers, 1252.

Murphy, G., & Murphy, L. B. (1931). *Experimental social psychology*. New York: Harper & Brothers.

Murphy, G., & Murphy, L. B. (1968). *Asian psychology*. New York: Basic Books.

Murphy, L. B. (1936). Sympathetic behavior in young children. *Journal of Experimental Education, 5*, 79–90.

Murphy, L. B. (1937). *Social behavior and child personality*. New York: Columbia University Press.

Murphy, L. B. (1938). Manuscript of *Parents Magazine* article, Sarah Lawrence College Archives, Bronxville, NY, Series 2, Box 2.

Murphy, L. B. (1942). The evidence for sympathy in young children. *Childhood Education, 18*, 58–63.

Murphy, L. B. (1956). Personality in young children. Volume 1: *Methods for the study of personality in young children*. Volume 2: *Colin—A Normal Child*. New York: Basic Books.

Murphy, L. B. (1962). *The widening world of childhood: Paths toward mastery*. New York: Basic Books.

Murphy, L. B. (1969). Interview with Lois Barclay Murphy. Conducted by Helen McMaster. Sarah Lawrence College Archives, Bronxville, NY. Series 1, Box 1.

Murphy, L. B. (1978). Roots of an approach to studying child development. In T. S. Krawiec (Ed.), *The psychologists: Vol. 3*. (pp. 166–180). New York: Oxford University Press.

Murphy, L. B. (1979). Interview with Phillip Holzman. Tape recording. Archives of the History of American Psychology, Akron, Ohio. Murphy Papers, M1250.

Murphy, L. B. (1980). On coping and change. The Catherine Molony Memorial Lecture, City College School of Education.

Murphy, L. B. (1983a). Lois Barclay Murphy. In A. N. O'Connell & N. F. Russo (Eds.), *Models of achievement: Reflections of eminent women in psychology* (vol. 1, pp. 89–107). New York: Columbia University Press.

Murphy, L. B. (1983b). Correspondence with Alice Ilchman. Lois Barclay Murphy Papers, Sarah Lawrence College Archives, Bronxville, NY. Series 1, Box 1.

Murphy, L. B. (1988). Interview with Lois Barclay Murphy. Conducted by Ms Ronnie Walker, Graduate Student in the Women's Studies Program at Sarah Lawrence College. Lois Barclay Murphy Papers, Sarah Lawrence College Archives, Bronxville, NY. Series 1, Box 1.

Murphy, L. B. (1990). *Gardner Murphy: Integrating, expanding, and humanizing psychology*. Jefferson, NC: McFarland.

Murphy, L. B., & Ladd, H. (1944). *Emotional factors in learning*. Sarah Lawrence College Publications. New York: Columbia University Press.

Murphy, L. B., & Moriarty, A. E. (1976). *Vulnerability, coping, and growth: From infancy to adolescence*. New Haven, CT: Yale University Press.

Myers, F. W. H. (1903). *Human personality and its survival of bodily death*. New York: Longmans, Green.

Pandora, K. (1997). *Rebels within the ranks: Psychologists' critique of scientific authority and democratic realities in New Deal America*. New York: Cambridge University Press. doi:10.1017/CBO9780511572975

Raushenbush, E. (Ed.), Murphy, L. B., Lerner, E., Judge, J., & Grant, M. (1942). *Psychology for individual education*. Sarah Lawrence College Publications. New York: Columbia University Press.

Scarborough, E., & Furumoto, L. (1987). *Untold lives: The first generation of American women psychologists*. New York: Columbia University Press.

Squires, S. (1989, December 13). From the mouths of babes, insights. *Washington Post*.

Walsh, M. R. (1985). Academic professional women organizing for change: The struggle in psychology. *Journal of Social Issues, 41*, 17–28. doi:10.1111/j.1540-4560.1985.tb01138.x

Watson, J. B. (1913). Psychology as the behaviorist views it. *Psychological Review, 20*, 158–177. doi:10.1037/h0074428

9

Roger Barker: *A Different Kind of Developmentalist**

M. M. SCOTT
Indiana University

Roger Barker is an interesting example of a developmentalist who made substantial contributions to the field by going in some directions that seemed initially to be away from traditional development. He began by being interested in children, how they develop, and what influenced this development. When his initial studies of children and their families in their own natural habitats produced, at best, conflicting results, he started over. Much in the spirit of Barbara McClintock, Nobel Prize winner for her seminal work in genetics, Barker abandoned accepted theory and methods and tried to "let the material tell him" (Keller, 1983, p. 179) how to proceed and what to look for. His discoveries led him to a deeper understanding of factors in the environment that have substantial influences not only on the behavior of children but on all of human behavior as well. He was given the American Psychological Association (APA) Award for Distinguished Scientific Contribution in 1963 for this work. He called his discoveries behavior setting theory.

Figure 9.1   Roger Barker.
(Courtesy of Phil Schoggen. With permission.)

* The author thanks Phil Schoggen and Allan Wicker for comments on an earlier version of this chapter. Phil Schoggen is also thanked for the picture of Barker.

Roger Barker was a bona fide developmentalist. He studied with developmentalists, published research on both children and the elderly in the principal journals, and was awarded some of the field's highest honors. In 1952 he was elected president of Division 7 (Developmental Psychology) of the American Psychological Association (APA). In 1957 he was elected president of the Society for Research in Child Development. In 1963, in addition to the APA award, he won the Kurt Lewin Award from the Society for the Psychological Study of Social Issues. He was named a fellow at the Center for Advanced Study in the Behavioral Sciences at Stanford in 1957–1958. Barker said that he was identified (by himself and others) during his early academic career as a child or developmental psychologist (Schoggen, 1991) and shifted from an individual view of behavior and development to an ecobehavioral view only following a substantial amount of research showing that the environment was at least as strong an influence on behavior as individual difference factors and sometimes an even greater influence. This led him to found a new field called ecological psychology that produced some very powerful theories (Scott, 2005).

But how did he get from a more traditional, individually focused view of development to a more ecologically focused one? To understand this shift it is helpful first to consider Barker's principal discovery, the behavior setting.

BARKER'S MAJOR CONTRIBUTION: BEHAVIOR SETTING THEORY

Barker and his colleagues at the Midwest Psychological Field Station in Oskaloosa, Kansas, discovered a feature of the environment that has a powerful effect on behavior. They called it a *behavior setting*. A behavior setting has two clusters of identifying properties or characteristics. First, it has a specific time, place, and objects. For example, behavior setting "IU basketball game" meets at 8:00 p.m. Friday in the IU field house and has hoops, balls, and clocks; behavior setting "Mrs. Smith's third grade class" meets from 8:30 a.m. until 2:30 p.m. in Room 103 and has desks, chairs, books, and crayons; behavior setting "Sunday worship service" meets at 11:00 a.m. in the Methodist church and has pews, hymnals, and an organ. Even if a complete list of all the time, place, and objects could be specified, they do not alone constitute a *behavior setting*. Second, a second set of characteristics is necessary. This is the attached, standing behavior patterns of the setting, that is, the "roles and rules" of the setting. For example, in a basketball game, some people run up and down the court trying to put the ball through the hoop, other people run up and down judging the moves of the players, and other people sit or stand on the sides watching, commenting, and cheering. In Mrs. Smith's third-grade class some people sit at desks, read, write, and sing, while one person stands at the front of the room or walks around giving instruction and helping people. In behavior setting Sunday worship service some people sit in pews, sing, listen, and watch neighbors, while other people lead songs, preach, or play the organ. An essential feature of a behavior setting is that both sets or clusters of characteristics are present for a setting to exist. It is this combination of both the physical and the social that constitutes a behavior setting and makes it different from almost all other behavior units. Many behavior units are constituted of *either* the physical (e.g., desks, books, trash cans, sidewalks) *or* the social (e.g., raise your hand before talking, focus on the arithmetic problems, deposit litter, stay off the grass). It is the combination of the two clusters that gives a behavior setting its power. Some psychologies imply that their behavior units link both physical and social aspects, but they do not specify how these are linked together or how they function together to direct behavior. Further, closer examination of these types of units shows that they often relate the social to the physical, or vice versa, rather than combining them into one unit and then studying behavior as a function of this combined unit.

A behavior setting exists at the *molar level*, that is, within the normal, everyday perspective of people who either enter or observe the setting. Each behavior setting is easily identified by both members and nonmembers and by both adults and children, although each group may understand the setting somewhat differently and play different roles in the setting. In fact, part of growing up (developing) is acquiring an increasingly complex view of behavior settings along with opportunities to play more roles and more complex roles in a variety of settings (Schoggen, 1991). Each behavior setting has a set of "circuits" that describes the operation of the setting and directs the behavior of people who enter it. A program circuit is composed of the rules and roles that are to take place to keep the setting functioning. A deviation countering circuit specifies how behavior outside these rules and roles will be dealt with. A vetoing circuit describes mechanisms for ejecting elements that cannot be corrected (either physical—the freezer case malfunctions in behavior setting grocery store; or the social—a prisoner begins singing loudly during court proceedings). Some settings are tightly structured, and others are less so, such as Dr. Smith's dental office versus City Park. Barker (1968) and Schoggen (1989) provided more complete descriptions of these circuits as well as the K-21 Index. This index is a measure of behavior setting characteristics that defines when a setting exists, when it does not, when it is part of another setting, or when it subsumes other smaller settings—called synomorphs.

Once in operation, settings then coerce all participants who enter them, including the initiator. If the setting does not quite work as intended, it can be altered, or, if that is not possible or the setting still does not work well (some limp along for years), various participants leave the setting. If enough leave, the setting will be terminated. In that case, the participants enter other settings. No person is not in a setting from birth to death. Settings are pervasive; they constitute the habitat for human behavior.

There are several sources for the power of a behavior setting (Scott, 2005). One of the most important is the *extraindividual nature* of the setting. That is, most people who enter a setting perceive the requirements of the setting and produce behaviors consonant with them. Those who do not do so either leave the setting (and enter others) or handle the setting in a variety of ways by the rules of the setting. For example, people in "basketball game" produce very similar behaviors despite great variety in things like personality or other individual differences. These same people, in behavior setting "church service," also produce behaviors very similar to each other, again despite substantial variety among themselves; that is, there is more similarity between the behavior of Joe and Harry in basketball (or church service) than there is between Joe in basketball game and Joe in church service. Barker gradually realized that the environment itself is organized on its own terms with directions toward behavior. This extraindividual nature of settings means that the people in a setting can be replaced and the setting still continues in a stable manner. For example, the Presbyterian worship service continued in much the same way over 20 years despite five changes in minister, six changes in musical director, and approximately 30% change in congregation. Louise Barker (Roger's wife) commented that ordinary people readily comprehend settings and their requirements; psychologists sometimes have more difficulty (Ozrek, 1987).

While many psychologies have focused on aberrant individuals, the power of behavior setting theory is that it focuses on understanding the predominant forces that direct behavior for most people and then specifies how people who do not produce the prescribed behavior are dealt with. This can be a very powerful source of information in understanding how individuals develop.

Another discovery that had broad implications for behavior in a number of settings was what Barker called "undermanning," now called underinhabiting (Scott, 2005; Wicker, 1984), underpopulated (Schoggen, 1989; Willems, 1990), or understaffing (Wicker, 1987). The research showed that people in settings where there are not quite enough people to carry out the functions of the setting produce different behavior than those in settings where there was a surfeit of people to play the roles. In the underinhabited setting people play more roles and a greater variety of roles, engage in more leadership roles, and exhibit greater satisfaction (Barker, 1968; Schoggen, 1989). Underinhabited settings also have an interesting effect on "marginal" people, those who had some deficit. They are more accepted in a setting. They were needed to keep the setting going, and they respond accordingly, producing behaviors that help the setting and also improve the people's behavior and increase their satisfaction and self-concept.

One very interesting study by Barker (1979b) considered the underinhabited aspects of frontier towns in the American West. He argued that this environment produces "frontier behavior" in the inhabitants that continued long after the frontier had passed. The inhabitants also carried these behaviors with them as they moved to new towns further west. This is yet another example of how behavior settings and their various characteristics influence behavior of individuals and groups both immediately and across time.

Barker's theoretical formulations earned accolades in psychology as well as other disciplines. His 1968 explication of this theory became a citation classic in psychology (Schoggen, 1992). Perhaps the most powerful judgment came from economist Karl Fox (1985): "We believe Barker's concept of behavior settings may come to play as important a role in the social sciences as the cell concept does in biology" (p. 173).

BARKER'S OTHER IMPORTANT CONTRIBUTIONS

Barker was also one of the founders of the field of rehabilitation psychology. A milestone in this area was his first grant, from the Social Sciences Research Council, to produce a monograph on the psychological aspects of disability (Barker, Wright, Meyerson, & Gonick, 1953). This work was important in rehabilitating injured veterans and later helped fuel the initiation of the fields of psychology of physical disability and of rehabilitation psychology including the establishment of Division 22 of APA, Rehabilitation Psychology. It also produced another "first" as Barker coined the term *somatopsychological relations*. At least some of his interest doubtless came from his own handicapping condition due to osteomyelitis.

Barker contributed substantially to the development of research methods for studying the uninterrupted environment. These methods contrasted in many ways from the dominant laboratory-experimental methods of the time. Since few such methods existed at the time, methodological work was necessary in addition to the theoretical. These methods have since migrated into many parts of psychology and other disciplines. They are rigorous and detailed and withstand the same scientific scrutiny as other methods in psychology and other disciplines.

A principal research strategy of the Field Station was to leave the environments in the town unaltered by the researchers. Barker described this method of research as *transducer* research, in which the scientists observe and record behavior without altering the environment. This was in contrast to more traditional *operator* research in which the scientists conduct experiments and give tests; that is, they operate on the environment and then look at what people do in response to these operations.

Barker's contributions to developmental psychology were many. He began studying elders in his dissertation. He followed this with studies of early and late maturing girls and continued a broad scope program of research to examine the relationship of development in children to their own natural habitats.

BARKER THE MAN

Barker was first and foremost a scientist. He was continually curious about the way development and human behavior work. He was also very persistent. He wrote that he first learned these strategies at Stanford (where "dogged does it" was the motto [Barker, 1979a]) and continued them in his studies with Lewin and then in his own work.

Barker was creative. He did not hesitate to enter new fields or seriously address the challenges of developing new theories and methods. Both behavior setting theory and the variety of methods he generated attest to this characteristic.

Barker frequently answered questions with a story or example illustrating his point. He was interested in helping people see for themselves the merit of his findings and of helping them to think independently about the matter under discussion. This was similar to his long discussions with Lewin of the work in progress. Barker was very independent, although quietly so, and he was experienced in taking unusual views and pursuing them.

Barker was also a very gentle person. He was soft-spoken and congenial and went out of his way to be helpful to others. He was always first among equals in research groups, but he was genuinely interested in hearing critiques and alternative views. After participating in a heated discussion on the scientific merits of a theory or data, he could always turn the atmosphere into a congenial, relaxed mood implying a "we're all in this together" attitude that encouraged and motivated other participants to continue their own thinking in the area. This was very motivating for students as well as for colleagues and other distinguished scientists. The picture at the beginning of this chapter expresses well this attitude.

Early History, Education, and Mentoring

Roger Garlock Barker was born in Macksburg, Iowa, in 1903, one of five children (including a sister who had Down syndrome and died in childhood). He lived in small towns in Iowa until he was 8 years old. Following the loss of his job, Roger's father moved the family to Palo Alto, California, where they occasionally lived with or near relatives. Following several other moves, including one to Canada, the family settled in Palo Alto. Barker described himself as shy and easily embarrassed when asked to perform during his childhood years, but he did well academically.

At age 14 Barker contracted osteomyelitis, an inflammatory and destructive bone disease causing pain, tenderness, and a variety of other symptoms. For the next 7 years Barker was an invalid and experienced many ineffective treatments, including two surgical interventions at the Mayo Clinic and bed rest in a sanatorium. He was also treated with a new German drug called aspirin. He had intermittent remissions of the disease during which he attended school briefly. He referred to this period as "the lost years," and they lasted through most of the rest of his high school years. Finally, he began to improve and became symptom free although he would continue to have flare-ups of the disease that sometimes lasted weeks or months. He wore braces on his legs for most of his life.

In 1924 Barker was admitted to the University of Redlands. The following year he transferred to Stanford, which was within cycling distance of his house. His years out of the formal education system had produced both advantages and disadvantages. He was bright, curious, and strong in independent study and self-direction. He lacked skills in paying attention to all subjects rather than only those in which he was interested, and he had to learn test-taking skills. After taking advantage of Stanford's fairly open and tolerant academic program, he reports "drifting" into a major in psychology because of some rather general senses of "doing good" and of psychology opening doors to a good future life (Barker, 1979a).

Following graduation Barker was admitted for graduate study at nearby University of California–Berkeley. The osteomyelitis flared up again, and he spent most of that year in bed. The following spring he returned to Stanford to do graduate work there. The Stanford psychology faculty was committed to details of obtaining and analyzing data, and from them he learned the nuts and bolts of investigations, although considerably less about the principles and theories of the discipline. His dissertation, completed in 1934, was done with Walter R. Miles and concerned the ability to do fatiguing muscular work in the elderly.

When Barker finished his PhD, there were no jobs. Calvin P. Stone offered him a postdoctoral research assistantship. He described these years as the most valuable at Stanford because they solidified his view of the importance of the influence of the environment on behavior. While working on Stone's studies of early maturing girls, a surprising finding emerged. The hypothesis that hormonal and other physical characteristics control social development turned out not to be true.

The environment apparently views the early maturing girls in ways different from later maturing girls and emits stimuli toward greater maturity earlier than is the case with the late maturing girls, who demonstrate similar physical characteristics, only later.

One other experience at Stanford would have profound and lasting effects on Barker's life. In 1927 he met Louise Dawes Shedd. In 1928 they both received BAs (he in psychology, she in biology), and they became engaged, marrying in 1930. They eventually had three children. As part of her work in biology, Louise went on various data collection trips in the natural habitats of local tide pools and Coastal Mountains and worked in the Hopkins Marine Station. She took Roger along, and he began what became a lifelong fascination with the theories and methods of natural habitat research. He later commented that he had been a naturalist for most of his career in psychology and that these experiences were very important in forming that view. A second important influence from Louise's life that affected Barker was that she was well connected socially. Her uncle, Ray Lyman Wilbur, was the president of Stanford at the time, and he was good friends with Lewis Terman, then chair of the psychology department. Louise's positive view of Barker's abilities were transmitted to Terman, who was interested in gifted people and took Barker under his wing and aided his career in several ways. Louise's early years in a missionary family in Iran and later years living with various family members in the United States (some of whom were U.S. presidential cabinet members and held other prominent positions) also helped the development of ecological psychology. As a variety of visitors came to the Field Station (e.g., leaders in psychology, funding agencies, and foundations), Louise was able to talk with them easily and knowledgeably. This was very helpful to Roger in getting grants and making contacts.

In 1935 Terman asked Barker if he was interested in a fellowship to work with Kurt Lewin at the University of Iowa Child Welfare Station. Barker agreed immediately and began one of the most important periods of his intellectual life. After several postdoctoral years and with no job in sight, there was "no choice really." Barker had met Lewin at Stanford but found his valences, psychological forces, and life spaces nearly incomprehensible and as easy to understand as "fairy dust." Lewin's theories, coming out of Gestalt psychology, were very different from the prevailing psychological theories in the United States at the time.

Barker was thrown into an ongoing project of Lewin's work on force fields. He joined the team composed of Lewin, Tamara Dembo, and Herbert Wright. There would be long discussions late into the night concerning whatever Lewin was thinking about his recent data. These discussions were theoretical, logical, and conceptual, whereas those at Stanford had been focused more on reliability, instrumentation, and other methodological issues. The watchword at Stanford had been "work hard;" the watchword at Iowa was "think hard." Although the transition was difficult for Barker, he acquired several concepts that would be crucial to his later work. These were the importance of the psychological environment, that molar level behavior has a strong effect on people's lives, and that people behave within dynamic systems that have overlapping parts (Lewin, 1935, 1936). Lewin's ideas that development and behavior occur within a total *lifespace* were consonant with Egon Brunswik's *probabilistic functionalism* (behavior is always functional at some level and is probabilistic rather than determined) and were a forerunner of current dynamic systems theories in development. Barker became concerned with the *texture* of the environment and with its intimate, *inextricable* relationship to behavior and development. These ideas formed the basis of Barker's work for the rest of his life.

Early Academic Career

Barker's first "real job" was at Harvard (1937–1938). Upon Lewin's recommendation Barker was hired as an instructor to teach Harvard's first undergraduate course in child development. He worked on the manuscript of *Frustration and Regression: An Experiment With Young Children* (Barker, Dembo, & Lewin, 1941), conducted some research, and got his college teaching career under way. He gave the child development lectures for men at Harvard and then repeated them for women at Radcliffe. This caused him to remember his grandmother having been a regular student in classes with men at the University of Iowa in 1867.

At the end of 1 year at Harvard Barker decided to leave rather than pursue another year or two as instructor. His very different theoretical stance, the physical isolation of his office, and other factors caused him to believe that he could not move forward in his career there.

Barker managed to find a position as assistant professor of child psychology at the University of Illinois (1938–1942). Several important influences emerged during this period. He began his own independent research program, first focusing on questions he had pursued at Stanford concerning the development of individuals and then gradually moving to focus on the environment. During his second year he was given partial leave of absence to attend a yearlong seminar in child development at the University of Chicago. Here he interacted with members of the newly formed Society for Research in Child Development and other luminaries (Ralph Tyler, Ernest Hilgard, Herbert and Lois Stolz, and Nevitt Sanford) as well as 12 or so resident members. This experience was valuable in that it deepened his knowledge of child development but also made him aware that "almost all scientific knowledge of children's behavior came from laboratories and clinics under conditions created by the investigators" (Barker, 1989).

It was here that Barker also produced another first in child development. In 1943 he published the first book of readings in child development, *Child Behavior and Development*, working with two former Iowa colleagues whom he recruited to help, Jacob S. Kounin and Herbert Wright. This anthology became a very popular book for developmental psychologists.

Two other experiences influenced the growing shift in Barker's mind from a traditional, individually oriented view of development to a broader one that examines the environment as a causative factor in development. One of Barker's duties at Illinois was to teach child psychology in various teachers' colleges around the state. As he traveled across this mostly flat agricultural land, he was impressed with the fact that there was a definite organization to the environment. Large open spaces were interspersed with small, clustered "cages" (towns) that enclosed children and their behavior. He began to wonder about the influence of these cages on children in somewhat the same way biologists study wildlife refuges. The seeds of the field station idea began to sprout.

The second experience at the University of Illinois was the reconnection with a childhood chum, Guy Smith from Des Moines, now an agronomist at the university, who talked about soils, yields, nutrients of grains, natural grasses, and other environmental factors. Barker realized that he would be embarrassed if he were asked similar questions about environmental conditions and child behavior yields in homes, schools, and other natural habitats.

After 4 years Barker perceived that a number of factors were emerging that were not consistent with the direction he now wanted his research to take. In addition, the Illinois weather in winter was not good for his osteomylitis. He had a recurrence during this period. He wrote to Terman at Stanford, and a position there was arranged for him as acting associate professor. Here he began work with his first graduate students (e.g., Paul Mussen and Lee Meyerson).

After 3 years, the regular staff began returning to Stanford, and Barker was out of a job. After a casual meeting with President Wallace Atwood of Clark University in the summer, he was then (to his surprise) offered the position of G. Stanley Hall Professor at Clark, where he went in January 1946. At Clark, Barker made the first concrete moves toward studying the behavior of children in their natural habitat. He and Louise moved to a small town near Worcester, Massachusetts, although it turned out not to have the requisite characteristics. Barker finished the monograph from his earlier grant and worked with colleagues Kurt Lewin and Fritz Heider (both of whom now lived nearby) and two promising graduate students, Chris Argyris and Howard Perlmutter. He also applied for and received a grant from the U.S. Public Health Service for a field study of the everyday lives of children of a single small town.

But Barker's life was set for another surprising turn. In 1947 he was offered the chairmanship of the psychology department at the University of Kansas, which had recently declined due to staff losses associated with the war. He was assured that he could recruit like-minded colleagues. Fritz and Grace Heider and Herbert Wright joined him, and, shortly Martin Scheerer, Alfred Baldwin, and Erik and Beatrice Wright. Along with Anthony Smith and Beulah Morrison, who were already at Kansas, this cadre of people formed a close-knit and intellectually consonant group that saw themselves theoretically as organismic psychologists with a Gestalt theoretical base. Importantly, Barker was given support for his ideas of studying behavior in the natural habitat. In fact, the dean of Arts and Sciences identified the small town that Barker had been hunting (Oskaloosa, Kansas), which became their main research base. The Midwest Psychological Field Station was established there in September 1947, in part with funds from the Public Health Service grant that he brought with him from Clark and in part with funds from the newly created National Institute of Mental Health. As he wrote, "We were all set for a congenial, productive Golden Age of our kind of psychology" (Barker, 1989, p. 26). Unfortunately, environmental events intervened. The University of Kansas was small (5000 students) and fairly stable but was soon swung into huge changes. Enrollment soon doubled and then tripled as returning veterans sought higher education. New staff had to be recruited to handle this load, and they brought a variety of theoretical positions with them. Other departments also made demands on psychology for courses for their students. The nature of the department and its objectives changed. Once again the environment had intervened. After 3 years he resigned as chair to devote more time to his research and the development of the Field Station in Oskaloosa. Barker would spend the rest of his life in Kansas.

THE MIDWEST PSYCHOLOGICAL FIELD STATION

As noted, Barker wasted no time in establishing the Midwest Psychological Field Station in Oskaloosa, Kansas, some 20 miles north of the main campus of the University of Kansas in Lawrence as a base from which to do research on children's behavior in the natural habitat. It was to become one of the most famous "laboratories" in psychology, although Barker would have looked askance at the use of the word *laboratories*, as this was exactly what he was trying to move away from.

Barker was the director of the Field Station for 25 years. He was principal investigator on most of its grants. He was its driving force. He directed numerous dissertations and collaborated with colleagues on almost all of the research conducted there. Examination of the work of the Field Station is, in fact, an examination of Barker's work and the progress of his thinking.

The Field Station had a substantial staff. Herbert Wright played an early role in the development of the station. After being recruited by Barker to join the endeavor, Wright and his wife, Lorene, moved to Oskaloosa and set up the offices of the Field Station in their home. Phil Schoggen was one of the first graduate students in the new program at Kansas. In January 1948, he and his wife, Maxine, also moved to Oskaloosa to work in the Field Station. Roger and Louise Barker soon followed (March 1948) with Louise now a full participant in the research. Paul and Natalie Gump joined the group in 1961. The Wrights stayed 7 years and then left to pursue research in cities. The Schoggens were there for 9 years overall. The Barkers and the Gumps remained at the Field Station throughout its life (and in Oskaloosa until Roger's and Paul's deaths). Over the course of its 25 years, the Field Station employed 9 professional staff, 5 research assistants, 48 graduate students, 19 field workers, 23 technical assistants, and 30 support staff. Various other individuals were associated with the station for shorter periods or for more limited tasks. See the special issue of *Environment and Behavior* (1990) on the Field Station for a more complete list of Field Station participants and products.

Barker (1989) gave a detailed description of the work, both conceptual and practical, that was done to develop new methods for this kind of research as well as the community involvement strategies necessary to embed the researchers in the community. He described the initiation of the field station idea while he was at the University of Illinois. Principles came together from the Hopkins Marine Field Station, from Guy Smith (his agronomist friend), his early life in Iowa, and the trips across Illinois' prairies (Barker, 1990).

In 1949 the Field Station moved from the Wrights' house to the second floor of the former bank building. Barker preferred it because of its large, walk-in vault in which the precious data could be stored relatively safely from the real threats of fire on the second floor of this old wooden building, or the fabled Kansas wind storms. The courthouse across the street had been destroyed by a tornado. Members of the field staff describe Barker insisting on closing and locking the vault and unplugging electrical machines whenever no one was in the office, including while taking coffee breaks at the café across the street.

Initially the methods were simply living in the town, participating in all its settings without interference and writing notes at the end of each day on what child behaviors had been observed. These methods were influenced by anthropologists whose work Barker and Wright admired. The research team initially continued the methods they had learned during their training. They interviewed parents, sat around in drugstores with stopwatches and checklists, and consulted an electronics expert about tagging children with transmitters. It soon became clear that more systematic data would be needed. After some initial false starts, the main method generated was a *specimen record.* An observer followed a child, without interference, and made running, narrative records *at the molar level* of whatever the child said and did and whatever was said and done to the child. Although early observation notes were written, Schoggen (1964) adapted a *Stenomask,* a device used in court reporting, for orally describing the child's behavior and the environment. These oral notes were transcribed into a detailed record immediately after the observation. One of the more famous of these records was published as *One Boy's Day* (Barker & Wright, 1951), in which 14 hours of 7-year-old Raymond Birch's life was now committed to paper. The method was described more fully by Wright (1967). Eventually 16 full day records of the behavior of children between the ages of 2 and 11 along with 4 records from children with serious physical impairments were collected. These are archived at the Spencer Library at the University of Kansas for use by interested investigators.

It did not take long to discover that children did not behave in "social interaction units." For example, Margaret's behavior in the drugstore bore only minimal relationship to her mother's social inputs (surprising no parent). Claire's efforts to get the dog to stop eating from her picnic plate had less to do with her personality than it did with the dog. Raymond's struggle to open the door against the strong Kansas wind was less related to his self-concept than it was to the force of the wind. Herb Wright then led the endeavor to analyze the records into their own, naturally occurring units, which were called *behavior episodes.* They were grounded in Lewin's theory of molar action. The number of episodes per day varied from about 1300 for the youngest children to about 500 for the older children and, inversely, had shorter durations for younger children and longer durations for older children. Episodes often overlapped, showing that children were involved in more than one thing at a time. About two-thirds of the episodes were social; however, the children were dominated by adults in only about one-third of the units, and more of the episodes ended satisfactorily than not (Schoggen, 1991).

One particular finding that emerged from these studies was important to child development and is illustrative of the contribution of these methods to psychology more broadly. Barker et al. (1941) had shown *in laboratory studies* that children respond to frustration with regression. In fact, this relationship took on something of the nature of a basic principle in development. When Fawl (1963) set out to study this relationship *in the natural habitat*, however, he found two surprising things: (1) Children are infrequently frustrated; and (2) when they are, they almost never respond with regression. This was one of the early studies that showed that investigations carried out in laboratories can produce very different results from those carried out in natural habitats. This theme was to be repeated many times.

It soon became clear that children's behavior could be predicted better from places than from people. Although individual differences are important, the first and primary influence on their behavior is the environment. And this environment could be seen to occur in observable, easily identifiable (by both researcher and participants) units. These units, called behavior settings, have specific, direct "intentions" toward the behavior of persons who enter them. In Barker's words, these behavior settings *coerce* behavior—not to the exclusion of individual variables but as a predominant force (Barker, 1968). The third-grade class emits signals for human behavior to all who enter, regardless of their personality. This is also true of the men's chorus and Lawyer Daggett's office. If people cannot produce the behavior required by the setting, they either leave or are vetoed by the setting. Settings do change over time, but when they restabilize they continue emitting signals to all who enter; that is, they are extraindividual. It also became apparent that these principles were true for adults as well as children, so the research thereafter expanded to include behavior of all participants in settings. A good bit of the rest of Barker's research effort and that of his colleagues was spent further investigating and explicating this idea. Barker believed that behavior settings are phenomena for which psychological theories are inadequate. It is, therefore, not surprising that many psychologists have had difficulty understanding these concepts.

Once all the behavior settings had been identified, Barker and his group developed a very large number of different analyses to make sense of them. For example, territorial range was defined as the number of different settings inhabited by a person or group. Adults had access to almost all settings in the town, elders had access to somewhat fewer settings, and children had access to the fewest settings. Habitat extent reflected the number of behavior settings during the study period, their occurrence (number of days), and their duration (number of hours per setting). For example, grocery businesses and school classes had a large habitat extent, whereas governor's visit and Fourth of July parade had lower habitat extents. Occupancy time data were the amounts of time spent in a setting by various people or groups. A variety of other characteristics of each behavior setting was also studied, such as action patterns, behavior mechanisms, inhabitant attributes, and behavior output (see Barker & Associates, 1978, for an early sampling of such studies.)

One very interesting measure was called "habitat claims." These are the human positions, slots, or tasks that needed doing for the settings of the town or school or organization to continue operating. They are the real-life demands of the environment on the people.

Once all the settings had been identified, interlinkages between settings could also be studied. For example, how much autonomy does each setting have over its program? What authority systems exist between settings?

Notice that these characteristics are not measures of what people think they did when reporting on their own behavior or what might have or should have happened. They are, instead, measures of what actually did happen. As such they are invaluable sources of the effects of the actual, real-life environment on behavior and can be studied in their own right or used for an endless variety of plans for changing the environment. These analyses permitted the examination of a very large number of questions concerning the actual, real-life habitats of people from any perspective of interest, such as education, religious, business, youth sport, philanthropy, elder habitats, and intergenerational activities. For more detail concerning these measures and their procedures see Barker (1968) and Schoggen (1989).

The studies of the Field Station also ranged into other cultures. One is reported in *Qualities of Community Life* (Barker & Schoggen, 1973). Two complete year-long behavior setting surveys were conducted simultaneously in Oskaloosa and in Leyburn, England, in 1954–55 and 1963–64. These surveys examined all the nonhome settings in each town for 1 year. The two communities were compared and contrasted across cultures as well as across time. It stands today as one of the most extensive examinations of whole environments ever conducted.

In the late 1950s Kansas was in a major school consolidation movement. The Field Station obtained U.S. Office of Education funding to conduct behavior setting surveys (and other studies) in entire schools the enrollments of which were large or small. Paul Gump joined the station in 1961 and became involved in these studies. This work eventually resulted in *Big School, Small School* (Barker & Gump, 1964), which also became a citation classic in psychology. The findings from these studies were among the first to show that size matters, and it matters in terms of outcomes for students. Students in smaller schools participate in more settings per individual (despite having fewer settings per school); they participate in a greater variety of tasks and take more leadership roles; they are more important in keeping the setting alive and functioning, and they recognize this and behave accordingly. There was also greater insecurity about maintenance of the settings and a lower level of maximal performance. Such results were repeated over a number of studies, and follow-up investigations of students from these same schools 15 year later showed that the differences persisted into their adult lives (Schoggen, 1991). This set of studies formed the early basis for underinhabiting theory. For the first time, a causal rather than a descriptive theory was produced.

During the 1960s two major projects predominated. Barker worked on the major theoretical explication of the work, *Ecological Psychology: Concepts and Methods for Studying the Environment of Human Behavior* (Barker, 1968), which stood for decades as the major theoretical treatise of this school of thought. It became a citation classic in psychology. Schoggen (1989) published a revision and extension of this work.

The second endeavor was a complete behavior setting survey of a small town near Oskaloosa that was being submerged by a U.S. Army Corps of Engineers' construction of a large dam. An initial setting survey had already been done on this town. The study found that 42% of settings were lost in the new town to which the citizens moved. The researchers pointed out that the data were collected soon after the move, however, so it is quite possible that settings that develop more slowly followed. Funding for a follow -up study could not be obtained.

In 1971 Barker resigned the Career Investigator Grant he had held since 1963 and retired in 1972. Paul Gump served as director of the station for the last several years until it was closed in 1972 as funding became more and more difficult to obtain. An important set of activities during these last years was the assembly, cataloging, and storing of the specimen records, behavior setting surveys, and other valuable materials produced by the Field Station over its 25-year history. These are now archived at the University of Kansas Archives in the Spencer Library. They have been and are being used by researchers from various disciplines.

The Midwest Psychological Field Station produced a substantial and influential body of work (*Environment and Behavior*, 1990, p. 545f). Nine books were published, two of which became citation classics in psychology (Barker & Gump, 1964, *Big School, Small School*; Barker, 1968, *Ecological Psychology*). *One Boy's Day* (Barker & Wright, 1951) reported an entire day in the life of 7-year-old Raymond Birch. *Midwest and Its Children* (Barker & Wright, 1955) reported the results of a behavior setting survey of an entire town for 1 year and is one of the earliest expositions of behavior setting theory and its possibilities as both a conceptual framework of the environment and the methods for studying that environment. *Qualities of Community Life* (Barker & Schoggen, 1973) presents the results of two year-long surveys at 10-year in intervals in two towns, Oskaloosa and Leyburn, England, and gives detailed pictures of the towns across time and across cultures.

A total of 16 chapters in books and 21 articles in major journals discussed various aspects of the work, both theoretical and methodological. A total of 20 dissertations and theses were produced, examining topics such as institutions for children with handicaps, children's naturally occurring problem solving, community leadership, Catholic schools, participation of marginal individuals in settings of differing sizes, and others. In the 10 years after the Field Station closed, a number of other publications described different aspects of the work there.

The work of Roger Barker and his colleagues at the Midwest Psychological Field Station has had broad and far-reaching implications for psychology and for other studies of human behavior. From this account it is easy to see that Barker and the Field Station were virtually synonymous. Barker *was* the Field Station. It was the operational base of his own work, and he, although a strong collaborator, was the power behind the research. "Behavior settings are constituent parts of institutions, communities, and societies. Changes come via the establishment, alternation, and termination of behavior settings" (Barker, 1989). Thus, the new field of *ecological psychology*, as Barker called the overall structure of his approach, has implications not only for basic research on human behavior but also for changing it. Settings begin (Smith's restaurant, Old Settler's ladies quilting club, Betty's nursery), and change (the library stayed open in the evenings) and are terminated (Henry's garage, Mt. Olive Church, high school Latin class). The environment for people's behavior changes. It is possible to observe and analyze these changes and to use these analyses as a basis for improving lives. Kelly (1990) pointed out applications of this strategy in environmental psychology, community psychology, cross-cultural psychology, and organizational psychology.

ECOLOGICAL WORK AFTER THE FIELD STATION

Two groups of people emerged during the latter period of the Field Station and following: the *classicists* and the *extenders* (Scott, 2005). The classicists thought that Barker's work on behavior settings as basic units of the environment was not complete and should be pursued directly and included L. Barker, P. Schoggen, M. Schoggen, and P. Gump. The extenders thought that the basic concept of the behavior setting is very important and should be maintained but that it might be strengthened and extended by adding to it and included A. Wicker, E. Willems, R. Bechtel, and perhaps others. What each person added depended on the environment in which each person found himself or herself and that person's research or application interests. A third group might be identified as those outside the Barker group whose work has strong ties to ecological psychology, behavior setting theory, or the natural habitat methods developed by Barker and his associates and includes people such as K. Fox and R. Taylor.

A variety of factors has been described that influenced the work of ecological psychologists following Barker (Scott, 2005). These include factors like changes in funding patterns and procedures, the types of institutions in which each person works, shifts in the dominant paradigms in psychology generally, larger cultural factors, and individual differences. These are relevant to the scope of Barker's influence and to his legacy.

After the Field Station closed Barker continued writing and speaking on a number of topics in ecological psychology until his death in 1990. Gump was frequently asked to speak and consult on matters of school size and other behavior setting applications until his death in 2004. Schoggen worked with Barker to finish *Qualities of Community Life* (Barker & Schoggen, 1973) and in 1989 offered a major revision and extension of Barker's *Ecological Psychology*. He has continued to write on the basic theory and consult on educational and other applications.

Wicker has continued writing and teaching ecological psychology and has extended the methods and theories. His *Introduction to Ecological Psychology* (1984) extended inhabiting level from the original one category of underinhabiting to two others—adequately inhabited and overinhabited—and included methods for identifying each. His other work included a major reconceptualization of behavior setting and inhabiting theory linking them into other areas of work in psychology (Wicker, 1987). He built on Barker's basic core concepts of a behavior setting but added information and reserves to the resources of a setting, and proposed a set of internal dynamics (e.g., individual differences and social factors) and contextual factors (e.g., setting history and linkages) that influence settings. One of his most interesting conceptualizations was that of the life cycle of settings; that is, each has a beginning phase, one or more relatively stable middle phases, and an ending phase. His work represents the strongest bridge between classical behavior setting theory and other elaborations. He has also extended the work into international settings and pragmatic applications (Wicker, 2009).

Willems extended the application of behavior setting theory to hospitals, reha-bilitation facilities, and architecture (Georgiou, Carspecken, & Willems, 1996; Willems, 1973a). He also studied a variety of methodological issues pertinent to natural habitat research and wrote a number of papers on theoretical integration of behavior setting theory with others (Willems, 1973b, 2000). Bechtel (1997) extended the view of natural habitats to extreme environments such as cold regions, arid zones, and the Mir Space Station.

The core group, or second generation after Barker, produced a number of stu-dents. These students (the third generation) also continued using behavior setting theory in a variety of ways. Kirmeyer (1978) studied understaffing in national parks and then moved into work environments, including police work (e.g., relationship of personality factors "Type A" to work stress). Blanchard (2004) examined online environments, identifying online communities called virtual behavior settings and later expanded this to work settings. She also studied "cyber loafing." Scott (1980; Scott & Hatfield, 1985) developed methods similar to specimen records and chronicles (chronologs and segment logs) as well as a time-weighted analytic strat-egy intended to increase the ecological validity of the analyses. Classrooms were studied across cultures (Scott, 1989), as were oral histories of ecological psycholo-gists (Scott, 2005). Scott also taught a doctoral seminar in ecological psychology at Indiana University for about 20 years. A number of students from this group have continued behavior setting work into the fourth generation. Several of these studies examined the behavior of atypical children in various settings, such as children who had hyperactivity (Hatfield, 1983), mental retardation (Rager, 1986), emotional problems (Argenbright, 1991), and autism (Ruble & Scott, 2002). Henry (2003) extended Blanchard's work on online virtual behavior settings. Heston (1995), in a complex study, experimentally varied inhabiting level and studied boys' reactions in a sport setting.

Behavior setting theory has spread to other disciplines; for example, Fox (1985) constructed an economic model based on behavior settings; Taylor (1997), in criminal justice, identified behavior settings in urban residential blocks and used those data for intervention in crime. The theory has also generated considerable international interest. For example, Kaminski (1983, 1989) presented some strong discussions of behavior setting theory and the field of ecological psychology in general. He recently (2009) applied Barker's ideas to athletic sport. Fuhrer (1990) considered the ecological–psychological gap.

CURRENT STATUS OF ECOLOGICAL PSYCHOLOGY

It is apparent that ecological psychology is alive and well, and work is being done from this perspective in a variety of places. Behavior setting theory is a powerful theory. Its power emanates from several sources (Scott, 2005) including its extra-individual nature, the requirement of linked physical and social features in the one unit, and the self-regulation of a setting via several internal mechanisms.

Willems (2000) suggested that ecological psychology has now been more widely accepted than is recognized by the core group as the basic principles have appeared in a number of places. In that sense it is like Lewinian psychology becoming so much a part of the general fabric of psychology that is taken for granted. Wicker (2002) pointed out that ecological psychology also shares a number of features with systems theory, which is currently very popular (although behavior setting theory is considerably more specific and detailed). Gump (2000) said that he was "continually surprised" by instances in which behavior setting theory pops up in the most unexpected places, having been living a secret but quite full-blown life.

Wicker (2002) noted that "the ecological perspective that emerged from the work of a few dedicated researchers in an obscure Kansas town more than 50 years ago has shown amazing survivability" (p. 124). Its international appeal is shown in a recent introductory text in Swedish. Wicker also reported a study by Kaminski showing that "journal citations to Barker's publications have occurred with nearly the same frequency in recent years as when the Midwest Field Station was operating. Roughly half of the citations appeared in a diverse set of non-psychological journals" (p. 124).

Roger Barker's contributions to development and to all of psychology are substantial. He generated a new theory of the environment and its influence on human behavior, behavior setting theory. He produced massive amounts of data to support his claim that this unit of the environment acts as a coercive force on behavior. He and his colleagues at the Midwest Psychological Field Station in Oskaloosa, Kansas, generated new methods of studying the environment and human development, the specimen record for studying individual behavior, and the behavior setting survey for studying specific units of the environment. This view of examining behavior from the standpoint of the natural habitat in which it occurs served as a strong countervailing force to the dominant paradigms of American psychology.

Barker generated a new field of psychology called ecological psychology. He was a substantial contributor to the field of development and was influential in the initiation of the field of rehabilitation psychology. He was recognized by many awards and honors for this work. It is an interesting paradox that such work has not yet moved into the mainstream of American psychology, although it is more recognized internationally. It may be, however, that his ideas have seemed so sensible to many people that, like Lewin's work, they have been incorporated into the mainstream without attribution. The future may bring a very different view of Barker and his work. In conclusion, it appears that Karl Fox's (1985) assertion that the concept of a behavior setting may come to play as important a role in the social sciences as the cell does in biology may well be justified.

SUGGESTED READINGS

Barker, R. G. (1968). *Ecological psychology: Concepts and methods for studying the environment for human behavior.* Stanford, CA: Stanford University Press.

This is the first and basic exposition of Barker's behavior setting theory and its methods. He describes the units of the environment (behavior settings), the basic methods for identifying them, and some of the findings, such as that behavior settings often play a greater role in people's behavior than do individual difference variables like personality and self-concept. A Psychology Citation Classic it was revised and updated in 1989 by Phil Schoggen as *Behavior Settings: A Revision and Extension of Roger G. Barker's "Ecological Psychology."*

Barker, R. G., & Gump, P. V. (1964). *Big school, small school: High school size and student behavior*. Stanford, CA: Stanford University Press.

A study of high schools of varying sizes, from 35 students to 2287 students, in which all behavior settings in each school that occurred during the entire school year 1959–1960, were identified, cataloged, classified, and then related to various student behaviors. Students in the small schools participated in more behavior settings per student and played more roles, more varied roles, and more leadership roles than students in large schools. A Psychology Citation Classic.

Barker, R., & Wright, H. F. (1971/1955). *Midwest and its children*. Hamden, CT: Archon.

A report of all the nonhome behavior settings in one town for a year. The book describes two of the main methods in the field of ecological psychology: (1) the behavior setting survey; and (2) the specimen record.

REFERENCES

Argenbright, G. A. (1991). A comparison of emotionally handicapped and unlabeled peers' conceptions of classroom behavior settings. *Dissertation Abstracts International: Section A. 52*(2), 468.

Barker, R. G. (1968). *Ecological psychology. Concepts and methods for studying the environment of human behavior*. Stanford, CA: Stanford University Press.

Barker, R. G. (1979a). Settings of a professional lifetime. *Journal of Social and Personality Psychology, 37*, 2137–2157. doi:10.1037/0022-3514.37.12.2137

Barker, R. G. (1979b). The influence of frontier environments on behavior. In J. O. Steffen (Ed.), *The American west: New perspectives, new dimensions* (pp. 61–93). Norman: University of Oklahoma Press.

Barker, R. G. (1989). Roger G. Barker. In G. Lindzey (Ed.), *History of psychology in autobiography* (vol. 8, pp. 2–35). Stanford, CA: Stanford University Press.

Barker, R. G. (1990). Recollections of the Midwest Psychological Field Station. *Environment and Behavior, 22*, 503–513. doi:10.1177/0013916590224007

Barker, R. G., & Associates. (1978). *Habitats, environments, and human behavior*. San Francisco: Jossey-Bass.

Barker, R. G., Dembo, T., & Lewin, K. (1941). Frustration and regression: A study of young children. *University of Iowa Studies in Child Welfare, 18*(1).

Barker, R. G., & Gump, P. V. (1964). *Big school, small school: High school size and student behavior*. Stanford, CA: Stanford University Press.

Barker, R. G., Kounin, J. S., & Wright, H. F. (Eds.) (1943). *Child behavior and development*. New York: McGraw-Hill.

Barker, R. G., & Schoggen. (1973). *Qualities of community life*. San Francisco: Jossey-Bass.

Barker, R., Wright, B. A., Meyerson, L., & Gonick M. R. (1953). *Adjustment to physical handicap and illness: A survey of the social psychology of physique and disability*. Bulletin No. 55. New York: Social Science Research Council.

Barker, R. G., & Wright, H. F. (1951). *One boy's day*. New York: Harper.

Barker, R. G., & Wright, H. F. (1971/1955). *Midwest and its children*. Hamden CT: Archon. (Original work published 1955.)

Bechtel, R. G. (1997). *Environment and behavior: An introduction*. Thousand Oaks, CA: Sage.

Blanchard, A. L. (2004). Virtual behavior settings: An application of behavior setting theories to virtual communities. *Journal of Computer-Mediated Communications, 9*(2). http://jcmc.indiana.edu/vol9/issue2/blanchard.html

Environment and Behavior. (1990, July). 22(4), 545f. (A special issue devoted to the Midwest Psychological Field Station.)

Fawl, C. L. (1963). Disturbances experienced by children in their natural habitats. In R. G. Barker (Ed.), *The stream of behavior: Explorations of its structure & content.* (pp. 99–126). New York: Appleton-Century-Crofts.

Fox, K. A. (1985). *Social systems accounts: Linking social and economic indicators through tangible behavior settings.* Boston: Reidel.

Fuhrer, U. (1990). Bridging the ecological-psychological gap: Behavior settings as interfaces. *Environment and Behavior, 22,* 518–537. doi:10.1177/0013916590224009

Georgiou, D., Carspecken, P. F., & Willems, E. P. (1996). An expansion of Roger Barker's behavior setting survey for an ethno-ecological approach to person-environment interactions. *Journal of Environmental Psychology, 16,* 310–333. doi:10.1006/jevp.1996.0027

Gump, P. V. (2000, April 13-14). *Interview with M. M. Scott.* Archives of the History of American Psychology, University of Akron. (Available in both tape and typescript format.) (See also M. M. Scott Papers, Collection number C370, Record Container 6, Office of University Archives and Records Management, Indiana University, Bloomington.)

Hatfield, J. G. (1983). The behavior of hyperactive children and unlabeled peers across classroom settings: An ecological analysis. *Dissertation Abstracts International: Section A.* 43(8), 2604.

Henry, D. J. (2003). *Computer mediated behavior settings: An application of behavior setting theory in on-line environments.* Unpublished doctoral dissertation, Indiana University, Bloomington.

Heston, M. L. (1995). Game inhabiting level effects on children. *Perceptual and Motor Skills, 81,* 523–527.

Kaminski, G. (1983). The enigma of ecological psychology. *Journal of Environmental Psychology, 3,* 85–94. doi:10.1016/S0272-4944(83)80022-X

Kaminski, G. (1989). The relevance of ecologically oriented conceptualizations to theory building in environment and behavior research. In E. H. Zube & G. T. Moore (Eds.), *Advances in environment, behavior, and design* (vol. 2, pp. 3–36). New York: Plenum.

Kaminski, R. (2009). Sport in the perspective of Barkerian psychological ecology. *International Journal of Sport Psychology, 40,* 50–78.

Keller, E. F. (1983). *A feeling for the organism: The life and work of Barbara McClintock.* New York: Freeman.

Kelly, J. G. (1990). The Midwest Psychological Field Station: Some legacies. *Environment and Behavior, 22,* 518–537. doi:10.1177/0013916590224008

Kirmeyer, S. L. (1978). Effects of work overload and understaffing on rangers in Yosemite National Park. *Dissertation Abstracts International: Section B.* 39 (3), 1543.

Lewin, K. (1935). *Dynamic theory of personality.* New York: McGraw-Hill.

Lewin, K. (1936). *Principles of topological psychology.* New York: McGraw-Hill. doi:10.1037/10019-000

Ozrek, A. M. (1987) Innovations in ecological psychology: Conversations with Roger and Louise Barker, *Journal of Counseling and Development, 65,* 233–237.

Rager, T. H. (1986). An ecological comparison of the effects of mainstreamed and non-mainstreamed settings on the behavior of EMR children. *Dissertation Abstracts International: Section A.* 47(5), 1692.

Ruble, L. A., & Scott, M. M. (2002). Executive functions and the natural habitat behaviors of children with autism. *Autism, 6,* 365–381. doi:10.1177/1362361302006004004

Schoggen, P. (1964). Mechanical aids for making specimen records. *Child Development, 35,* 985–988.

Schoggen, P. (1989). *Behavior settings: A revision and extension of Roger G. Barker's "ecological psychology."* Stanford, CA: Stanford University Press.

Schoggen, P. (1991). Ecological psychology: One approach to development in context. In R. Cohen & A. Siegel (Eds.), *Context and development* (pp. 281–301). Hillsdale, NJ: Erlbaum.

Schoggen, P. (1992). Roger Garlock Barker (1903–1990). *American Psychologist, 47,* 77–78. doi:10.1037/0003-066X.47.1.77

Scott, M. M. (1980). Ecological theory and methods for research in special education. *Journal of Special Education, 14,* 279–294. doi:10.1177/002246698001400303

Scott, M. M. (1989). Pupil occupancy time in classroom settings across cultures. *Journal of Cross-Cultural Psychology, 20,* 244–266. doi:10.1177/0022022189203002

Scott, M. M. (2005). A powerful theory and a paradox: Ecological psychologists after Barker. *Environment and Behavior, 37,* 295–329. doi:10.1177/0013916504270696

Scott, M. M., & Hatfield, J. G. (1985). Problems of analyst and observer agreement in naturalistic narrative data. *Journal of Educational Measurement, 22,* 207–218. doi:10.1111/j.1745-3984.1985.tb01059.x

Taylor, R, B. (1997). Social order and disorder of street blocks and neighborhoods: Ecology, microecology, and the systemic model of social disorganization. *Journal of Research in Crime and Delinquency, 34,* 113–155. doi:10.1177/0022427897034001006

Wicker A. W. (1984). *Introduction to ecological psychology.* New York: Cambridge University Press. (Original manuscript published 1979.)

Wicker, A. W. (1987). Behavior settings reconsidered: Temporal stages, resources, internal dynamics, context. In D. Stokols & I. Altman (Eds.), *Handbook of environmental psychology* (pp. 97–122). New York: Wiley.

Wicker, A. W. (2002). Ecological psychology: Historical contexts, current conception, prospective directions. In R. B. Bechtel & A. Churchman (Eds.), *Handbook of environmental psychology* (pp. 114–126). New York: Wiley.

Wicker, A. W. (2009, May). *Toward a pragmatic ecological psychology.* Invited address presented at the meeting of the Man-Environment Research Association, Tokyo.

Willems, E. P. (1973a). Behavior-environment systems: An ecological approach. *Man-Environment Systems 3,* 79–110.

Willems, E. P. (1973b). Behavioral ecology and experimental analysis: Courtship is not enough. In J. R. Nesselroade & H. W. Reese (Eds.), *Life-span developmental psychology. Methodological issues* (pp. 127–148). Oxford: Academic Press.

Willems, E. P. (1990). Inside Midwest and its Field Station: The Barker effect. *Environment and Behavior, 22,* 468–491. doi:10.1177/0013916590224004

Willems, E. P. (2000, February 21–22). *Interview with M. M. Scott.* [Part of the Oral Histories of Ecological Psychologists Project.] Archives of the History of American Psychology, University of Akron. Available in both tape and typescript formats. (See also M. M. Scott Papers, Collection number C370, Record Container 7, Office of University Archives and Records Management, Indiana University, Bloomington.)

Wright, H. F. (1967). *Recording and analyzing child behavior.* New York: Harper & Row.

10

Robert W. White:
A Life in the Study of Lives

SUZANNE C. OUELLETTE
The City University of New York

I judged it good pedagogy, both for interest and for sound thinking, to anchor the subject right at the outset in real people's lives. (White, 1987, p. 32)

Imagine it is 1958. The United States and Russia are launching satellites; Egypt and Syria form the United Arab Republic; Elvis Presley is inducted into the U.S. army; Fidel Castro launches the Cuban revolution; the United States sends Marines into Lebanon to support its government; there is the first protest against nuclear weapons; and Paul Robeson sings at Carnegie Hall. You are sitting in an abnormal psychology class at Harvard University. It is a very large and popular class filled with psychology majors, but there are also students from other social and physical and biological science disciplines and the humanities. At the front of the class is a very tall but gentle-looking man. As he speaks, he seems deeply engaged with what he is talking about yet also very focused on the students. You are taken by this engagement, passion,

because this professor also seems generally reticent, shy even. For this class, he reviews a life history, a case study for which he has completed the first of three planned interview sessions; the second will happen in 10 years, the third in 20 years. You recognize the positive responses of those around him. For everyone in the room, and unusually for a psychology classroom, Professor Robert W. White is generating excitement about peoples' lives.

Figure 10.1   Robert W. White.
(Courtesy of David White. With permission.)

The life of the woman he talks about, the choices she has made, the things she has struggled to attain, and what she has learned through her relationships with other people are all fascinating to you. In his very calm, polite, and balanced style, Professor White reveals details and patterns. He focuses on her curiosity, what she has explored in various parts of her life, her accomplishments, and the extent to which she has changed through her life. There is little talk about her unconscious or irrational drives or reinforcement schedules. As you listen, you cannot help wondering how much Professor White's life is like or different from the life he is telling. You are drawn even more, however, to thoughts about connections between your own life and hers. You find yourself thinking about ways that you have, like her, contended with people and things in your life—ways that you would like to think you might make choices the way she did and ways that you hope you would be able to make other kinds of decisions.

Different from your experience of too many other psychology classes, you find yourself thinking and feeling, "This is why I decided to major in psychology." You are seeing and understanding something about other people and yourself that you did not see and understand before. You are feeling really smart and listened to. Encouraged by Professor White's words about how psychology is now practiced, you leave the class reflecting on your choice to seek a career in psychology. You wonder how that choice reflects your values and other commitments and how relevant it is to the needs of people in 1958. You decide to go hear that lecture being given in the history department on race relations in the United States. Also, remembering Professor White's comments about the importance of art in peoples' lives, you choose to swing by the library to pick up that novel you have been meaning to read.

Professor White leaves the class to go to his office to work a bit on his monograph, "Motivation Reconsidered: The Concept of Competence" (White, 1959). Published the next year, this piece becomes a classic and foundation for much later research, including some of what we now know as the popular field of positive psychology. After a couple of hours, he is off to a faculty meeting of Harvard's uniquely interdisciplinary Department of Social Relations, a department that he chairs. He slows his pace, however, when he remembers that stomach ulcer that tends to flare at times like this. At home, after dinner with his wife, Patsy, his high school age son, David, and Flicka, a much loved old dog, White checks in with David on how his clarinet practice is going, and then he and Patsy attend a meeting for a mental health clinic that they have helped establish in their town. Finally, at the very end of the day, White settles down for some serious planning of the family's summer. High on his list of anticipated activities is his serving as the organist for the Episcopal Church in Dublin, New Hampshire. Before turning off the light, he decides to review, one more time, his notes for tomorrow's social relations class.

AIM AND STRUCTURE OF THE CHAPTER

This vignette was inspired by White's advice to anchor the topic under discussion in real lives. Although a fictional image of White is presented here, it is based on material from White's own writings about his teaching, especially his memoir about his life as a personality psychologist (1987), and interviews with students and colleagues who knew him in the classroom. The other lives that the vignette seeks to bring into play are yours, the reader's. In this chapter, the author asks you to put your own life as someone interested in psychology in the foreground as you read. That is what White did. White's distinctive work was enabled by his willingness to challenge what he read in psychology through his examination and reflection upon his own life. He came to understand others' lives through his inquiries into himself, into his life as lived with specific others around him, and in his own society and the world more broadly understood. Use him as a model here. As you read what follows, imagine yourself in dialogue with his life and his work. Let that dialogue provoke for you some ideas and questions about your journey in psychology, including the doubts, struggles, challenges, and joys of the journey. The intention of the chapter's author is to promote what White would have called progress in lives.

In what follows, the author applies White's advice about how to do a life history (White, Riggs, & Gilbert, 1976) in a brief biography, offers some background on his early life, and provides a chronological sketch that seeks to bring in the many dimensions of White's life. Then zooming in on a particularly important turning point in his professional life, the author tries to sketch the general contours of White's contributions as a psychologist and his commitment to the study of lives through his appreciation of history and the humanities. The chapter closes with statements about how White's work remains important in contemporary psychology. There is now an increasingly strong interest in the study of lives in most of the social sciences. All of the following will set the stage for a renewed appreciation of White's work: a growing openness to qualitative methods, the influence of narrative studies, the loosening of borders between psychology and other disciplines, a concern with the relevance of social science research to the pursuit of justice, and postmodern notions such as reflexivity. Because of the intellectual concerns it shares with these currently expanding fields, contemporary students and faculty find their needs addressed in White's work. In a reconsideration of White's contributions, we look backward as a way to look ahead. The link between present and past is especially clear as we appreciate White's emphasis on the place of history in the study of lives and his recognition of the importance of the humanities, art, and literature for doing psychology.

A key source for this chapter is a memoir that Robert White wrote in 1987 about his long career as a teacher, writer, and researcher. White wrote the book 20 years after his retirement from Harvard. His retrospective view was broad as it took in many parts of psychology and the society in which it sat. The book is remarkably modest, humorous, and challenging. He was intent on sharing his personal reflections about what it meant to practice psychology. He challenged students and faculty to identify and evaluate how our selection of psychology as an academic specialty fits within the broad-based value commitments of our own lives. From the memoir, we learn ways to use personal experience and to develop the self as a research tool—skills that White characterized as prerequisites for good research. Another key source is a chronology (D. White, personal communication, January 11, 2004) of White and his family life that White's son David assembled at his father's request and in collaboration with his father. It begins in 1943 at David's birth and ends in 1992 when White was living quietly but still writing, visiting, and corresponding with former students and colleagues, consulting as a trustee emeritus for three schools, enjoying his garden, and listening to music. Other sources are more of White's publications, others' writings about White, and communications with those who did life history interviews with White and people who knew him.

BIOGRAPHICAL SKETCH

Robert W. White's life corresponded almost exactly with the full 20th century. He was born in 1904 and died at the age of 96 in 2001. His parents were of Anglo-Saxon heritage and from families with deep roots in New England. His father's family was New England Congregationalist; they had been small-business people and before that farmers. His mother's family was Episcopalian and very upper class. White was raised in comfortable circumstances in affluent suburbs of Boston, with yearly summer vacations in Maine. He was the youngest of three children, with a brother 6 years and a sister 3 years older than he. The family was a religious one with strong connections to the Episcopalian church during White's youth. Parents shared with their children the importance of a strong sense of commitment to community service and the development and practice of personal responsibility for the common good.

White's lawyer father was "deeply immersed in the idea of service" (Sollod & White, 1980, p. 13). Wanting his sons to have the same sort of social commitment, he sent them to public high school. At the time for college, White followed in the footsteps of his father, uncle, and brother and entered Harvard College in 1920. He remained there until 1926 and gained both an undergraduate and master's degree in history with particular interest in social, intellectual, and economic history. White never took a psychology course as an undergraduate and master's student. The closest he came was a sociology course and its introduction of McDougall's social psychology. He did a thesis on the English laws of primogeniture and when and how these were changed in the original 13 colonies of the United States. Throughout his time at Harvard, White pursued his very early interests and training in music and took organ lessons. He practiced daily. At 19, he became a church organist. By this point he had lost his sense of personal connection with institutional religion but was drawn to the church as a place where he could play the instrument he loved.

Unlike his pathway to college, White did not follow his father's and older brother's footsteps and become a lawyer; instead, he chose to teach. White's first academic job was teaching freshman history at the University of Maine in Orono. He was able to pair this with a job as a church organist. After 2 years in Maine, he decided to shift from history to psychology and returned to Harvard for graduate work. His return was much to the chagrin of Edwin G. Boring, then chair of the psychology department, who was not pleased by someone coming to do graduate work in his department without any background in psychology (Bales, Maybury-Lewis, Maher, & White, 2002). There was also distress for White. He could not do his graduate work in psychology and take a job as an organist. With the 80-hour week that Boring deemed essential for a psychologist in training, White had little time for the organ. He focused on his studies. Nonetheless, following 2 years of study from 1928 to 1930, he postponed further graduate school and went to Rutgers where he taught psychology at the New Jersey College for Women (now Douglass College) for 3 years. He went back to Harvard to complete his PhD from 1933 to 1937.

While a graduate student, White became associated with the Psychological Clinic at Harvard, initially when Morton Prince was its director and then under the directorship of Henry Murray. As his dissertation and a contribution to Murray's (1938) *Explorations in Personality*, White conducted a study of individual differences in hypnotizability, that is, hypnotic susceptibility. White viewed hypnosis as an interpersonal event. Hypnotizability represented a kind of capacity on the part of the person being hypnotized that emerged in the interpersonal setting. White did not connect hypnosis with any kind of esoteric unconscious depths.

White's teaching career after his degree was spent at Harvard. Following his death, the *Harvard University Gazette* described him as a professor "known for his availability to students, his willingness to listen, and his spareness of speech. About his writing, a former student once commented, 'even the footnotes are human'" (*Harvard University Gazette*, March 1, 2001). In 1937, White completed the PhD and was named both interim director of the Psychological Clinic (Murray had taken a leave) and instructor at Harvard. Until 1950, he held various research associate and lecturer positions. In 1950, in his late 40s, he was appointed professor of clinical psychology. From 1957 to 1962, he served as chair of the Department of Social Relations. He retired as emeritus professor in 1968. In a memorial statement placed in the records of the meetings of the Harvard Faculty of Arts and Sciences, his colleagues noted along with White's teaching, research, and writing contributions the uniqueness of his administrative contribution. They wrote that White managed "with kindness and tact to deal with the inevitable vicissitudes of the activities of strong minded colleagues from diverse disciplines. He truly reflected a combination of scholarship and gentleness not often seen" (Bales et al., 2002).

At age 36, 3 years following completion of his degree and appointment at the clinic, White married Margaret Ley Bazeley, whom he called "Patsy" and credited in his books with having helped him in the gathering and interpretation of life history data and his research with children. Theirs was a more than 41-year marriage that ended with Patsy's death in 1982. Although their life together was a very busy one on many private and public fronts, Patsy frequently spent time away from home and the family because of her health problems. They had two sons. The elder son, David, was close to his parents and to their love of music. He is now a music librarian. The younger son, Timothy, was born with Down syndrome and although raised outside the home remained in frequent contact with his family until his death at age 21.

White lived in homes in New England throughout all of his adult life. The chronology (D. White, personal communication, January 11, 2004) by David White depicted many households that were always very active and filled with many kinds of relatives, friends, and caretakers in residence. And there were the seemingly ever-present and greatly loved dogs. Robert White and his wife were also very involved in their communities, largely in schools, organizations that provided mental health services, and musical organizations. With regard to the last, there were small groups in which they played music and major cultural institutions like the Marlboro Festival for which they were major supporters. White's playing of the organ remained a passion throughout his life, as did his connection with art in general. In his remarks at his father's memorial service, David (D. White, personal communication, February 17, 2001) said that although teaching and university administration had filled much of his life his father "was a writer and musician from his heart and soul."

THE PROFESSIONAL PORTRAIT

A Turning Point

Critical in study of lives research is the recognition of what the person being portrayed casts as important turning points in her or his life. Made clear by the story he told in his memoir and in interviews, a key turning point in White's life was his leaving Maine and teaching history for graduate work in psychology at Harvard. As White later put it, he moved from studying "national histories to studying individual histories. That puts it well enough, the emergence in me of a greater interest in individual lives … rather than social movements" (Sollod & White, 1980, p. 4). The facilitator for this transition was Donald MacKinnon (who would go on to do important psychological studies of personality and creativity). MacKinnon had just spent a year at Harvard's Psychological Clinic with Morton Prince and Henry Murray, and he sparkled with enthusiasm about psychology. White was struck by his positivity and definiteness. In their small group of four young instructors at Orono, MacKinnon emerged as the one with the most opinions—he took positions on things and was enthusiastic about sharing them. White saw himself as being without that kind of assertiveness and confidence and wanted to learn something from MacKinnon about how one grows those things in oneself. In later life, White reflected often on his encounter with MacKinnon and shared that he had erroneously thought that one got to be the way MacKinnon was through studying psychology. Nonetheless, there was something modern about psychology and its break with traditional forms of thinking like those embodied in most religious systems that appealed to White. At 23, he felt he needed to make this kind of change.

When he arrived at Harvard, White joined the Psychological Clinic and became involved in research for the classic volume, *Explorations in Personality* (Murray, 1938). By the time of his arrival, Murray was already moving in the direction of dynamic psychology, with a psychoanalytic bent and attachment to Carl Jung. This troubled White. He found Murray too reductionistic in his emphasis on the unconscious and the Freudian and other infantile complexes. He was critical that in spite of all the methodological procedures employed with participants in the explorations study Murray was willing to overlook the taking of life histories that would cover the person's contemporary interests. Murray was willing to stop at early childhood memories and childhood secrets. White wanted to know from the young college student participants what they were like in grammar and high school, what their early friendships were like, and in what and whom they were now interested. Unlike many of the other researchers and students at the clinic, White did not go into psychoanalysis. As he later told Sollod, "I thought I would do without analysis and see what happens. And it wasn't that I felt that I didn't have problems, I felt I had plenty of problems but I had the feeling, 'Well, I'll work on them, I'll solve them myself in some way'" (Sollod & White, 1980, p. 11).

Studying Persons the Long Way

From his first days at Harvard, White turned to doing a psychology that focuses on the fullness of individual lives and on issues that involve conscious efforts and competence. This remained his focus throughout his professional life.

Robert White, in his commitment to the investigation of persons through what he called "the long way," did the study of individual lives in context over and over again. Barenbaum and Winter (2002) show in their very helpful review of the place of case studies and life histories in the history of psychology White's was a rare practice. Although prominent personality psychologists like Henry Murray and Gordon Allport wrote frequently about the value and necessity of life studies, they rarely produced them in the finished and full-blown form expected, given all that they promised. White actually did that work. Doing what Elms (1994), a key contributor to psychobiography, says is essential for the survival of a psychology that takes individuals seriously, he did the life histories. White published many studies of individual lives so that others could have both conceptual and methodological models from which to build a field.

A Psychologist and Historian

Although White formally abandoned the job of history teacher and frequently cited his conversion from the study of the history of nations to psychology and individuals by MacKinnon, he never really left a historical way of thinking in his scholarship. The writer of his obituary for the *New York Times* described him in the opening line as "a Harvard psychologist who brought a historian's perspective to the study of personality" (McCoubrey, 2001). White (1972, 1976) began *The Enterprise of Living*, the book that he described as a critical teaching tool and culmination of his "ventures into life histories," with a depiction of the historical setting in which he lived, wanting the reader to understand the context to which his book was a reaction and response:

> In a period of history marked by an unparalleled rate of change in the conditions of life, we human beings are more than ever before a puzzle to ourselves.... Yet if we aspire to improve the current social order, we are apt to be discouraged by the slow progress of cooperative endeavors and the fitful enthusiasm of participants. And we are certainly in no position to feel satisfied with our accomplishments in the way of peace and social justice. With justification we continue to be puzzled, frustrated, at times harrowed by our failure to live as we are convinced it might be possible to live. (pp. 3–4)

White's was not the abstract, universalizing way of working that has been aptly criticized by many contemporary critics of psychology. White presented a psychology modestly and seriously addressed to the particular problems and questions of its own historical period, as those problems and questions were actually experienced in the lives of ordinary people. As he prepared the different editions of textbooks like *The Abnormal Personality*, from 1948 to 1981, he changed what he wrote in important ways over the years. He was aware of the influences of time and place on his work. What was happening in the world, country, university, and psychology were all part of what he contended with as he wrote, and his writing changed as he addressed critical world events, evolving value climates, different intellectual trends and prejudices, and new research findings and their interpretations.

What remained constant across the different editions of the abnormal psychology text was White's commitment to presenting actual persons. He showed them as whole persons living with some form of what others label a mental disorder or disability. They struggle to remain aware, coherent, and effective as they contend with the many psychological, embodied, and social challenges of their diagnoses. In his commitment to this way of writing about people, White has contemporary counterparts in writers like Hornstein (2009). For White and Hornstein, as the interpersonal, institutional, social, and other challenges faced by people called mentally ill change, so does what they as psychologists write.

In his practical guides for how to do case studies, White remained the historian. In the outline that he offered on how to do a study of a life in the *Case Workbook in Personality* (White, Riggs, & Gilbert, 1976), he presented the depiction of the historical epoch as the first step in the work. This is where the psychologist who seeks to describe and understand another's life needs to begin. Historical epoch, as lived through a particular family constellation, is the first of what he calls the "chief areas in which personal growth takes place." Given that he did his case studies within a long time frame, from the mid-1930s to the late 1970s, he studied and detailed many historical epochs, as different from each other as are the U.S. Midwest in the McCarthy era and New York City's Spanish Harlem in the 1960s. White's message through his case reports is very clear. To do life studies well, the psychologist needs to understand the social, cultural, and political events and trends that characterize the time and place during which the particular life under study is being lived. This includes the histories of other individuals, families, and communities that mattered in that single life.

White's work with history showed how a biographer can be serious about both social context and the psychological reality of lives. He worked with an analytic scheme that did not force him to choose one over the other. He dedicated a long section, a chapter titled "The Shaping of Lives by Social Forces," in *Lives in Progress* (White, 1952, 1966, 1975) to a description of the many ways an individual, in this case Hartley Hale, was shaped by the culture and society of which he was a member. White did a thorough investigation of some of the key historical issues that defined Hale's context, such as the cultural ideal of competitiveness and faith in material progress so prominent between the two World Wars. And he did it as a psychologist. White recognized the value of sociological social science, yet he didn't trade in his psychologist hat. He kept it on as he showed the distinctive ways through which Hale resided in his context and contended with the dominant norms and ideologies, with his unique organization of coping styles, initiative, sense of competence, ways of identifying with others, and hopes.

There was yet another approach to history that White introduced. His life studies reflect his awareness that the life he sought to understand had both a past and a future. His analyses included a search for what came before and what might come after. In his long view of a life, he recognized the current state as what had evolved from something prior to it, and, just as important, an appreciation of how and why individuals were always involved in change. White kept the reader aware that what one observes in and concludes about the present are likely to be quite different from what one might see and learn in a later part of that life. Recognizing that history presents an ongoing series of new opportunities and challenges to individuals, White advised us in *The Enterprise of Living* to leave room for the many new ways that individuals will rise to these in pursuit of their own distinctive purposes and projects:

> …But there is a touch of creation in almost everything we do. New situations are always a little different from those that have gone before, so that there is room for initiative and innovation in every event. Actual living is at least to some extent a venture into the unknown, and it is thus inherently an enterprise. (White, 1972, 1976, p. 524)

A Psychologist and Humanist   White's words here may easily move the reader to self-reflection, to an appreciation of how one's own life is always somehow changing, in growth. White, however, also wanted us to read this as a directive to how we approach the lives of others. And here is the big challenge: How does one write another's life history and leave room for the innovative, the not yet? There is an important parallel between White's quest and the contributions of the philosopher Paul Ricoeur (1977). Found to be very helpful to contemporary researchers who seek to pursue a narrative psychology is Ricoeur's idea that a narrative can be understood through both a progressive and a regressive hermeneutics. The story another tells about one's life needs to be seen as revealing not only long-standing efforts to contend with what has happened in one's past but also future concerns and anticipations of what is yet to come in one's life. White would have agreed with this approach to interpretation.

White called for case studies that end in a spirit of questioning, openness, and humility. These qualities constituted an ethical stance in White's work and enabled the reader to remain curious about what comes next, and the participant or collaborator in the study free to go on to do what no one might have predicted. White's view of life studies is a gift to a teacher of contemporary courses in the study of lives. Current students, in part as a result of their familiarity with postmodern and poststructuralist ideas and critical cultural studies, are frequently made uncomfortable by case studies and psychobiographies presented as the "final word" on another's whole life (cf. Rosenwald, 2003). Students are mistrustful of texts that claim full explanation of a person's present behavior in terms of early life determinants or a set of fixed unconscious processes that are unaffected by any environmental influences. They want room to be able to ask questions like "Who am I to say this about another?" and "How am I to know that this is about another person and not just me?" They also want to be able to write about the movement in a life that continues after they stop writing. White's approach offers a way of addressing the questions that feminist practitioners of the study of lives like Hornstein (1994) and Josselson (1996) raised about the ethics of life history research and the responsibilities we take on as we write the lives of others. I think White would have understood Hornstein's rule not to reveal something about the life of her subject (in Hornstein's case, Frieda Fromm Reichmann) that she would not be able to tell a friend about her friend's life. He would support Josselson's urging that we consider the influence of our own narcissism on how we write and what we do with what we write about another (through conference papers, publications, and other public statements).

The consideration of creativity, openness, and ethics brings us to another of White's special kinds of inspiration: the way he directed us to look beyond the typical borders of psychology. The complexity of personality was a defining issue in White's work. It appeared in his comments on others' work, such as in his early critique of Hull's views of hypnosis, his case studies, and his reflections on his own life. With regard to the last, note the extent to which White in his memoir presented self-confidence as a contested concept. For White, it was a reason for both admiration and regret about another person's self-display.

To capture the complexity in others' lives and one's own, White advised us to go beyond the ways of seeing that typically characterize psychology done strictly as a science in what is thought to be the physical science mode. He told us to draw on other ways of seeing that are practiced in the arts, humanities, and literature. White did this throughout his life. For example, when he sought to describe the psychological consequences of prejudice in the lives of Black Americans, he turned to the novels of Black writers like Richard Wright and James Baldwin for their depictions of human character. His special attachment to music emerged in his psychological work. His strong and long-lasting tie to music was well expressed in that wonderful statement he wrote to Jim Anderson about hearing Erik Erikson deliver a paper on a child: "It was like hearing great music for the very first time" (Anderson, personal communication, August, 2000). In his memoir, he made use of musical terms like *scherzo* and *divertimento*. These introduced playfulness but also suggested metaphors that could usefully be mined in research on lives (cf. Gregg, 1995).

White was clear about the dangers connected with personality psychologists' failure to take advantage of other fields of human endeavor. In a letter to Rae Carlson in May 1983, White wrote:

> Personologists must have a basic conviction that people's lives are worth studying in themselves. Knowledge of a lot of lives can be a source of wisdom, a liberal education, just as knowledge of history and the social sciences contributes to wisdom and liberal education. Personologists do not regard the study of lives merely as a source of hypotheses for more controlled investigations, although it can be used for this purpose. Understanding lives is an end in itself.... A personologist's sense of identity should not be founded on being a scientific psychologist. Considering the fairly small range of problems of personality that can be drawn into experimental or quantitative forms, defining oneself simply as a scientist pushes away the whole background of humanistic study—biography, history, social sciences—and confines the personologist to

the fringes of people's lives. In the realm of lives, thinking of oneself only as a scientific psychologist is a serious form of constriction.

ONGOING INFLUENCE OF WHITE'S WORK

White's work provides students a way of coming back to a psychology that is concerned with persons as individuals. For me, as a faculty member in a social/personality psychology program with strong commitments to social justice research, students have often had their heads turned by postmodern and critical scholarly currents in the academy. For many graduate students, encounters with Foucault, critical psychology, feminism, queer theory, and other sources of inspiration have left them doubtful that they can place whole persons at the center of their focus and do systematic and useful scholarly work. White corrects for that. White's demonstration of the importance of history for psychological study together with his emphasis on doing psychology as the study of lives provide a way of recapturing students' attention and keeping the person in a broad view. White rejoins the individual with society, culture, and the political. He enables us to recognize the power of structures that contemporary scholarship has so emphasized and not to let go of concerns with persons, personality, and individual development.

White also provides responses to a second kind of threat that psychology students concerned about social issues often feel. Given the current emphasis on biology, genes, and functional magnetic resonance imaging (fMRI) machines, students need some reassurance that what Runyan calls the "softer" ways of doing psychology still matter (Runyan, 2005). White offers a compelling vision of the meaningfulness of what a psychology of the whole person can contribute to society generally and to those who practice psychology. White's work reflects an inspiring sensibility that in no small part is based in his willingness to join psychology with other social science disciplines and the arts and humanities. Students can follow White as he struggles throughout his work to find his place in the discipline and then experience psychology's worth as he stretches it beyond its typical disciplinary borders.

There are many signs that this is a time for enthusiastic receptivity within psychology for a researcher who placed such a strong emphasis on the study of lives. Several publications within mainstream psychological arenas make the point. There is the recent *Handbook of Psychobiography* edited by Todd Shultz (2005) that is chock-full of life studies. Oxford University Press, the press that published this handbook, also recently initiated a new series of short biographies. A recent entry is a life study of George W. Bush by Dan McAdams (McAdams, 2010). There are several collections of women's lives by feminist authors. In these, one finds work like that of Brinton Lykes (1994), who intensively studies individual women's lives lived in the rich diversity and challenge of the structures associated with gender, sexual orientation, race, ethnicity, and other power relations. Gary Gregg's (2007) recent book on young adults in Northern Africa brings back personality and culture studies through his integration of the study of lives tradition and solid cultural and political analysis. Some important books also offer analysis of the lives of the people who shaped the very ways we now think about lives, such as Amy Demorest's (2005) book on Sigmund Freud, B. F. Skinner, and Carl Rogers that shows the links between their lives and their work. There are pieces that combine biography and social and cultural history. Good examples of this are in the work of Ian Nicholson, especially his studies of the early stages of Gordon Allport's (Nicholson, 2003) life and work and his amazing chapter on S. S. Stevens (Nicholson, 2005) in the Schultz handbook.

A growing number of reports of narrative and other forms of qualitative research not only present the results of particular studies of lives but also attend to important problems such as how to train others to do life studies within the typical constraints of university settings. An issue of the series on the narrative studies of lives devoted to teaching is a good example of this (Josselson, Lieblich, & McAdams, 2003). Schultz's (2005) handbook for psychobiography provides students with specific conceptual and methodological strategies that they need to do their own research in this arena. Professors who teach the study of lives may soon find themselves relying a little less on the sociology and anthropology sections of the library for syllabus entries (cf. Plummer, 1995). Thanks to researcher/teacher/ editors like Weis and Fine (2000), who brought together important examples of both what goes right and what goes wrong as students launch into qualitative research, psychology students can now read what their peers and mentors in their chosen field write. This matters seriously for the maintenance and evolution of the study of lives tradition in psychology.

With all of these resources at hand, current students of psychology can practice the kind of study of lives that Robert White hoped would one day thrive in and outside the academy. As psychologists, we can now do what others in fields such as history, anthropology, and sociology have been able to do—namely, use the study of an individual life as the means for *revealing* social structures and ideologies. We learn about society and culture as we learn about the particular unique person. White's hold on a historical way of working and his willingness to go beyond the boundaries set for psychology as a science continue to be important guides for personally and collectively meaningful research.

SUGGESTED READINGS

White, R. W. (1948). *The abnormal personality*. New York: Wiley.

    In his first book, White used what he had learned from his teaching experiences and wrote with students in mind. The book was a big success and went through four later editions, the last in 1981. For more than 2 decades, it was the leading textbook in abnormal psychology. White does not offer disembodied diagnostic categories. Instead we find life histories of individuals living in their social and historical contexts as they contend with what others label a mental disorder. His focus is on the development of the neurotic symptoms with less attention to psychoses.

White, R. W. (1952, 1966, 1975). *Lives in progress: A study of the natural growth in personality*. New York: Holt, Rinehart, & Winston.

    White provides us with studies of the lives of three psychologically healthy individuals—we meet them in all of their complexity, indeed as lives in progress, over time, first when they are college age, then again as young adults, and then finally in mid-adulthood. Chapters in the book formally present different psychological perspectives through which the life histories could be differently and richly understood.

Lives in Progress offers the study of lives as a legitimate alternative approach to a discipline of psychology too often preoccupied with single variables and neglectful of whole individual persons.

White, R. W., Smith, M. B., & Bruner, J. (1956). *Opinions and personality*. New York: John Wiley & Sons.

White, Smith, and Bruner wrote a book that recognized the wisdom of the idea that the personal is the political and that the political is the personal. Through three case studies, the book examines the connections between a person's political views and her or his personality and development.

White, R. W. (1959). Motivation reconsidered: The concept of competence. *Psychological Review*, 297–333.

This is thought to be White's chief theoretical contribution to psychology, a monograph in which he provided a new way of thinking about human behavior that emphasized our inclinations to be curious, to explore our environments, to be effective and competent in the world. White filled out the possibilities of what it means to be human. He enabled us to see much more than we do in the portrayals that are based in simple behavioristic drive-reduction theories or psychodynamic motivational conflict frameworks of the mid-twentieth century.

REFERENCES

Bales, R. F., Maybury-Lewis, D. H. P., Maher, B. A., & White, S. H. (2002). FAS Memorial minute: Robert Winthrop White. *Harvard University Gazette*, May 23. Retrieved from http://www.news.harvard.edu/gazette/2002/05.23/18-memorialminute.html

Barenbaum, N., & Winter, D. (2002). Personality: Case studies and life histories in personality psychology. In I. B. Weiner (Series Ed.) & D. K. Freedheim (Vol. Ed.), *Comprehensive handbook of psychology: Vol. 1. History of psychology* (pp. 177–203). New York: Wiley.

Demorest, A. (2005). *Psychology's grand theorists: How personal experiences shaped professional ideas*. Mahwah, NJ: Erlbaum.

Elms, A. C. (1994). *Uncovering lives: The uneasy alliance of biography and psychology*. New York: Oxford University Press.

Gregg, G. (1995). Multiple identities and the integration of personality. *Journal of Personality, 63*, 617–641. doi:10.1111/j.1467-6494.1995.tb00508.x

Gregg, G. (2007). *Culture and identity in a Muslim society*. New York: Oxford University Press.

Harvard University Gazette, March 1, 2001, R. W. White, personality psychologist, dies at 96. Retrieved from http://www.news.harvard.edu/gazette/2001/03.01/04-white.html

Hornstein, G. A. (1994). The ethics of ambiguity: Feminists writing women's lives. In C. E. Franz & A. J. Stewart (Eds.), *Women creating lives: Identities, resilience, & resistance* (pp. 51–70). Boulder, CO: Westview Press.

Hornstein, G. A. (2009). *Agnes' jacket: A psychologist's search for the meaning of madness*. New York: Rodale Books.

Josselson, R. (1996). On writing other people's lives: Self-analytic reflections of a narrative researcher. In R. Josselson (Ed.), *The narrative study of lives: Vol. 4. Ethics and process* (pp. 60–72). Thousand Oaks, CA: Sage.

Josselson, R., Lieblich, A., & McAdams, D. (Eds.). (2003). *Up close and personal: The teaching and learning of narrative research*. Washington, DC: American Psychological Association.

Lykes, M. B. (1994). Speaking against the silence: One Maya woman's exile and return. In C. E. Franz & A. J. Stewart (Eds.), *Women creating lives: Identities, resilience, and resistance* (pp. 97–114). Boulder, CO: Westview Press.

McAdams, D. (2010). *George W. Bush and the redemptive dream: A psychological portrait.* New York: Oxford University Press.

McCoubrey, C. (2001, February 20). Robert White, psychologist who specialized in personality, dies at 96. *New York Times.*

Murray, H. A. (1938). *Explorations in personality.* New York: Oxford University Press.

Nicholson, I. (2003). *Inventing personality: Gordon Allport and the science of selfhood.* Washington, DC: American Psychological Association. doi:10.1037/10514-000

Nicholson, I. (2005). From the book of Mormon to the operational definition: The existential project of S. S. Stevens. In W. T. Schultz (Ed.), *Handbook of psychobiography* (pp. 285–298). New York: Oxford University Press.

Plummer, K. (1995). Life story research. In J. A. Smith, R. Harre, & L. Van Langenhove (Eds.), *Rethinking methods in psychology* (pp. 50–63). Thousand Oaks, CA: Sage.

Ricoeur, P. (1977). *Freud & philosophy: An essay on interpretation.* New Haven, CT: Yale University Press.

Rosenwald, G. C. (2003). Task, process, and discomfort in the interpretation of life histories. In R. Josselson, A. Lieblich, & D. McAdams (Eds.), *Up close and personal: The teaching and learning of narrative research* (pp. 135–150). Washington, DC: American Psychological Association. doi:10.1037/10486-008

Runyan, W. M. (2005). Evolving conceptions of psychobiography and the study of lives. In W. T. Schultz (Ed.), *Handbook of psychobiography* (pp. 19–41). New York: Oxford University Press.

Schultz, W. T. (Ed.). (2005). *Handbook of psychobiography.* New York: Oxford University Press.

Smith, M. B., Bruner, J. S., & White, R. W. (1956). *Opinions and personality.* New York: John Wiley & Sons.

Sollod, R. N., & White, R. W. (1980). Robert W. White and the origins of the concept of competence: An interview. Interviewed by R. N. Sollod, *The Sollod Papers.* Archives of the History of American Psychology, Box M1045, University of Akron.

Weis, L., & Fine, M. (Eds.). (2000). *Speed bumps: A student friendly guide to qualitative research.* New York: Teachers College Press.

White, R. W. (1948, 1956, 1964, 1973) [with N. F. Watt], 1981 [with Watt]. *The abnormal personality.* New York: John Wiley & Sons.

White, R. W. (1952, 1966, 1975). *Lives in progress: A study of the natural growth of personality.* New York: Holt, Rinehart & Winston.

White, R. W. (1959). Motivation reconsidered: The concept of competence. *Psychological Review, 66,* 297–333. doi:10.1037/h0040934

White, R. W. (1972, 1976). *The enterprise of living: A view of personality.* New York: Holt, Rinehart & Winston.

White, R. W. (1987). *A memoir: Seeking the shape of personality.* Marlborough, NH: Homestead.

White, R. W., Riggs, M. M., & Gilbert, D. C. (1976). *Case workbook in personality.* New York: Holt, Rinehart & Wilson.

11

Joseph McVicker Hunt:
Golden Age Psychologist

WADE E. PICKREN
Ryerson University

In 1951, Joseph (Joe) McVicker Hunt left New York City for the Department of Psychology at the University of Illinois. Hunt had already made several important contributions to American psychology by this time, but the move to Illinois led him into a golden period of work and influence from the time he arrived until his retirement in 1974 and even into a long and active retirement. These were the peak years of his intellectual and professional life. He initially served as the coordinator of training in clinical and counseling psychology.

He was the director of the influential Ford Foundation Grant for the Behavioral Sciences, and, as detailed in this chapter, he made his most important and substantive contributions to the understanding of the development of human intelligence while at Illinois.

Figure 11.1   Joseph McVicker Hunt, 1952.
(Courtesy of the University of Illinois at Urban-Champaign Archives. With permission.)

This was the Golden Age of American psychology (Rice, 2005), and Illinois was among the most gilded centers of psychology. Hunt joined an impressive roster of American psychologists at the University of Illinois—Raymond Cattell, Lyle Lanier, Paul T. Young, and Charles Osgood were leaders in the field, junior faculty included Robert Glaser and Arthur Irion, and present at the university were such prominent psychologists as O. Hobart Mowrer, Society for the Study of Psychological Issues cofounder Ross Stagner, and comparative psychologist turned clinical psychology pioneer C. M. "Red" Louttit (Farreras, 2005). Also at the university was George Stoddard, by this time a grand old man of American psychology.

Into this favorable atmosphere Joe Hunt brought a solid record of achievement and the honor of having been elected as the president of the American Psychological Association. He had built this stellar professional life on a foundation of education and training in Nebraska and New York. But it all began in western Nebraska, a state that was the birthplace of a number of other important pioneers of psychology.

O! NEBRASKA: FROM SCOTTSBLUFF TO LINCOLN

Willa Cather's trilogy of prairie novels—two of which are set in Nebraska—tells about the rich and often difficult life on the prairies (Cather, 1913, 1915, 1918). Nebraska farm life proved a rich soil for the growth of American psychologists for such pioneers as Harry Kirke Wolfe (1858–1918; see volume 5), Harry L. Hollingworth (1880–1956; see volume 2), and Leta Stetter Hollingworth (1886–1939, see volume 1). All spent some or all of their formative years on Nebraska farms. Wolfe returned to teach at Nebraska after earning his doctoral degree with Wilhelm Wundt and taught three future American Psychological Association (APA) presidents at the University of Nebraska.

It was on a farm in a setting much like that described by Cather where Joseph McVicker Hunt was born on March 19, 1906. His parents, R. Sanford and Carrie Pearl (McVicker) Hunt, were both graduates of the University of Nebraska at Lincoln, and that is where Joe enrolled in the mid-1920s. By his own admission (Hunt, 1974), Joe was a busy student with many interests, both academic and nonacademic. He participated in football and wrestling, became president of both the Student Christian Association and the League of Industrial Democracy, wrote for the student newspaper, and sold life insurance on the side for a little spending money.

Joe had great difficulty in choosing his undergraduate major. He tried several, beginning with business, then switched to philosophy, then on to biology and then to sociology. In addition to classes for his various majors, Joe enrolled in courses in chemistry, physics, mathematics, economics, English, and history, that is, almost everything but psychology. Joe Hunt had eclectic intellectual interests to say the least, but his curiosity also helped prepare him for a fruitful career as a person capable of drawing from diverse knowledge traditions. By his junior year, Joe realized that he was not sure of what he wanted to do for a career. Nevertheless, he became engaged to Esther Dahms that year, with a plan for teaching English in Japan after graduation as a way to defer the need to make a decision. Those plans for teaching fell through, but not his engagement, and he and Esther were married on Christmas Day 1929 and remained married until her death in 1989.

So how did Joseph McVicker Hunt get to psychology? His journey into psychology began with the return of another Nebraskan to the university. Joy Paul Guilford (1897–1987), born in Marquette, earned his BA and MA at Nebraska and then his doctoral degree at Cornell in 1927. After teaching for a year at the University of Illinois and the University of Kansas, Guilford returned to his alma mater to direct the psychology laboratory. On the advice of his sociology professor that psychology would be a good supplement for work in sociology, Joe enrolled in the senior course in psychology taught by Guilford. He liked the course well enough that when Guilford asked him to consider graduate work in psychology under his (Guilford's) direction, Joe accepted, even though the graduate assistantship in psychology paid less than ones in zoology or sociology. So in September 1929, Joe Hunt became a graduate student in psychology at the University of Nebraska.

Guilford headed the one-person graduate program in psychology at Nebraska. Joe Hunt began his MA in 1929 with four other graduate students. The small size of the graduate program did not prevent the students from getting a thorough education in psychology. Joe and the other students were thoroughly immersed in statistics, psychometrics, and laboratory research. Guilford pushed the students to learn on their own and to pursue interests beyond the formal course instruction. As often happens in graduate school settings, Joe mingled with students from other graduate programs and was an active participant in informal seminars that drew from sociology, biology, psychology, and other fields.

It was in one such group that Joe Hunt became intrigued with psychoanalytic theory. He had already decided to use the personality traits of introversion and extraversion, as described by William McDougall, for his master's thesis. However, discussions with other students, combined with reading the work of Sigmund Freud and Carl Jung, convinced Hunt of the importance of early life experience in shaping personality. This was his first direct foray into developmental issues, and it was soon followed by another, more practical, set of experiences.

The director of the Nebraska Home for Dependent Children, an orphanage, decided that having the children undergo intelligence testing would help in adoption placement. When he asked Guilford for assistance, Guilford assigned Joe Hunt to the task. Joe, of course, had no experience and no training in intelligence testing. He borrowed the 1916 version of the Stanford-Binet Tests of Intelligence from the psychology department, books on testing from the library, and set out to learn how to be a tester. He practiced on the children of friends and finally began testing the children at the home. Given his later seminal work on intelligence and children's development, this proved to be one of those life-altering events.

Joe earned his MA in 1930 and that fall became an assistant instructor at the university. He was responsible for directing the laboratory experiences for the introductory psychology course as well as for a course on psychological testing. Not only did he teach and conduct psychological tests for the Home for Dependent Children, but he also began to offer psychotherapy under the auspices of the university's Psychological Clinic at the fresh young age of 24. Perhaps his most remarkable case was that of a young woman diagnosed as a psychoneurotic, whom Joe treated with a combination of dream analysis and hypnotherapy.

HEADING EAST: CORNELL, BROWN, AND NEW YORK CITY

After a year of teaching, Joe and Esther departed for his doctoral study at Cornell University in Ithaca, New York. His doctoral supervisor at Cornell was another Nebraskan, Madison Bentley, who had also done his graduate work at Cornell.

Moving to Cornell was definitely moving to the mainstream of American experimental psychology from the frontier of Nebraska. The psychology department had been led for many years by E. B. Titchener, one of the giants of early experimental psychology (see Volume 1). Although Titchener's structural approach to psychology had yielded pride of place to the functionalism of William James and others, Cornell was still one of the preeminent graduate programs in American psychology at this time.

For Joe Hunt, doctoral work at Cornell helped him begin the formation of a rich network of friends and colleagues that became instrumental to his own rise to prominence in American psychology. He earned his PhD in 1933 with a thesis on perceptual judgment, but this was done more to please Bentley than out of a deep commitment to perceptual research. What was more important for Hunt was the opportunity to review the extant experimental psychological literature on mental disorders (Hunt, 1936). As it turned out, doing the review helped prepare him for the next step in his career.

Growth and Diversification of Psychology between the World Wars

Before turning to Hunt's next move, though, it would be instructive to look at experimental psychology at this time in relation to trends in the field and to place Hunt in his cohort. By the 1930s, American psychology had quietly begun to diversify its topics and methods. Traditional textbook historical accounts (e.g., Schultz & Schultz, 2008) typically relate how neobehaviorism came to dominate American psychology in the 1930s. As far as it goes, this is true, but it does not go far enough. The number of laboratory-based experimental psychologists was actually quite small even among the members of the APA. However, the leaders of the APA tended to be those who were or had been experimentalists, and the rhetoric they used made it seem as though the only real science of psychology was that practiced in traditional laboratories.

The growth and diversification of psychology had begun after World War I ended. Applied psychology grew rapidly in the period between the World Wars (Napoli, 1981), as the percentage of APA members—and a significant number of psychologists were not APA members—reporting applied and professional work increased from 9.3% in 1916 to 39% in 1940 (Finch & Odoroff, 1939, 1941). Psychologists began to work in an astonishing array of settings: schools, clinics, hospitals, prisons, industry, advertising, and many others (see Finch & Odoroff, 1939, 1941; Napoli, 1981). It was during this period that psychology truly found a fit with the larger American society and took on its particularly American hue (Pickren, 2010).

Psychology also diversified in its attempts to address social issues (e.g., Nicholson, 1997). In fact, it was in the mid-1930s that a group of mostly junior psychologists founded the Society for the Psychological Study of Social Issues (Finison, 1979, 1986), along with the formation in New York City of the Psychologists League, whose members actively sought social change and increased employment of psychologists.

New topic areas and fields in psychology also emerged. Social and personality psychology became distinct fields (Nicholson, 2003), as did developmental psychology

(Smuts, 2008). What later became Industrial and Organizational Psychology but was then typically referred to as Business Psychology, took off from its prewar beginnings at places like the Carnegie Institute of Technology. Psychologists from several fields began to study psychopathology. New tests were introduced, including the Rorschach Projective Technique, which rapidly became the most widely used test, and the Minnesota Multiphasic Personality Inventory (Buchanan, 1994). These tests were used in clinics, hospitals, and private offices throughout America, and their use helped lay the foundation for the explosive growth of the redefined field of clinical psychology after World War II.

The Remarkable Cohort of Psychologists Between the World Wars

Hunt was trained as a psychologist as part of what, in retrospect, was a remarkable group of psychologists. This cohort led the way in the postwar boom in psychology. Only a few names are listed here to give a sense of this dynamic group: Theodora Abel, Donald Adams, J. F. Brown, C. R. Carpenter, Ward Halstead, Molly Harrower, E. R. Hilgard, Carlyle Jacobsen, Elaine Kinder, Otto Klineberg, Carney Landis, Donald Lindsley, C. M. Louttit, Norman Maier, Abraham Maslow, Neal Miller, O. H. Mowrer, Carl Rogers, T. C. Schneirla, David Shakow, B. F. Skinner, Robert White, and Herman Witkin, just to name a small number. Given the size of the field at the time, this proved to be a rich period for the training of psychological scientists and clinicians. It was this group that was able to seize the day after World War II and lead psychology into its Golden Age of the 1950s and 1960s (Rice, 2005).

Clinicians and scientists are mentioned, though, of course, psychologists were trained as scientists first and then took up clinical work. David Shakow, founder of the training model that still guides most North American clinical psychology PhD programs, developed his clinical expertise with a long stint as research director at Worcester State Hospital. There he trained many of those who went on to become leaders in modern clinical psychology. Molly Harrower earned her doctorate with Kurt Koffka at Smith in 1934 and turned first to hospital-based neuropsychological research with Kurt Goldstein and Wilder Penfield and then developed the Group Rorschach during WWII and became one of America's leading clinical psychologists after the war. Neal Miller earned his PhD at Yale (1935) after a year of didactic psychoanalysis in Germany and then began one of the most distinguished careers in all of American science, including seminal research on learning theory and psychoanalysis, and the development of biofeedback. And the examples go on and on of important and transformative research and practice by this cohort; this was perhaps the most illustrious group ever to emerge together in American psychology. Joe Hunt was an important member of this group.

From NRC Fellow to Personality and the Behavior Disorders

Once Hunt completed his doctoral degree in 1933, he was faced with a quandary. This was the Great Depression, and jobs were few. Many young psychologists and recent graduates simply could not find academic employment, and when they did it was often more a matter of underemployment. The leadership of APA refused to get involved in the employment issue, which created disgruntlement and led to such new organizations as the Psychologists League in New York (Finison, 1978).

A small number of young psychologists were able to obtain one of the few postdoctoral fellowships then available, those from the National Research Council (NRC). The NRC fellowships had been created in 1919 for young scientists in physics and chemistry; they were extended to the medical sciences in 1922 and then to biological sciences, including psychology, in 1923. Between 1923 and 1945, 93 young psychologists held NRC fellowships, some, including Joe Hunt, for 2 years (National Research Council, 1945). (Many of the young psychologists mentioned in the previous section also held NRC fellowships.)

Hunt's fellowship was awarded for research on the topic "An investigation of the immediate antecedents of psychological activity in the abnormal." With $2070 of fellowship support, he spent the first year at the New York Psychiatric Institute with Carney Landis, William Hunt, the young Joseph Zubin (Zubin & Zubin, 1977), and the renowned Rorschach specialist Zygmunt Piotrowski (Pickren, 2000). As Hunt (1974) noted in his autobiography, he brought a certain kind of narrow-mindedness to the Institute, which initially hampered his ability to benefit from the rich setting. A number of studies were under way at the time Hunt was a fellow there, especially those on schizophrenia, and he was able to gain experience working with seriously mentally ill patients in a research setting. As he noted, perhaps the biggest benefit for him was the extension of his personal and professional network, as he met some of the leaders of psychology who were based in New York City, including Gardner Murphy, Albert Poffenberger, and Robert S. Woodworth (see volume 6).

Hunt applied for and received a second year of his NRC fellowship. With that support, he spent a year at Worcester State Hospital in Massachusetts. David Shakow was the chief psychologist at Worcester and was leading a highly productive research team on schizophrenia (see Shakow, 1972, for a substantive history of this research). As noted, this was the period when Shakow was developing his model of training clinical psychologists as scientists-practitioners, a model that was institutionalized in 1949 at the Boulder Conference (Raimy, 1950). Shakow accepted as students and trainees a number of foreign students who went on to important careers in clinical psychology after the war (Woodward, 2010), and these students helped expose Hunt to many of the nuances of clinical work with seriously mentally ill patients. Most of all, this was a year for Joe to gain rich clinical experiences. He was further exposed to the Rorschach and the seminars on psychoanalysis led by Earl Zinn, a former student of G. Stanley Hall. As in New York, so in Worcester, the personal contacts proved just as important as the psychological research. While in Worcester, Hunt made a close connection with the psychologists at Clark University in Worcester. This group included Donald B. Lindsley and Edward Kemp, but most importantly it was led by Walter Hunter, a key figure in American psychology at that time. Hunt made a favorable impression on Hunter, and when the latter moved to Brown University in 1936 he invited Joe Hunt to become an instructor on the staff of the psychology department. Before going to Brown, though, Hunt taught at the University of Nebraska for the fall term of 1935 and then spent a half-year at St. Elizabeth's Hospital in Washington, DC, where he served under one of the great figures of American psychological medicine, William Alanson White. It is worth noting that at both Worcester State Hospital and St. Elizabeth's Joe's interest in the importance of early life experiences was heightened, primarily within a psychoanalytic framework.

Finally, Joe Hunt had a regular academic appointment. As he later put it, Brown University was an "advantageous place to begin an academic career" (Hunt, 1974, p. 157). The faculty was small, and there were frequent opportunities for scholarly interaction with colleagues from multiple departments. Hunter attracted quite a few talented young psychologists to the department, and there was a palpable excitement in the laboratories (Arkowitz & Bartlett, 2002). In addition to the opportunities at the university, the department also had close connections with the nearby Butler Hospital and the Bradley Home in East Providence.

Over the next 10 years, Brown University emerged as a center of research in experimental psychopathology, much of it attempts to investigate Freudian concepts in the laboratory with animals. This was happening in other psychology departments as well (Hornstein, 1992; Pickren, 1995). Some years ago, in correspondence with Neil Bartlett who was a graduate student in the late 1930s and early 1940s at Brown, Bartlett confided that the psychologists on the staff believed that "somehow science must seize on his [Freud's] ideas, straighten them out, and turn the magic of science and the laboratory on it and then we will truly have a theory and a practice to worship" (Neil Bartlett, personal communication, February 9, 1995).

Two of Hunt's collaborators at Brown during this period were Harold Schlosberg and Raymond R. Willoughby. Hunt and Schlosberg conducted research on hoarding in rats while also attempting to induce neuroses in them experimentally (Hunt & Schlosberg, 1939). In the hoarding study, one group of infant rats was given access to an unlimited food supply and the other group experienced irregular feedings. As might have been predicted by Freudian theory, the irregularly fed rats tended to hoard their food as adults, while the unlimited feeding group did not. Hunt interpreted these findings as support for the psychoanalytic assertion that early life experience is a determinant of adult behavior (Hunt, 1941).

Hunt collaborated with Ray Willoughby on a study that compared deprivation and frustration as possible sources of hoarding behavior in rats. They concluded that, in their study, deprivation provided a more powerful explanation than frustration. This work was published in the new journal *Psychosomatic Medicine* (Hunt & Willoughby, 1939) and is a good example of the extension of psychological research into medical questions.

Perhaps the most important accomplishment of Hunt during his 10 years at Brown was the production of the magisterial *Personality and the Behavior Disorders* (Hunt, 1944). Truly one of the landmark publications (in two volumes) of midcentury American psychology, the two volumes both summarized extant work relevant to personality and mental disorders as well as providing a template for future research. The two volumes, much like their editor, were eclectic and wide-ranging. Contributors included experimental psychologists, psychiatrists, psychoanalysts, endocrinologists, internists, neurologists, sociologists, and anthropologists. From the ranks of psychology, junior and midcareer psychologists dominated, indicating the changing interests and experimental emphases under way in psychology that would rapidly accelerate after the war.

Psychodynamic, if not strict psychoanalytic, approaches infused most of the chapters by psychologists and psychiatrists. Hunt initially took on authorship of two chapters—one on the general meaning of abnormality and one on the concept of psychological deficits. Space considerations led him to withdraw his chapter on the meaning of abnormality, but the chapter on deficits (with Charles Cofer) was a masterly summation of what was then known about the development of psychological deficits.

The two volumes were published in 1944 and garnered praise from across the domains covered by the book. Not only did the publication serve as a benchmark for what was known and as a signpost to future research, but it also propelled Joe Hunt into the forefront of his generation of American psychologists.

Expanding Opportunities in New York City, 1946–1951

Before long, Hunt was looking for new employment. Although he had an extremely productive career at Brown with accompanying rise in professional stature, his salary and prospects at Brown had not risen with him. Now deeply embedded in the elite professional network of Eastern psychologists, Joe began to look for new opportunities. This led to a collaborative research project with John Dollard, then of Yale's Institute of Human Relations (Morawski, 1986). Dollard had been requested by the Institute of Welfare Research, a branch of the Community Service Society of New York City, to evaluate the success of the institute's case-work. To what extent, the institute wanted to know, did the interventions improve the lives of their clients? The collaboration with Dollard led in 1946 to the position of director of the institute, which Hunt held for 5 years.

This was the beginning of the great growth period of American psychology, which reflected the thorough psychologization of American society (Smith, 1997). Suddenly, it seemed, psychological expertise was in demand. At the institute, Hunt hired a competent and dedicated professional staff made up primarily of psychologists. They developed tools to assess client change, which were later adapted to suit college counseling centers (Hunt, LaForge, Ewing, & Gilbert, 1959).

There was a great increase in the training of psychologists, especially in clinical and counseling psychology, which is elaborated next. Hunt became involved in training programs both at Teachers College (Columbia) and at New York University. At Teachers College, Hunt was recruited by Laurence Shaffer to teach the clinical students, and at New York University (NYU) Lyle Lanier enlisted him to teach methodology. As was the norm for Hunt, these proved to be important personal as well as professional connections. Shaffer and Hunt worked together in the leadership of APA during this time, with Hunt elected president for 1951–1952, and Shaffer immediately succeeding him. Lyle Lanier left NYU in 1951 to become chair at the University of Illinois and recruited Hunt to become a professor there. During his time at the institute, Joe made another important personal and professional connection. Joe met and became friends with Don Young, the executive director of the Russell Sage Foundation. Not long after leaving New York, the Sage

Foundation funded his return to research and writing on the impact of early life experience on later development.

THE GOLDEN AGE OF PSYCHOLOGY

American psychology was a growth industry in the quarter century after the end of World War II. The number of psychologists grew so rapidly that one person noted that if the current rate of growth continued, by 2010 every person in the world would be a psychologist. In 1950, there were 1498 APA members; in 1960, APA membership was 14,569. Clearly, something happened.

American science, including psychology, was transformed by the events of World War II. For the first time on a large scale, scientists and government agencies developed close relationships, as the government invested heavily in scientific research related to war needs and recruited scientists to serve both in uniform and in advisory capacities. Psychologists became heavily involved in many areas of research, as they applied their skills to serve their nation (Capshew, 1999; Herman, 1995; Hoffman, 1992). For the first time, too, psychologists benefited from sizable government contracts and grants that facilitated their basic as well as applied research. Clinical psychology, a minor field before the war, experienced rapid growth as the military's needs required an increase in personnel devoted to psychological assessment. By 1943, it became clear that the army did not have enough psychiatrists to deliver psychological counseling or therapy to soldiers in the field or in military hospitals, so psychologists were recruited to become psychotherapists. By the end of the war, the number of army clinical psychologists was 450, and at least a quarter of their time was spent offering therapy and counseling to soldiers (see Pickren & Rutherford, 2010, Chapter 9).

The war also made mental disorders salient to American political and military leaders. While 14 million Americans served in uniform during the war, nearly 2 million men were rejected by the Selective Service on the grounds of psychiatric problems or mental deficiencies. Of those who were inducted, nearly 500,000 were discharged due to mental problems. These numbers do not reveal how many suffered during the war but were able to return to service due to treatment or passage of time. Certainly, it is known that many suffered from what was then labeled combat stress or combat fatigue (Shephard, 2000).

One item that caught policymakers' eyes after the war was the high percentage (60%) of veterans with psychiatric disorders in Veterans Administration (VA) hospitals (Baker & Pickren, 2007). What made this situation worse was the acute shortage of mental health professionals in America. There were simply not enough psychiatrists or psychiatric nurses to meet the pressing needs of the veterans, let alone the general population. As a result, two large-scale training programs were instituted, one in the VA and one in the newly created National Institute of Mental Health (Pickren & Schneider, 2005). Four professions were targeted for growth: psychiatry, psychiatric nursing, social work, and clinical psychology. Over the next 4 decades, hundreds of millions of dollars were invested in the training of mental health professionals. The growth of the psychological professions altered the landscape of American life.

Concurrent with the emphasis on training more mental health professionals was a new emphasis on funding research relevant to mental health. On July 3, 1946, President Harry Truman signed into law the National Mental Health Act (NMHA; Public Law 487, 79th Congress). The act created the National Institute of Mental (NIMH) as one of the institutes within the National Institutes of Health (Grob, 1991; Strickland, 1972). Funding of research actually began in 1948. The first director, psychiatrist Robert Felix, took a very liberal approach to what constituted appropriate research. He argued that since we do not understand clearly what causes mental illness NIMH should fund as much research as possible. This policy, especially during the first 20 years when Congress was authorizing an abundance of funds, had important ramifications for psychology. The range of topics considered suitable for federal support was broad. As a result, many areas of psychology received generous financial support. Research in comparative psychology, social psychology, cognitive psychology, even ethnomusicology and many others was supported. This helped diversify psychology beyond the mainstream emphasis on variants of learning theory. As psychology grew in resources, the field also became more attractive for graduate students, both for native and international students. All of these events, together with the growth of American military, economic, and political power, made American psychology the center of the discipline. Joe Hunt was at the center of the center.

IN THE HEARTLAND AGAIN: APA AND THE *JOURNAL OF ABNORMAL AND SOCIAL PSYCHOLOGY*

The APA had reorganized itself during WWII, in part due to pressure from the American Association for Applied Psychology (AAAP). The new organization arose from the demand for a national organization that would meet the needs of the rapidly growing number of psychologists who were engaged in applied and professional fields (Farreras, 2005; Napoli, 1981). The growth of the AAAP membership led to a realization on the part of some of the APA leaders that a change in APA's structure was desirable, especially better to meet the nation's wartime needs. The two organizations merged under the name of the APA (Hilgard & Capshew, 1992).

The APA emerged from the war much stronger than when the war began, with new headquarters in Washington, DC, a new organizational structure, and a very capable executive officer in Dael Wolfle (Coon & Sprenger, 1998; Pickren & McKeachie, 2003). It was now a part, if a minor part, of the dense network of governmental and nonprofit organizations in Washington, DC. This was the period when the US federal government began the current era of funding scientific research on a larger scale than ever before in American history. As noted, the membership of the APA grew rapidly in this period, with many members receiving funding and becoming part of the funding apparatus of numerous federal agencies, including NIMH, the VA, and the National Science Foundation.

With the inauguration of the large-scale VA Clinical Psychology Training Program in 1946 and the generous funding of clinical training by NIMH beginning in 1948, the APA also had to take on the responsibility for accrediting training programs (Baker & Pickren, 2007; Farreras, 2005). The APA was also pushed to provide a training model for clinical psychologists that would serve as the template for accreditation. With the support of the NIMH, a training conference was held at the University of Colorado in Boulder in 1949. The participants drew upon the work of David Shakow (Baker & Benjamin, 2005; Committee on Training in Clinical Psychology, 1947; Shakow, 1942) to devise the scientist-practitioner model, colloquially known as the "Boulder Model." For more than 60 years this model, with a modest amount of tweaking, has been the standard for training clinical psychologists for the doctor of philosophy degree.

In the great growth in the number of psychologists previously mentioned, a significant number were in clinical and counseling psychology. This new emphasis on the application of psychology to mental health problems reflected the wishes of those who were now the new stakeholders in psychology and other mental health professions, federal policymakers and politicians (Pickren, 2007). The infusion of capital funds into research and training by government agencies shaped the direction of psychology in America, essentially transforming its implicit utilitarianism into an explicit utilitarian expression.

The new applied emphases were also reflected in the leadership of the APA after the war; among the presidents in the immediate postwar period were Carl Rogers, Laurence Shaffer, and Joseph McVicker Hunt. Joe had become involved in the leadership of American psychology through first becoming involved in the Eastern Psychological Association (EPA). At this time, EPA was the leading regional association of psychologists, and many future APA presidents were first EPA presidents. This was the case for Joe Hunt, too. By the late 1940s, Joe was on the APA council of representatives and then on the board of directors. He was elected president in 1950 and began his 1-year term after the APA meeting in 1951. Even after his presidency, Joe remained involved and was one of the key movers in the development of a program of awards and honors within the APA, including the association's most prestigious awards, the Distinguished Contribution Awards. He was also instrumental in establishing the charitable arm of the APA in 1953, which became known as the American Psychological Foundation. As first president of the foundation, Joe initiated the Gold Medal Award to recognize those who had made important lifelong contributions to psychology.

When Hunt moved to the University of Illinois in 1951 to become a professor of psychology, he had already served 2 years as the editor of the *Journal of Abnormal and Social Psychology,* the leading psychological journal in the clinical field. At the university, his primary role was to direct the programs in clinical and counseling psychology. Thus, Joe was part of the mammoth effort to train enough mental health professionals to meet the demands of policymakers and the public.

INTELLIGENCE, EXPERIENCE, AND EDUCATION: HUNT'S REVITALIZED RESEARCH PROGRAM

Even in his student days at the University of Nebraska, Joe Hunt was interested in the role of early life experiences in shaping human personalities. Admittedly, this interest was not well developed, consisting mostly of reading some of Freud's work and debating Freudian psychology with other students. By the time he was hired at Brown University (1936), Joe was more knowledgeable than before, though now he was in the circle of influence of Clark Hull, who sought to domesticate Freudian theory by subjugating it to Hullian drive-reduction theory (Morawski, 1986). As noted already, Joe and his colleagues at Brown used animal models to investigate the role of early experience in laboratory rats, primarily through frustration and hoarding studies. Other duties and opportunities took him away from this line of research, and he was unable to return to it until he was established at the University of Illinois in the 1950s. However, once he resumed his reading and research on early life experiences, his scholarship became highly important in a reformulation of intelligence and experience. The result led to Hunt becoming a national leader in early childhood education and to notoriety as a developmental psychologist, a rather new identity for him.

As mentioned previously, when he was director of the Institute for Welfare Research, Joe became friends with Don Young, the executive director of the Russell Sage Foundation. Young had shown interest in supporting Joe's desire to study early child experiences and the role of parenting. Now at Illinois, Joe sought and received support from the Russell Sage Foundation to survey the parenting and childhood literature. As historians Julia Grant (1998) and Ann Hulbert (2004) documented, Americans have a long history of seeking advice about child rearing. In the twentieth century, John B. Watson and Arnold Gesell stood out as psychologists who offered such advice, and by the 1950s many others had entered the field, perhaps none as well known as psychiatrist Benjamin Spock. His guide to baby and child care, first published in 1946, was the most popular of all time in the English language, yet there were other voices, too.

In the midst of all this sometimes contradictory advice, Joe Hunt sought to understand what behavioral science had to tell us about child rearing. The Sage Foundation provided Hunt with summer stipends for several years to give him time to review the literature and produce an authoritative book on the subject. What Hunt soon realized was that he had to escape his allegiance to the theories of his friends in the neobehaviorist tradition to come to a fresh understanding of child development (Hunt, 1974).

Hunt never produced the volume on child rearing and behavioral science. Instead, his reading and research led him to take up the old question about nature and nurture in children's intellectual development. As he delved into the literature, he found that he had to lay aside the assumptions of many of his colleagues in mainstream psychology about the fixed nature of intelligence. In its place, Hunt drew on many sources that led him to conclude that intelligence is malleable and that experience is crucially important. His sources included the research of Donald Hebb and colleagues on intelligence as a problem-solving capacity largely derived from past experiences (Hebb, 1949); the research of Robert Gagné on adult problem solving and learning complex skills (summarized in Gagné, 1965); and perhaps most importantly, his rediscovery of the work of Jean Piaget on the development of intelligence in children.

In his autobiography, Hunt (1974) stated that it was while he was a graduate student at Cornell that he was first exposed to the theories of Jean Piaget. At the time he discounted them, but now he found much that resonated with his developing theory about the relationship between intelligence and experience. Piaget's observations on the importance of the child's interactions with the environment for intellectual development, his genetic epistemology if you will, through successive stages leading to greater cognitive complexity were crucial in persuading Hunt to pay careful attention to the interactive effects of intelligence and environment. Rather than authoring the promised volume on behavioral science and child rearing, Hunt produced instead one of the most important volumes of 20th-century American psychology, *Intelligence and Experience* (Hunt, 1961).

The volume served as one of the two major reintroductions of Jean Piaget to American psychologists and developmentalists. (The other volume was John Flavell's [1963] *Developmental Psychology of Jean Piaget*). The exposition and discussion of Piaget's theories take up almost four chapters in Hunt's book. At the time, it was by far the most complete articulation of Piaget extant in English. Hunt took Piaget's notions about the child's cognitive development seriously. He also set Piaget's ideas alongside other experimental work drawn from many lines of research. The result was an exposition that contained many provocative ideas and questions for the stimulation of further research. When Flavell's volume appeared 2 years later, there followed what eventually became a tidal wave of investigations predicated upon Piagetian notions—and American developmental psychology was transformed. In some accounts, it was from this time that developmental psychology in the United States began its growth toward maturity as a scientific discipline.

INTELLIGENCE, ENVIRONMENTS, AND AMERICAN EARLY CHILDHOOD EDUCATION

The publication and positive reception of *Intelligence and Experience* (Hunt, 1961) brought Joe Hunt to the attention not only of his fellow psychologists but also of policymakers and presidents in American public life. He became a much sought after speaker in both psychology and education circles. He also became involved in the series of events that led to one of the major changes in 20th-century public policy related to the education of children.

Hunt was contacted in early 1962 by New York social psychologist Martin Deutsch. Deutsch and his wife, Cynthia Deutsch, had begun investigating the question of what would happen if children from impoverished environments were exposed to enriched environments prior to beginning school. They established the Institute for Developmental Studies at NYU, which served as the institutional base for their research. In New York City, disparities in educational opportunities and classroom performance between poor Black and White children and those children who were middle class were widely known. The Deutsch's received approval from the New York City Board of Education in 1958 to work with schoolchildren in Harlem to determine if the children would benefit from a richer environment.

The rationale for their study was provided by the work of David Krech and Mark Rosenzweig at the University of California–Berkeley on enriched environments. Krech and Rosenzweig began their work in the 1950s after both took positions at the university. Both were influenced by the work of Donald Hebb. Rosenzweig recounted how in a Harvard summer course in the late 1940s he had heard Hebb tell the story about raising rats in his home, where he allowed them to explore their environments freely and where his children played with them. He then conducted research on them using standard laboratory tasks (Rosenzweig, personal communication, September 12, 2002). Hebb indicated that these home-reared rats performed much better on problem-solving tasks than those rats raised in the typical laboratory environment.

Krech, meanwhile, brought questions about possible biological or neurological bases of differences in problem solving among rats of similar strains. Krech and Rosenzweig, later joined by chemist Edward Bennett and neuroanatomist Marion Diamond, formalized this provocative report in a series of studies on what they called enriched environments; they were interested, in particular, in the impact on the brain of being raised in such environments. After raising rats in the two conditions, enriched and standard, the researchers ran them in typical laboratory tasks that called for displays of problem solving. Afterward, the rats were sacrificed, and their brains were autopsied. The brain sections of those rats that had been reared in enriched environments indicated a much richer network of neural connections than those of rats reared in standard laboratory environments. Not surprisingly, the work of Krech and his colleagues received a great deal of publicity, both in scientific circles and in popular media outlets. Hunt's book seemed to validate their work and vice versa.

Returning to the work of Martin and Cynthia Deutsch in New York City, the Deutsches recruited 4-year-old children from three Harlem school districts to attend a special class several mornings a week. These classrooms were enriched environments; that is, there were materials there for the children to stimulate them in several domains. When the children began school the following year, they showed greater gains than similar children who had not had this enriched experience.

When Joe Hunt's book appeared in 1961, it had great relevance for the work of Martin and Cynthia Deutsch. As noted, Martin Deutsch contacted Joe Hunt and got him involved in the discussions then just beginning among educators, social scientists, and policymakers about the role of the federal government in improving early childhood education among the poor. In early fall 1962, Deutsch invited Joe to give a talk at Arden House, Columbia University, to a group meeting to discuss the role of preschool enrichment programs for disadvantaged children. Joe's talk, later published as "The Psychological Basis for Using Pre-School Enrichment as an Antidote for Cultural Deprivation" (Hunt, 1964), became widely influential in the debates then under way about such enrichment programs and the government's role in supporting them.

This was the era of presidents John Kennedy and Lyndon B. Johnson (1960–1968) in which they and their staffs believed that it was important for the federal government to be involved in improving society and the lives of America's citizens. The "War on Poverty" was a phrase used by government leaders to indicate their intention to improve life by addressing structural disparities in American life. Lyndon Johnson, who succeeded John Kennedy as president after Kennedy was assassinated in November 1963, initiated various programs under the banner of the War on Poverty, including a Presidential Task Force on Education, led by psychologist John Gardner. Gardner recruited a number of psychologists to participate in the development of reports on preschool programs. The task force drew on the research and writing of Hunt, Deutsch, Lois Barclay Murphy (see Chapter 1 in this volume) and others to formulate a plan for improving educational opportunities for preschool children. Out of this work came the blueprint for the national preschool program Head Start. The first Head Start program was run for 8 weeks in summer 1965. It was then institutionalized to become a part of the regular school year and soon was in place in schools around the country. Thus, Joe Hunt played a part in a change in educational policy and helped initiate Head Start.

Once involved in early childhood education policy, Joe Hunt became a leader. He was asked by President Johnson to head the White House Task Force on Early Childhood Development. Its blue-ribbon report, "A Bill of Rights for Children," was cited by President Johnson in 1967 as the basis for several new offices and programs meant to improve the lives of children. Included in the implementation of the report's recommendations were federal funds for research on children's education. Out of this grew a federally funded National Laboratory for Early Childhood Education. This was a network of extant centers where early childhood research was being conducted. Joe hoped to be able to get these centers truly to work together on important problems. The Coordination Center for the National Laboratory was located at the University of Illinois under Joe's direction. However, as Hunt reported in his autobiography, it proved nearly impossible for the centers fully to work together in a coordinated fashion. Each center already had its own research program, and the leaders found it difficult either to give up their own programs or to incorporate new intercenter research. Joe eventually stepped aside as the director of the Coordination Center, though he did continue to serve on its National Advisory Board. One final note from this period of national leadership on early childhood education policy is that Joe was named to the advisory board of the then new Children's Television Workshop in 1968. While on the board, he played an advisory role in the development of the popular children's television show *Sesame Street*.

RETIRED AND PRODUCTIVE

Joe Hunt retired from the full-time faculty at the University of Illinois in 1974. However, as professor emeritus, he remained active in research, writing, and consulting as well as singing in his church choir for many years. By all accounts, he maintained his rich network of friendships, both personal and professional, until he died. Doubtless the reader has detected that Joe Hunt was a very sociable person, someone who loved good conversation, human companionship, and the pleasure of his family. This stood him in good stead as he grew older.

Even though Joe retired, he remained involved in research and some teaching. For example, just before he retired he edited *Human Intelligence* (Hunt, 1972) and continued his work with Ina Uzgiris in developing an ordinal scale of child development based on Piagetian concepts of sensorimotor development (Uzgiris & Hunt, 1975). The esteem and high regard that his former students and his colleagues held for him were expressed in a *Fetschrift* published in 1977 (Uzgiris & Weizmann, 1977).

Joe Hunt received many awards and honors in his life. As noted, he served as president of APA (1951–1952), held an NIMH Research Career Award (1962–1974), and was awarded the Gold Medal of the American Psychological Foundation (1970). He was also the recipient of the G. Stanley Hall Award from APA Division 7 (Developmental Psychology) and the Distinguished Contribution Award of APA Division 12 (Clinical Psychology).

By the time he retired, Joe had made substantive contributions to the fields of psychopathology, psychological assessment, and psychological treatment. His most enduring contributions, however, were in developmental psychology. Through his work he showed the importance of the malleability of the human child and the necessity for understanding the role of the environment in shaping the person. His career came to full expression just as American psychology entered its Golden Age. Joseph McVicker Hunt died on January 9, 1991, at a retirement home in Urbana, Illinois. His life and work not only reflected the Golden Age but also helped make it brighter.

SUGGESTED READINGS

Hunt, J. M. (Ed.). (1944). *Personality and the behavior disorders* (2 vols.). New York: Ronald Press.

    The two volumes represent a landmark of American research and theorizing about the multiple facets of human personality and problems that emerge in its development. The chapters, especially those by psychologists, were excellent summaries of the contemporary state of the field and perhaps more importantly served as templates for what still needed to be done. After World War II, many of the volumes' contributors then engaged in work laid out by the book.

Hunt, J. M. (1961). *Intelligence and experience*. New York: Ronald Press.

    The book is often cited as playing a vital role in redirecting psychologists' attention away from the notion that intelligence is a fixed, inherited set of abilities and toward a deeper consideration of the importance of the environment, especially in early childhood years. The book also served as the first major reintroduction of Piaget's rich body of work on child cognitive development.

REFERENCES

Arkowitz, H., & Bartlett, N. (2002). The Brown University psychology department, Spring 1941: An historic photograph. *Journal of the History of the Behavioral Sciences, 38*, 57–60.

Baker, D. B., & Benjamin, L. T., Jr. (2005). Creating a profession: The National Institute of Mental Health and the training of psychologists, 1946–1954. In W. E. Pickren & S. F. Schneider (Eds.), *Psychology and the National Institute of Mental Health: A historical analysis of science, practice, and policy* (pp. 181–207). Washington, DC: American Psychological Association. doi:10.1037/10931-006

Baker, R. R., & Pickren, W. E. (2007). *Psychology and the Department of Veterans Affairs: A historical analysis of training, research, practice, and advocacy.* Washington, DC: APA Books. doi:10.1037/11544-000

Buchanan, R. D. (1994). The development of the Minnesota Multiphasic Personality Inventory. *Journal of the History of the Behavioral Sciences, 30*, 148–161. doi:10.1002/1520-6696(199404)30:2<148::AID-JHBS2300300204>3.0.CO;2-9

Capshew, J. H. (1999). *Psychologists on the march: Science, practice, and professional identity, 1929–1959*. New York: Cambridge University Press. doi:10.1017/CBO9780511572944

Cather, W. (1913). *O! pioneers*. Boston: Houghton Mifflin.

Cather, W. (1915). *The song of the lark*. Boston: Houghton Mifflin.

Cather, W. (1918). *My Ántonia*. Boston: Houghton Mifflin.

Committee on Training in Clinical Psychology. (1947). Recommended graduate training program in clinical psychology. *American Psychologist, 2*, 539–558. doi:10.1037/h0058236

Coon, D. J., & Sprenger, H. A. (1998). Psychologists in service to science: The American Psychological Association and the American Association for the Advancement of Science. *American Psychologist, 53*, 1253–1269. doi:10.1037/0003-066X.53.12.1253

Farreras, I. G. (2005). The historical context for National Institute of Mental Health support of American Psychological Association training and accreditation efforts. In W. E. Pickren & S. F. Schneider (Eds.), *Psychology and the National Institute of Mental Health: A historical analysis of science, practice, and policy* (pp. 153–179). Washington, DC: American Psychological Association. doi:10.1037/10931-005

Finch, F. H., & Odoroff, M. E. (1939). Employment trends in applied psychology. *Journal of Consulting Psychology, 3*, 118–122. doi:10.1037/h0054724

Finch, F. H., & Odoroff, M. E. (1941). Employment trends in applied psychology, II. *Journal of Consulting Psychology, 5*, 275–278. doi:10.1037/h0059312

Finison, L. J. (1978). Unemployment, politics, and the history of organized psychology, II: The Psychologists' League, the WPA, and the National Health Program. *American Psychologist, 33*, 471–477. doi:10.1037/0003-066X.33.5.471

Finison, L. J. (1979). An aspect of the early history of the Society for the Psychological Study of Social Issues: Psychologists and labor. *Journal of the History of the Behavioral Sciences, 15*, 29–37. doi:10.1002/1520-6696(197901)15:1<29::AID-JHBS2300150104>3.0.CO;2-C

Finison, L. J. (1986). The psychological insurgency: 1936–1945. *Journal of Social Issues, 42*, 21–33. doi:10.1111/j.1540-4560.1986.tb00202.x

Flavell, J. H. (1963). *The developmental psychology of Jean Piaget*. Princeton, NJ: Van Nostrand. doi:10.1037/11449-000

Gagné, R. M. (1965). *The conditions of learning*. New York: Holt, Rinehart, & Winston.

Grant, J. (1998). *Raising baby by the book: The education of American mothers*. New Haven, CT: Yale University Press.

Grob, G. N. (1991). *From asylum to community: Mental health policy in modern America*. Princeton, NJ: Princeton University Press.

Hebb, D. O. (1949). *The organization of behavior: A neuropsychological theory*. New York: Wiley.

Herman, E. (1995). *The romance of American psychology: Political culture in the age of experts*. Berkeley: University of California Press.

Hilgard, E. R., & Capshew, J. H. (1992). The power of service: World War II and professional reform in the American Psychological Association. In R. B. Evans, V. S. Sexton, & T. C. Cadwallader (Eds.), *The American Psychological Association: A historical perspective* (pp. 149–175). Washington, DC: American Psychological Association.

Hoffman, L. E. (1992). American psychologists and wartime research on Germany, 1941–1945. *American Psychologist, 47*, 264–273. doi:10.1037/0003-066X.47.2.264

Hornstein, G. A. (1992). The return of the repressed: Psychology's problematic relations with psychoanalysis, 1909–1960. *American Psychologist, 47*, 254–263. doi:10.1037/0003-066X.47.2.254

Hulbert, A. (2004). *Raising America: Experts, parents, and a century of advice about children*. New York: Vintage.

Hunt, J. M. (1936). Psychological experiments with disordered persons. *Psychological Bulletin, 33*, 1–58. doi:10.1037/h0059407

Hunt, J. M. (1941). The effects of infant feeding-frustration upon adult hoarding in the albino rat. *Journal of Abnormal and Social Psychology, 36*, 338–360. doi:10.1037/h0053489

Hunt, J. M. (Ed.). (1944). *Personality and the behavior disorders* (2 vols.). New York: Ronald Press.

Hunt, J. M. (1961). *Intelligence and experience.* New York: Ronald Press.

Hunt, J. M. (1964). The psychological basis for using pre-school enrichment as an antidote for cultural deprivation. *Merrill-Palmer Quarterly of Behavior and Development, 10*, 209–248.

Hunt, J. M. (1972). *Human intelligence.* New York: Transaction Books.

Hunt, J. M. (1974). A professional odyssey. In T. S. Krawiec (Ed.), *The psychologists* (vol. 2, pp. 134–202). New York: Oxford University Press.

Hunt, J. M., LaForge, R., Ewing, T. N., & Gilbert, W. M. (1959). An integrated approach to research on therapeutic counseling with samples of results. *Journal of Counseling Psychology, 6*, 46–54. doi:10.1037/h0045391

Hunt, J. M., & Schlosberg, H. (1939). General activity in the male white rat. *Journal of Comparative Psychology, 28*, 23–38. doi:10.1037/h0062976

Hunt. J. M., & Willoughby, R. R. (1939). The effect of frustration on hoarding in rats. *Psychosomatic Medicine, 1*, 309–310.

Morawski, J. G. (1986). Organizing knowledge and behavior at Yale's Institute of Human Relations. *Isis, 77*, 219–242.

Napoli, D. S. (1981). *Architects of adjustment: The history of the psychological profession in the United States.* Port Washington, NY: Kennikat Press.

National Research Council. (1945). National research fellowships, 1919–1945. Washington, DC: Author.

Nicholson, I. (1997). The politics of scientific social reform, 1936–1960: Goodwin Watson and the Society for the Psychological Study of Social Issues. *Journal of the History of the Behavioral Sciences, 33*, 39–60. doi:10.1002/(SICI)1520-6696(199724)33:1<39::AID-JHBS2>3.0.CO;2-F

Nicholson, I. A. M. (2003). *Inventing personality: Gordon Allport and the science of selfhood.* Washington, DC: American Psychological Association. doi:10.1037/10514-000 PMid:18175615

Pickren, W. E. (1995). Psychologists and physicians in the borderlands of science, 1900–1942. *Dissertation Abstracts International, 56*, 11B (UMI No. 6373).

Pickren, W. E. (2000). Zygmunt Piotrowski. In Alan E. Kazdin (Ed.), *Encyclopedia of Psychology* (vol. 6, pp. 200–201). Washington, DC: American Psychological Association.

Pickren, W. E. (2007). Tension and opportunity in post WWII American psychology. *History of Psychology, 10*, 279–299. doi:10.1037/1093-4510.10.3.279

Pickren, W. E. (2010). Hybridizing, transforming, indigenizing: Psychological knowledge as mélange. *Boletín de la Sociedad de Historia de la Psicología, 44*, 6–12.

Pickren, W. E., & McKeachie, W. (2003). Dael Lee Wolfle (1906–2002). *American Psychologist, 58*, 758–759. doi:10.1037/0003-066X.58.9.758

Pickren, W. E., & Rutherford, A. (2010). *A history of modern psychology in context.* New York: Wiley.

Pickren, W. E., & Schneider, S. F. (Eds.). (2005). *Psychology and the National Institute of Mental Health: A historical analysis of science, practice, and policy.* Washington, DC: APA Books.

Raimy, V. (1950). *Training in clinical psychology.* Englewood Cliffs, NJ: Prentice Hall.

Rice, C. E. (2005). The research grants program of the National Institute of Mental Health and the golden age of American academic psychology. In W. E. Pickren & S. F. Schneider (Eds.), *Psychology and the National Institute of Mental Health: A historical analysis of science, practice, and policy* (pp. 61–111). Washington, DC: APA Books. doi:10.1037/10931-003

Schultz, D. P., & Schultz, S. E. (2008). *A history of modern psychology*, 9th ed. Belmont, CA: Thomson.

Shakow, D. (1942). The training of the clinical psychologist. *Journal of Consulting Psychology, 6*, 277–288. doi:10.1037/h0059917

Shakow, D. (1972). The Worcester State Hospital research on schizophrenia (1927–1946). *Journal of Abnormal Psychology, 80*, 67–110. doi:10.1037/h0033412

Shephard, B. (2000). *A war of nerves*. Cambridge, MA: Harvard University Press.

Smith, R. (1997). *The history of the human sciences*. New York: Norton.

Smuts, A. B. (2008). *Science in the service of children, 1893–1935*. New Haven, CT: Yale University Press.

Spock, B. (1946). *The common sense book of baby and child care*. New York: Duell, Sloan, & Pearce.

Strickland, S. P. (1972). *Politics, science, and dread disease: A short history of United States medical research policy*. Cambridge, MA: Harvard University Press.

Uzgiris, I., & Hunt, J. M. (1975). *Assessment in infancy: Ordinal scales of psychological development*. Urbana: University of Illinois Press.

Uzgiris, I., & Weizmann, F. (Eds.). (1977). *The structuring of experience*. New York: Plenum Press.

Woodward, W. R. (2010). Russian women émigrés in psychology: Informal Jewish networks. *History of Psychology, 13*, 111–137. doi:10.1037/a0018531

Zubin, D., & Zubin, J. (1977). From speculation to empiricism in the study of mental disorder: Research at the New York State Psychiatric Institute in the first half of the twentieth century. *Annals of the New York Academy of Sciences, 291*, 104–135. doi:10.1111/j.1749-6632.1977.tb53064.x

12

Sidney W. Bijou:
*Outstanding (and Out Standing) in His Fields**

EDWARD K. MORRIS

University of Kansas

In his conclusion to *The Innocents Abroad*, Mark Twain (1869) observed, "Travel is fatal to prejudice, bigotry, and narrow-mindedness…" (p. 243). Sidney William Bijou (1908–2009) traveled a lot. He traveled in search of a point of view that would unify and advance psychology as a natural science. He traveled from field to field, among them, mental testing, psychometrics, animal models of psychopathology, abnormal child psychology, basic and

Figure 12.1 Sidney W. Bijou, 1982. (Courtesy of Jude Bijou. With permission.)

---

* Except where noted, all biographical material is taken from Bijou's autobiographical writings (i.e., Bijou, 1996, 1999, 2001); a partial biography (i.e., Morris, 2008); obituaries and in memoriams (e.g., Ghezzi, 2010); published interviews (i.e., Krasner, 1977; Wesolowski, 2002); audio interviews (i.e., with Peterson, 1998; copy with the author); personal communications with his son and daughter (Bob and Jude Bijou) and his colleagues (i.e., Bob Peterson, Bill Redd); a file of personal papers (e.g., "Personal History," correspondence, clippings; originals with Jude Bijou); Etzel, LeBlanc, and Baer's (1977) vita-like listing of his contributions; his last known vita (November, 17, 1999); and his website (*www. sidneywbijou.com*). Where these sources were at variance with one another, I relied mainly on Bijou's vita and Etzel, LeBlanc, and Baer (1977).

applied child psychology, and developmental theory. He traveled from system to system: psychoanalysis, neo-Gestalt field theory, and four varieties of behaviorism. Although his destinations were sometimes unexpected, his travels were not haphazard. As Louis Pasteur noted, "Chance favors only the prepared mind" (Vallery-Radot, 1927, p. 88). Bijou was always preparing. He took numerous courses outside his academic programs, read well beyond his required curricula, and audited classes even as a faculty member. As a result, his travels were progressive, selected by their approximations to the psychology he was seeking. He eventually found it in the integration of two systems—an integration of his own making. By the time he retired, he had earned awards for lifetime achievements in several fields. In some of them, he was an outstanding contributor to the end. In others, he was left out standing in them at the end. This is part of his story.

EDUCATION AND PROFESSIONAL TRAINING

Bijou's parents—Leon Bijou (1874–1947) and Lea Babert Bijou (1883–1966)—were born in France but immigrated to the United States soon after the turn of the century, settling in Arlington, Maryland. Leon was a custom tailor and dry cleaner, Lea a homemaker. Born on November 12, 1908, Bijou was the youngest of four children, but eventually an only child, as his siblings died of natural causes. Raised by a loving and supportive mother, proud of her son, he returned her love fully. In 1918, the family moved to Brooklyn, New York, to be near relatives. In the process, Bijou missed a year of school, struggled with his grades, and took evening classes in preparation for college. He graduated from high school in 1928, interested in mechanics and athletics. Mechanics exemplified the scientific values of prediction and control espoused by Francis Bacon (1561–1626) (Smith, 1992). They may have shaped Bijou's search for a natural science of psychology, but not seamlessly.

Lehigh University and the University of Florida

That fall, Bijou enrolled at Lehigh University on a football scholarship to major in electrical engineering. However, the dual demands of athletics and engineering proved too great, and he turned instead to business administration. Without a scholarship, though, Lehigh was too expensive, so he transferred to the University of Florida in 1930 where the tuition and cost of living were lower. Between transferring and an appendectomy, he lost another year of school. He graduated in 1933 in business administration, yet with waning interest in it. He spent increasing time reading psychology, in particular, about psychotherapy, dreams, and hypnosis, trying to understand his own "shy and withdrawn behavior." His degree was fortuitous, however: Research administration would figure in his success. As for psychology, his interest was not unusual or atypical. In Progressive, modernist America, psychology promised practical advice for self-improvement and advancement (Burnham, 1968).

Columbia University

Bijou returned to New York City in 1933 to make his fortune on Wall Street, but he could not even find a job. It was the Depression. The next year, though, he married his partner in life, Janet Rose Tobias. Supported by her teacher's salary, he took undergraduate courses to prepare for Columbia University's master's program in psychology, which he entered in 1935. Among its faculty members were Henry E. Garrett, Elizabeth B. Hurlock, Albert T. Poffenberger, Carl J. Warden, and Robert S. Woodworth. In Woodworth's course on contemporary psychology, he found the plethora of psychology's systems "bewildering." He wanted to know which of them held the greatest promise for psychology as a natural science. "Woodworth remarked," Bijou wrote later, "that psychology was in a state of flux and only a genius could unify the field and move it in the direction of the natural sciences" (Bijou, 1999, p. 179).

Psychoanalysis   Bijou had already considered one system—psychoanalysis. It was deterministic and, he thought, capable of accounting for both individual behavior and cultural practices. Before entering Columbia, he took a course from the psychoanalyst Fritz S. Wittels at the New School for Social Research, but came away unsatisfied. The system's data were clinical cases, which constrained its generality, while its constructs were so ambiguous as to preclude verification (e.g., sublimation, the superego). Whether Bijou was sophisticated enough about psychological science prior to entering Columbia to draw these conclusions is, for the moment, unknown. On one hand, his interests in mechanics and engineering suggest that he was analytic; however, these capacities do not always generalize to psychology. On the other hand, what he read in psychology at Florida might not have been the field's most critical literature. If not, then his conclusions might have been, in part, later reconstructions. Not until Bijou's materials are cataloged at the Archives for the History of American Psychology at the University of Akron might we verify when and how he reached the conclusions he wrote later that he reached earlier.

Child Clinical Psychology   Although Bijou set psychoanalysis aside, two events outside of his courses drew him to child clinical psychology. The first was an elective summer school course he took at the Letchworth Village State School in Thiells, New York. The school was a residential facility for "mental defectives and epileptics" administered by the New York State Department of Mental Hygiene. The course sought "to stimulate more widespread interest in mental deficiency; to encourage medical students and graduates in the study of the many ramifications of the subject; to afford training toward clinical and research studies for qualified non-medical students; and to correlate the problems of mental deficiency with recent advances in allied biological and sociological sciences" (News and Notes, 1935, p. 1447). Bijou was stimulated. He interacted with the head psychologist, Elaine F. Kinder, and professionals in allied sciences and professions and learned about the problems of providing services in large institutions. He was disappointed, though, by the limited contributions clinical psychologists made to the education and training of the residents. At the time, clinicians were psychometricians and mental testers who assisted physicians and psychiatrists in diagnosis and classification. They would not become psychotherapists until after World War II (Capshew, 1999).

Classical Behaviorism

The second event was his master's thesis, but not before he had encountered classical behaviorism. In Woodworth's course, he learned about John B. Watson's (1878–1956) founding of behaviorism in the early decades of the twentieth century. Watson accounted for behavior largely in terms of Ivan P. Pavlov's (1849–1936) science of conditional reflexes, making his behaviorism a mechanistic stimulus-response (S→R) psychology. In subsequently reading Watson's (1919) *Psychology from the Standpoint of a Behaviorist* and *Behaviorism* (Watson, 1930), Bijou was impressed by his research with animals and children, practical orientation, and optimism about the future of psychology. Watson was "ultrascientific" and, perhaps, the future of psychological science.

Enthused yet naïve, Bijou wrote Watson, then vice president of the J. Walter Thompson advertising agency, describing his interests and asking him to recommend a thesis topic. Watson responded, suggesting that he study how young children learn "muscle sense" (e.g., proprioception), for example, "how … does little Jimmy know that his arms are stretched out at shoulder length when his eyes are closed?" (Bijou, 1999, p. 180). Bijou found Watson's recommendation "most appealing," but could not find anyone to supervise the research. Sorely disappointed, he turned to a project begun by one of his instructors on the measurement of nonverbal intelligence in young children with intellectual disabilities. Garrett, Columbia's specialist in tests and measurement, found the project acceptable and served as his advisor. The project was also acceptable to Bijou. It was consistent with his child clinical interests and allowed him to administer intelligence tests to children. He received his master's degree in 1937 (see Bijou, 1938). Although he never returned to classical behaviorism, he remained interested in research with children.

Neo-Gestalt Field Theory

Bijou did not pursue a doctorate at Columbia because he found the program too eclectic. It had no "point of view." However, he took additional courses while working part time as a school psychologist. One was on Gestalt and organismic psychology, taught by George W. Hartmann at Teacher's College. In it, Bijou was drawn to Kurt Lewin's (1890–1947) field-theoretic psychology (Lewin, 1935, 1936).

Influenced by field theory in physics (see Einstein & Infeld, 1938), Lewin was extending Gestalt psychology's holistic approach to sensory perception (e.g., seeing wholes, not parts) to the relation between people (P) and their environments (E) in a dynamic field of mutually interdependent forces, among them barriers, conflicts, interruptions, and needs. Their relation was not biological or physical, but psychological. For instance, children's behavior toward some adults as authority figures was due to their perceptions of those adults, not to the adults per se. Not all adults are authority figures for all children. Lewin depicted the person–environment relation in his equation, $B = f(P,E)$. When he later claimed, "There's nothing so practical as a good theory," by theory, he meant models or equations, such as his, that depict a unit of analysis and its participants, not formal propositional theory.

The latter meaning has become an origin myth in experimental psychology (on origin myths, see Samelson, 1974). When Bijou told Hartmann of his reservations about Columbia, Hartmann suggested that he study with Lewin at the University of Iowa. Perhaps Lewin would unify and advance psychological science.

Child Clinical Psychologist

Instead, Bijou took a position as a clinical psychologist at the State Hospital and Mental Hygiene Clinic in Farmhurst, Delaware. There, he administered more than 33 different psychological tests to over 2000 individuals across a range of ages, disabilities, and settings but was disappointed again. His duties entailed testing and report writing, not education and training. However, he did collaborate with Joseph F. Jastak, the clinic's chief psychologist. Jastak thought that mental diagnoses should be based on more than just aptitude. They should include, at least, some measure of achievement. Unable to find a brief achievement test, he and Bijou constructed their own—the Wide Range Achievement Test (WRAT)—a 15-minute test of reading, spelling, and arithmetic (Jastak & Bijou, 1938). The WRAT was a success then and later, for instance as a screening instrument in the Head Start programs of the 1960s, and is broadly administered in revision today. Bijou was, by then, a mainstream clinician. He also joined his first professional organization, the American Psychological Association (APA), which marked the beginning of his lifelong support of the profession.

University of Iowa

In 1939, Bijou rededicated himself to psychological science and applied to the Department of Psychology at the University of Iowa to work with Lewin. He was accepted and offered an assistantship. On his arrival however, he discovered that Lewin was not in the department, but at the university's associated Child Welfare Research Station, later named the Institute of Child Behavior and Development. To retain his assistantship, Bijou had to remain in psychology, so he elected a concentration in "learning" and was assigned Kenneth W. Spence (1907–1967) as his advisor. For his assistantship, he worked with Charles R. Strother in the Psychological and Speech Clinic, testing children and adults who had speech disorders.

Bijou took Lewin's course, Theory of Psychology and Personality Development, as Lewin was also becoming interested in social behavior. He was, for instance, conducting research on the effects of authoritarian, democratic, and laissez-faire leadership styles on children's peer interactions. This was a precursor to his "action research" concerning cultural practices (e.g., democracy), in which context he observed, "If you want truly to understand something, try to change it." Bijou found Lewin "stimulating," but his psychology unsatisfying:

> [H]e had a problem that bothered him to the very end of his career: how does one know what the individual's perceptions are. Or, in other words, how does one know what the environment means to the person. Lewin said you have to interpret the environment in terms of the eyes of the individual. Well, how

does one do that? Lewin's solution was to ask him. But all you can get from that is a correlation between what a person says and what he does, and Lewin really didn't want that. He wanted a functional field system. (Krasner, 1977, p. 598; see also Bijou, 1999, p. 181)

By then, Bijou was being drawn to Clark L. Hull's (1884–1952) mediational neobehaviorism, eventually seeing Hull as "the genius destined to bring psychology to the threshold of the natural sciences" (Bijou, 1999, p. 182).

Mediational Neobehaviorism   Among the highlights of Bijou's graduate training was Spence's course on theories of conditioning and learning (e.g., Guthrie, Tolman, Hull), along with those taught by the logical positivist Gustav Bergmann on the philosophy of science and the history of psychology, by the applied statistician Everett F. Lindquist on advanced statistics for small sample research, and by the department chair John A. McGeoch on systematic psychology and human learning, mainly memory, which Bijou audited. Two other highlights were Spence's Monday Night Group—an informal seminar devoted to a close reading of Hull's (1943) manuscript for *Principles of Behavior* (and memorizing its postulates)—and the rivalry between Spence and Lewin and their students. Spence's students included I. E. (Iz) Farber, G. Robert Grice, Arthur L. Irion, Howard H. and Tracy S. Kendler, Margaret Kuenne, and Benton J. Underwood. They conducted basic research on learning and motivation with rats in mazes. Lewin's students included Leon Festinger, Ronald O. Lippitt, and Ralph K. White. They conducted applied research, also on learning and motivation, but with children in social situations. Iowa was an exciting place to be a graduate student (see Cantor, 1991).

Bijou was still interested in child clinical psychology, but the department had no program to accommodate him. It did, though, allow him to specialize in experimental psychopathology. For his dissertation he investigated "experimental neuroses" in rats in an extension of Ivan Pavlov's studies of neuroses in dogs. However, whereas Pavlov used a classical conditioning preparation, Bijou used an instrumental conditioning preparation, but did not know it. Reflex and instrumental behavior were, at the time, often conflated. For the first part of his dissertation, he modified a Skinner box and refined his research methods (Bijou, 1942). For the second part, he investigated experimental neurosis by having rats make increasingly difficult visual discriminations between two sources of light as they moved together. This caused the rats to become increasingly "neurotic"—struggling, squealing, and biting (Bijou, 1943).

As a Hull–Spence behaviorist, Bijou was thoroughly trained in between-subject research designs in which independent variables (e.g., rewards, cues for food) were differentially correlated with experimental and control groups. He was also trained in hypothetico-deductive theorizing about organismic (O) variables (e.g., drives, habit strength) that mediate the relation between stimuli (S) and responses (R) in an S→O→R psychology. This was a form of methodological behaviorism in which behavior is what psychologists study, but is not their subject matter. Their subject matter is the mediators. Bijou graduated from Iowa in 1941 as Spence's second doctoral student and lifelong friend—Bijou's son's middle name is Kenneth.

PROFESSIONAL LIFE: TEACHING, RESEARCH, AND SERVICE

Bijou's first postdoctorate position was as a research assistant and staff consultant at the Wayne County Training School in Northville, Michigan, a residential facility for predelinquent youths with mild intellectual disabilities. Because the Depression had curtailed university hiring, the facility's superintendent, Robert Haskell, was able to attract outstanding scientists and scholars, among them Samuel A. Kirk, Boyd R. McCandless, Alfred A. Strauss, and Heinz Werner. McCandless and Werner became renowned in developmental psychology, Kirk in special education, and Strauss in learning disabilities. Bijou collaborated on research with McCandless and Werner (e.g., on language) and became lifelong friends with Kirk. He was emerging as a mainstream developmental psychologist—an applied developmental psychologist.

During World War II, he took a commission in the army. Initially, he administered intelligence tests at army induction centers. Later, he gave aptitude tests to pilots, navigators, and bombardiers in John Flanagan's unit in the Army Air Force. Finally, he oversaw psychological services for the army's rehabilitation centers, working with Paul McReynolds, Lawrence F. Shaffer, and Merrill Roff. As the war ended and he returned to the training school, Sid and Janet started a family: Robert (Bob) Kenneth Bijou was born in 1945 in Louisville, Kentucky; Judith (Jude) Ann Bijou was born in 1946 in Ann Arbor, Michigan. Bob and Jude were Sid's partners in life, too. Although Bijou would later nominate two of his contributions to psychology as his "greatest achievements," in private he said that raising Bob and Jude was the greatest achievement of them all. The family was close, warm, and mutually supportive.

Indiana University

Skinner's Methods and Science   In 1945, B. F. Skinner (1904–1990) was hired to chair the Department of Psychology at Indiana University. He had earned renown for innovations in research methods and apparatus, among them strategies and tactics for within-subject research, the cumulative recorder, and the eponymous Skinner box. He had established an empirical-inductive science of instrumental behavior, which he called *operant* behavior. This is behavior that operates on the environment and is strengthened by its consequences, not elicited by antecedents. His science became known as the experimental analysis of behavior (Skinner, 1938; see Iversen & Lattal, 1991; the *Journal of the Experimental Analysis of Behavior* was established in 1958).

Unlike Watson's unit of analysis—the S→R relation between formal instances of stimuli and responses—Skinner's was an R↔S relation between codefining classes of responses and stimuli. In practice, though, he conceptualized it as a lineal three-term contingency comprising functional relations among operant responses (R_O), their reinforcing consequences (S^R), and their cues or discriminative stimuli (S^D). In his account, behavior is not responding per se, but the three-term contingency itself: B = $S^D{\rightarrow}R_0{\rightarrow}S^R$. As for biology, history, and motivation, these were "third variables," which he held constant in research. They influenced the functional relations between the first two variables—responses and stimuli—not as hypothetical mediators between them, but as their context. However, Skinner never included third variables in his unit of analysis, leading to misunderstandings (e.g., his putative dismissal of biology). In his science, behavior was both what was studied and the subject matter. Public behavior was studied directly; private behavior was considered by inference. Mediational terms such as drive, expectations, and perception describe functional relations that need explaining. They are not explanations, a point he had just made in articulating the philosophy of his science—radical behaviorism (Skinner, 1945). His science and its philosophy eventually became the basis of today's discipline of behavior analysis. For a Hull–Spence neobehaviorist such as Bijou, however, Skinner's psychology could not be the future of psychological science.

Bijou at Indiana   As the department's chair, Skinner was soon searching for a director of its newly accredited clinical training program, especially for one with an "experimental-learning" orientation. Bijou was hired in 1946. In addition to directing the clinical program, he set up a laboratory to continue his animal research and taught a course on experimental psychopathology. In the latter, he drew heavily on Hull's colleagues at Yale's Institute of Human Relations (est. 1929; see Morawski, 1986), among them, John Dollard, Carl I. Hovland, Neal E. Miller, O. Hobart Mowrer, and Robert R. Sears. They had founded social learning theory in its dynamic form, using Hull's drive-reduction learning theory to account for psychoanalytic observations about personality and social development. For this, they operationally defined and conducted research on, for example, aggression, frustration, identification, and dependence. Sears, for instance, was using projective doll play techniques to study family dynamics. This involved observing and recording how children played with dolls, denoted as family members, and interpreting the dolls' interactions and thus the children's fantasy play in terms of social learning theory constructs (e.g., frustration, dependence).

Indiana was as exciting as Iowa had been, but the rivalries were more intense, this time among the Skinnerians (e.g., Skinner, William K. Estes, Norman Guttman), the Hullians (e.g., Bijou, Douglas A. Ellson, William S. Verplanck), and the interbehaviorists—notably J. R. Kantor (1888–1984)—and their students (Capshew, 1988). Spence had not covered Skinner in his learning and conditioning course, so Skinner's behaviorism was largely new to Bijou, as was Kantor's interbehavioral psychology. Thus, Bijou attended their classes: a joint Skinner–Kantor seminar, "Theory Construction in Psychology;" a seminar by Skinner that was a precursor to *Science and Human Behavior* (Skinner, 1953); Kantor's undergraduate psychopathology course; and a faculty–student seminar on Hull and Skinner. At the same time, two graduate students were making some of the first applications of Skinner's science: Joel Greenspoon demonstrated the operant conditioning of adult verbal behavior, and Paul R. Fuller conditioned the arm movement of a "vegetative idiot." Bijou was Fuller's clinical supervisor. He also served as the secretary-treasurer of the Indiana Association of Clinical and Applied Psychologists, marking the start of his long-standing service to state, regional, national, and international organizations.

Kantor's Philosophy

In Bijou's conversations with Kantor, Kantor took issue with Hull's making mediational constructs, not behavior, psychology's subject matter. He criticized Hull's implicit reductionism: The mediators had to be physiological, or else they were fictions. And, he was critical of Hull's exclusive use of deductive theorizing; inductive methods have a place in science, too. Although a stern critic, Kantor did have a constructive program. This was his interbehavioral psychology (Kantor, 1938).

Interbehavioral psychology was a naturalistic, field-theoretic system, whose unit of analysis was the psychological event: PE = C(k, sf, rf, hi, st, md). Among its participants were the environment and the organism, which were, respectively, inorganically and organically constituted. They also had physical forms: the environment's stimulus forms, for instance, a box of crayons, and the organism's response forms, for instance, putting a box of crayons on a desk. The forms, in turn, had reciprocally defining functions: stimulus functions (sf) and response functions (rf). The stimulus function of a box of crayons might be a paperweight, while the response function of placing it on the table might be to hold down drawings. Kantor depicted their relation as rf $\leftrightarrow$ sf, which was much like Skinner's R$\leftrightarrow$S relation, but Kantor's PE included more. It included the field's history (hi), which established the rf $\leftrightarrow$ sf relations; setting factors (st), which influenced their occurrence; and a sensory medium (md) of contact between the environment and the organism. His C stood for the interdependence of the field's participants and his k for the field's uniqueness. Interbehavioral psychology contrasted almost as much with Hull–Spence neobehaviorism as had Lewin's field-theoretic psychology, so it too could not be the future of psychological science for Bijou.

University of Washington

In 1948, Bijou moved to the University of Washington as a faculty member in the Department of Psychology and as the director of the Institute of Child Development, where he could work with children again. The institute had been directed by Stevenson Smith, a protégé of Edwin R. Guthrie's (1886–1959), but was little more than a testing and guidance clinic in the psychology department. By 1950, Bijou had moved the clinic—named the Child Development Clinic—to a building that housed the university's nursery school classrooms, where he also set up a laboratory to study child behavior. This constituted the "new" Institute of Child Development. By 1955, he was elected president of the Washington State Psychological Association and appointed a consulting editor for *Child Development*.

In establishing a research program at Washington, Bijou began using Sears's doll play techniques, but became dissatisfied with them and their theoretical grounding. Unlike his between-subject research with rats, doll play research was poorly controlled, and the results were purely correlational, for instance, correlations among the experimenter's instructions, the children's play, the particular dolls, and the play materials (e.g., doll houses). Moreover, a theory, the subject matter of which was hypothetical mediators provided Bijou with little methodological guidance for research with individual children. In rethinking his research, he recalled his discussions with Skinner about within-subject designs, read Skinner's (1953) just published *Science and Human Behavior*, and decided to give Skinner's methods and science a try. This was a bold move. It took him afield from mainstream neobehavioral and developmental psychology.

Basic Research   In his first try, Bijou (1955) built a quasi-operant apparatus: a box with a hole into which children dropped a ball, the consequences of which were automatically delivered trinkets and the return of the ball to a receptacle for the next drop. He also combined Hullian and Skinnerian research designs. One group of nine 4-year-old children received a trinket for the first six times they dropped the ball in the hole (a continuous schedule of reinforcement), followed by 3.5 minutes during which no trinkets were delivered for further responses— extinction. A matched group of children also received six trinkets for dropping the ball, but received them indeterminately over the first 30 responses (an intermittent schedule of reinforcement), followed by the extinction condition. The results replicated those of Skinner's science: Intermittent schedules of reinforcement produced more resistance to extinction than continuous schedules. The mean numbers of responses were 22 and 15, respectively.

However, Bijou was not satisfied. First, although the between-subject differences were statistically significant, they were small. The preparation was perhaps suitable for statistical control in testing theories about hypothetical mediating variables, but not for demonstrating experimental control of individual children's behavior. Second, the within-subject differences across the conditions were not replicated within individuals. Bijou (1957) rectified this by following Skinner's methods more scrupulously. To reduce response variation caused by balls missing the hole, he built a lever-press apparatus for delivering the trinkets and added a cumulative recorder that automatically plotted responding and trinket delivery over time. With these, he demonstrated experimental control of response rates and response patterns on different schedules of reinforcement within individual children. This study "inspired" Bijou and his colleagues, who now included Donald M. Baer, a 1957 department hire from the University of Chicago, to extend this line of research, develop a related one, and begin a new one.

In extending the research, they replicated Skinner's methods and findings with other schedules of reinforcement as well as on conditioned reinforcement, escape and avoidance, and discriminative stimulus control. Funded by the National Institute of Mental Heath (NIMH), Bijou hired Robert Orlando from the University of Connecticut to conduct similar research with children with intellectual disabilities in a laboratory Bijou had set up at the Rainier State School in Buckley, Washington. Although Skinner's methods and findings were being replicated at the time by Ogden R. Lindsley with adult psychiatric patients at the Metropolitan State Hospital (Waltham, MA) (Rutherford, 2009, pp. 47–52), Bijou was the first to establish a systematic program of such research with children (Kazdin, 1978, pp. 179–181; Rutherford, 2009, pp. 54–56). Looking backward, its importance was the extension of Skinner's methods and findings to human behavior, which supported the continuity of behavioral processes from nonhumans to humans. Looking forward, its importance was the promise of a natural science of human behavior. When Bijou was later asked what he thought were his "greatest achievements," he nominated this research with children as one of two.

Translational Research   The related line of research inspired by Bijou's (1957) study was an extension to everyday child behavior. The most notable line of these studies was the synthesis and analysis of imitation and generalized imitation, the latter a higher-order operant. When combined with research in other laboratories on, for instance, cooperation, and with Bijou's basic research, this became the subfield of Skinner's science known as the experimental analysis of human behavior (see Lattal & Perone, 1998). As a consequence of Bijou's success, Skinner's methods and science became the first cornerstone of his theory of child development, which he was just beginning to consider.

Applied Research   The third line of research inspired by Bijou's (1957) study was the application of Skinner's science to problems of social importance. He began planning it with Jay S. Birnbrauer, a 1961 department hire from Indiana University, but they had to set it aside while Bijou took a 1-year NIMH senior fellowship with Skinner at Harvard.

Harvard University

At Harvard, Bijou conducted research on concept formation with children at the Walter E. Fernald State School in Waltham, Massachusetts, programming stimuli to establish left-right spatial discriminations. In addition, he attended Harvard's Pigeon Staff meetings; audited Skinner's undergraduate course, Natural Science 114 Human Behavior; and learned programmed instruction from James G. Holland in Skinner's Teaching Machine Project. He also visited the Northeast's model programs for the education and training of children, among them Omar K. Moore's Responsive Environments program in Hamden, Connecticut; Burt Blatt's psychoeducational clinic in Boston, and David Zeaman's project at the Mansfield State Training School in Mansfield, Connecticut. He found them "relatively ineffectual" and vowed to do better.

Back at Washington

Back at Washington in 1962, he returned to his applied line of research, which eventually encompassed four programs. Of all the foundations of behavior modification, or what is now called applied behavior analysis (see Cooper, Heron, & Heward, 2007; the *Journal of Applied Behavior Analysis*, established in 1968), these were arguably the most influential (Kazdin, 1978, p. 273; Krasner, 1977, p. 587). For Bijou, they were the second of his two "greatest achievements."

Applications in Special Education   The first program was his collaboration with Birnbrauer (e.g., Birnbrauer, Wolf, Kidder, & Tague, 1965). At the Rainier

State School, they established an experimental classroom, which Birnbrauer directed with the assistance of Montrose M. Wolf, a 1962 Institute hire from Arizona State University. They developed a token economy system for motivating students and refined time-out procedures for reducing their problem behavior. For the curriculum, Bijou, Birnbrauer, and the classroom teachers—Celia Tague and John D. Kidder—wrote programmed instructional materials for reading, writing, and arithmetic (Bijou et al., 1966). The classroom became a model for individualized instruction in special education. Its reading curriculum was marketed successfully as the Edmark Reading Program.

Early Childhood   The Institute's nursery school was the site of the second program of applied research, which was prompted by R. Florence Harris, the school's psychoanalytically oriented director. She confided in Wolf about a toddler who had regressed from walking to crawling soon after the birth of a sibling. The teachers had been providing her with compensatory attention when she was on the floor, but to no discernible effect. Wolf suggested that they attend to her only when she was walking or standing, not crawling or sitting on the floor. The effect was dramatic, as were those when the contingencies were reversed and then reinstated (Harris, Johnston, Kelly, & Wolf, 1964). Related procedures were used in three other studies to eliminate whining, crying, and aggression and to increase social interactions and motor skills. Of these, "Effects of Social Reinforcement on Isolate Behavior of a Nursery School Child" (Allen, Hart, Buell, Harris, & Wolf, 1964) became a citation classic (Allen, 1983).

Applications in Autism   As the institute's work became better known, Bijou began receiving requests for services, one of them from a physician at the Washington State Psychiatric Hospital for Children. He asked if Bijou would work with a young "schizophrenic" boy who had recently had eye surgery, but would not wear his glasses. Without them, he would go blind. He was also nonverbal and had severe challenging behavior, which made Bijou apprehensive about taking the case. However, he had observed Charles B. Ferster and Marian K. DeMeyer's successful program of operant research with children with autism at the Indiana University Medical School and thus accepted the challenge. It was the Institute's third program of applied research.

Bijou served as the liaison to the hospital, made Wolf the case consultant, and enlisted the assistance of Todd R. Risley, then a graduate student, and Hayden L. Mees, the hospital's psychologist. They developed interventions for the boy's tantrums, self-destructive behavior, and eating and bedtime problems; taught him to speak; and trained hospital personnel to carry out these interventions. The interventions were successful enough that he was dismissed from the hospital 7 months later, yet he still needed intensive treatment in the Institute's nursery school. He was integrated into public school the next year; eventually graduated from high school, indistinguishable from his peers; and had a life. Published as "Application of Operant Conditioning Procedures to the Behavior Problems of an Autistic Child" (Wolf, Risley, & Mees, 1964), this was the first systematic extension of behavior analysis to autism. It, too, became a citation classic. Today, applied behavior analysis is the most effective evidence-based treatment for autism (Myers, Johnson, & the Council on Children with Disabilities, American Academy of Pediatrics, 2007), due, in part, to its further development by O. Ivar Lovaas, another Washington doctorate and Institute staff member.

Clinic and Home: Parent Training   The fourth program of applied research began at the Child Development Clinic. It was on parent training. In analyzing children's asocial behavior (e.g., incessant demands), Robert G. Wahler experimentally demonstrated that it was commonly maintained by parent attention (e.g., acquiescing to demands). He also demonstrated that parents could reduce asocial behavior by ignoring it and attending instead to prosocial behavior, which suggested that parents might serve as therapists for their children (Wahler, Winkel, Peterson, & Morrison, 1965). Robert P. Hawkins experimentally demonstrated that they could serve as therapists in their homes with their children, using time-out for asocial behavior and attention, praise, and affection for prosocial behavior (Hawkins, Peterson, Schweid, & Bijou, 1966).

From Washington to Illinois

Under Bijou's vision and guidance, the Institute made Washington as vibrant as Iowa and Indiana had been. Although commonplace now, the success of the institute's programs of applied research was dramatic and unexpected in its day, especially for children with developmental and intellectual disabilities. They were considered beyond habilitation and placed in institutions for care, at best. Although the Institute was productive, this was not reflected in Bijou's publication record because of his professional and personal style. As Baer described it:

> Bijou's style [was] ... extremely generous. Bijou's pattern was to set up young people like me in a good situation, to talk a lot in ways that would be stimulating and provocative, and then to just watch us go do our own work as a result of that and to, in effect, encourage us to publish ourselves. Bijou never asked to share publications in anything I did by myself.... Bijou just constantly pushed people like me and Birnbrauer and Wolf into these kinds of adventures and then let us reap the benefits of them. (Interview with Terry Knapp, Lawrence, KS, summer 1984; copy with the author)

Bijou's professional service may also have been a factor. By 1958, he was the representative from APA's Division 7 for Developmental Psychology to APA Council and soon on the nomination committee for the Society for Research in Child Development. In 1963, he became the founding editor of the *Journal of Experimental Child Psychology.*

The institute's success notwithstanding, Bijou left Washington because its relations with the psychology department had grown acrimonious. The facts of the matter were multiply determined and interpreted. Bijou's description should suffice for now:

> I left because a majority of the psychology department were antagonistic toward the program. It seemed that the better known our work became, the more antagonistic they became. Among other things, when members of the child development program received attractive offers from other universities, no attempt was made to keep them at Washington with counteroffers. So when Don decided to go to Kansas, Jay to North Carolina, and Mont to Arizona, I decided to make my dissatisfaction known by leaving, too. (Bijou, in Krasner, 1977, p. 594)

Bijou had established programs of basic and applied research that were outside mainstream neobehaviorism and developmental psychology. As Robert F. Peterson, a student at Washington at the time, later commented, Bijou was "one of those 'gentle giants' in the profession" who pioneered by following 'the road less taken'" (personal communication, August 31, 2007). The road he took was behavior analysis.

University of Illinois

Bijou remained in psychology, though. Recruited by special educators and attracted to the psychology department, he moved to the University of Illinois in 1965 as a professor of psychology, a member of the Institute for Research on Exceptional Children, and soon a professor of Educational Psychology. His hiring helped establish the university's focus on applied behavior analysis with children (Goodall, 1972; Kazdin, 1978, p. 273). Several colleagues from Washington joined him, including Barbara D. MacAulay, Marion A. Ault, and Howard N. Sloane. Among his colleagues in the psychology department, only Wesley C. Becker was a behavior analyst, but others were soon hired: Peterson, Warren M. Steinman, Gladys B. Baxley, and later William H. Redd. Bijou was a mentor to them, encouraging their research, assisting their writing, and teaching them how to be mentors themselves (William H. Redd, personal communications, June 24, 2007 and November 1, 2007).

The focal point of Bijou's research and administrative activities at Illinois was the Child Behavior Laboratory (CBL), which he founded and directed until 1972. It eventually comprised administrative offices, research rooms, and, at its core, two experimental classrooms, modeled after those at the Rainier State School. Bijou supported the CBL, its staff, and his students with grants from NIMH, the U.S. Office of Education, and the National Institute of Child Health and Human Development. Although his publication record was stronger at Illinois than at Washington, his contributions were more refinements and extensions of his earlier work than they were ground-breaking. He put it this way:

> Well, our program went on pretty much the way it was set up in Seattle and we kept on pretty much doing what we were doing there, but I don't think we were breaking new ground at that particular time. We were more or less consolidating and not in any sense doing anything different. I felt that my job was done, so to speak. At least we started the programs [at Illinois] and got them running and so on. (Interview with Robert F. Peterson, Reno, NV, July 8, 1998; audio copy with the author)

As was Bijou's style, he was too humble. What he started and got running was a career's worth of contributions for many others.

Among his contributions were methods for integrating descriptive and experimental research in the natural environment, in particular, for assessing, analyzing, and intervening on functional relations among behavior, its consequences, and their antecedents. The seminal publication was Bijou, Peterson, and Ault's (1968) "A Method to Integrate Descriptive and Experimental Field Studies at the Level of Data and Empirical Concepts," one of his two publications he said had "the greatest impact on psychologists and students" (Bijou, 2001, p. 117). He also promoted home-based parent interventions, notably David E. and Marsha S. Shearer's Portage Early Childhood Education Project in Portage, Wisconsin. Then, nearing retirement, he revamped his undergraduate lecture course in child development into a Personalized System of Instruction (Keller, 1968). In conducting and publishing research on the course's effectiveness, defined in terms of student learning, he engaged the scholarship of learning before its time (see Boyer, 1990). In service, he played a significant role in association governance, on journal editorial boards and task forces, and on the organizational committee for what became the Association for Behavior Analysis (ABA). In recognition of his contributions, he began to receive awards, among them the Research Award from the American Association on Mental Deficiency (now on Intellectual and Developmental Disabilities). Near retirement, his colleagues honored him with a Festschrift at the 1974 APA convention (see Etzel, LeBlanc, & Baer, 1977). He was beloved for his generosity and for making everyone around him better.

The Behavior Analysis of Child Development

Although Bijou said his basic and applied research with children were his two greatest professional achievements, another one was almost as great, but never completed or fully sustained. It was his theory of child development—the behavior analysis of child development. At Washington, he and Baer taught a child development course using Mussen, Conger, and Kagan's (1956) *Child Development and Personality*. However, they wanted a text that was consistent with the concepts and principles they were using in their research, so they wrote several short books explicating Bijou's theory. Skinner's science was one cornerstone of it, but Bijou thought it insufficient. Recalling his discussions with Kantor at Indiana, he delved into interbehavioral psychology (e.g., Kantor, 1959) and found it "compatible" with Skinner's science, but broader. It was broader theoretically, practically, and substantively: (1) Its unit of analysis is field-theoretic, not lineal; (2) it explicitly includes the field's history and setting factors as participants, which would enhance prediction and control; and (3) it addresses topics such as developmental stages. Kantor's philosophy was the second cornerstone of Bijou's theory. When he decided to "coordinate" it with Skinner's, he saw that his near quarter-century search for a "point of view" was complete: "I was now convinced that the work of two geniuses—Skinner and Kantor—could be integrated into a psychological system that would meet the criteria of a natural science" (Bijou, 1999, p. 187).

Bijou and Baer's (1961) first book, *Child Development: A Systematic and Empirical Theory*, was the other of Bijou's two publications he said had "the greatest impact on psychologists and students" (Bijou, 2001, p. 117), as well as "the best thing we put out" on his views (Bijou, interview with Robert F. Peterson, July 8, 1998; copy with the author). In it, they defined psychological development as "progressive changes in the way an organism's behavior interacts with the environment" (p. 1). Following Skinner, they conceptualized responses and stimuli as class concepts (R↔S) but courted misrepresentation by depicting the unit of analysis as B = f(S). However, they elaborated. The S comprises two subclasses: S_1 for current stimuli and S_2 for their phylogenetic and ontogenetic histories. S_1 also comprises two subclasses. Following Kantor, one was stimulus functions, that is, stimuli defined in relation to responses, for instance, the authoritativeness of adults, which makes some children comfortable but others uneasy. The other subclass of S_1 stimuli was setting events—events that influenced stimulus functions, for instance, the effects of an experimenter's instructions to a child engaged in doll play that a particular doll is a father, not a brother. In addition to describing their theory, this book was an early and widely influential primer of Skinner's science.

It was also revised twice and became more interbehavioral in the process. In the first revision, Bijou and Baer (1978) replaced B = f(S) with field-theoretic language. They characterized behavior as an *interaction* between responses and stimuli, not as a form of responding. They characterized the interaction as *reciprocal*: stimulus functions cannot be defined independently of response functions and vice versa. And, they characterized the reciprocal interactions as *interdependent*, not as dependent or independent. With this, Bijou had solved, for himself, Lewin's problem: How do we know what a person's perceptions are or what the environment means to the person? For Bijou, they were the reciprocal and interdependent relations between a person's response functions, for instance, acquiescing to a child's demands, and the environment's stimulus functions, for instance, a child's demanding behavior. The publicly evident functional relations could be described, predicted, and in principle controlled.

In the book's second revision, Bijou (1993) integrated biology more fully into his theory. First, he noted that biology participates in all behavior; behavior could not occur without it. However, biology is not a basis of response functions unless it also has stimulus or setting event functions. Second, unlike Skinner, he set nature and nurture aside as a false dichotomy. The issue is not how much one or the other contributes to development but *how* they contribute—both 100%. For this, he turned to developmental systems theory, in particular, to Susan Oyama's (1989) contributions. On this view, nature and nurture are not independent sources of variance for development but are, respectively, the product and process of development from the point of conception forward. To quote Oyama (1989), "…nature is the product of the process of the developmental interactions we call nurture" (p. 5).

As for Kantor's developmental stages, Bijou and Baer addressed them in their next two books. The stages were neither biologically based nor age determined, but descriptive of children's predominant interactions with their environments.

The foundational stage extends from prior to birth through infancy. It is marked by reflex behavior, a transition from uncoordinated to coordinated exploratory behavior, and the emergence of early perceptual, emotional, social, and verbal behavior (Bijou & Baer, 1965). The basic stage extends from the end of infancy through early childhood. It is marked by the elaboration of play, the development of knowledge and problem solving, and the emergence of individually characteristic behavioral repertoires (Bijou, 1976). The societal stage is marked by the start of socialization outside the family and immersion into the community, but Bijou did not write a book about it, in part, because he found so little behavior-analytic material available.

Bijou's integration of Skinner's radical behaviorism and Kantor's interbehavioral psychology was a unique achievement of his own making, albeit far from complete as a theory of child development, which he readily acknowledged (interview with Robert F. Peterson, Reno, NV, July 8, 1998; audio copy with the author). It was also not a theory in the traditional sense, like Arnold L. Gesell's, Erik Erikson's, or Jean Piaget's. Compared with theirs, the experiential, observational, and experimental basis of Bijou's theory yielded but a sketch of children's development. This was, however, perhaps an unfair comparison. Bijou's theory was a theory more in Lewin's sense: a model of an integrated field and its participants. Fair or not, the comparison left Bijou outside of mainstream developmental theory.

His pragmatism also left him outside developmental psychology's philosophy of science. His pragmatism resonated with Lewin's observation about action research: "If you want truly to understand something, try to change it." Bijou's basic and applied research entailed experimental and practical control—change in child behavior. In learning to change it or what controlled it, Bijou increasingly understood behavior. This was Charles S. Peirce's (1839–1914) pragmatic criterion of truth—and Bijou's (see Lattal & Liapple, 2003)—but not the criterion of truth in developmental psychology. The latter's criteria were either theoretical coherence or the correspondence between theory and data, neither of them tested in action. Bijou's pragmatism also resonated with Lewin's point, "There's nothing so practical as a good theory," in that theory, in Lewin's sense, was good for practice. That is, it was good for changing socially important behavior, not just for formal propositional deductions for research.

Today, Bijou's behavior analysis of child development lies outside mainstream developmental research, theory, and philosophy. However, it retains a place within behavior analysis, with occasional updatings (e.g., Gewirtz & Pelaez-Nogueras, 1992; Schlinger, 1995) and extensions (e.g., Novak & Pelaez, 2004) and some promising advances, among them, behavioral cusps (Rosales & Baer, 1997) and relational frame theory (Hayes, Barnes-Holmes, & Roche, 2001).

"RETIREMENT"

Bijou retired from the University of Illinois in 1975 as a professor emeritus, but his retirement was in name only. He remained active in teaching, research, and service for another 25 years—almost another career.

University of Arizona

In 1975, he moved to the University of Arizona as an adjunct professor in the departments of psychology and of special education and rehabilitation. There, he rejoined Kirk and Ralph Wetzel, who had been a student at Washington. He consulted on research, training, and demonstration projects; taught graduate seminars; and continued his scholarship, for instance, a program of research based on Kantor's (1977) book *Psychological Linguistics* (Bijou, 1989). In service, he was elected the third president of ABA and traveled extensively, disseminating behavior analysis in Mexico, Central and South America, Japan, and Europe (see, e.g., Rayek & Ribes-Inesta, 1977). A natural science of behavior is a science without borders.

In recognition of his contributions, he received more awards, among them the Distinguished Scientist Award from the National Association of Retarded Citizens (now the ARC) and awards from three fields represented by APA divisions: the Don Hake Basic/Applied Award (now the Translational Research Award) from Division 25 for the Experimental Analysis of Behavior (now Behavior Analysis) for "individuals whose work spans basic and applied research and represents the cross-fertilization of the two areas;" the Edgar A. Doll Award from Division 33 for Mental Retardation and Developmental Disabilities (now Intellectual and Developmental Disabilities), which is its "highest recognition of a career marked by outstanding scientific contributions to the field of intellectual and developmental disabilities;" and the G. Stanley Hall Award from Division 7 for Developmental Psychology for:

> Distinguished contributions to developmental psychology, including contributions in research, student training, and other scholarly endeavors. Evaluations are based on the scientific merit of the individual's work, the importance of this work for opening up new empirical or theoretical areas of development psychology, and the importance of the individual's work in linking developmental psychology with issues confronting the larger society or with other disciplines. (retrieved from http://ecp.fiu.edu/apa/div7/?d=gstanleyhall)

University of Nevada–Reno

In 1993, Bijou moved to the University of Nevada–Reno as a distinguished professor emeritus of psychology. There, he helped establish the department's behavior analysis program, cofounded its Early Childhood Autism Program, taught and advised graduate students, and continued to publish (e.g., Bijou & Ribes, 1996). He also garnered additional awards: one for International Contributions to Behavior Analysis from ABA and one for Distinguished Service to Behavior Analysis from the Society for the Advancement of Behavior Analysis.

Retirement

When Janet died on December 16, 2000, Sid finally retired. He moved to Santa Barbara, California, to live with Jude and be closer to Bob further north in Mill Valley. For nearly a decade, though, he remained professionally involved, corresponding with and receiving visits from former students and colleagues and from other scientists and scholars. On June 11, 2009, he died at home, still active at age 100. As Jude and Bob wrote of the moment, "A peaceful, natural death, as he was getting ready for another day. A life well lived to the very last moment." Developmental psychology was fortunate to have had such a kind, gentle man in the field for so many years. He was selfless in being brave and brave in being selfless. He was a gem.

CONCLUSION

Sidney William Bijou traveled a lot. He traveled across many fields in developmental psychology and across many systems. Finding eclecticism bewildering, he sought a point of view. This presupposed, of course, that eclecticism is bewildering and that psychology could have a point of view. Bijou supposed so. However, not any point of view would do. It had to unify and advance psychology as a natural science. This presupposed that psychology could be unified and a natural science. Bijou supposed this, too. The points of view Bijou considered were psychoanalysis, neo-Gestalt field theory, and four varieties of behaviorism. Eventually, he settled on an integration of two of the latter, his own integration: Skinner's experimental analysis of behavior provided methods and a science, while Kantor's interbehavioral psychology provided a philosophy. This presupposed that psychology could be their integration. Bijou supposed so.

As psychology evolved from classical behaviorism to mediational neobehaviorism to cognitive psychology, Bijou increasingly stood outside the mainstream of developmental research, theory, and philosophy. However, he was not alone. Psychology encompassed (and encompasses) other nonmediational, nonreductionistic, and nonmechanistic programs, among them ecological approaches to cognition and perception, selectionist accounts of intelligence, and developmental systems theory (Morris, 2003). Eventually, these programs—not cognitive psychology (see Leahey, 1992)—may prove revolutionary in psychology. Historiography that addresses them at the time of the putative cognitive revolution may provide a fresh perspective on what actually happened then and since then and on developmental psychology's future. This may be especially true where misunderstandings play a role in shaping history and historiography—for instance, misunderstandings that all behaviorisms are stimulus-response psychologies and none are field theoretic. Like travel, the study of history is fatal to prejudice, bigotry, and narrow-mindedness.

SUGGESTED READINGS

Bijou, S. W., & Baer, D. M. (1961). *Child development: A systematic and empirical theory.* New York: Appleton-Century-Crofts.

This was the first edition of Bijou and Baer's first book on child development. It described the theory's rudiments, among them its assumptions about theory (e.g., empirically based, inductively derived), the field of child development (e.g., its relations with biology and cultural anthropology), and the nature of development (e.g., "progressive changes in the way an organism's behavior interacts with the environment," p. 1). It also provided a primer of the basic principles of respondent behavior (e.g., conditioning), operant behavior (e.g., reinforcement, discrimination), and their interaction (e.g., emotional behavior, self-control).

Bijou, S. W., Peterson, R. F., & Ault, M. A. (1968). A method to integrate descriptive and experimental field studies at the level of data and empirical concepts. *Journal of Applied Behavior Analysis, 1,* 175–191.

Bijou et al. argued that descriptive studies of behavior in the natural environment should be integrated with experimental studies in those settings (e.g., at home). They assumed that behavior is the interaction between organisms and their environments and that behavioral concepts (e.g., shyness) are descriptive concepts, not explanatory constructs (e.g., shyness). They described how to define and record behavior; train observers and assess their agreement; and collect, analyze, and interpret data. They concluded by explaining the benefits of integration (e.g., experiments suggested by descriptions and vice versa).

Bijou, S. W. (1979). Some clarifications of the meaning of a behavior analysis of child development. *Psychological Record, 29,* 3–13.

Bijou addressed five misunderstandings of his developmental theory, among them that it was an S→R learning theory; that it regarded children as passive, not active, organisms; and that it had harmful effects when applied. He argued, in turn, that behavior analysis is not a learning theory but a system of psychology with a science and a philosophy; that it is a theory not about children but about their behavior, conceptualized as a field of factors, all of them unique and thereby active; and that it is not inherently harmful, especially where it addresses the function of behavior, not just its form, thereby precluding cultural irrelevance.

REFERENCES

Allen, K. E. (1983). The week's citation classic. *Current Contents, 38,* 22.

Allen, K. E., Hart, B. E., Buell, J. S., Harris, F. R., & Wolf, M. M. (1964). Effects of social-reinforcement on isolate behavior of a nursery school child. *Child Development, 35,* 511–518.

Bijou, S. W. (1938). The performance of normal children on the Randall's Island performance series. *Journal of Applied Psychology, 22,* 186–191. doi:10.1037/h0059986

Bijou, S. W. (1942). The development of a conditioning methodology for studying experimental neurosis in the rat. *Journal of Comparative Psychology, 34,* 91–106. doi: 10.1037/h0063146

Bijou, S. W. (1943). A study of "experimental neurosis" in the rat by the conditioned response technique. *Journal of Comparative and Physiological Psychology, 36,* 1–20.

Bijou, S. W. (1955). A systematic approach to an experimental analysis of young children. *Child Development, 26,* 161–168.

Bijou, S. W. (1957). Patterns of reinforcement and extinction in young children. *Child Development, 28,* 47–54.

Bijou, S. W. (1976). *The basic stage of early childhood development.* Englewood Cliffs, NJ: Prentice-Hall.

Bijou, S. W. (1979). Some clarifications of the meaning of a behavior analysis of child development. *Psychological Record, 29,* 3–13.

Bijou, S. W. (1989). Psychological linguistics: Implications for a theory of initial development and a method for research. In H. W. Reese (Ed.), *Advances in child behavior and development* (vol. 21, pp. 221–241). Orlando, FL: Academic Press.

Bijou, S. W. (1993). *Behavior analysis of child development.* Reno, NV: Context Press.

Bijou, S. W. (1996). Reflections on some early events related to behavior analysis of child development. *Behavior Analyst, 19*, 49–60.

Bijou, S. W. (1999). Empirical behaviorism. In W. T. O'Donohue & R. Kitchener (Eds.), *Handbook of behaviorism* (pp. 179–193). New York: Academic Press.

Bijou, S. W. (2001). Child behavior therapy: Early history. In W. T. O'Donohue, D. A. Henderson, S. C. Hayes, J. E. Fisher, & L. J. Hayes (Eds.), *A history of the behavioral therapies: Founders' personal histories* (pp. 105–124). Reno, NV: Context Press.

Bijou, S. W., & Baer, D. M. (1961). *Child development: A systematic and empirical theory.* New York: Appleton-Century-Crofts. doi:10.1037/11139-000

Bijou, S. W., & Baer, D. M. (1965). *Child development: The universal stage of infancy.* New York: Appleton-Century-Crofts.

Bijou, S. W., & Baer, D. M. (1978). *Child development: A behavior analysis approach.* Englewood Cliff, NJ: Prentice-Hall.

Bijou, S. W., Birnbrauer, J. S., Kidder, J. D., & Tague, C. (1966). Programmed instruction as an approach to the teaching of reading, writing, and arithmetic to retarded children. *Psychological Record, 16*, 505–522.

Bijou, S. W., Peterson, R. F., & Ault, M. A. (1968). A method to integrate descriptive and experimental field studies at the level of data and empirical concepts. *Journal of Applied Behavior Analysis, 1*, 175–191. doi:10.1901/jaba.1968.1-175

Bijou, S. W., & Ribes, E. (Eds.). (1996). *New directions in behavior development.* Reno, NV: Context Press.

Birnbrauer, J. S., Wolf, M. M., Kidder, J. D., & Tague, C. (1965). Classroom behavior of retarded pupils with token reinforcement. *Journal of Experimental Child Psychology, 2*, 219–235. doi:10.1016/0022-0965(65)90045-7

Boyer, E. (1990). *Scholarship reconsidered: Priorities of the professoriate.* San Francisco: Jossey-Bass.

Burnham, J. C. (1968). The new psychology: From narcissism to social control. In J. Braeman, R. H. Bremner, & D. Brody (Eds.), *Change and continuity in twentieth century America: The 1920s* (pp. 351–398). Columbus: University of Ohio Press.

Cantor, J. H. (Ed.). (1991). *Psychology at Iowa: Centennial essays.* Hillsdale, NJ: Erlbaum.

Capshew, J. H. (1988). The legacy of the laboratory (1888-1988): A history of the Psychology Department at Indiana University. In E. Hearst & J. H. Capshew (Eds.), *Psychology at Indiana University: A centennial review and compendium* (pp. 1–83). Bloomington: Indiana University Psychology Department.

Capshew, J. H. (1999). *Psychologists on the march: Science, practice, and professional identity in America, 1920–1969.* Cambridge, UK: Cambridge University Press. doi:10.1017/CBO9780511572944

Cooper, J. O., Heron, T., & Heward, W. (2007). *Applied behavior analysis*, 2d ed. Upper Saddle River, NJ: Pearson.

Einstein, A., & Infeld, L. (1938). *The evolution of physics.* New York: Simon and Schuster.

Etzel, B. C., LeBlanc, J. M., & Baer, D. M. (Eds.). (1977). *New developments in behavioral research: Theory, method, and application.* Hillsdale, NJ: Erlbaum.

Gewirtz, J. L., & Pelaez-Nogueras, M. (1992). B. F. Skinner's legacy to infant behavioral development. *American Psychologist, 47*, 11, 1411–1422. doi:10.1037/0003-066X.47.11.1411

Ghezzi, P. M. (2010). In memoriam: Sidney W. Bijou. *Journal of Applied Behavior Analysis, 43*, 175–179. doi:10.1901/jaba.2010.43-175

Goodall, K. (1972, November). Shapers at work. *Psychology Today, 6*(6), 53–63, 132–138.

Harris, F. R., Johnston, M. K., Kelly, C. S., & Wolf, M. M. (1964). Effects of positive social reinforcement on regressed crawling of a nursery school child. *Journal of Educational Psychology, 55*, 35–41. doi:10.1037/h0042496

Hawkins, R. P., Peterson, R. F., Schweid, E., & Bijou, S. W. (1966). Behavior therapy in the home: Amelioration of problem parent-child relations with the parent in the therapeutic role. *Journal of Experimental Child Psychology, 4*, 99–107. doi:10.1016/0022-0965(66)90054-3

Hayes, S. C., Barnes-Holmes, D., & Roche, B. (Eds.). (2001). *Relational frame theory: A post-Skinnerian account of human language and cognition.* New York: Kluwer Academic/Plenum.

Hull, C. L. (1943). *Principles of behavior.* New York: Appleton-Century-Crofts.

Iversen, I. H., & Lattal, K. A. (Eds.). (1991). *Techniques in the behavioral and neural sciences: Experimental analysis of behavior, Parts 1 and 2.* Amsterdam: Elsevier.

Jastak, J. F., & Bijou, S. W. (1938). *Wide Range Achievement Test.* Wilmington, DE: Guidance Associates.

Kantor, J. R. (1938). The nature of psychology as a natural science. *Acta Psychologica, 4*, 1–61. doi:10.1016/S0001-6918(39)90002-8

Kantor, J. R. (1959). *Interbehavioral psychology.* Chicago: Principia Press.

Kantor, J. R. (1977). *Psychological linguistics.* Chicago: Principia Press.

Kazdin, A. E. (1978). *History of behavior modification: Experimental foundations of contemporary research.* Baltimore: University Park Press.

Keller, F. S. (1968). Good-bye teacher. *Journal of Applied Behavior Analysis, 1*, 79–89. doi:10.1901/jaba.1968.1-79

Krasner, L. (1977). An interview with Bijou. In B. C. Etzel, J. M. LeBlanc, & D. M. Baer (Eds.), *New developments in behavioral research: Theory, method, and application* (pp. 587–599). Hillsdale, NJ: Erlbaum.

Lattal, K. A., & Liapple, J. S. (2003). Pragmatism and behavior analysis. In K. A. Lattal & P. N. Chase (Eds.), *Behavior theory and philosophy* (pp. 41–61). New York: Kluwer Academic/Plenum.

Lattal, K. A., & Perone, M. (Eds.). (1998). *Handbook of research methods in human operant behavior.* New York: Plenum.

Leahey, T. H. (1992). Mythical revolutions in the history of American psychology. *American Psychologist, 47*, 308–318. doi:10.1037/0003-066X.47.2.308

Lewin, K. (1935). *A dynamic theory of personality.* New York: McGraw-Hill.

Lewin, K. (1936). *Principles of topological psychology.* New York: McGraw-Hill. doi:10.1037/10019-000

Morawski, J. G. (1986). Organizing knowledge and behavior at Yale's Institute of Human Relations. *ISIS, 77*, 219–242.

Morris, E. K. (2003). Behavior analysis and a modern psychology: Programs of direct action. In K. A. Lattal & P. N. Chase (Eds.), *Behavior theory and philosophy* (pp. 275–298). New York: Kluwer Academic/Plenum.

Morris, E. K. (2008). Sidney W. Bijou: The Illinois years. *Behavior Analyst, 31*, 179–203.

Mussen, P., Conger, J., & Kagan, J. (1956). *Child development and personality.* New York: Harper.

Myers, S. M., Johnson, C. P., & the Council on Children with Disabilities, American Academy of Pediatrics (2007). Management of children with autism spectrum disorders. *Pediatrics, 120*, 1162–1182. doi:10.1542/peds.2007-2362

News and notes (1935). *American Journal of Psychiatry, 91*, 1447.

Novak, G., & Pelaez, M. (2004). *Child and adolescent development: A behavioral systems approach.* Thousand Oaks, CA: Sage.

Oyama, S. (1989). Ontogeny and the central dogma: Do we need a concept of genetic programming in order to have an evolutionary perspective? In M. R, Gunnar & E. Thelen (Eds.), *Systems and development: The Minnesota symposium on child psychology* (vol. 22, pp. 1–34). Hillsdale, NJ: Erlbaum.

Peterson, R. F. (1998). Interview with Sidney W. Bijou. Santa Barbara, CA.

Rayek. E., & Ribes-Inesta, E. (1977). The development of behavior analysis in Mexico: Sidney W. Bijou's contribution. In B. C. Etzel, J. M. LeBlanc, & D. M. Baer (Eds.). *New developments in behavioral research: Theory, method, and application* (pp. 601–603). Hillsdale, NJ: Erlbaum.

Rosales. J., & Baer, D. M. (1997). Behavioral cusps: A developmental and pragmatic concept for behavior analysis. *Journal of Applied Behavior Analysis, 30,* 533–544. doi:10.1901/jaba.1997.30-533

Rutherford, A. (2009). *Beyond the box: B. F. Skinner's technology of behavior from laboratory to life, 1950s–1970s.* Toronto: University of Toronto Press.

Samelson, F. (1974). History, origin myth, and ideology: "Discovery" of social psychology. *Journal for the Theory of Social Behaviour, 4,* 217–231.

Schlinger, H. D. (1995). *A behavior-analytic view of child development.* New York: Plenum.

Skinner, B. F. (1938). *The behavior of organisms.* New York: Appleton-Century.

Skinner, B. F. (1945). The operational analysis of psychological terms. *Psychological Review, 52,* 270–277, 291–294. doi:10.1037/h0062535

Skinner, B. F. (1953). *Science and human behavior.* New York: Macmillan.

Smith, L. D. (1992). On prediction and control: B. F. Skinner and the technological ideal of science. *American Psychologist, 47,* 216–223. doi:10.1037/0003-066X.47.2.216

Twain, M. (1869). *Innocents abroad.* Hartford, CT: American Publishing.

Vallery-Radot, R. (1927). *The life of Pasteur.* Paris: Hatchet.

Wahler, R. C., Winkel, G. H., Peterson, R. F., & Morrison, D. C. (1965). Mothers as behavior therapists for their own children. *Behaviour Research and Therapy, 3,* 113–124. doi:10.1016/0005-7967(65)90015-X

Watson, J. B. (1919). *Psychology from the standpoint of a behaviorist.* Philadelphia: Lippincott. doi:10.1037/10016-000

Watson, J. B. (1930). *Behaviorism.* Chicago: University of Chicago Press.

Wesolowski, M. D. (2002). Pioneer profiles: A few minutes with Bijou. *Behavior Analyst, 25,* 15–27.

Wolf, M. M., Risley, T. R., & Mees, H. (1964). Application of operant conditioning procedures to the behavior problems of an autistic child. *Behaviour Research and Therapy, 1,* 305–312. doi:10.1016/0005-7967(63)90045-7

13

John Paul Scott:
The Study of Genetics, Development, and Social Behavior

DONALD A. DEWSBURY

University of Florida

Although developmental animal research has been an important part of psychology since its early years as a discipline (e.g., Small, 1899; Watson, 1903), its connection to human developmental psychology has sometimes been lost in recent literature. As several authors have pointed out, this is unfortunate (e.g., Kazdin & Rotella, 2009). It is appropriate to include John Paul Scott in this compilation because of his contributions to the field of developmental psychology in addition to related areas. His greatest impact came as the chair of the Division of Behavior Studies at the Jackson Laboratory in Bar Harbor, Maine, where he conducted landmark studies of the development of canine behavior; he later directed a Center for Research on Social Behavior at Bowling Green State University. His developmental work focused on the processes of socialization. Scott also established the importance of the critical period hypothesis that he adapted from embryology.

Figure 13.1   John Paul Scott. (Courtesy of the Center for Archival Collections, University Libraries, Bowling Green State University, Bowling Green, OH. With permission.)

John Paul Scott was a man on a mission to reduce strife in the world. He was concerned with war and peace and the betterment of humanity. Scott viewed his times as dominated by periods of war and economic strife and felt that these problems required alleviation. He believed, however, that an important route toward these goals lay in the study of animal behavior. Scott's belief that betterment of the human condition might be facilitated through research on nonhuman animals was sincere and deeply held, not just a casual statement designed to secure federal funding. In his view this required a developmental approach in basic research. Overall, one might list as the themes of his work: behavior genetics, development, social behavior, aggression, and violence.

Scott's career represents a fascinating journey from geneticist to developmentalist and functioning psychologist. The mission underlying this journey remained the betterment of the human condition through a better understanding of aggression, violence, and war and their determinants. Driven by this goal, Scott was a rather serious and dedicated man, not prone to be the life of the party, but sincere—and genuine.

EARLY LIFE AND EDUCATION

Scott was born December 17, 1909, the year of the Darwin centennial, in Kansas City, Missouri (Dewsbury & Panksepp, 2001; Scott, 1985; Stuckey, 2001). Paul was the second of six children of Eulalia Vivian (Armstrong) Scott and John W. Scott. John W. was a parasitologist and the chair of the Department of Zoology at the University of Wyoming; he had a master of arts degree in psychology and is known, in part, for a classic study of the behavior of the sage grouse. His son John Paul Scott (1985) listed several formative events from his early years. When the family spent a year in Virginia Paul was an outsider and became the target of bullies; this sensitized him to issues of violence. Back in Laramie he became a star scholar and athlete. He then enrolled at the University of Wyoming. During his sophomore year Paul spent a summer at the Marine Biological Institute in Woods Hole, Massachusetts. There his love of biology was strengthened, he developed an affinity for the idyllic life in a research institute, and he conducted his first study of behavior—the response to light of brittle stars, a species of invertebrates. This experience appears to have started him toward a career at a similar institution. As an undergraduate, Scott took psychology courses from department chair June Etta Downey, the first woman to chair a psychology department at a major university. He finished at the university with a record that enabled him to become a Rhodes Scholar at the University of Oxford. At Oxford Paul studied zoology, but the Oxford zoology program at that time had little on the study of behavior. He also spent a few weeks at yet another research institute, the Zoological Station at Naples.

Scott wrote some poems and short stories and reached a choice point as he harbored interest in becoming a writer. Wanting to marry and recognizing the financial problems of a professional writer, he chose graduate school in zoology at the University of Chicago. There Scott met two of the lasting influences on his professional life. Sewall Wright, his dissertation advisor, was one of the world's leading geneticists and one of the developers of the modern evolutionary synthesis. With Wright, who knew little of behavior, Scott studied the embryology of a mutation Wright had discovered, polydactyly (extra digits) in guinea pigs. Scott (1937) found that the gene had its effect by stimulating growth at a critical period in development. He would carry the theme of critical periods throughout much of his career; it became especially important to his work in developmental psychology.

The other major Chicago influence was ecologist Warder Clyde Allee, whom Scott (1985) regarded as the only major zoologist at the time working on problems of behavior. Working with some of Wright's *Drosophila*, Scott conducted his first study of behavior genetics. But Allee appears to have had a more subtle influence on Scott as well. A member of the Society of Friends, Allee was a humane man who was concerned with using his science to promote human welfare. This would become a major part of Scott's life work.

In 1933 Scott married Sally Fisher, the daughter of acclaimed novelist Dorothy Canfield Fisher. Children soon followed. Sally worked closely with Paul, mainly in transcribing his work, but also wrote 22 children's books of her own.

When Paul completed his PhD at Chicago in 1935 he regarded himself as a qualified researcher in developmental genetics (Scott, 1985). But 1935 was a bad time to be job hunting, so he accepted a position inconsistent with his lofty research goals, at Wabash College in Indiana.

Because stories such as this must, of necessity, be told in a linear manner, they miss some of the more complex dynamics of development. Other events in Scott's life interacted with his experiences at Chicago and elsewhere. At the macro level Scott grew up in a difficult time. Prior to his fifth birthday the Germans invaded Belgium and World War I had begun. Somewhat later, economic turmoil and the stock market crash gripped much of the world. He saw the impact in Europe during his years at Oxford. There were military conflicts in Spain and China and then World War II. He reflected that at the end of World War II, when he was 36, he had known just 16 years that had not been affected by war and economic disaster (Scott, 1985). His experience with bullying, the climate of war and poverty, experiences in Europe, and interaction with Allee all were factors, among others, in convincing Scott to seek scientific solutions to pressing social problems. Although he chose to do this with research on nonhuman animals, this goal nevertheless provided the foundations of his science. Earlier, as war progressed, Scott (1942b, p. 40) called for research to find "non-military methods of winning the war."

EARLY CAREER

Scott stayed at Wabash College for 10 years. One particularly important experience he recalled occurred when a group of faculty members hosted students at a Senior Study Camp. As a ploy he attacked the social scientists for their lack of rigor compared with his in biological science. This contrast led to much discussion and thought. He wrote that this experience convinced him that the methods of the biological sciences could be applied to social phenomena. He recalled that he saw a clear path toward a science he called *sociobiology*. He was not interested in simplistic application of animal research to humans; rather, he wished to use the methods of biology to better understand human behavior. The sociobiology he envisioned was quite different from that later promulgated by E. O. Wilson (1975), who popularized the term. Scott (1986) criticized Wilson's use of the term for what he believed to be its overreliance on evolutionary genetics. Scott (1967) also used the term *evolutionary psychology* in a different sense than it is now used but well before it came into common usage.

In 1938 Scott took a year off from Wabash to go to Boston to work in libraries and elsewhere to teach himself the literature of the social sciences with the goal of producing a book. Unable to serve in World War II because of his age, parental status, and chronic stomach problems, he decided to reaffirm his determination to apply science to the problems of war. Back at Wabash, Scott rented a farm so that he could study the social behavior of sheep. He also spent the summers of 1938 and 1939 at yet another research institute, the Jackson Laboratory, studying the aggressive behavior in inbred strains of house mice (usually defined as the product of at least 20 generations of brother–sister matings and thought to be close to identical twins; Scott, 1942a). This linked to the similar contemporaneous research in Allee's laboratory.

THE JACKSON LABORATORY

After 10 years at Wabash, Scott's family was completed with two sons and two daughters. He felt that he had found his life's work but felt unable to realize his goals in the college environment of Wabash. Meanwhile, Alan Gregg of the Rockefeller Foundation wanted to increase awareness among social scientists of the role of genetics in human behavior. The Jackson Laboratory, founded by Gregg's old classmate C. C. Little, was a leading facility for research in genetics, as the world's leading repository of inbred strains of mice, though the emphasis was on cancer research. Gregg focused on putting a behavior program there. He was especially interested in the possible use of dogs in the research, partially because they are more social and their behavior is easier to study. It was decided that the behavior laboratory was to be established in Bar Harbor. By this time Scott was regarded as the only person in the country with formal training in genetics who also had an interest in behavior, and he was offered the position, which became that of the chair of the Division of Behavior Studies; he accepted and remained there for 20 years.

Scott's administrative style was modeled after the style he encountered at Woods Hole and was consistent with his ideals: democratic organization, with the program run by the scientists involved therein. He soon organized a Summer Investigators Program, patterned after others, such as that at Woods Hole in which he had earlier participated (Scott, 1978b). The Bar Harbor program brought immediate results in terms of productive and helpful colleagues. One of the participants, John L. Fuller, returned as a staff member a year later and became Scott's closest colleague and collaborator. This was the period of Scott's most important and influential work. The dog program flourished and an appreciable amount of research was also done on mice. The many products of those years are summarized in the following sections.

BOWLING GREEN

Eventually conditions at the Jackson Laboratory changed with a new administration and altered working conditions; the behavior program was not supported as it had been previously (Scott, 1978b). By 1959 Scott became restless and contemplated a move. He wrote "feelers" to such people as Frank Beach, Leonard Carmichael, Lee Dice, and Robert Sears. He sought a better environment in which to integrate research results, but he made no immediate move. Scott spent the academic year 1963–1964 at the Center for Advanced Study in the Behavioral Sciences at Stanford University and in 1965 moved to Bowling Green State University as a research professor and director of graduate studies and later at Ohio as Regents professor of psychology, with few formal duties. The Jackson Laboratory behavior program was phased out. During this period he also held secondary positions at Tufts University, the University of Connecticut, and the University of Chicago for varying periods.

At Bowling Green Scott organized and directed a Center for Research on Social Behavior. Although he established a dog colony there and participated in some important research, his emphasis shifted somewhat as he turned his attention toward more integrative projects and assumed administrative responsibilities. The center attracted numerous students and visitors. Scott's attention during this period shifted to issues of adjustment, attachment, and implications for human psychiatric problems. He developed a systems approach to agonistic behavior and related phenomena. A member of the American Psychological Association (APA), he joined Divisions 26 (History) and 28 (Psychopharmacology) and was elected a Fellow of Divisions 1 (General), 3 (Experimental), 6 (Behavioral Neuroscience and Comparative Psychology), and 48 (Peace Psychology). He retired as a Regents research professor in 1980.

Sally died in 1978, and the next year Paul married his long-time associate Mary-'Vesta Marston. John Paul Scott died in Toledo, Ohio, on March 26, 2000.

THE JACKSON LABORATORY DOG PROGRAM

Funded by the Rockefeller Foundation, with later help from the National Institutes of Health, the Ford Foundation, the National Science Foundation, and the National Institute of Mental Health, Scott and Fuller operated the behavior program and collected data on dog behavior for 13 years (Dewsbury, 2011; Scott & Fuller, 1965a). It was housed at the Hamilton Station facility, several miles from the main laboratory. About 300 puppies were raised at the laboratory during this period. Most dogs were reared under standardized conditions in pens with litter mates. Most were of five breeds: African basenjis, beagles, cocker spaniels, Shetland sheep dogs (Shelties), and wire-haired terriers. What is remarkable about this substantial study, and nearly unique in the literature, is the study of an appreciable group of pure-bred dogs, not those of mixed breeds, with controlled histories, under controlled and uniform laboratory conditions. In recent years there has been a resurgence of interest in dog behavior, especially in the study of cognition. Virtually all of that work is being conducted with pets of varying breeds and developmental histories; this contrasts with the more controlled genetics and environmental conditions in Bar Harbor.

To ensure uniform procedures, the staff developed a 72-page *Manual of Dog Testing Procedures* (Staff, 1950). This included a description of the physical environment, social environment, nutrition, and veterinary procedures, a series of performance tests, and physical and physiological observations. A battery of 30 tests was used on the dogs. Uniform procedures were developed so that each dog was tested in a specific way at a specific age. There were dominance tests, climbing and leash control tests, emotional reactivity tests, relationship tests, barrier tests, maze tests, delayed response tests, retrieving tests, and the like. As these tests were spaced through the first year of life, the staff generated an ontogenetic history of the five breeds of dogs.

Because they were interested in genetic influences on behavior, Scott and Fuller chose two breeds, cocker spaniels and basenjis, for a Mendelian genetic analysis. This entails breeding F_1 crosses between the two breeds as well as the F_2 ($F_1 \times F_1$), and the backcrosses between the F_1 and each parental breed.

Several scientists, including Anne Anastasi (Anastasi, Fuller, Scott, & Schmitt, 1955), helped them analyze some 8000 bits of data they generated, many of them with multiple measures. Their 50×50 correlation matrix was a challenge for the computers of the day. Surely, their analyses of more than 40 years ago were not as sophisticated as those of today, but they were considerable for the time.

The data were interesting, however. Correlations among the tests were generally low, suggesting that they were not tapping a single factor. Although there were many breed differences, no one breed outshone all of the others. Scott interpreted this to mean that there is no general intelligence factor (such as Spearman's g) but rather that different breeds do poorly or well on different tasks. Breeds differed in the display of apparent fear in test situations. Although all acted fearful in some situations, they reacted most fearfully in different conditions, depending on breed. Surely, this apparent fear affected their performance in these tasks. Performance in problem-solving tasks appeared to be as much affected by fear reactions as by any cognitive ability. The culmination of the project was Scott and Fuller's (1965a) classic, *Genetics and Social Behavior of the Dog*.

When heritability coefficients were determined, all of the traits showed some heritability. Overall, the average for behavioral traits was around 27% of the variance due to breed differences. However, one must remember what this means and does not mean. The heritability coefficient does not show what percentage of a trait is heritable; only what percentages of the variability within the sample under specific test conditions can be attributable to genetic differences. Environmental factors are also important. For example, growing up in a litter with other puppies of a dog's own breed versus another breed affected performance. Heritability is one of the most misunderstood measures in psychology. Thus, one must not overinterpret heritability coefficients.

Scott was trained as a geneticist and never shied away from the view that genetics are important influences on behavior. Indeed, he expressed this on the pages of the *American Psychologist* in 1949. However, he placed the genetic influences in an interactionist, developmental, rather than a deterministic, framework. As

Scott (1985) put it, "Genetics does not put behavior in a straitjacket" (p. 416). One can see Scott's shifting orientation toward developmental and away from genetic emphases. This was affirmed in a 1988 interview with historian Diane Paul. She expressed some surprise that Scott appeared to shift so much from an emphasis on genetics to one on plasticity and the flexibility of behavior. Scott concurred, noting that the basic patterns of behavior appeared quite similar across breeds; what differs is the ease with which these behavioral patterns can be elicited. He added that emotional reactivity has an important role in this.

One interesting outgrowth of the dog program was the training of guide dogs for the blind. Clarence J. Pfaffenberger, a trustee of Guide Dogs for the Blind in San Rafael, California, visited the laboratory with an interest in the breeding of guide dogs. With a grant to help improve the training of these dogs, Pfaffenberger began work with Scott, Fuller, and Benson Ginsberg through regular consulting. This resulted in a 1976 volume, *Guide Dogs for the Blind, Their Selection, Development, and Training* (Pfaffenberger, Scott, Fuller, & Bielfelt, 1976). Fuller (1985) concluded that the social bond between dog and human is critical.

RESEARCH WITH HOUSE MICE

Although Scott was brought to Bar Harbor primarily to study dogs, both his background and the resources available led him and his associates to work with house mice, the species for which the Jackson Laboratory is most widely known, as well. As noted, well before moving to Bar Harbor, Scott had spent the summers of 1938 and 1939 as a visitor there studying strain differences in fighting behavior among males (Scott, 1942a). This work was followed up by others. He revisited and expanded these findings with mice while also working with the dogs. Scott became as interested in experiential effects on agonistic behavior (roughly including both attack behavior and withdrawal and other reactions to attack) as in genetic influences. A series of studies revealed the effects of victory and defeat and the deleterious effects of the latter (e.g., Scott & Marston, 1953).

Another phenotype that became much studied was audiogenic seizures in mice. The researchers would place a mouse in a washtub and ring a bell mounted on the tub. Some strains showed a brief startle reaction; others would sometimes engage in frantic running, have full seizures, and perhaps even die. Calvin Hall worked on this behavior during Scott's first summer on the staff in Bar Harbor, and Fuller and others followed it up.

DEVELOPMENT, EARLY EXPERIENCE, AND CRITICAL PERIODS

As noted, interlaced with the genetic analyses were studies of early experience and a variety of developmental studies of mice and dogs; this research might be of greatest interest to readers of this volume. It was a time of great interest in the effect of early experience on later behavior. Among the influences were the arrival of European ethology, including Konrad Lorenz's studies of imprinting in fowl, and interest in Freud's theories. In addition, such topics as the primacy effect in human verbal learning and the maturation of the nervous system were undergoing study. This work also followed on the heels of the classic work of Rene Spitz on the deleterious effects of rearing in hospitals and foundling homes and in the context of research by John Bowlby on attachment. Later, the 1950s then saw a mushrooming of research on effects of early experience; the US government's Head Start program began in 1965. Recall also that, while still a graduate student, Scott had studied critical periods in the embryology of guinea pigs. The times were ripe.

In 1948 Scott obtained one of the first grants from the recently established National Institute of Mental Health (MH123) to study the effects of early experience on fighting behavior in mice. He organized a major conference on the topic of early experience and hired Emil Fredericson and John A. King to work on it. Their work (e.g., Fredericson, 1951) and that of others revealed that there are times in the early development of rats and mice when the animals appear especially sensitive to environmental stimuli, such as handling or cold. This work, and that of others, led to a vast outpouring of research on early experience during the 1950s and 1960s led primarily by two scientists, Victor Denenberg and Seymour Levine, both of whom had been summer investigators at the Jackson Laboratory (e.g., King, 1958).

The research for which Scott may be most widely known, that on critical periods in dogs, was conducted in this context. Scott and Marston (1950) studied the development of 73 puppies from seven different breeds. They found that social development could be usefully divided into four periods. The neonatal period lasts between birth and about 2 weeks (the opening of the eyes). Locomotor and ingestive patterns of behavior were adapted simply to neonatal life. The transition period runs between about 2 and 3 weeks, at which time the puppy leaves the nest and notices more of its environment. More adult-like patterns of locomotion and ingestion develop at this time. The socialization period runs from about 3–4 weeks to about 12 weeks, by which time the puppy has been weaned. During this time juvenile patterns recede, and the puppy makes contact with individuals other than the parents. The juvenile period stretches from the end of the socialization period to about 6 months or older (i.e., from weaning to sexual maturation). All behavioral patterns except sex and reproduction are developed by this time.

One important practical application of these results concerns the adoption of puppies by humans. It is during the socialization period, between about 4 and 10 weeks, that puppies are most effectively introduced into a human home. Earlier than that the puppies are not ready. Later than that, attachments may already be formed elsewhere. This is important because dogs introduced too early may not do well, and those introduced too late may never fully adjust to people. It was found that dogs isolated past the socialization period might show a pattern of emotional disturbance—kennel dog syndrome or separation syndrome. The link to the work of Spitz and others should be apparent.

Scott also believed that there is indeed a critical period for learning. In essence, he would not say that one cannot teach an old dog new tricks, only that it is much easier in young dogs. Some old adages really can be supported with data. Scott tried to apply this concept of critical periods to other species, including humans, in this and later publications (e.g., Scott, 1962) and thus demonstrate the generality of the critical-period notion. He believed that human parents could learn to introduce new material to their children more effectively if their critical periods were understood.

Later, Scott, Stewart, and DeGhett (1974) expanded the approach most broadly into a general theory of critical periods applicable to a variety of living systems. In this systems approach they noted that the critical period can be understood in terms of the various organizational processes occurring during the relevant period. Thus, for example, during the socialization period of puppies they are learning to discriminate familiar from unfamiliar, organizing a separation distress response, developing mature visual and auditory systems, and improving long-term associative learning and memory. To understand any critical period one must analyze the underlying processes characteristic of the period. They also expanded the theory to disorganizational processes of later life.

The critical-period notion has been important in developmental social psychology. Surely, it existed before Scott, but he helped to develop and expand the concept and the underlying principles. Scott's approach was not without critics (Schneirla & Rosenblatt, 1963; Scott, 1963). Schneirla and Rosenblatt envisaged a more complex and progressive pattern of adjustment and regarded Scott's approach as too simple. Some would argue that these are best regarded as "sensitive" periods because of the gradual onset and offset and the fact that the precise timing can be modified by various treatment factors. However, Scott (e.g., 1962) understood that these periods could be altered somewhat, and the basic concept remains influential.

A natural outgrowth of this work was that on attachment, separation, anxiety, and depression. This was an interest in Bar Harbor, where, for example, Elliot and Scott (1961) found that the most severe emotional reactions to separation occur near the end of the critical period for socialization. Some of the research in the Bowling Green colony was directed at these issues (e.g., Scott, Stewart, & DeGhett, 1973). Scott et al. developed a broad review of research on dogs and other species to summarize the knowledge of the time. As might be expected, they listed both genetic and experiential-situational determinants of distress at the absence of the familiar and fear of the strange. They viewed prolonged separation as often leading to depression, depending on developmental history. Scott et al. noted that the same class of drugs that relieves depression in human patients also appears to work with dogs, suggesting similar mechanisms. They postulated "a general motivational system associated with attachment, separation, and allelomimetic [i.e., contagious or imitative] behavior" (p. 29) in both humans and nonhumans. Scott et al. concluded that "the response of depressed activity may be protective and adaptive and prevent exhaustion in hopeless situations" (p. 29).

Scott's developmental interests were elaborated in his *Early Experience and the Organization of Behavior* (1968). He pulled together diverse articles by various authors dealing with critical period phenomena in *Critical Periods* (1978a). His book on *Separation and Depression* (Scott & Senay, 1973) deals with that aspect of his developmental work.

It may seem odd that a program that started out directed at understanding genetic factors would wind up with so much emphasis on development. Indeed, Scott (1986) reflected "as a trained geneticist, it sometimes seemed to me I've spent most of my life saying 'No, no, genetics can't do that.'"

OTHER ASPECTS OF SCOTT'S CAREER

Aggression, War, and Peace

As noted already, war seemed to Scott to be an ever-present background in his life and much of his focus was on aggression and peace. Scott (1986, p. 16) recalled "my whole idea, all the way along, has been that what we're trying to do is use the research on animals to understand human behavior and so to modify it and improve it where possible." He showed this commitment in personal interactions, in scientific articles, and in books. Scott defined *agonistic behavior* as "a system of related behavior patterns having a common function of adaptation to situations of conflict between members of the same species" (1970, p. 568). He saw the need for an inclusive term that would incorporate both the aggressive aspects of conflict situations and aspects of passivity, withdrawal, submission, and retreat. Although Scott was cautious about direct extrapolations from the conflict situations in non-human animal to humans, he came to believe that human harmony is to be found in social relationships and organized societies (Scott & Scott, 1971). He believed that "disaggregation of systems on any level may lead to maladaptive violence" (Scott, 1975, p. 235).

In about 1942 Scott wrote a book manuscript entitled *The New American Destiny*, for which he was unable to find a publisher. This material became the foundation for *Aggression* (1958a). There one sees his early views on the multicausal determination of aggression at the levels of the organism, society, and ecology. The theme of social control was developed in his 1971 *Social Control and Social Change*, edited with his first wife, Sarah. At the organismic level, he coedited *The Physiology of Aggression and Defeat* with Basil Eleftheriou (Scott & Eleftheriou, 1971). Scott's interdisciplinary approach in developing the Bowling Green Center for Research on Social Behavior is apparent in *Violence in Animal and Human Societies*, edited by Arthur G. Neal (1976), for which he wrote a chapter on the control of aggression in human and animal societies. The book includes chapters by Bowling Green biologists, historians, sociologists, and psychologists.

Scott's most mature thinking appeared in his *The Evolution of Social Systems* (1989). Here Scott rejected unidirectional approaches regarding aggression to adopt a mature systems approach. In this approach, systems are characterized by multidirectional interactions at the levels of the genotype, physiological system, organism, society, and ecosystem. One sees the familiar, complex diagrams of the ways all of these elements influence each other. This is an antireductionistic, antimechanistic approach. Although genetic influences are important in this approach, they are embedded in, and affected by, feedback processes.

Scott firmly believed that there is no innate drive to aggression, as proposed by some scientists. He was among the scientists who met in Seville, Spain, in May 1986 and was one of 20 founding signatories to the Seville Statement on Violence (UNESCO, 2009). In essence, according to this statement there is no evidence for an inherited need or instinct specifically evolved for aggression. This was one of Scott's core beliefs, though not all scientists would agree that the matter is so clear-cut.

The Eugenics Problem

Although it represents but a small part of his work, Scott's relationship to eugenics is somewhat complex. He recognized the difficulties and limitations of the eugenic approach. In a 1936 article "A Challenge to the Eugenist," and such publications as Scott and Fuller (1965b) and Scott and Scott (1971) and his 1988 interview with Diane Paul, Scott clearly dissociated himself from the traditional approaches of the eugenics movement. For example, Scott and Scott (1971, p. 4) wrote that "cultural change proceeds so rapidly compared with biological change that the selection methods useful in animal breeding would be ineffectual in producing social change even if they were compatible with human social organization."

However, during at least part of his career Scott was a member, director (1959–1963), and vice president (1964–1965) of the American Eugenics Society (O'Keefe, 1993). He also published three articles in the journals of the American Eugenics Society (Allen, Kirk, Scott, Shapiro, & Wallace, 1961; Fuller & Scott, 1954; Scott, 1953). Two are basically reports of the dog research along with a few comments concerning the complexities of the concept of intelligence and some speculations about the relevance of the research for understanding genetics and behavior in humans. By contrast, the article by Allen et al. is a statement of the eugenic position from a Special Committee of the Board of Directors of the American Eugenics Society, of which Scott was a member. The committee sought means to encourage increased research and improved communication to modify the "tendency for individuals to have more or fewer children in proportion to their success or achievement in their particular environment" (p. 183).

Surely, Scott advocated increased knowledge of heredity in all species, including humans. He was also vitally concerned with improving society. These were united in this movement at this time. During the 1960s the eugenics movement was actively differentiating itself from the coercive policies of pre-WWII eugenics and trying to bring social and biological scientists together to forge new policies in a manner consistent with "the ideals of individuality, diversity, and liberty" (Ramsden, 2009, p. 853; see also Ramsden, 2008). It is likely that this combination of ideals, united in this way, would have appealed to Scott at this time and thus attracted him to the movement.

Scott the Organizer

Scott possessed an ability to organize scientists toward specific goals. Part of this was his organization of three important scientific conferences and several scientific societies. The first of the conferences was the Conference on Genetics and Social Behavior, which he organized in Bar Harbor soon after his arrival there (Scott, 1946, 1947a). In summer 1946 he gathered an elite multidisciplinary group of scientists for one of the first such postwar scientific gatherings. The goals were to assess the then-current state of knowledge on genetics and behavior, especially social behavior, and to plot the future for the field, both in Bar Harbor and elsewhere. Among the psychologists who attended were Robert M. Yerkes (chair),

Calvin Stone, O. H. Mowrer, Henry Nissen, Harry Harlow, Clifford Morgan, Frank Beach, Neal Miller, Gardner Murphy, and Lois Barclay Murphy. There was great interaction at the meeting because participants were not to prepare papers in advance and were to meet and live in one building. Participants advised the Jackson Laboratory staff to concentrate on laboratory studies of the larger species, dogs, because they could not be housed in university facilities. Work was to be directed especially at genetic influences, and the summer investigator program was strongly supported. This conference was a landmark event in the development of the field of behavior genetics (Dewsbury, 2009).

Functioning as Secretary of the Committee for the Study of Animal Societies Under Natural Conditions, Scott organized a 1947 Conference titled "Methodology and Techniques for Studying Animal Societies Under Natural Conditions" in Jackson Hole, Wyoming, under the aegis of the New York Zoological Society (Scott, 1947b).

In 1951 Scott organized his Conference on Early Experience and Mental Health at the Jackson Laboratory. He brought together a group of scientists interested in animal behavior and clinical psychologists interested in research on mental health. One can see the shift in his interest to bring in experiential factors as well as those of genetics. There was much discussion of the nature–nurture problem with an emphasis on a variety of epigenetic approaches. Among the scientists attending were John E. Anderson, Frank Beach, Leonard Carmichael, Calvin Hall, Donald O. Hebb, J. M. Hunt, Karl H. Pribram, and John Whiting. As with the 1946 conference, the conference was organized with both plenary sessions and breakout sessions for committees to construct and later read their reports to the whole group. General chair Carmichael summarized the view that "the study of the basic mechanisms of behavior in higher mammals which cannot speak assumes such great modern significance for one who would understand the biological and psychological basis of human behavior" (Scott, 1951, p. 32).

Scott was also deeply involved in the founding of the Behavior Genetics Association, the Animal Behavior Society (ABS), the International Society for Research on Aggression (ISRA), and the International Society for Developmental Psychobiology (ISDP). In this list we see most of Scott's lasting topics of interest, his ability to facilitate scientists to address them, and his sense of the timing in forming such organization.

Scott, C. R. Carpenter, and T. C. Schneirla, working as part of the Committee for the Study of Animal Societies Under Natural Conditions, laid the groundwork for the Animal Behavior Society. In those days the American Society of Zoologists (ASZ) and the Ecological Society of America (ESA) met under the aegis of the American Association for the Advancement of Science (AAAS). Following up on the committee, Scott annually organized a session on "Animal Behavior and Sociobiology"—possibly the first published use of the latter term (see also Scott, 1950). Eventually the group formally affiliated as a division/section of the ASZ and ESA. At the 1964 AAAS meeting in Montreal the decision was made to form a separate organization, the Animal Behavior Society. Scott is properly regarded as the founder of that organization because he had been the founding chair of the division/section that developed into the ABS. He received the Society's first

Distinguished Animal Behaviorist Award, its highest honor, in 1990. It has been highly successful and today is the largest organization of animal behaviorists in the Western Hemisphere.

The field of behavior genetics evolved as a distinct subdiscipline during the period of the Bar Harbor work. The Bar Harbor scientists played a pivotal role in the development of this field as Hall's (1951) classic chapter and Fuller and Thompson's (1960) book helped to define it (see Dewsbury, 2009). These personnel, including Scott, Fuller, W. R. Thompson, Hall, Benson Ginsburg, and others, were instrumental in forming the group that became the Behavior Genetics Association (BGA; Dewsbury, 2009). Ginsburg hosted the first formal meeting of the BGA. Fuller and Scott were the second and fourth presidents, respectively; Thompson was the sixth. Scott and Fuller were given its 1987 Dobzhansky Award. The association still presents an annual Fuller and Scott Award for early career scientists contributing to behavior genetics and a Thompson Award for graduate student presentations.

The International Society for Research on Aggression (ISRA) is a society of scholars and researchers interested in the scientific study of violence and aggression. It was founded at the International Congress of Psychology meetings in Tokyo in 1972. A group of scientists, led by Saul Rosenzweig and Scott, founded the organization; Scott served as the second president after Rosenzweig.

Scott was also involved in the founding of the International Society for Developmental Psychobiology and, in 1972–1973, served as its fourth president. He was a member of the International Society for Political Psychology (member of the governing council, 1983–1984), the Association for Politics and the Life Sciences, and the International Peace Society (Stuckey, 2001).

Scott the Educator

Scott was very much concerned with teaching the next generation the merits of science as he practiced it. He was active in developing a summer investigator's program in Bar Harbor not only for active scientists but for undergraduates, graduate students, and post-doctoral students as well. He taught short courses during these summers. I was a summer student between my undergraduate and graduate student careers. There was a wonderful mix of people from all of these levels. A lunch discussion could include Scott, Fuller, Walter Stanley, Denenberg, and Joseph Church as well as graduate students and undergraduates (e.g., Carolyn Rovee-Collier). The Jackson Laboratory was a stimulating environment for a student to experience. Scott also encouraged some of his assistants, such as Philip H. Gray and Mary-'Vesta Marston (later his second wife), to pursue further study and complete doctoral degrees. One of the reasons Scott left Bar Harbor was that he wanted to return to a university setting (Scott, 1986).

In 1988 Scott wrote to many alumni of the Jackson Lab behavior program with several questions about their experiences and later careers. The replies reside in the Archives of the History of American Psychology in Akron, Ohio. Michael W. Fox (1988) wrote of his indebtedness to Scott and that his "memory of him at Hamilton Station is filled with respect, gratitude and appreciation." Daniel G. Freedman (1988) called Scott an "ideal boss." He added "once he was confident in the student (me), he let him go his own way, just the sort of environment I've always flowered in.... Don't parrot me, but do your own thing and do it well."

Beginning in 2007, with no knowledge of Scott's earlier effort, I also contacted many of the alumni of the Bar Harbor behavior program at various levels as well and received some interesting replies. A few are summarized here, and they as well as those from the Akron archives will be dealt with in more detail elsewhere. Carolyn Rovee-Collier wrote that "my research experience at Jackson Lab changed my life and was ultimately responsible for my graduate career and ultimate success as an experimental psychologist" (personal communication, December 31, 2007). Victor Denenberg (personal communication, December 21, 2007) recalled that "it was fun to be at Ham Station in the summer.... I've always thought that the relaxed genial nature at Ham was set by Paul. It wasn't that he did any specific thing to create this atmosphere. Rather, just by being himself (low-keyed and genial), he set the tone for all of us." Consistent with my view of Scott, Jerome Kagan, who spent a summer at the laboratory as a graduate student in 1953, remembered Scott as "gentle and with humility" (personal communication, August 14, 2007). Some responses were more measured; a couple of respondents regarded Scott as too philosophical and removed from the day-to-day data collection.

Limitations and Criticisms

As with all scientists, Scott had some views that were not universally accepted and he was criticized by some other scientists. In a chapter of this sort one is tempted to celebrate the person rather than prepare a more critical history. A more honest approach, in my view, is to discuss the warts as well as the contributions. Some scientists believed that the resources of the Jackson Laboratory would have been better spent and had more significant scientific impact if it had been used to study dog–dog interactions rather than dog–human ones or if more experimental, rather than observational, methods would have been used (e.g., Schneirla & Rosenblatt, 1963). After supporting the program from its inception, the Rockefeller Foundation officials and their consultants (e.g., Carpenter, 1955) became somewhat disenchanted with it and terminated funding in 1958. Scott's situation with the foundation in 1955 was eerily similar to that experienced by Robert Yerkes at the Yerkes Laboratories of Primate Biology in the 1930s (see Dewsbury, 2006).

Late in Scott's career, some criticized him for not keeping up with the times as behavioral ecology and a science of sociobiology different from his evolved; however, Scott's resistance was based on his views of the science more than a failure to keep up. Many social psychologists will disagree with his belief that "social psychology has produced only two reliable phenomena: critical periods and social facilitation" (Scott, 1985, p. 421). Some critics went so far as to question the existence of critical periods (e.g., Beach, 1951).

Scott's broad interest in animal behavior is revealed in his *Animal Behavior* (1958b); the book went through three editions. There and elsewhere Scott (e.g., Scott, 1950) promulgated a system for classifying behavioral patterns according to which there are nine functional categories: ingestive behavior; shelter-seeking; agonistic behavior; sexual behavior; epimeletic (care-giving) behavior; et-epimeletic (care-soliciting) behavior; eliminative behavior; allelomimetic (contagious or imitative) behavior; and investigative behavior. This system and its neologisms, proposed by Scott in a number of publications, did not find wide use in the field.

Some of Scott's major goals were to use basic research better to understand human aggression and war, to facilitate peace, and to use research on nonhuman animals to improve conditions for children (e.g., Scott, 1957). Although his work revealed much about aggression in animals, it is difficult to discern any noticeable effect on peace and tranquility in humans. One might wonder, however, how many basic scientists have had such effects; Scott aimed high. Similarly, his research revealed much about basic developmental processes but appears to have had little, if any, effect on human child rearing and development.

However, scientific fashions change with the times. Viewing Scott's work from the perspectives of 2011 sheds a softer light on his approaches than in some of the perspectives of his time. For example, the critical period notion still influences some scientists (e.g., Coppinger & Coppinger, 2001). Whereas many scientists in Scott's day favored the study of intraspecific interactions, many today argue that because the domestication of dogs occurred in a human context, it is dog–human interactions that deserve priority. Miklósi, Topál, & Csányi (2004) wrote that "earlier studies of social learning in dogs were concerned mainly with within-species learning…. The ethological question is whether dogs are able to learn from their heterospecific companions" (p. 1001). According to Tomasello (in Morrell, 2009, p. 1065) "dogs are collaborating with us; they aren't doing this with other dogs."

Honors

As might be expected, Scott received various honors. His election to fellow in several APA divisions, elections as president in three societies, and ABS Distinguished Animal Behaviorist Award have already been mentioned. Scott was also a fellow of the AAAS, the ABS, and the New York Zoological Society. He was a member of Phi Beta Kappa and Sigma Xi. Scott received the Jordan Prize of the Indiana Academy of Sciences, the Dobzhansky Award from the BGA, a Special Achievement Award from Bowling Green, and both a Distinguished Alumnus Award and an Outstanding Achievement Award from the University of Wyoming.

SCOTT THE MAN

What kind of person was Scott? He did not perceive himself as a messiah, genius, scholar, or promoter, which were his four categories in his taxonomy of individuals. He wrote that "if I have an outstanding characteristic, it lies in a combination of qualities, rooted in the desire to organize the world in a meaningful and understandable combination of symbols" (Scott, 1985, p. 429). He mentioned that he was capable of hard work, liked to explore, and had an interest in ideas. He regarded himself as something of a rebel intellectually. Perhaps most critically, he wrote, "I like to get things done" and that "if there is a theme that runs through my whole life, it is that of organization" (Scott, 1985, p. 395). He was good at organizing both facts and people.

Jack King, a colleague of Scott's in Bar Harbor, kept in contact with him for the rest of Scott's life; he provided an incisive summary of Scott's work and personality. King (2006) regarded Scott above all as a man on a mission. Paul sincerely believed that his ideas and values could be used to improve humankind. He thought that his science and organizing ability could contribute to human welfare. He wanted to reduce violence and competition in the world. He turned his attention to genetics and development because he believed, rightly or wrongly, that in this way one could modify behavior for the benefit of humankind. Paul was generally noncompetitive and not one to put on airs:

> He was a calm, friendly, helpful, and supportive individual…. He was not vain. He directed his personal ambition through an influence on others in a mild, non-assertive manner. He was confident in his goals and was determined in his mission without strongly urging or coercing the uninitiated. If anyone showed a sincere interest in his goals, he treated them as equal. (King, 2006, p. 3)

Scott was a good family man with four children and a happy home life. He had faith in humanity and democracy. He was a humanist and liberal democrat who believed in a strong central government. He was "a serious, driven man without hyperbole or flamboyance, almost a teetotaler. No back slapping, joke telling, or jovial charm, just honest, serious friendship with a dash of warmth" (King, personal communication, January 5, 2009).

I kept in periodic touch with Paul for nearly 30 years after my summer in Bar Harbor. I believe King's assessment to be accurate and incisive. Many espouse idealistic values, but Scott really seemed to live them. Frankly, I found him often to be a rather dull speaker and lecturer who lacked the dynamism of some of his colleagues of the time. But one would walk away and realize that he had expressed some important ideas and that he was well worth one's attention. He was serious and seemed to believe that the message he promulgated was more important than the style in which this was done. It probably was. He managed to influence many people in a mild, but effective, manner.

There were many facets to John Paul Scott and his career. The study of development was but one facet, but a very important one. Like all of us, he was many things. Scott conducted significant research, organized institutions, conferences, and academic societies and participated in efforts to try to improve humanity. Though trained as a geneticist, he came to adopt a developmental approach in the belief that, with better conditions, humanity could be improved. He sought world peace and domestic tranquility not as casual phrases but as bases for his life work. World peace was beyond him, but he influenced many people along the way.

SUGGESTED READINGS

Dewsbury, D. A. (Ed.) (1985). *Leaders in the study of animal behavior: Autobiographical perspectives.* Lewisburg, PA: Bucknell University Press. (Republished as Dewsbury, D. A. (Ed.). (1989). *Studying animal behavior: Autobiographies of the founders.* Chicago: University of Chicago Press.)

The volume includes autobiographical chapters by Scott and Jackson Laboratory personnel J. L. Fuller and J. A. King.

Scott, J. P. (1958a). *Aggression.* Chicago: University of Chicago Press.

    Here, Scott reviewed the genetic, physiological, psychological, social, and ecological influences on aggression and concluded that there is no evidence of a drive for aggression. He viewed aggression as stimulated by external events and suggested that peaceful living might be possible with control of the environmental stimulants to aggression.

Scott, J. P. (1962). Critical periods in behavioral development. *Science, 138,* 949–958.

    Written for a broad scientific audience, Scott developed the theory of critical periods and the developmental processes underlying them. He suggested that the timing of these periods is not absolute and that parents should understand these periods so that efforts at child rearing can be timed to be maximally effective.

Scott, J. P., & Fuller, J. L. (1965a). *Genetics and the social behavior of the dog.* Chicago: University of Chicago Press.

    Scott and Fuller summarize their long-term program of research on the genetics and development of five breeds of dogs. No one breed is superior to others. They speculate about the implications for humans and the possibility of promulgating stable social organizations through cultural evolution.

REFERENCES

Allen, G., Kirk, D., Scott, J. P., Shapiro, H. L., & Wallace, B. (1961). Statement of the eugenic position. *Eugenics Quarterly, 8,* 181–184.

Anastasi, A., Fuller, J. L., Scott, J. P., & Schmitt, J. R. (1955). A factor analysis of the performance of dogs on certain learning tests. *Zoologica, 40,* 33–46.

Beach, F. A. (1951, September 20). [Letter to J. P. Scott.] J. P. Scott papers, Archives of the History of American Psychology, Akron, OH.

Carpenter, C. R. (1955, November 2). [Letter to Robert S. Morrison]. Record Group 200A, Series 12, Box 134, Folder 1194, Rockefeller Archive Center, North Tarrytown, NY.

Coppinger, R., & Coppinger, L. (2001). *Dogs: A startling new understanding of canine origins, behavior, and evolution.* New York: Scribner.

Dewsbury, D. A. (2006). *Monkey farm: A history of the Yerkes Laboratories of Primate Biology, Orange Park, Florida, 1930–1965.* Lewisburg, PA: Bucknell University Press.

Dewsbury, D. A. (2009). Origins of behavior genetics: The role of the Jackson Laboratory. *Behavior Genetics, 39,* 1–5. doi:10.1007/s10519-008-9240-1 PMid:19020968

Dewsbury, D. A. (2011, February 21). A history of the behavior program at the Jackson Laboratory: An overview. *Journal of Comparative Psychology.* doi: 10.1037/a0021376

Dewsbury, D. A., & Panksepp, J. (2001). John Paul Scott (1909–2000). *American Psychologist, 56,* 454. doi:10.1037/0003-066X.56.5.454

Elliot, O., & Scott, J. P. (1961). The development of emotional distress reactions to separation in puppies. *Journal of General Psychology, 99,* 3–22.

Fox, M. W. (1988, May 28). [Questionnaire in response to J. P. Scott] J. P. Scott papers, Archives of the History of American Psychology, Akron, OH.

Fredericson, E. (1951). Competition: The effects of infantile experience upon adult behavior. *Journal of Abnormal and Social Psychology, 46,* 406–409. doi:10.1037/h0063046

Freedman, D. G. (1988, September 10). [Questionnaire in response to J. P. Scott] J. P. Scott papers, Archives of the History of American Psychology, Akron, OH.

Fuller, J. L. (1985). Of dogs, mice, people, and me. In D. A. Dewsbury (Ed.), *Leaders in the study of animal behavior* (pp. 93–118). Lewisburg, PA: Bucknell University Press.

Fuller, J. L., & Scott, J. P. (1954) I. Heredity and learning ability in infrahuman mammals. *Eugenics Quarterly, 1,* 28–43.

Fuller, J. L., & Thompson, W. R. (1960). *Behavior genetics.* New York: Wiley.

Hall, C. S. (1951). The genetics of behavior. In S. S. Stevens (Ed.), *Handbook of experimental psychology* (pp. 304–329). New York: Wiley.

Kazdin, A. E., & Rotella, C. (2009). Like a rat. Retrieved 17 November, 2009 from http://www.slate.com/id/2234707/http://www.slate.com/id/2234707/

King, J. A. (1958). Parameters relevant to determining the effect of early experience upon the adult behavior of animals. *Psychological Bulletin, 55,* 46–58. doi:10.1037/h0041002 PMid:13505967

King, J. A. (2006). John Paul Scott (1909–2000). Unpublished manuscript.

Miklósi, Á., Topál, J., & Csányi, V. (2004). Comparative social cognition: What dogs can teach us. *Animal Behaviour, 67,* 995–1004. doi:10.1016/j.anbehav.2003.10.008

Morell, V. (2009). Going to the dogs. *Science, 325,* 1062–1065. doi:10.1126/science.325_1062 PMid:19713504

Neal, A. G. (Ed.). (1976). *Violence in animal and human societies.* Chicago: Nelson Hall.

O'Keefe, K. (1993). *American Eugenics Society 1922–1994.* Retrieved August 16, 2010 from http://www.all.org/abac/contents.txt

Paul, D. (1988). Interview with John Paul Scott. Cassette tape provided by Diane Paul.

Pfaffenberger, C. J., Scott, J. P., Fuller, J. L., & Bielfelt, S. M. (1976). *Guide dogs, their selection, development, and training.* Amsterdam: Elsevier.

Ramsden, E. (2008). Eugenics from the New Deal to the Great Society: Genetics, demography and population quality. *Studies in History and Philosophy of Biological and Biomedical Sciences, 39,* 391–406. doi:10.1016/j.shpsc.2008.09.005 PMid:19026971

Ramsden, E. (2009). Confronting the stigma of eugenics: Genetics, demography and the problems of population. *Social Studies of Science, 39,* 853–884. doi:10.1177/0306312709335406 PMid:20506743

Schneirla, T. C., & Rosenblatt, J. S. (1963). "Critical periods" in the development of behavior. *Science, 139,* 1110–1114. doi:10.1126/science.139.3559.1110

Scott, J. P. (1936). A challenge to the eugenist. *Journal of Heredity, 27,* 261–264.

Scott, J. P. (1937). The embryology of the guinea pig. III. Development of the polydactylous monster. A case of growth accelerated at a particular period by a semi-dominant lethal gene. *Journal of Experimental Zoology, 77,* 123–157. doi:10.1002/jez.1400770107

Scott, J. P. (1942a). Genetic differences in the social behavior of inbred strains of mice. *Journal of Heredity, 33,* 11–15.

Scott, J. P. (1942b). Science and social action. *Science, 96,* 39–40. doi:10.1126/science.96.2480.39-b.

Scott, J. P. (1946). *Minutes of the conference on genetics and social behavior.* Bar Harbor, ME: Roscoe B. Jackson Memorial Laboratory.

Scott, J. P. (1947a). The Conference on Genetics and Social Behavior at the Roscoe B. Jackson Memorial Laboratory. *American Psychologist, 2,* 176–177. doi:10.1037/h0054358

Scott, J. P. (1947b). Formation of a Committee for the Study of Animal Societies under Natural Conditions. *American Psychologist, 2,* 212. doi:10.1037/h0058706

Scott, J. P. (1949). Genetics as a tool in experimental psychological research. *American Psychologist, 4,* 526–530. doi:10.1037/h0061504 PMid:15397959

Scott, J. P. (1950). The social behavior of dogs and wolves: An illustration of sociobiological systematics. *Annals of the New York Academy of Sciences, 51,* 1009–1021. doi:10.1111/j.1749-6632.1950.tb27330.x

Scott, J. P. (1951). *Minutes of the Conference on the Effects of Early Experience on Mental Health.* Bar Harbor, ME: Roscoe B. Jackson Memorial Laboratory.

Scott, J. P. (1953). New directions in the genetic study of personality and intelligence. *Eugenical News, 38,* 97–101.

Scott, J. P. (1957). Animal and human children. *Children, 4,* 163–168.

Scott, J. P. (1958a). *Aggression.* Chicago: University of Chicago Press.

Scott, J. P. (1958b). *Animal behavior.* Chicago: University of Chicago Press.

Scott, J. P. (1962). Critical periods in behavioral development. *Science, 138,* 949–958. doi:10.1126/science.138.3544.949 PMid:13992547

Scott, J. P. (1963). "Critical periods" in the development of behavior. *Science, 139,* 1115–1116. doi:10.1126/science.139.3559.1115 PMid:17813014

Scott, J. P. (1967). Comparative psychology and ethology. *Annual Review of Psychology, 18,* 65–86. doi:10.1146/annurev.ps.18.020167.000433 PMid:5333431

Scott, J. P. (1968). *Early experience and the organization of behavior.* Belmont, CA: Brooks/Cole.

Scott, J. P. (1970). Biology and human aggression. *American Journal of Orthopsychiatry, 40,* 568–576. doi:10.1111/j.1939-0025.1970.tb00715.x

Scott, J. P. (1975). Violence and the disaggregated society. *Aggressive Behavior, 1,* 235–260. doi:10.1002/1098-2337

Scott, J. P. (Ed.) (1978a). *Critical periods.* Stroudsburg, PA: Dowden, Hutchinson & Ross.

Scott, J. P. (1978b, September 29). Letter to Mrs. Jean Holstein. Joan Staats Library, Jackson Laboratory, Bar Harbor, ME.

Scott, J. P. (1985). Investigative behavior: Toward a science of sociality. In D. A. Dewsbury (Ed.), *Leaders in the study of behavior: Autobiographical perspectives* (pp. 389–429). Lewisburg, PA: Bucknell University Press.

Scott, J. P. (1986, August 22). Interview with Susan Mehrtens of August 19, Bar Harbor, ME. Transcription in the Jackson Laboratory Oral History Collection, American Philosophical Society Library, Philadelphia, PA.

Scott, J. P. (1989). *The evolution of social systems.* New York: Gordon and Breach.

Scott, J. P., & Eleftheriou, B. E. (Eds.) (1971). *The physiology of aggression and defeat: Proceedings of a symposium held during the meeting of the American Association for the Advancement of Science in Dallas, Texas, December, 1968.* Washington, DC: American Association for the Advancement of Science.

Scott, J. P., & Fuller, J. L. (1965a). *Genetics and the social behavior of the dog.* Chicago: University of Chicago Press.

Scott, J. P., & Fuller, J. L. (1965b, March 6). What dogs can tell us about man's future. *Saturday Review, 48,* 47–51.

Scott, J. P., & Marston, M-'V. (1950). Critical periods affecting the development of normal and mal-adaptive social behavior of puppies. *Journal of Genetic Psychology, 77,* 25–60.

Scott, J. P., & Marston, M-'V. (1953). Non-adaptive behavior resulting from a series of defeats in fighting mice. *Journal of Abnormal and Social Psychology, 48.* 417–428. doi:10.1037/h0058844

Scott, J. P., & Scott, S. F. (Eds.) (1971). *Social control and social change.* Chicago: University of Chicago Press.

Scott, J. P., & Senay, E. C. (1973) (Eds.). *Separation and depression: Clinical and research aspects: A symposium presented at the Chicago meeting of the American Association for the Advancement of Science, 27 December 1970.* Washington, DC: American Association for the Advancement of Science.

Scott, J. P., Stewart, J. M., & DeGhett, V. J. (1973). Separation in infant dogs: Emotional response and motivational consequences. In J. P. Scott & E. C. Senay, *Separation and depression: Clinical and research aspects: A symposium presented at the Chicago meeting of the American Association for the Advancement of Science, 27 December 1970* (pp. 3–32). Washington, DC: American Association for the Advancement of Science.

Scott, J. P., Stewart, J. M., & DeGehtt, V. J. (1974). Critical periods in the organization of systems. *Developmental Psychobiology, 7,* 489–513. doi:10.1002/dev.420070602 PMid:4615003

Small, W. S. (1899). Notes on the psychic development of the young white rat. *American Journal of Psychology, 11,* 80–100. doi:10.2307/1412730

Division of Behavior Studies Staff. (1950). *Manual of dog testing techniques.* Bar Harbor, ME: Roscoe B. Jackson Memorial Laboratory.

Stuckey, R. L. (2001). Obituaries of the members of the Ohio Academy of Science report of the Necrology Committee, 2001. John Paul Scott (1909–2000). Retrieved September 15, 2010 from http://www.allbusiness.com/north-america/united-states-ohio/837509-1.html

UNESCO. (1986). Seville statement on violence, Spain, 1986. Retrieved December 23, 2009 from http://portal.unesco.org/education/en/ev.php-URL_ID=3247&URL_DO= DO_TOPIC&URL_SECTION=201.html

Watson, J. B. (1903). *Animal education: An experimental study of the psychical development of the white rat, correlated with the growth of its nervous system.* Chicago: University of Chicago.

Wilson, E. O. (1975). *Sociobiology: The new synthesis.* Cambridge, MA: Harvard University Press.

14

Eleanor J. Gibson:
*Learning to Perceive, Perceiving to Learn**

HERBERT L. PICK

University of Minnesota

Imagine you were Eleanor Jack Gibson arriving in New Haven in 1934 to undertake graduate study in psychology at Yale. You had been an honors student at Smith College, received your BA, and then gone on for a MA at Smith. Your undergraduate study led you to a strong interest in animal psychology. So you went to Yale with the goal of working with the well-known comparative psychologist, Robert Yerkes. You went to his office to introduce yourself, tell him of your plan, and ask him to take you on

as an advisee. He told you abruptly that he accepted no women to work in his laboratory. That might have been an overwhelming encounter, but you had the perseverance to investigate other possibilities, including listening to advice from a number of more advanced graduate students. You decided to approach Clark Hull, another noted scholar

Figure 14.1   Eleanor Gibson with granddaughter, 1979. (Courtesy of David Rosenberg. With permission.)

* The author gratefully acknowledges the very helpful discussions of portions of this paper with Anne D. Pick. He is also most appreciative to Jean Gibson and David Rosenberg for the photograph of Eleanor Gibson.

at Yale. His area of research involved development of a systemic approach to learning.

FROM SMITH COLLEGE TO YALE UNIVERSITY AND BACK AGAIN

Eleanor Jack was born in Peoria, Illinois in 1910 and grew up with a businessman father, homemaker mother, and a younger sister. She attended Smith College and graduated magna cum laude in Spring 1931. She was awarded a teaching assistantship for the following year with her teaching duties to take up half her time and work on an MA the other half. She chose as her adviser James Gibson who had also been her experimental psychology instructor. They fell in love and married in summer 1932. She continued her teaching duties and completed her MA. She applied and was accepted by Yale to study for her PhD.

Clark Hull, to whom she turned after being rejected by Yerkes, was also a leading scholar of the time. His work was focused on developing a formal hypothetico-deductive theory of learning. In his approach learning was motivated by reinforcement from drive reduction. However, he used concepts of differentiation and generalization to explain some of the more complex and interesting properties of animal learning. For example, how was it that an animal trained to make a response to one stimulus would show transfer or interference when tested with other stimuli? Hull's system had been developed and tested primarily with animals—rats. Eleanor proposed to him that she would try to elaborate the system and adapt it to, and test it on, human verbal learning.

Although Hull was much more receptive to Eleanor than Yerkes, initially he was a little skeptical, possibly because of how ambitious her proposal was. He wanted to see some concrete evidence that a formal extension to verbal learning might be possible. She apparently convinced Hull. And in fact she completed her dissertation in 1938 and published several article series based on it in the late 1930s and early 1940s. One of these (Gibson, 1940) was a key theoretical and empirical exposition of this series. Her theoretical analysis, applied to the learning of verbal lists, begins with the notion that discrimination of the items is a fundamental part of the learning process. Preexisting or acquired discrimination or differentiation of the items on the list can explain much about transfer and interference of the learning to subsequent lists. This differentiation can be experimentally manipulated. Eleanor's analysis, published 70 years ago, has been cited numerous times over the years, most recently twice in 2010 (Criss, 2010; Dopson, Esber, & Pearce, 2010).

Eleanor Gibson's experience at Yale foreshadowed two threads that were reflected in much of her career. One was her treatment as a woman scientist. The other was the theoretical (and empirical) interest in differentiation as an essential part of the learning process. In the first half of the 20th century (even through much of the entire century) there was substantial bias against female scientists and academics. Its effect on Eleanor's academic career was a constant background. However, one place that prejudice was not so manifest even in the 1930s was at Smith College. As part of her undergraduate study at Smith she was encouraged to take laboratory courses in experimental psychology in which experiments at the then current frontiers of the field were actually carried out. Indeed one experiment conducted by a lab partner and herself in collaboration with their instructor was published just 1 year after she graduated from Smith (Gibson, Jack, & Raffel, 1932).

Eleanor's PhD dissertation was completed in, and was part of, the behaviorist era that continued for the next several decades. A basically very simple experimental procedure called *discrimination learning* became popular during that period. Experimental participants (often animals or children) were repeatedly presented a pair of stimuli over a series of trials. Their task was to learn consistently to choose one of the pair for a small reward given on each trial for a correct response. If the stimuli were quite similar, participants initially confused them and only gradually came reliably to respond correctly, that is, to demonstrate discrimination learning. They learned to make one response to the positive stimulus and a different one or no response to the negative stimulus. One theoretical interpretation of this result was that learning a different response to the two stimuli made them more distinctive—this finding was designated as acquired distinctiveness of cues.

An alternative interpretation, favored by Eleanor, was that to associate a different response with each member of the pair, the two stimuli already needed to be discriminated. In fact, such a perspective was described in detail by Gibson and Gibson (1955). Their perspective did not deny that the stimuli became more discriminable on the basis of experience with them. Rather, they argued that improvement did not depend on associating different responses to the two stimuli; it did depend on detecting more aspects or characteristics of the stimuli. This improved detection formed the basis of perceptual learning—a very general theoretical view of perceptual learning that emphasized differentiation rather than enrichment. A classical view of perception and perceptual learning was that there is insufficient information in the stimulation impinging on the senses to account for our (usually veridical) complex perception. The impoverished stimulation has to be *enriched* by information from prior associations or innate brain mechanisms. The perspective of the Gibsons, in contrast, was that there is sufficient information to account for our complex perception if one *differentiates* and attends to the correct variables.

In this paper, Gibson and Gibson (1955) described an experiment in which a set of different but initially confusable stimuli were presented to participants one by one. The experimental task was to say whether each stimulus was the same as a standard. At first there were many errors of confusion, but with repeated exposure to the members of the set accuracy of selection of only matches to the standard increased without any explicit knowledge of results or learning of distinctive responses. The members of the set of initially confused stimuli varied on three physical dimensions. Participants seemed to become more sensitive to these variations with repeated exposure. (Also, as was pointed out in this paper, such improvement was quite similar to that found in psychophysical experiments with repeated exposure to the stimuli.)

After receiving her PhD in 1938, Eleanor was promoted to assistant professor at Smith College. She was able to continue her teaching, albeit with a heavy teaching load. Nevertheless, she was able to complete several articles for publication based on her dissertation. The young Gibson academic couple maintained an active professional and social life until December 1941, when the United States entered the Second World War.

THE IMPACT OF WAR AND A MOVE TO CORNELL

The outbreak of the war soon led to James Gibson entering the Army Air Force. His assignment involved the development of tests for selection of aircraft crews. He left in spring 1942 and was initially stationed in Fort Worth, Texas, and then in Santa Ana, California. Eleanor accompanied him to these posts. While he was thus able to continue his professional scientific activity, there was no parallel opportunity for her. Although with some change of emphasis, she was able to keep up with the psychological field to some extent by reading and discussions with her husband. However, her full-time activity was not in psychological science. Indeed, the Gibsons had their first child, Jerry, just before they moved to Texas, and their second child, Jean, while in Texas. So Eleanor spent a good deal of time engaged in maternal activity. Nevertheless, she preserved a long-term goal of combining a personal family life with a professional academic career.

At the end of the war in 1946 the Gibson family returned to Northampton, Massachusetts, and Smith College. In 1947 Eleanor and her husband resumed their academic duties. She continued as assistant professor with a very heavy teaching load. They both were somewhat frustrated by the lack of time for research. James already had established a reputation as a perception researcher. He was soon offered a position at Cornell University, where the psychology department had a PhD program and a strong experimental psychology faculty. In spite of nepotism rules that would preclude Eleanor from having a faculty position there, they decided to move. She felt there would be ample opportunity to engage in research. They left for Ithaca, New York, in 1949.

In fact, Eleanor was able to get started in research very soon. Her first activity was on a project with Cornell psychology department professor Howard Liddell involving classical conditioning of sheep and goats. Liddell's laboratory was housed in a converted barn and appropriately called the "behavior farm." In addition to carrying out conditioning experiments, Eleanor hoped to develop a project of her own investigating mother/infant relations and rearing patterns in the farm animals. That work was not brought to fruition due to complications in the farm management.

More successful continuation of her research career was possible with a project Eleanor undertook with funding from the army to study the perception of distance in natural settings. Her particular interest was whether perception of distance could be trained. This aim fit in well with what was beginning to be the main focus of her research career, the study of perceptual learning. Even though the topic of learning was emphasized in the psychology of this period, the focus was on response learning and the association of responses. There was not much interest in perceptual learning, that is, how perception improves with experience. The experimental setting she used for the investigation of distance perception was one typical of size constancy experiments of that time. In those experiments observers had the task of judging the size of a nearby object in relation to one far away whose retinal image would be much smaller than that of the nearer one. Eleanor was not interested in the constancy problem but in the perception of distance itself. Her experiments on this topic were conducted in large outdoor fields rather than in the purified setting of indoor laboratories. Initial experiments made it clear that, if observers judge the distance of objects in some metric units such as yards or other scale of distance and if they received correction, their accuracy improved. However, was that improvement just development of a more accurate concept of the metric scale? Or did their perception itself improve? Further experiments indicated there was no improvement in perceptual sensitivity. The experiments did show, however, that observers were generally very good at judging distances over large areas of ground (Gibson, Bergman, & Purdy, 1955).

PERCEPTUAL LEARNING

Although the distance judging experiments did not demonstrate actual improvement in perception, Eleanor began thinking about alternative ways of providing perceptual experience. Recall that the experiment reported in the study by Gibson and Gibson (1955) found improvement in perception with repeated exposure to stimuli, without any information about the results of judgments or any learning of associated responses. What other situation would provide such repeated exposure and no learned responses? Controlled rearing of animal participants would fit the bill. She teamed up with another Cornell departmental colleague, Richard Walk. They raised rats with triangular and circular cutouts fixed to the sides of their cages (Walk & Gibson, 1956). Their results indicated that such early experience facilitated later discrimination learning between triangles and circles in comparison with a control group reared with no objects on the sides of their cages. Note that such rearing ensures prolonged early experience and no differential response learning specifically associated with the triangles and circles. In a series of subsequent studies they determined that it was exposure to the fixed cutouts or other solid objects on the sides of the cages that was important. Triangles and circles painted on the sides of the cages did not result in facilitation. However, research on this project came to a halt when Walk left Cornell and closed down his animal laboratory. This again is an instance of the disadvantage of nepotism rules of the time, mainly affecting wives.

This rat-rearing study represented a foray into developmental psychology, a direction that Eleanor was able to continue with studies of children and reading. Could her perspective on perceptual learning (and development) as increasing sensitivity to more aspects of stimulation be extended to the early stages of learning to read? Eleanor took the opportunity to investigate this question as part of her participation during the 1960s in an interdisciplinary Project Literacy, which was concerned with basic research on children's development of reading skills. One of Eleanor's studies was motivated by her perceptual learning view that discrimination would precede identification (Gibson, Gibson, Pick, & Osser, 1962). Before learning to identify and name letters one must perceive that they are different from one another. The study covered children of ages 3 to 7 years and used an artificial alphabet of nonsense (but letter-like) shapes. The youngest of these children differentiated shapes only on the basis of the same properties as real objects among which they distinguished in their environment. With increasing age and school attendance, children also came to differentiate shapes differing by properties of letters of English. Even the oldest children, however, were relatively poor at differentiating shapes that distinguished neither real objects nor English letters. Eleanor followed up this initial research on reading with a number of studies investigating more complex processes of reading. Over a decade of investigation of research on reading culminated in a collaborative book on the psychology of reading (Gibson & Levin, 1975).

FINALLY, A FULL PROFESSORSHIP

About this time period Eleanor began to receive considerable recognition for her theoretical and empirical productivity. Within the Cornell Department of Psychology she was awarded a full professorship in 1966, and her work was further recognized by Cornell in 1972 with the award of the Susan Linn Sage endowed professorship. Beyond the university she received the Distinguished Contribution Award from the American Psychological Association in 1968.

In the years following the Gibson and Gibson (1955) article on perceptual learning as differentiation or enrichment, Eleanor intensively studied perceptual development. That concentration was reflected in a chapter in a handbook of research methods in child development (Gibson & Olum, 1960) and in an *Annual Review of Psychology* chapter on perceptual learning (Gibson, 1963), among other related writings. Soon afterward, she took her differentiation perspective and views of perceptual learning a major step further by writing the book *Principles of Perceptual Learning and Development* (Gibson, 1969). This book essentially defined the field of perceptual learning. In a defining statement she wrote, "Perceptual learning then refers to an increase in the ability to extract information from the environment, as a result of experience and practice with stimulation coming from it…But modification goes on in development too, and I have found it impossible to arrive at a theory without considering both learning and development" (Gibson, 1969, pp. 3–4).

THE VISUAL CLIFF

The book is a compilation of what was known about the increasing ability of children to extract information. But it is much more than that. She not only integrated changes of perception in learning with development but also included many topics of how perception changes with experience and development. Among the many topics she considered were the effect of transformation of the stimulus array (distorting spectacle experiments), the issue of transfer of perceptual learning between sense modalities, and how controlled rearing affects the development of perception.

That latter topic is obviously an important one in the study of the effect of experience on perception. Eleanor herself had used this method in the experiments she and Richard Walk conducted rearing rats with objects attached to the sides of their cages (Walk & Gibson, 1956). Recall that the results of her study of young children's discrimination of letter-like forms reflected their perception of real world objects. Object perception was indeed one general focus of Eleanor's research that spanned a number of years.

This interest in object perception was further exemplified by an experiment demonstrating the sensitivity of young children to dynamic stimulus information for objects (Carroll & Gibson, 1981). Three-month-old infants were presented with a gradually approaching planar object. Such stimulation provides optical flow information for an approaching object. The infants' responses indicated avoidance, for example, by trying to move their head away as indicated by increasing pressure against a head rest. In contrast, if they were presented with an aperture such as a window frame approaching at the same rate there was no such avoidance response.

Embedded in this study were two important shifts in Eleanor's theoretical approach. First, perception of affordances was central to perceptual learning and development. The concept of affordance refers to the fit between an organism's capabilities and properties of the environment that support (or fail to support) action. So, for example, an object of a given size is graspable by a child with an appropriate hand size. Or, a step is climbable by a person with appropriate leg length and strength and balance. Thus, an affordance is a relation between organism and environment. Importantly, there is perceptual information about this relation. Perceivers are, or can become, sensitive to such information. In short, applied to perceptual learning and development, with increasing experience children become more sensitive to such relationships. As their skills change so does their sensitivity to the changed relation between their capability and relevant properties of the environment. Thus in the previous example an approaching object affords possible (harmful) contact. But an approaching window or doorway affords free passage. These examples also illustrate the second and related shift in her thinking. The information for affordances is often dynamic. It involves some aspect of stimulation changing over time.

Both aspects of Eleanor's thinking were manifest in her study of infants' sensitivity to the differences in affordance of objects. She asked whether infants are sensitive to substantive characteristics of objects. Are they rigid or flexible? To find this out, she applied a habituation procedure that, in principle, goes back to her early concern with generalization and differentiation. In the procedure, used today by many infant researchers, babies are presented repeatedly with one stimulus until they lose interest in it (habituation). They will generalize that loss of interest to similar stimuli. However, they will recover their interest to a novel stimulus if they discriminate it as different from what they have become used to (dishabituation).

In one experiment, the dynamic feature of stimulation was used to investigate infant sensitivity to the rigidity and elasticity of objects (Gibson, Owsley, & Johnston, 1978). Three-month-old infants were exposed repeatedly to objects undergoing rigid transformations, such as displacing horizontally, vertically, and approaching/receding. After they lost interest in such stimuli, they displayed generalization (continued low interest) to a new rigid transformation (e.g., rotation) but renewed interest to a new deforming elastic transformation. Apparently, they generalized to the new stimulus that specified the same affordance but differentiated a new stimulus that specified a different affordance.

A similar, but even more dramatic, experiment was conducted by Gibson and Walker (1984). They exposed 1-month-olds to an unseen rigid or elastic nipple in their mouth. After they had experienced such a nipple for a short period of time, they were shown visually a pair of nipples side by side, one undergoing a rigid transformation and the other an elastic transformation. These 1-month-olds generalized their oral tactual/haptic perceptual experience to the very different visual display. This generalization was indicated by preference for looking at the nipple exhibiting the novel transformation. The common feature that was generalized was the substance/composition of the objects, which provides a particular affordance for manipulation. (This is one of a very few examples of generalization and differentiation across sense modalities with such young infants.)

Another direction of Eleanor's research on affordances may have had its root in the perceptual learning studies of rats reared with objects on the sides of their cages. In one of those experiments (Walk, Gibson, & Tighe, 1957) a group of rats was raised in the dark to be compared with animals reared with geometric forms. When the animals reached maturity the researchers wanted to be sure that the dark-reared animals were not simply blind, so they devised a test of their vision. Each animal was placed on a narrow board separating the two sides of a large plate of glass. On one side of the board was a checkered wallpaper pattern directly under the glass. On the other side of the board there was the same pattern visible on the floor several feet below. Almost all the rats in both groups, when exploring, crawled off the board onto the side with the pattern directly underneath the glass, the "shallow" side. All the animals could see well enough to avoid the visual drop-off. The "visual cliff" test was born.

Initially the visual cliff was exploited as a test of distance or depth perception in a variety of animal species: rats, chickens, kittens, and human babies. Some, such as chickens, show discrimination of deep from shallow essentially at birth. Other species display it at different periods of development. For example, kittens display depth perception soon after birth when their visual system has become functional, and human babies display it after their locomotor system has become functional and they begin to crawl (Walk & Gibson, 1961).

However, Eleanor began to think about the visual cliff and its relation, more generally, to affordances for locomotion. She hypothesized that besides the perception of depth and avoidance of a deep drop-off, another reason crawling infants might avoid the deep side of the visual cliff is that there simply was no textured surface that provided information for the affordance of locomotion. One bit of evidence that led to this idea was an experiment showing that if the texture on the shallow side of a visual cliff is very fine infants will no longer move off the center board onto that side (Walk & Gibson, 1961). This condition was tried out in one experiment to equate the size of this texture stimulation projecting to the eye from the two sides of the visual cliff. In the original form of the cliff the same texture pattern was used on both the deep and the shallow sides. That arrangement resulted in a much finer projection to the eye from the deep side.

Thinking along these lines led Eleanor and her colleagues to a series of experiments on the effects of surface characteristics on the locomotion of infants and toddlers (Gibson, Riccio, Schmuckler, Stoffregen, Rosenberg, & Taomina, 1987). Crawling and newly walking infants were provided the opportunity to traverse pathways with different surfaces. The infants were placed on a starting platform in front of a pathway across which they could locomote to their parent or caregiver. In one experiment, infants were faced with a textured surface or a completely homogeneous black velvet surface. Both the crawlers and the newly walking infants crossed both surfaces to their parent, but they were much slower to initiate movement across the homogeneous surface. In a follow-up experiment the two types of pathway surfaces were presented side by side, and the infants could choose which surface to cross. Here almost all infants, both walkers and crawlers, chose the textured surface and avoided the homogeneous surface.

The same experimental setting was used to investigate other surface properties. For example, what would happen if a rigid static surface were paired with an undulating waterbed surface? In such an experiment each surface was covered with cross-hatch patterns. Again, crawling and newly walking infants were called to by a parent. The crawling infants showed no preference for one pathway over the other, but interestingly the walkers overwhelmingly chose the rigid surface. However, the few walkers who did choose to cross the waterbed surface got down and crawled. It is clear that babies so young are sensitive to the surface qualities and what they afford for locomotion.

Eleanor went on to investigate perceptual aspects of locomotion more generally. Besides analyzing perception of surface qualities she considered both balance and maintenance of posture while locomoting as well as orientation and way-finding. Her analysis and work are summarized in an article outlining a developmental theory of mobility (Gibson & Schmuckler, 1989).

AN ACTIVE RETIREMENT

Many of the experiments based on the concept of affordance were conducted after Eleanor's formal retirement in 1979. She continued to engage in research as professor emerita until 1987, when she gave up her laboratory and moved to Vermont. Even after that she was invited to spend extended periods of time at a number of universities and colleges including Emory University, the University of Connecticut, the University of South Carolina, Indiana University, and Middlebury College. She continued to engage in considerable writing and even conduct some research. During the period before and after her retirement Eleanor received considerable additional external recognition: honorary degrees from Smith College, Emory University, the University of South Carolina, Middlebury College, and Yale University. She was elected to the National Academy of Science and was a recipient of the National Medal of Science.

As may be obvious in much of the previous discussion, a functional orientation permeated Eleanor's general theoretical perspective about differentiation. This was apparent all through her research career. It was already evident in the first published experiment she did as an undergraduate. In that experiment participants were classically conditioned upon the sound of a buzzer to withdraw their right middle finger from a shock-delivering electrode. After conditioning they were tested with the buzzer sounding when their left middle finger was placed on the electrode. A large proportion of her participants showed intermanual transfer of the withdrawal response. She interpreted this as indicating that what was being conditioned was not a specific reflex reaction of a muscle or a muscle group but rather a more general withdrawal response. The response had a function.

Later on, her functional orientation was further manifest in the content of the problems she investigated. Her research on the perception of distance in wide-open natural spaces thus contrasted with the laboratory studies common at the time. The initial use of the visual cliff in the study of depth perception is another obvious functional problem in distance perception, and it was possible to apply it to research with preverbal children and animals.

Her reading research was another example. What are the perceptual units in children's learning to read—letters, letter clusters, words? Here she applied her differentiation perspective to the discrimination of letters, for example, in analyzing the distinctive features that enable beginning readers to perceive when two letters are different from each other.

When graduate students would ask Eleanor about what use there is to a lot of theorizing about perceptual learning, how it could be applied, she was fond of answering, "There is nothing so practical as a good theory."

Her functional orientation came explicitly into its own when she began to focus on the affordance concept. It was apparent in her research on the perceptual sensitivity of infants to the rigidity and flexibility of objects. This is clearly a dimension of difference with functional implications as to how an object can be manipulated. Similarly, the rigidity and flexibility of surfaces has functional implications for locomotion. It is worthy of note that these properties had not previously been of interest to investigators of perceptual development.

This chapter has emphasized Eleanor's ideas and intellectual acumen. In so doing, not much attention has explicitly been paid to the programmatic quality of her work, to the elegance of many of her experimental procedures or to her intellectual toughness. However, these characteristics are clearly there for readers who want to delve further. But let us conclude on a more personal note.

All through this chapter, reference was made more or less formally to "Eleanor." However, already as an undergraduate student she was known to her friends as Jackie. This diminutive nickname was adopted by her colleagues at Smith College and was well suited to the collegial atmosphere at Cornell. There were a number of other faculty members who went by similar nicknames: Robbie MacLeod, Jimmy Gibson, Julie Hochberg, Olie Smith. And this is how they and Jackie were addressed by both fellow faculty and by graduate students. The psychology department was a small and close-knit family.

All this fit in well with Jackie's style. She developed close personal relations with her students. One aspect of that style was manifest when a young graduate student would approach her with the kernel of an idea. Often her reaction would be a positive but relatively subdued, "That's interesting." Then she would ponder the idea overnight or for a day or two and come back with a much more meaningful and elaborated gem for which she gave the originating student full credit. Of course, she also gradually incorporated the student as a full and equal partner. It was this personal thoughtfulness and profound serious attention that enabled her relations with students to be familiar while at the same time preserving their deep respect.

Eleanor "Jackie" Gibson lived a long and productive life, loved by family and friends, admired and respected by her colleagues. She died on December 30, 2002, in South Carolina.

SUGGESTED READINGS

Gibson, E. J. (1969). *Principles of perceptual learning and development*. New York: Appleton-Century-Crofts.

This is the first major statement of the domain of perceptual learning and development. It integrates the experimental research and theoretical analyses available to that time. It was also one of the earliest attempts to relate comprehensively perceptual learning and perceptual development. A full 30 years later this effort was brought up to date and elaborated from an ecological perspective with the publication of Gibson and Pick (2000).

Gibson, E. J. (1991). *Odyssey in learning and perception*. Cambridge, MA: MIT Press.

This is a collection of many of Eleanor Gibson's most important papers between 1932 and 1988. The volume is divided into six sections roughly chronologically but more significantly by the domains of her thinking and research during the course of her career. The first section reflects the experimental psychology of the era in which she entered the field of scientific psychology. The papers of the final section capture the ecological perspective on perceptual learning and development. They provide vivid evidence of her impact on psychology. Particularly interesting is her own commentary at the beginning and end of each section.

Gibson, E. J., & Schmuckler, M.A. (1989). Going somewhere: An ecological and experimental approach to development of mobility. *Ecological Psychology, 1*, 3–25.

This is an interesting example of how Eleanor Gibson uses her experimental research to relate her ecological and functional perspectives.

REFERENCES

Carroll, J. J., & Gibson, E. J. (1981). *Differences of an aperture from an object under conditions of motion by three-month-old infants.* Paper presented at the meeting of the Society for Research in Child Development. Boston, MA.

Criss, A. H. (2010). Differentiation and response bias in episodic memory: Evidence from reaction time distributions. *Journal of Experimental Psychology: Learning, Memory, & Cognition, 36*, 484–499. doi:10.1037/a0018435

Dopson, J. C., Esber, G. R., & Pearce, J. M. (2010). Differences in the associability of relevant and irrelevant stimuli. *Journal of Experimental Psychology: Animal Behavior Processes, 36*, 256–267. doi:10.1037/a0016588

Gibson, E. J. (1940). A systematic application of the concepts of generalization and differentiation to verbal learning, *Psychological Review, 47*, 196–229. doi:10.1037/h0060582

Gibson, E. J. (1963). Perceptual learning. *Annual Review of Psychology, 14*, 28–56. doi: 10.1146/annurev.ps.14.020163.000333

Gibson, E. J. (1969). *Principles of perceptual learning and development*. New York: Appleton-Century-Crofts.

Gibson, E. J., Bergman, R., & Purdy, J. (1955). The effect of prior training with a scale of distance on absolute and relative estimations of distance over ground. *Journal of Experimental Psychology, 50*, 97–105. doi:10.1037/h0048518

Gibson, E. J., Gibson, J. J., Pick, A. D., & Osser, H. (1962). A developmental study of the discrimination of letter-like forms. *Journal of Comparative and Physiological Psychology, 55*, 897–906. doi:10.1037/h0043190

Gibson, E. J., & Levin, H. (1975). *The psychology of reading*. Cambridge, MA: MIT Press.

Gibson, E. J., & Olum, V. (1960). Experimental methods of studying perception in children. In P. H. Mussen (Ed.), *Handbook of research in child development* (pp. 311–373). New York: Wiley.

Gibson, E. J., Owsley, C. J., & Johnston, J. (1978). Perception of invariants by five-month-old infants: Differentiation of two types of motion. *Developmental Psychology, 14,* 407–415. doi:10.1037/0012-1649.14.4.407

Gibson E. J., & and Pick, A. D. (2000). *Perceptual learning and development: An ecological approach.* New York: Oxford University Press.

Gibson, E. J., Riccio, G., Schmuckler, M. A., Stoffregen, T. A., Rosenberg, D., & Taomina, J. (1987). Detection of the traversability of surfaces by crawling and walking infants. *Journal of Experimental Psychology: Human Perception and Performance, 13,* 533–544. doi:10.1037/0096-1523.13.4.533

Gibson, E. J., & Schmuckler, M. A. (1989). Going somewhere: An ecological and experimental approach to development of mobility. *Ecological Psychology, 1,* 3–25. doi:10.1207/s15326969eco0101_2

Gibson, E. J. & Walker, A. (1984). Development of knowledge of visual and tactual affordance of substance. *Child Development, 55,* 453–460. doi:10.2307/1129956

Gibson, J. J., & Gibson, E. J. (1955). Perceptual learning: Differentiation or enrichment? *Psychological Review, 62,* 32–41. doi:10.1037/h0048826

Gibson, J. J., Jack, E. J., & Raffel, G. (1932). Bilateral transfer of the conditioned response in the human subject. *Journal of Experimental Psychology, 15,* 416–421. doi:10.1037/h0071059

Walk, R. D., & Gibson, E. J. (1956). The effect of prolonged exposure to visually presented patterns on learning to discriminate them. *Journal of Comparative and Physiological Psychology, 39,* 239–242.

Walk, R. D., & Gibson, E. J. (1961). A comparative and analytic study of visual depth perception. *Psychological Monographs, 75,* No. 15.

Walk, R. D., Gibson, E. J., & Tighe, T. J. (1957). Of light- and dark- reared rats on a visual cliff. *Science, 126,* 80–81. doi:10.1126/science.126.3263.80-a

15

Mamie Phipps Clark:
*Developmental Psychologist, Starting From Strengths**

ALEXANDRA RUTHERFORD
York University

A child can pick up race prejudice at 10 o'clock in the morning. It's in the air. It's on the face of some people when they look at Negroes…. M. P. Clark as cited in "Control Prejudice." (1968, p. 7)

About 3 months after the assassination of America's best-known civil rights activist and integrationist Dr. Martin Luther King Jr., an article titled "Control Prejudice" appeared in the *Billings Gazette.* "Race prejudice is everywhere," it began, "and parents who want to guard against it must work on it every day" (July 29, 1968, p. 7). The article went on to quote Dr. Mamie Phipps Clark, a "prominent psychologist and mother of two children" (p. 7), who outlined a number of strategies parents could use both in the home and outside it to promote racial understanding and fight

Figure 15.1   Mamie Phipps Clark. (Courtesy of the Archives of the History of American Psychology, The Center for the History of Psychology–The University of Akron, Robert V. Guthrie papers. With permission.)

* The author would like to thank Kelli Vaughn for her assistance compiling material on Mamie Phipps Clark. The research for this chapter was supported by a Social Sciences and Humanities Research Council of Canada Standard Research Grant.

prejudice early in their children's development. These strategies included providing children with opportunities to learn about people from different cultures and religions, reading to them from books with multiethnic characters and taking an active stand against discriminatory remarks and behaviors when they occurred.

Dr. Clark concluded by stating that the primary goal of these strategies is to help all children develop respect for others, especially others who are unlike themselves. Central to her philosophy of respect was the belief that all people, no matter how disadvantaged, have strengths that could be identified and built upon, that families and communities are important sources of these strengths, and that central to the task of helping any child develop optimally is a simultaneous focus on these strengths and the structural factors that might suppress them. She put this philosophy into practice as the executive director of the Northside Center for Child Development in New York City, which she cofounded in 1946 with her husband, Kenneth Bancroft Clark. Northside is, to this day, a multidisciplinary, multiethnic service for children, adolescents, and parents with psychological and educational needs in the Harlem community. Mamie Clark's vision for Northside and her implementation of this vision for over 30 years attest to her enormous contribution to strengthening and improving the lives of disadvantaged children and their families. Her philosophy also exemplifies the conjoining of the social welfare and psychological outlooks on child development, a process that had begun in the first White House Conference on Child Health and Protection in 1930 and that became the "dominant framework for understanding the social and psychological effects of racism" at midcentury (Selig, 2006, p. 138).

FAMILY STRENGTH

Mamie Katherine Phipps (b. April 18, 1917, d. August 11, 1983) experienced firsthand the value of a strong family and community. Born in 1917 in Hot Springs, Arkansas, she was the daughter of a prominent physician, Harold H. Phipps, and Katie Florence Phipps, a homemaker. Like all children in the United States at the time, she attended a racially segregated school. In Hot Springs there was one White school and one Black school, from first through twelfth grade. The schools were located at opposite ends of town so that many students passed each other on the way to their respective schools. Racial tension erupting into fights was not uncommon. In this environment, Phipps recalled developing a protective armor that she carried with her at all times, but she was also aware that her position as the daughter of a well-respected physician (her father also managed a resort hotel for vacationers) accorded her certain privileges not extended to other Blacks in the community. As Lal (2002) pointed out, Black physicians, like Black lawyers, were extremely rare in the first half of the 20th century, with the ratio of Black physicians to the Black population as a whole a meager 1 in 3,194. The Phipps family was privileged with respect to class, but this did not mean they were immune to the racism that was all-pervasive in their small southern town.

However, despite the economic privations of the Great Depression, the omnipresent awareness of racism, and the direct experience of legalized discrimination, Phipps described her childhood as comfortable, happy, and secure. Adversity produced increased family cohesion:

> I had a very happy childhood. I really did. We were comfortable, and we lived through the Depression, but somehow it seemed to strengthen the family ties, rather than anything else. I remember the Depression very well. I remember that we had to cut back on all kinds of things that we had always had in our lives. But it wasn't really that much of a hardship. And at the end of it, I went to college. (M. P. Clark, 1976, p. 3)

In a later autobiographical reflection, she reiterated the importance of a "warm and protective extended family" in giving her the foundation for later career satisfaction (Clark, 1983, p. 269).

Coping with the facts of everyday life in the Jim Crow South required resilience and determination, and Phipps drew on both of these qualities in her decision to pursue post-secondary education. Noting that "in 1934, a southern Negro aspiring to enter an academic college had relatively few choices" (Clark, 1983, p. 269), Clark chose one of the very few options open to her. At the age of 16, with the support of her parents who were determined that she should get the best education possible, she traveled over 1000 miles by train to enroll at Howard University in Washington, DC. To ensure his daughter's safety on her first few trips to and from college, Harold Phipps bought her a compartment and instructed her to keep the shades down and stay inside. He made arrangements with the porters to look after her and ensure that she got meals. Security, even in the midst of a hostile environment, was a consistent feature of Phipps's upbringing (Lal, 2002).

Initially, Phipps thought she would major in mathematics. She quickly discovered, however, that the segregated public school system in Hot Springs had not prepared her to meet the intellectual demands of her new environment. Howard University employed some of the nation's most exciting Black intellectuals of the 1930s, including Alain Locke in philosophy, Ralph Bunche in political science, and Francis Cecil Sumner in psychology. Phipps soon realized that there were huge gaps in her education, not only in mathematics but also in English and foreign languages. With typical resilience she acted quickly to compensate:

> Well, I had to study harder. I really did…. I went to summer school the first two summers when I was in college, to make up the deficiencies…. But I was taking five courses in summer school, and that's a lot of courses…. (M. P. Clark, 1976, p. 12)

She caught up, but her interest in mathematics was soon replaced by a new interest: psychology.

PSYCHOLOGY: THE SILENT CHALLENGE

Mamie Phipps's initial desire to pursue mathematics at Howard quickly gave way to an interest in child development and psychology, partly due to the lack of encouragement given female students in mathematics (Clark, 1983, p. 270), and partly due to the encouragement of her future husband, Kenneth Bancroft Clark (see Jackson, 2006; Keppel, 2002; Phillips, 2000). Clark, a fellow student who was studying psychology, described it as a stimulating field that would fit with her interest in children and, he noted (perhaps optimistically), would provide future job opportunities. He introduced her to the head of the psychology department, Francis Cecil Sumner, who was the first African American to receive a PhD in psychology (see Guthrie, 1998, pp. 214–232; Sawyer, 2000), and she changed her major in her sophomore year. There were no Black women on the staff of the department. She reported retrospectively that the absence of Black women with advanced degrees in psychology at Howard (and indeed anywhere) itself represented a "silent" challenge (Clark, 1983, p. 268).

Mamie Phipps and Kenneth Clark came to share significantly more than just an interest in psychology and were married in April 1938 in Stafford, Virginia, when Mamie was finishing her senior year. As Kenneth later described his first meetings with his future wife:

> She was a freshman when I was a senior. I knew that she was going to be a part of my life from that point on, and that nothing was going to interfere with that fact, including the star basketball player—you know, the other competitors who thought that they had more to offer an attractive, and at that time, comparatively well-to-do young woman, whose father was a physician. (K. B. Clark, 1976, p. 73).

Mamie graduated with her bachelor's degree and spent the summer working as a secretary in the law offices of Charles Hamilton Houston, the dean of Howard Law School and a lead attorney for the National Association for the Advancement of Colored People (Jackson & Weidman, 2006; Lal, 2002). She described this experience as "an enormously instructive and revealing one in relation to my own identity as a 'Negro'" (Clark, 1983, p. 268). There, she witnessed the excitement of early planning for the eventual repeal of the *Plessy v. Ferguson* ruling of 1896 that had upheld the constitutionality of the separate but equal doctrine that permitted racial segregation for almost 50 years.

In the fall, she began her master's degree program with an interest in developmental psychology. Kenneth, who was doing his doctoral training at Columbia University, suggested that she travel to New York and talk with psychologists Ruth and Eugene Horowitz (later Hartley) about their work on self-identification in nursery school children (see Horowitz, 1939). Thus, after a visit to an all-Black nursery school in Washington, DC, that resulted in an offer to do research with the children and after her meeting with the Horowitzes, she decided to merge her interests in race and child development in her master's research, resulting in her thesis, "The Development of Consciousness of Self in Negro Pre-school Children" (Clark, 1939).

In this work, Mamie Clark explored the development of racial identity in 150 Black children in segregated nursery schools in the Washington, DC, area using a modification of a picture technique that had been pioneered by Ruth and Eugene Horowitz. A version of the study was published later that year with her husband as first author (Clark & Clark, 1939). In the published study, boys and girls aged 3, 4, and 5 years were presented with a set of pictures portraying various combinations of White boys, "colored" boys, and irrelevant figures (clown, dog, lion, hen). The boys were asked, "Show me which one is you," and the girls were asked to point out the figure that was like their brother, male cousin, or a male playmate (Clark & Clark, 1939, p. 594). The Clarks concluded that in the whole sample, choices of the colored boy increased with age, and for boys at least there was a distinct increase in awareness of self between the ages of 3 and 4. Ultimately, however, the technique would have to be refined to say anything about the development of self-awareness in girls or to generate a more nuanced picture for self-identification processes in older children.

The Clarks also analyzed the data with respect to choices of White versus colored boys when the sample was divided into light, medium, and dark-skinned children. This analysis showed that dark-skinned children were significantly more likely than their light-skinned peers to choose the colored boy over the White boy (Clark & Clark, 1940). They also gathered more data in "mixed" New York City nursery schools, where both Black and White children attended a school with White teachers. They concluded that compared with the segregated sample, children in the mixed nursery school seemed to develop a consciousness of self and sense of racial identification somewhat later (Clark & Clark, 1939).

Ultimately, the results of these studies, along with the acknowledged limitations of the method, produced more questions than they answered. Thus, Kenneth and Mamie prepared a proposal for further research on racial identification in Negro children that included new methods: a coloring test and a doll test (as noted in Clark, 1983, p. 269). They submitted their proposal to the Julius Rosenwald Fellowship program in 1939 and were awarded the fellowship in 1940 (with renewals in 2 subsequent years). The value of the initial fellowship was $1500, and 68 were awarded from a pool of 600 applicants (Rosenwald Awards made to 68 students, 1940, p. 26).

The mandate of the Rosenwald Fund was to advance the lives of Black Americans and to improve race relations. Until the late 1920s, the fund had concentrated its attention on building schools for Black communities in the rural South. Following an extensive reorganization in 1928, the fund shifted its focus from building schools to building people. The philosophy behind the fellowship program that supported the Clarks' work was that providing talented and promising Blacks with the resources necessary to undertake advanced training, to pursue professional careers, and to work toward social justice would "give the lie to the notion of racial inferiority" (Perkins, 2003, p. 345). It would demonstrate that "Black achievements were limited not by inherent inadequacy, but by the barriers of institutionalized racism, social isolation, educational deprivation, and lack of economic opportunity" (Perkins, 2003, p. 345). The fellowship allowed Mamie to enter Columbia University, where her husband had just been awarded his PhD in 1940, and for the couple to continue their research. That year, Mamie gave birth to their first child, Kate. Their son, Hilton, was born in 1943.

At Columbia, Mamie Clark chose to work with White psychologist and well-known eugenicist and racist Henry Garrett rather than with Kenneth's more sympathetic mentors Gardner Murphy and Otto Klineberg. Garrett had considerable statistical expertise, which was important for Mamie's work, but, as Kenneth later reported, she felt that working with Murphy or Klineberg would be "too easy" (K. B. Clark, 1976, p. 91); she wanted to show Garrett firsthand that a Black student could perform just as well as a White student. In Mamie's own understated words, Garrett was "not by any means a liberal on racial matters" (Clark, 1983, p. 270). Clark received her PhD in 1943. Her dissertation was titled "The Development of Primary Mental Abilities with Age" (Clark, 1944). It was a factor analytic study of intelligence conducted on children in the New York public school system. Garrett promptly assumed she would return to the South to teach in a Black high school, an assumption that Mamie later reported "amused" her (Clark, 1983, p. 270). A few years after her graduation, Mamie Clark would indeed meet Henry Garrett in the South—in a Virginia courtroom where a school desegregation case was being heard. Garrett was there to testify on the side of segregated schools, arguing that Black and White children had different talents and abilities that justified separate education. Clark gave testimony to support integration. It was the last time she would see her former supervisor.

With their PhDs completed, Mamie and Kenneth Clark became the first two African Americans to receive doctorates in psychology from Columbia University, and only the seventeenth and twenty-second African Americans, respectively, to receive psychology doctorates in the United States (Phillips, 2005).

THE DEVELOPMENT OF RACIAL IDENTIFICATION AND PREFERENCE

Although Mamie Clark's dissertation was a developmental study of mental ability, at the same time that she was conducting this research she was also continuing her collaboration with Kenneth on their Rosenwald-funded studies of racial identification in children. These studies were completed by 1943 (according to Clark, 1983, p. 270), but reports on the findings did not begin to appear in print until 1947 (Clark & Clark, 1947, 1950). As Kenneth Clark later reported:

> Mamie and I were into the racial preferences and identification of Negro student research.... It was an extension of her Master's thesis on racial identification of Negro students. That was the thing that came to be known as the "Dolls Test" that the Supreme Court cited. The record should show that was Mamie's primary project that I crashed. I sort of piggybacked on it. (K. B. Clark, as cited in Nyman, 2010, p. 76)

In their 1947 report, the Clarks presented the results from one of their new methods of assessing racial identification and preferences: the Dolls Test. In this test, Black children ages 3 through 7 were presented with four dolls that were identical except for skin and hair color. Two of the dolls had brown skin and black hair, and two of the dolls had white skin and yellow hair. To assess racial preference, the children were presented with the four dolls and responded to the following requests by picking one of the dolls and handing it to the experimenter: "1) Give me the doll that you like to play with or like best; 2) Give me the doll that is a nice doll; 3) Give me the doll that looks bad; and 4) Give me the doll that is a nice color" (Clark & Clark, 1947, p. 169). The children were then asked to make racial identifications (e.g., "Give me the doll that looks like a colored child") and self-identification ("Give me the doll that looks like you").

The Clarks tested 253 Black children, 134 of whom attended segregated nursery and public schools in the South (Arkansas) and 119 of whom attended racially mixed schools in the Northeast (Massachusetts). They found that by age 7, 87% of the children correctly self-identified by choosing the brown doll as the one that looked like them. In terms of racial preference, the majority of Black children chose the white doll as the doll they wanted to play with (67%), indicated that the white doll was the nice doll (59%), indicated that the brown doll looked bad (59%), and chose the white doll as having the nice color (60%). The Clarks also analyzed the children's doll preferences by age and by light, medium, and dark skin-color groups. At the very end of their report, they compared the doll preferences of Northern children and Southern children. Although the pattern of preferences found in the overall sample held for the Northern and Southern groups analyzed separately, the Clarks did find that Southern children in segregated schools were slightly less pronounced in their preference for the white doll compared with Northern children. For example, while 68% of Northern children identified the white doll as the nice doll, 52% of Southern children made this identification. While 72% of Northern children chose to play with the white doll, 62% of Southern children made this choice.

In 1950, the Clarks published another study in which they expanded on the "dynamics of racial attitudes in Negro children" (Clark & Clark, 1950, p. 341). In this paper, they reported on the results from a coloring test given to the 5, 6, and 7 year olds in their sample. Children were asked to color a line drawing of a boy or girl "the color that you are" and then to color a second drawing "the color you like little boys [or girls] to be" (p. 342). They found that, as in other studies, racial self-identification was fairly accurate by age 7 (97%) but that 52% of the sample used white or a color other than brown to indicate the color they liked little boys or girls to be. Again, they presented results from the Southern and Northern children separately. As in the Dolls Test, Southern, segregated children were somewhat less pronounced in their rejection of the color brown, with 30% not using the color brown in response to the preference question, compared with 64% of the Northern children rejecting the color brown. The Clarks suggested that this represented more emotional conflict in the Northern children and returned to the Dolls Test to substantiate this interpretation with observations of the children's behavior and the comments the children made to explain their choices. For example, while 9% of the Southern children who explained their preference did so in an evasive or irrelevant way, 40% of the Northern children gave evasive responses. The Clarks concluded that the "Northern group (even at this age) generally tends to repress or attempt to escape from the apparently painful fact of the meaning of color differences in American society" (Clark & Clark, 1950, p. 348). Conversely, the Southern children were more likely to give matter-of-fact explanations and, in two cases, identified the black doll with the racial epithet "nigger."

In explaining why they did not publish their study for several years after its completion, Kenneth Clark later explained:

> Mamie and I knew that it was important, but I think we tended to assess its importance in terms of its effect upon us. It was a terribly disturbing bit of research for us…. It was disturbing for me to see the children in the test situation placed in this terrible conflict of having to identify with dolls to which they had previously ascribed negative characteristics. (K. B. Clark, as cited in Nyman, 2010, pp. 76, 77)

The Clarks were of course distressed when the children cried or ran out of the room when asked to respond to the identification question, but as Kenneth also remarked:

> Equally disturbing was seeing the Southern children accommodating to this, accepting this as a God-given. I remember one little boy … as if it was yesterday. He looked up into my face and he smiled pointing to the brown doll he said, "That's me. That's a nigger. I'm a nigger." That hurt me as much as the Northern children who cried. In fact, I thought the crying was more healthy as a response than this seemingly humorous, total acceptance of rejected status. I don't want to get too sentimental about this. In fact, I try to put that away sometimes. (K. B. Clark, as cited in Nyman, 2010, p. 77)

The Clarks' studies of racial identification and preference among Negro children and their growing reputations as experts in this area soon came to the attention of the National Association for the Advancement of Colored People (NAACP) lawyers working to end the racial segregation of public schools in the United States. Both Kenneth and Mamie Clark were called to give expert testimony on the effects of racial segregation and racism on the personality development of Black children in several lower court school desegregation trials, including the one in Virginia where Mamie Clark ran up against her former PhD supervisor.

In 1950, Kenneth Clark was commissioned to write a report for the Mid-Century White House Conference on Children and Youth, which he titled *Effect of Prejudice and Discrimination on Personality Development* and which summarized research findings in this area (Clark, 1950). When his mentor, Otto Klineberg, was approached by Robert Carter, an NAACP Legal Defense Fund lawyer, because of his previous work on race and prejudice, Klineberg quickly referred Carter to Kenneth Clark (see Benjamin & Crouse, 2002; Kluger, 1975; Phillips, 2000). In September 1952, along with Isidor Chein and Stuart Cook, Clark wrote a document called "The Effects of Segregation and the Consequences of Desegregation: A Social Science Statement" (Clark, Chein, & Cook, 2004). The document reviewed the body of social psychological research on the effects of segregation and its role in maintaining prejudice as well as work on the potential effects of desegregation. Included were references to the Clarks' own studies on racial preference in children in segregated versus desegregated schools. Signed by

32 prominent social scientists, including Mamie Phipps Clark, the Social Science Statement, as it would come to be known, would play an important role in the 1954 Supreme Court Decision in *Brown v. Board of Education of Topeka*, which struck down the legality of segregation by race in public schools. Submitted as an Appendix to the appellants' briefs, and cited by Chief Justice Earl Warren, it stands as the first use of social science research in a Supreme Court decision (for more on the role of social science in the *Brown v. Board* decision, see Jackson, 2005; Keppel, 1995; Kluger, 1975; Schmidt, 2006).

THE BIRTH OF NORTHSIDE

Although Henry Garrett's assumption that, upon completion of her PhD, Mamie Clark would return to the South to teach high school was clearly racist and sexist, his attitudes were not unlike those of many Americans in the period leading up to and persisting after the *Brown v. Board* decision (for assessments of the impact of *Brown v. Board*, see Pettigrew, 2004; Weinstein, Gregory, & Strambler, 2004). This racism and sexism made being female and Black distinct liabilities in terms of securing a professional position in the 1940s. Thus, despite her husband's recent academic appointment at the City College of New York (he was the City College's first African American instructor; Markowitz & Rosner, 2000), it was very clear to Clark that full-time university appointments for doctoral-level Black women psychologists were nonexistent. Consequently, she looked for research positions outside academia. Her first job was with the American Public Health Association, where she was charged with analyzing data being collected for a national study of nurses. It was a thoroughly demoralizing first post-PhD work experience. Despite her qualifications—the only other PhD psychologist was a White woman—as a Black woman and the only Black person on the staff, Clark was subjugated and humiliated. She later recalled:

> I got a job with the American Public Health Association, and it was absolutely the most ghastly experience I'd ever had in my life. And it was my first job experience. It had nothing to do with children. It had to do with public health. And I said to Kenneth one night, I said, "Kenneth, I just can't work with people. And certainly not these kinds of people." I said, "I have to do something by myself." (M. P. Clark, 1976, p. 31)

Clark endured this situation for a year to gain experience but then took a job as a research psychologist for the U.S. Armed Forces Institute, New York Examination Center at Teachers College, Columbia University (Guthrie, 1998, p. 206), a position she found satisfying but likened to a "holding pattern" (Clark, 1983, p. 272). She then secured a position doing psychological testing at a private agency serving homeless Black girls, the Riverdale Home for Children. There, her earlier resolve to do something by herself began to take shape. Working at Riverdale convinced her that there were almost no resources, especially mental health resources, for neglected and abandoned minority children in New York City, and specifically in the Harlem community.

For over a year, with Kenneth, she approached a number of agencies that they hoped would be willing to start a program to provide such services, specifically psychological testing, remedial programs, and social support for these underserved children. As she explained:

> Kenneth and I went to most of the existing agencies in Harlem, because it was our first thinking that this service should be a part of a larger agency, and we went for example to the Urban League. We went to the Children's Aid Society. We went to the Community Service Society. We even talked to a few ministers, thinking it could be part of a church program, in terms of location if nothing else…. For the most part, the agencies seemed to feel that it wasn't a service that they weren't performing. They seemed to feel that it was something they were already doing—which they weren't, really. So we just realized that we weren't going to get it open that way. So we decided to open it ourselves. (M. P. Clark, 1976, p. 39)

Thus, with a loan of $936 from Harold Phipps, Mamie and Kenneth Clark opened a basement office in the Paul Dunbar Apartments on the north side of Harlem in February 1946. They named it the Northside Testing and Consultation Center but in 1947 changed the name to the Northside Center for Child Development. For the next 30 years, Mamie Clark's vision would drive Northside (for a detailed history of Northside, see Markowitz & Rosner, 2000).

Northside's primary and overarching objective was (and still is) to provide psychological and educational services to minority children and their parents to help them cope with and overcome the pervasive impact of racism, discrimination, and disadvantage. The Clarks' philosophy of treatment and their vision for Northside grew out of the social science research at the time (including their own) that showed the pernicious effects of racial discrimination and resulting social inequities on personality development. The two-pronged emphasis on both individual maladjustment and the role of the environment in producing that maladjustment at times collided with prevailing psychiatric thought that was predominantly psychoanalytic and tended to focus exclusively on intrapsychic deficiencies. However, even when to do so meant loss in funding from psychoanalytically inclined board members (see Markowitz & Rosner, 2000), the Clarks consistently promoted the understanding and treatment of children's emotional and behavioral difficulties holistically from a strengths-based, psychosocial, and environmental perspective while acknowledging the damage that racism brought about for both Black and White children.

This meant that the services offered at Northside were eclectic and multifocal and underwent constant revision to meet the needs of families and of the community. For example, when it became clear early in the center's history that minority children were overrepresented in classes for the mentally deficient (known as Classes for Children of Retarded Mental Development), the staff at Northside retested children and showed that most did not meet the criteria for this designation (most had IQs above 70) but were subjected to social and educational neglect (Clark, 1983, p. 273). They then developed remedial reading classes that became a core component of client services. The success of these efforts provided acceptance of the center in the larger Harlem community, a community where the stigma attached to having psychological problems was high, as it was in American society generally. As Mamie Clark noted, "Although at that time there was a climate of not accepting psychiatry or anything clinical, people did come" (M. P. Clark, 1976, p. 41).

Thus, instead of identifying the weakness or pathology of the family, Northside would "start with what's strong in this family and pick it up and work with it" (M. P. Clark, as cited in Markowitz & Rosner, 2000, p. 48). This emphasis on strengths was an antidote to a growing belief in the cultural deprivation hypothesis, widely espoused by liberals and social scientists. This hypothesis, in brief, stated that hundreds of years of racism had weakened the personalities of Blacks and wreaked havoc with the structures of their communities and families. It had displaced the Black man as head of his household by depriving him of his opportunity to be the primary breadwinner, thus creating deviant (at least by White standards) matriarchal family structures and social pathology. This belief, espoused by prominent Black social scientists as well as by Whites (e.g., Frazier, 1939; Kardiner & Ovesey, 1951), resulted in little attention paid to the uniqueness and strength of Black social practices, cultures, and communities but did call for an end to racism to undo the damage being done to Blacks by Whites. There was a subtle slide, however, so that by the mid-1960s, amid escalating discourse about the "culture of poverty"—that poverty was more than economic deprivation, it was a way of life passed down through generations—Black families were increasingly seen as beyond help and responsible for their own problems. Psychological therapy, rather than structural reforms, was becoming the key to change.

In the context of belief in the cultural deprivation hypothesis, it is important to note that at Northside, the emphasis was on finding the strengths in the family and building on those strengths. There was strong resistance to narrowing services to psychological and psychiatric treatment only and a rejection of the pathologizing of the Black family. As Markowitz and Rosner (2000) noted of this period in Northside's development, "In March, 1965, Mamie Clark called the staff together to … 'define our approach to treatment at Northside' and avoid the traps of the cultural deprivation hypothesis as it applied to children" (p. 135).

Another critical aspect of Northside's service philosophy was that all children, regardless of race, should be served by a multiracial and multidisciplinary team of professionals and paraprofessionals. Despite differences in race, class, and professional status among the staff, Mamie Clark strove to maintain a nonhierarchical atmosphere. This reflected not only the center's eclecticism but also the Clarks' unwavering belief in the pernicious effects of racial segregation on all children and the desire to present a model of integration in its very structure. To appreciate how radical this position was at the time, Markowitz and Rosner (2000) noted the extent of Supreme Court sanctioned segregation, not only in the South but in the North as well: "When the Clarks initiated Northside, Jackie Robinson had not yet been allowed to play baseball in Brooklyn; the Yankees would not even consider integrating their team until another decade had passed" (p. 20).

Mamie Clark also believed in providing a pleasing physical environment for the children and their families. The offices at Northside, whether in the original basement or in the later multifloor facility in Schomburg Towers to which Northside relocated in 1974, were safe, attractive, and stimulating for the children and parents served within their walls. In fact, on the thirtieth anniversary of Northside in 1976, Kenneth Clark recalled the reaction of one of the parents at the grand opening of the new facilities, who remarked, "Oh my God! It looks as if it were for rich kids!" (Cummings, 1976, p. 31). Indeed, as Lal (2002) noted, Mamie Clark herself embodied and enacted what has been termed *uplift ideology*, the belief that cultivating self-improvement and respectability would diminish White racism and elevate the moral and material conditions for Black people. Accordingly, it was often remarked that Mamie Clark herself was the picture of poise and respectability, both in demeanor and appearance. In the 1960s, she was a member of a committee to rename the section of Harlem where Northside was located *Central Park North* in the hopes that a name change, although symbolic, would also create more pleasing connotations and lead to physical upgrades in the community. As the *New York Times* reported, "The new name, Mrs. Clark said, 'will have the same connotation, we hope, as Central Park South, which is a pretty nice place.' 'We want the place to look like Central Park South,' said Mrs. Clark, a fashionable figure in an apricot silk sheath, off-white pumps, and a single strand of pearls" (Pace, 1965, p. 41). The committee's efforts were not uncontroversial. Many in the Harlem community saw this as meaningless window dressing.

BEYOND NORTHSIDE

In addition to her work at Northside, Mamie Clark was active in the larger Harlem community and the greater New York City area. She worked with Kenneth on the Harlem Youth Opportunities Unlimited project as well as being a member of its advisory board. She also served on advisory boards to the National Headstart Planning Committee of the Office of Economic Opportunity. In 1973, she was awarded the American Association of University Women achievement award for her "admirable service to the field of mental health" (Dr. Mamie Clark, recipient of AAUW achievement award, 1973, p. 7). Beyond psychology and child development, she served on the boards of numerous educational and philanthropic institutions, including the Mount Sinai Medical Center, the New York Public Library, the Museum of Modern Art, and the New York City Mission Society. In brief, Mamie Clark was deeply involved in her community (see Phillips, 2005).

Clark was the executive director of Northside until her retirement in 1979. Her death from lung cancer followed shortly thereafter in 1983. She was buried in Mount Hope Cemetery in the town of Hastings-on-Hudson where she and her husband had been living for many years and where Kenneth Clark continued to live until he passed away in 2005 (Jones & Pettigrew, 2005). As one of her staff members characterized her directorship of the center:

> When an unusual and unique person pursues a dream and realizes that dream and directs that dream, people are drawn not only to the idea of the dream, but to the uniqueness of the person themselves. I think this is what Dr. Mamie was like … Northside, including today's school, really revolved on her ingenuity, her dream…. (Johnson, 1993, as cited in Markowitz & Rosner, 2000, p. 246)

And finally, as Lal (2002) wrote:

> Mamie Clark's comprehensive efforts to ameliorate the pain attached to skin color have had a lasting impact in the fields of child development and the psychology of race. Her vision of social, economic, and psychological advancement for African American children resonates far beyond the era of integration. (p. 20)

SUGGESTED READINGS

Clark, K. B., & M. K. Clark (1939). The development of consciousness of self and the emergence of racial identification in Negro preschool children. *Journal of Social Psychology: SPSSI Bulletin, 10,* 591–599.

    This published report, based on Mamie Clark's master's thesis research at Howard University, explored the development of racial identity in 150 Black children in segregated nursery schools in the Washington, D.C., area using a modification of a picture technique that had been pioneered by Ruth and Eugene Horowitz. The study was the first in a series of studies that modified and refined various projective techniques for assessing not only racial identification but also racial preference in "Negro" children.

Clark, K. B., & Clark, M. P. (1947). Racial identification and preference in Negro children. In T. M. Newcomb & E. L. Hartley (Eds.), *Readings in social psychology* (pp. 169–178). New York: Holt.

    This publication is the report of the now famous Dolls Test—the method pioneered by the Clarks to assess racial identification and preference in "Negro" children, both in the segregated South and in the integrated North. The major finding was that the majority of Black children chose the white doll as the doll they wanted to play with (67%), indicated that the white doll was the nice doll (59%), indicated that the brown doll looked bad (59%), and chose the white doll as having the nice color (60%). This finding was cited, along with the results of many other studies, in the 1952 Social Science Statement authored by Clark et al. (2004) that was submitted as an Appendix to the brief prepared by the National Association for the Advancement of Colored People Legal Defense and Education Fund. This brief was influential in the Supreme Court Case *Brown v. Board of Education*, which struck down the legality of segregation by race in the public schools in the United States. The Dolls Test has subsequently been replicated or modified by other researchers, with sharply differing results (see Farrell & Olson, 1983; Jordan & Hernandez-Reif, 2009).

REFERENCES

Benjamin, L. T., Jr., & Crouse, E. M. (2002). The American Psychological Association's response to *Brown v. Board of Education:* The case of Kenneth B. Clark. *American Psychologist, 57,* 38–50. doi:10.1037/0003-066X.57.1.38

Clark, K. B. (1950). Effect of prejudice and discrimination on personality development, *Fact Finding Report Mid-Century White House Conference on Children and Youth,* Children's Bureau-Federal Security Agency (mimeographed).

Clark, K. B. (1976). Reminiscences of Kenneth B. Clark. In the Oral History Research Office. Collection of the Columbia University Libraries (OHRO/CUL). Retrieved from http://www.columbia.edu/cu/lweb/digital/collections/nny/clarkk/audio_transcript.html

Clark, K. B., Chein, I., & Cook, S. W. (2004). The effects of segregation and the consequences of desegregation: A (September 1952) social science statement in the *Brown v. Board of Education of Topeka* Supreme Court case. *American Psychologist, 59,* 495–501. doi:10.1037/0003-066X.59.6.495

Clark, K. B., & Clark, M. K. (1939). The development of consciousness of self and the emergence of racial identification in Negro preschool children. *Journal of Social Psychology: SPSSI Bulletin, 10,* 591–599.

Clark, K. B., & Clark, M. P. (1939). Segregation as a factor in the racial identification of Negro pre-school children: A preliminary report. *Journal of Experimental Education, 8,* 161–163.

Clark, K. B., & Clark, M. P. (1940). Skin color as a factor in racial identification of Negro pre-school children. *Journal of Social Psychology, 11,* 159–169. doi:10.1080/0022454 5.1940.9918741

Clark, K. B., & Clark, M. P. (1947). Racial identification and preference in Negro children. In T. M. Newcomb & E. L. Hartley (Eds.), *Readings in social psychology* (pp. 169–178). New York: Holt.

Clark, K. B., & Clark, M. P. (1950). Emotional factors in racial identification and preference in Negro children. *Journal of Negro Education, 19,* 341–350. doi:10.2307/2966491

Clark, M. P. (1939). The development of the consciousness of self in Negro pre-school children. In *Archives of Psychology.* Washington, DC: Howard University.

Clark, M. P. (1944). Changes in primary mental abilities with age. *Archives of Psychology,* no. 291. New York: Columbia University.

Clark, M. P. (1976). Reminiscences of Mamie Phipps Clark. In the Oral History Research Office. Collection of the Columbia University Libraries (OHRO/CUL). Retrieved from http://www.columbia.edu/cu/lweb/digital/collections/nny/clarkm/index.html

Clark, M. P. (1983). Mamie Phipps Clark. In A. N. O'Connell & N. F. Russo (Eds.), *Models of achievement: Reflections of eminent women in psychology* (pp. 267–277). New York: Columbia University Press.

Control prejudice (1968, July 29). *Billings Gazette,* p. 7.

Cummings, J. (1976, November 1). Harlem center aids disturbed children. *New York Times,* p. 31.

Dr. Mamie Clark recipient of AAUW achievement award (1973, September 19). *Fairbanks Daily News,* p. 7.

Farrell, W. C., & Olson, J. L. (1983). Kenneth and Mamie Clark revisited: Racial identification and racial preference in dark-skinned and light-skinned Black children. *Urban Education, 18,* 284–297. doi:10.1177/004208598301800302

Frazier, E. F. (1939). *The Negro family in the United States.* Chicago: University of Chicago Press.

Guthrie. R. V. (1998). *Even the rat was white: A historical view of psychology,* 2d ed. Needham Heights, MA: Allyn and Bacon.

Horowitz, R. E. (1939). Racial aspects of self-identification in nursery school children. *Journal of Psychology, 7,* 91–99. doi:10.1080/00223980.1939.9917623

Jackson, J. P. (2005). *Social scientists for social justice: Making the case against segregation.* New York: New York University Press.

Jackson, J. P. (2006). Kenneth B. Clark: The complexities of activist psychology. In D. A. Dewsbury, L. T. Benjamin, & M. Wertheimer (Eds.), *Portraits of pioneers in psychology* (vol. 6, pp. 273–286). Washington, DC: American Psychological Association.

Jackson, J. P., & Weidman, N. M. (2006). *Race, racism, and science: Social impact and interaction.* New Brunswick, NJ: Rutgers University Press.

Jones, J,. & Pettigrew, T. F. (2005). Kenneth B. Clark (1914–2005). *American Psychologist, 60,* 649–651. doi:10.1037/0003-066X.60.6.649

Jordan, P., & Hernandez-Reif, M. (2009). Reexamination of young children's racial attitudes and skin tone preferences. *Journal of Black Psychology, 35,* 388–403. doi:10.1177/0095798409333621

Kardiner, A., & Ovesey, L. (1951). *The mark of oppression: Explorations in the personality of the American Negro.* Cleveland, OH: World.

Keppel, B. (1995). *The work of democracy: Ralph Bunche, Kenneth B. Clark, Lorraine Hansberry, and the cultural politics of race.* Cambridge, MA: Harvard University Press.

Keppel, B. (2002). Kenneth B. Clark in the patterns of American culture. *American Psychologist, 57,* 29–37. doi:10.1037/0003-066X.57.1.29

Kluger, R. (1975). *Simple justice: The history of Brown v. Board of Education and Black America's struggle for equality.* New York: Random House.

Lal, S. (2002). Giving children security: Mamie Phipps Clark and the racialization of child psychology. *American Psychologist, 57,* 20–28. doi:10.1037/0003-066X.57.1.20

Markowitz, G., & Rosner, D. (2000). *Children, race, and power: Kenneth and Mamie Clark's Northside Center.* New York: Routledge.

Nyman, L. (2010). Documenting history: An interview with Kenneth Bancroft Clark. *History of Psychology, 13,* 74–88. doi:10.1037/a0018550

Pace, N. (1965, September 7). New name given to 110th St. area. *New York Times,* p. 1.

Perkins, A. (2003). Welcome consequences and fulfilled promise: Julius Rosenwald fellows and *Brown v. Board of Education. Journal of Negro Education, 72,* 344–356. doi:10.2307/3211252

Pettigrew, T. F. (2004). Justice deferred: A half century after *Brown v. Board of Education. American Psychologist, 59,* 521–529. doi:10.1037/0003-066X.59.6.521

Phillips, L. (2000). Recontextualizing Kenneth B. Clark: An Afrocentric perspective on the paradoxical legacy of a model psychologist–activist. *History of Psychology, 3,* 142–167. doi:10.1037/1093-4510.3.2.142

Phillips, L. (2005). Mamie Phipps Clark. In S. Ware & S. Braukman (Eds.), *Notable American women* (pp. 125–126). Cambridge, MA: Harvard University Press.

Rosenwald Awards made to 68 students (1940, April 30). *New York Times,* p. 26.

Sawyer, T. F. (2000). Francis Cecil Sumner: His views and influence in African American higher education. *History of Psychology, 3,* 122–141. doi:10.1037/1093-4510.3.2.122

Schmidt, C. (2006). The children of *Brown:* Psychology and school desegregation in midcentury America. In B. Beatty, E. D. Cahan, & Grant, J. (Eds.), *When science encounters the child: Education, parenting, and child welfare in 20th-century America* (pp. 175–194). New York: Teachers College Press.

Selig, D. (2006). The whole child: Social science and race at the White House conference of 1930. In B. Beatty, E. D. Cahan, & Grant, J. (Eds.), *When science encounters the child: Education, parenting, and child welfare in 20th-century America* (pp. 136–156). New York: Teachers College Press.

Weinstein, R. S., Gregory, A., & Strambler, M. J. (2004). Intractable self-fulfilling prophecies: Fifty years after *Brown v. Board of Education. American Psychologist, 59,* 511–520. doi:10.1037/0003-066X.59.6.511

16

Lawrence Kohlberg:
Moral Biography, Moral Psychology, and Moral Pedagogy

JOHN R. SNAREY

Emory University

Lawrence Kohlberg (1927–1987) completed his BA in psychology in just one year, and his subsequent doctoral dissertation launched his start as a developmental psychologist. His fast-track education and career, however, were each made possible by a prior decade of intellectual work and reflection about moral issues. This cognitive-ethical combination allowed him to found a new branch of life span developmental psychology—moral development and moral education. I first met Professor Kohlberg in the fall term of 1976 when I began my doctoral studies at the Harvard Graduate School of Education. I gradually got to know him well over the next decade as his student, research colleague, and personal friend. I now believe that to understand Lawrence Kohlberg's contributions to developmental psychology best, one needs to begin with his life story. With this in mind, the first section of this chapter is devoted to Kohlberg's moral biography, the second section maps out the development of Kohlberg's moral psychology, and the third section charts the development of Kohlberg's moral pedagogy.

Figure 16.1 Lawrence Kohlberg with the author's infant son, 1984.

277

KOHLBERG'S MORAL BIOGRAPHY

A fundamental dimension of being human is the inevitable necessity of making moral judgments. Kohlberg observed that children, adolescents, and adults are all, in a broad sense, moral philosophers. Thus, it is not surprising to find that themes of moral conflict and choice helped shape Kohlberg's own boyhood, young adulthood, and professional years.

Boyhood Years

"Laurie," as his family called him, was born October 25, 1927, in Bronxville, New York. He was the youngest of four children (Marjorie, Roberta, Alfred, and Laurence) born to Alfred Kohlberg (1887–1960), a Jewish German entrepreneur, and Charlotte Albrecht (1900–1991), a Christian German chemist. Fair-haired Laurie's early home life was marked by the privileges of great wealth, made possible by his father's import business (Herzstein, 2006; Keeley, 1969). It was also, however, marked by upheaval and dispersion. Just before Laurie was 4 years old, his father and mother separated and maintained a rotating 6-month custody arrangement from 1933 to 1938. Perhaps it was this disorder that motivated a boyhood ritual, which he recalled to a friend: "I couldn't have been more than six. Alone, I took the Popsicle sticks I had been saving and placed them carefully in a stack meant to be a pyre. With a prayer to whatever indeterminate God there be, I took matches and lit the pyre in hopes of atonement and forgiveness" (Fowler, Snarey, & DeNicola, 1988, p. 2). As a young boy, Kohlberg understood religion as a way of bartering with God, and, thus, according to his own subsequent developmental theory, he was much like other similarly aged children. Nevertheless, Kohlberg's peers recognized his intellectual precociousness. When he graduated from junior high school, the class prophecy section of the yearbook forecast that he would become known as "the great scientist and Nobel Prize winner" (Fowler et al., p. 7).

A judge dissolved the custody order in 1938 and allowed each Kohlberg child to choose the parent with whom he or she wanted to live. There is some uncertainty about when each child made his or her choice, but 3 years later 14-year-old Laurie and his older sister, Roberta, were living in Bronxville with Alfred Kohlberg as their custodial parent. Alfred hired a tutor to coach Laurie in Greek and Latin to prepare him to enter Phillips Academy, an elite preparatory high school in Andover, Massachusetts. His classmates there remembered him as a genuine intellectual who loved Plato, rebelled against arbitrary social conventions (and was often placed on probation), and was always ready for an adventure (Fowler et al., 1988; Morrison, 2007).

As a high school student during World War II, Kohlberg's identity formation was centered by his Jewish German heritage as he witnessed incidents of anti-Semitism and closely followed current events involving the Nazis' treatment of European Jews. His father, Alfred, also had become involved in aiding European Jews in his role as the chair of the United Jewish Appeal, but he loathed socialistic Zionism and was so ashamed of Jews who had become communists that he founded the right-wing American Jewish League against communism. Laurie would not adopt all of his father's goals.

Early Adulthood Years

Instead of following his prep school peers to an Ivy League college, the adventurous 18-year-old Kohlberg joined the U.S. Merchant Marines in 1945. For the next 2 years, he sailed on the USS *George Washington* and traveled in Europe, where he witnessed the aftermath of World War II and met Holocaust survivors. By the time his tour of duty ended, he had become a nonviolent activist on behalf of victims of the war. Consequently, he returned to Europe in 1947 as a crew member on the ship *Paducah*, which had been renamed the *SS Redemption* and outfitted by the Haganah (the Jewish defense organization in Palestine) to smuggle European Jewish refugees through the British blockade and relocate them in Palestine, which was a British-controlled territory at the time (Kohlberg, 1948). Kohlberg decided that establishing a Jewish state served a higher moral purpose than obeying the law and, therefore, participated in civil disobedience. He willingly broke British law for what he believed was a just cause—assisting Jewish war refugees to emigrate. While en route to Palestine in October, the ship was intercepted by the British; the crew and the approximately 1500 refugees all were interned on Cyprus. Three months later, the Haganah provided the British with forged papers with false names and obtained the release of Kohlberg and others. Kohlberg made his way to Palestine and was there during the first phase of the 1948 war that established the state of Israel, but he refused to participate in the fighting. He lived on an Israeli *kibbutz* (a socialist collective community) until he was able to leave the country (Fowler et al., 1988; Snarey, 1982).

Kohlberg returned to the United States in summer 1948. His war experiences had crystallized his Jewish identity and intensified his moral commitment to advance social justice for all. Perhaps symbolic of his identity achievement, he changed his first name from Laurence to Lawrence and his nickname from Laurie to Larry. The youthful Kohlberg had contributed in some small way to the care of Holocaust survivors and the founding of a nation. Yet related moral questions were soon unveiled: Was responding to the tragedy of the anti-Semitic European Holocaust by expelling Palestinian Arabs from their ancestral homeland a fully just resolution? Did this end justify the Haganah's methods? "When is it permissible to be involved with violent means for supposed just ends?" (Brabeck, 2000, p. 453).

Larry Kohlberg took the questions raised by his wartime experiences to the University of Chicago, where he enrolled in Hutchins College in fall 1948. He read the great books of numerous psychologically inclined philosophers and philosophically inclined psychologists. In addition to his beloved Plato and Socrates, he studied John Locke, John Stuart Mill, Immanuel Kant, Thomas Jefferson, and John Dewey, among others. At that time at the University of Chicago, course credit could be obtained by merely passing the final examination. Kohlberg took exams to obtain credits for 3 additional years of courses and completed his BA degree in 1 year (Reed, 1997).

Kohlberg was initially torn between becoming a lawyer or a clinical psychologist as a practical way to work toward social justice, but he decided to follow neither of those paths. He chose to pursue his graduate studies in academic psychology at the University of Chicago and embarked on a quest for the cognitive-developmental foundations of universal moral principles. His choice resulted in part from the continued influence of the great philosophical questions he had pondered aboard the *S.S. Redemption,* in Palestine, and at the University of Chicago: "What is virtue?" and "What is justice?" Kohlberg noted that he studied "psychoanalysis under Bruno Bettelheim, humanistic psychology under Carl Rogers, and behaviorism under Jacob Gewirtz" (Kohlberg, 1985b, p. 13). Although Kohlberg emphasized that he learned from each, he was dissatisfied with the answers provided by these dominant schools in psychology. Kohlberg (1958) proposed that the foundational virtue is justice, which he defined as fairness and equal respect for all people, and that the methods of developmental psychology are critical to understanding changing conceptions of justice across the life span.

At age 31 in 1958, Kohlberg completed a groundbreaking doctoral dissertation, based on the interviews he conducted with 84 adolescent boys in Chicago about several moral dilemmas. The boys were asked, for instance, "Should Heinz steal a drug to save the life of his wife or should he obey the law and let his wife die for lack of the drug? Why or why not?" (This dilemma, of course, mirrored the personal dilemma Kohlberg faced when he purposely violated British law to help the survivors of the Holocaust establish a new nation.) As Kohlberg examined the boys' answers to his dilemmas, he identified distinct age-related differences in the complexity of the moral reasoning they used to reach and justify their moral decisions. Although psychologists at that time were reluctant to utter the "m" word or otherwise depart from relativistic ideas, Kohlberg's revolutionary dissertation laid out six cognitive-developmental stages of moral judgment, at each of which persons constructed increasingly complex and progressively more useful understandings of morality.

Kohlberg had married Lucille Stigberg in 1955. Now, as he was finishing his doctoral studies, they began a family. Their first son, David Kohlberg, was born in 1958, the same year he completed his dissertation.

Professional Years

Kohlberg moved from Chicago to New Haven, Connecticut, in 1958 to begin his career as assistant professor of psychology at Yale University. He was at Yale when Stanley Milgram conducted his classic obedience experiments, and Milgram acknowledged Kohlberg's developmental critique in a brief footnote to *Obedience* (Milgram, 1974, p. 205). Kohlberg stayed in New Haven until 1961, when he became a fellow at the Center for Advanced Study in the Behavioral Sciences in Palo Alto, California. His second son, Steven Kohlberg, was born in August 1962 in nearby Santa Clara, California. In that same year he accepted an offer from the University of Chicago to return and join their faculty. First as assistant professor and then as associate professor at Chicago, he continued to take a bold stand for the validity of universal moral principles and for psychology as an inherently moral science. He did so at a time when the world had been shaken by the immoral horrors of the Holocaust. Noting that the Holocaust incongruously occurred in a country noted for its citizens' high level of education, flourishing arts, and complex culture, Kohlberg wondered what factors promote the development of people's moral maturity.

After 6 years at Chicago, he joined the faculty of Harvard University as a full professor in the Graduate School of Education in 1968. There he expanded his efforts to identify educational methods that would promote an individual's moral development, and in 1974 he founded the Center for Moral Education and Development. It quickly became a whirlwind of research, training, and educational activities. As the center's influence widened, a constant stream of scholars came from across the nation and around the world, seeking Kohlberg's advice and enjoying the synergy of working with him. With his students, Larry was even more generous with his time and ideas. He did not hesitate to become involved in their lives; he knew them as people as well as degree candidates. Larry was frequently their co-celebrant on holidays and at major life events. He listened to his students' viewpoints in a manner that recalled his own teacher, Carl Rogers, and helped them to extend their ideas. Many of his students became his colleagues and personal friends. They in turn went on to develop the field he had founded in their unique way.

The 1980s were unusually generative years as Kohlberg brought major projects to completion and reaped the rewards of his labor. The first volume of his collected essays on moral development, *The Philosophy of Moral Development*, was published in 1981. The empirical findings from his 20-year longitudinal study of 58 of his original 84 American males were published as a *Society for Research on Child Development Monograph* in 1983 (Colby, Kohlberg, Gibbs, & Lieberman, 1983). The next year saw the publication of the second volume of his collected essays, *The Psychology of Moral Development*. With Ann Colby, in 1987 he published the long-awaited two-volume moral stage scoring manual, *The Measurement of Moral Judgment*. With Clark Power and Ann Higgins, he completed a volume on moral education, published posthumously in 1989 as *Lawrence Kohlberg's Approach to Moral Education*.

While Kohlberg's professional and publishing successes were growing, his physical health, in contrast, was declining. During a trip to Central America in 1973, Kohlberg contracted a particularly severe and painful form of giardiasis (a disease of the digestive system caused by the parasite *Giardia lamblia*). Tragically, the parasitic infection slowly drained his physical health over the next 13 years (Rest, Power, & Brabeck, 1988). The health of his family life also was declining; Larry and Lucy separated in 1974 and finally divorced in 1985. To complicate matters, interpersonal and university politics also infected his professional social world during these years (Havens, 1993). Nevertheless, Kohlberg maintained a high level of productive scholarship. His physical energy and emotional serenity were both nourished, in part, by the almost mystical perspective he derived from the experiences he had on Cape Cod during his summers. From his concurrent knowledge of his own limits and his sense of oneness with something more, Kohlberg became increasingly open to religious-like perspectives, which moderated the question of why be moral in a world that is largely unjust. But perhaps mystical conceptions, in the end, also failed him. Suffering under much physical pain and mental depression, Lawrence Kohlberg apparently surrendered his life to the waters of the Atlantic Ocean on January 17, 1987. Even though Kohlberg died during the sixtieth year of life, his voice can still be heard in the ongoing study of *moral psychology* and *moral education.*

THE DEVELOPMENT OF KOHLBERG'S MORAL PSYCHOLOGY

Kohlberg's dissertation (1958), early professional articles (e.g., Kohlberg, 1963), and popular publications (e.g., Kohlberg, 1968) initiated a new field of study, the psychology of moral development. His stage model of moral development remains his best-known contribution to moral psychology, although he augmented it with two additional models to provide a more comprehensive view of moral cognition and development. Altogether, he created three models to conceptualize his understanding of morality: (1) moral stages, which chart the steps in an individual's moral development; (2) moral types, which map within-stage content differences; and (3) social-moral atmosphere levels, which map a group's moral climate.

Moral Stages

As early as 1950, when Kohlberg began to construct a universal, nonrelative theory of justice, he discovered the relevance of the views of developmental psychologist Jean Piaget (1896–1980; see Chapter 9 in this volume), who had found that cognitive development plays a part in moral development. The incorporation of Piaget's ideas led Kohlberg to search for the cognitive-developmental foundations of universal moral principles. His 1958 dissertation proposed six stages of moral development, in contrast to Piaget's two (heteronomy and autonomy), and took a bold stand for the validity of universal justice-oriented moral principles. He based these stages of social-moral reasoning on the understanding that mental structures or cognitive schemata are evolving within the developing brain.

Subsequently, through the course of 20 years of repeated interviews with his original research participants as well as other research samples, he observed that when participants' thought structures were inadequate to solve social-moral dilemmas, their thought structures would change in a predictable pattern of six stages. More specifically, his research suggested the following hypotheses: Each stage represents a qualitatively different way people resolve moral dilemmas. The stages form an invariant sequence: People do not skip stages or reverse their order. Kohlberg theorized that the six stages are hierarchically integrated—higher stages are better in the sense that a person who reasons at a higher stage can understand the moral reasoning used by those at lower stages—but the converse would not be true. Kohlberg also hypothesized that these stages are universal: They apply to all human beings in all cultures, even though many persons do not progress through all of the stages (Colby et al., 1983).

Kohlberg's stages of moral development were organized into three levels, with two stages each, for a total of six stages (Colby & Kohlberg, 1987; Kohlberg, 1984). Kohlberg referred to the first two stages as the level of *preconventional morality* because children at this level (typically aged 4 through 10 years) do not yet understand socially customary or conventional forms of morality as anything more than the arbiter of penalties for breaches in conduct. Stage 1, which Kohlberg called the *punishment and obedience orientation,* is evident among young children who unquestioningly orient to authority figures and believe that the physical consequences of action determine its goodness or badness. They avoid breaking rules set by external authorities for obedience's sake, to avoid punishment, and to avoid doing physical damage to people or property. Justice is punishing the bad in terms of "an eye for an eye and a tooth for a tooth." Kohlberg illustrated this concept by quoting his 4-year-old son who had stopped eating meat because he said it is "bad" to kill animals. One night, after Kohlberg had read him "a book about Eskimo life that included a description of a seal-killing expedition," his son became angry and said, "There is one kind of meat I would eat, Eskimo meat. It is bad to kill animals, so it's all right to eat Eskimos" (Kohlberg, 1981, pp. 14–15, 46, 143). Stage 2, termed *individualism, instrumental purpose, and exchange*, is more commonly the experience of school-aged children who follow rules only when it is in their immediate interest to do so, especially when it leads to an equal exchange, a good deal. What is moral is a reciprocal type of concrete exchange ("You scratch my back, and I'll scratch yours."). The justification for being moral is to take care of one's own needs in a world in which one must recognize that other people also have their own interests, which may conflict with one's own.

Kohlberg referred to the third and fourth stages as the level of *conventional morality.* These are the stages in which the majority of people spend most of their lives—meeting the requirements of societal or group expectations, maintaining familial expectations, and justifying the maintenance of the conventional social order. Stage 3, *mutual interpersonal expectations and conformity*, is a moral orientation that equates what is morally right with what is perceived to be "good" and "nice" by others. The justifications for acting morally focus on the desire to be seen as a good person in one's own eyes and those of others. For instance, one day when Kohlberg's son was in the second grade he came home from school and told his father that he did not want to be one of the "bad boys." Asked, "Who are the bad boys?", he replied, "The ones who don't put their books back where they belong and get yelled at" (Kohlberg, 1981, p. 6). Stage 4 was referred to by Kohlberg as the *social system and conscience maintenance* stage because at Stage 4 people believe that the "moral right" stems from their allegiance to a particular social system. Thus they equate morality with the legal system, or with the moral rules of a social institution. The justifications for being moral are to keep the institution functioning, to maintain self-respect for having met one's defined obligations, and to avoid setting a socially disruptive precedent.

Kohlberg referred to the last two stages as *postconventional* or *principled morality* because here the moral agent defines moral values or principles as existing before and having priority over the social conventions maintained by societies and institutions. The postconventional level reflects a moral philosophy in which moral principles are separable from the authorities or persons who hold them, they are open for debate and generally agreeable to individuals who seek to live in a fair and just society, and they withstand tests of logical comprehensiveness. This allows the moral agent to use those principles critically to question socially agreed upon standards and arrangements (e.g., slavery) in relation to individual rights and duties of all members of the society. Stage 5 is characterized by a focus on *prior human rights* and the *social contract*. A social system is understood, ideally, as a social contract freely entered into. Persons at Stage 5 justify upholding the social contract because it preserves one's own rights and the rights of others, ensures impartiality, and promotes the greatest good for the greatest number of people. People who reason at Stage 5 believe that the purpose of society is to protect individuals' rights and to promote communal welfare. Stage 6 moral judgments employ what Kohlberg called *universal ethical principles* to resolve moral dilemmas. These principles encapsulate respect for the dignity of all human beings and the universality of basic human rights. All persons are viewed as free and autonomous, as ends in themselves and not simply as means to an end. Persons at Stage 6 make sense of a moral dilemma by imaginatively taking the roles of all participants to ensure that all receive fair, just consideration and choose what they believe is right action as a matter of conscience, in accordance with self-chosen ethical principles.

Moral stages, for Kohlberg, were not simply moral ideals, ideal types, or virtual models of reasoning but were actual cognitive-developmental stage structures that evolve in the social-moral brain. His sweeping approach received both academic acclaim and public media attention. Scholars, of course, also intensely scrutinized his work, which led to several critiques of his theory. These challenges focused on (1) stage validity, (2) cross-cultural universality, (3) moral action applicability, (4) gender inclusiveness, and (5) racial-ethnic inclusiveness (Levine, Hewer, & Kohlberg, 1983; Siddle-Walker & Snarey, 2004). Despite a number of necessary qualifications and caveats, however, Kohlberg's stage model remains theoretically forceful and pedagogically useful. It continues to generate innovative research into the nature of moral thought and action, the causes of delinquency and criminal behavior, the nature of human nature, and the understanding that persons are moral agents (Gibbs, 2010).

Moral Types

Kohlberg recognized that moral stages did not address important within-stage variations, often seen between different people whose moral judgment interviews are scored at the same moral stage. To account for these differences, he returned to a Piagetian-like conception of morality as two substages (heteronymous and autonomous) within each of his stages. Eventually, however, Kohlberg and his colleagues dropped the "substage" language because research showed that this approach did not satisfy strict Piagetian stage criteria; type change, for instance, did not represent a consistently invariant sequence from A to B (Tappan, Kohlberg, Schrader, Higgins, Armon, & Lei, 1987).

Kohlberg then turned to the tradition of sociologist Max Weber and identified the two forms as "ideal types," that is, abstractions that define the extreme forms of the possible properties of each stage. More specifically, Kohlberg and colleagues defined Type A (heteronomy) and Type B (autonomy) as two subtypes that may occur within any stage (e.g., Stage 2A and Stage 2B). These subtypes are defined by variations in the content of moral judgments, including notions of freedom from external constraints, ideas about the human construction of rules and law, and issues of who is to be included in the moral domain (Kohlberg, 1984). Moral types are, in essence, a way to include information about the content of a person's reasoning that is ignored when the reasoning is evaluated only by stage definitions (i.e., by the cognitive structure of a person's reasoning). Thus, what Kohlberg originally saw as a pioneering, but developmentally restricted, conception of morality in Piaget's work, was retrieved to describe apparent cycles of variation between heteronomy and autonomy within each stage.

When analyzing a moral dilemma interview for moral types, Kohlberg and his colleagues used nine distinguishing criteria or "content themes," which they derived from the psychological and philosophical works of Piaget and Immanuel Kant (Schrader, Tappan, Kohlberg, & Armon, 1987). If a participant emphasized practical concerns, held an instrumental view of persons, considered only the self-interests of the persons' involved, and made judgments that are justified on an external basis with unilateral obedience to rules and laws in a rigid fashion without regard for justice or fairness, the dilemma response would be scored as an example of Type A or heteronymous morality. If a participant reasoned in a way that reflects a clear hierarchy of moral values, in which persons are treated as ends in themselves, the other person's perspective in the dilemma is understood, and rules are considered as flexible and can be adapted to achieve the most fair and just solution, the dilemma response would be scored as an example of Type B or autonomous morality. Many interviews, of course, were mixed types.

Kohlberg's moral types proved to be a robust model for understanding how moral reasoning translates into actual moral behavior. In a number of studies reviewed in Kohlberg's (1984) chapter on "The Relationship of Moral Judgment to Moral Action" in his collected works, those subjects with a Type B moral orientation were more likely to act in concordance with their moral judgments and values, even when those values conflicted with a prevailing rule or authority. This conclusion was supported by Kohlberg's follow-up study of persons involved in Stanley Milgram's (1974) classic obedience experiment. In Milgram's original study, an experimenter assigned a naive subject to the role of teacher, who is asked to "shock" someone assigned to the role of student under the guise of studying the effects of punishment on learning (memorizing word pairs). Most of the participants complied and administered shocks to the end of the scale, 450 volts. This included 63% of the men in the first study. Kohlberg was Milgram's colleague at Yale University at the time of the original studies (1958–1962) and was able to reinterview 27 students who had participated in one of Milgram's replication studies. When Kohlberg's standardized scoring system became available in the 1980s, those interviews were rescored for moral stage and moral type. Students who scored at higher stages were significantly more likely to quit the experiment. Most surprisingly, however, Kohlberg found that a full 86% of the participants who used moral reasoning Type B quit the experiment regardless of moral stage. None of the participants who used moral Type A reasoning quit, and only 18% of those who had an "ambiguous" score in terms of moral type stopped participating in the experiment (Kohlberg, 1984).

In sum, Kohlberg's moral typology expanded his stage theory in three respects: (1) moral types address primarily the content of moral reasoning (in contrast to moral stages, which focus primarily on the structure of moral reasoning); (2) either type may occur in persons at any stage and at any age in the lifespan, thus accounting for observed within-stage variability; and (3) moral type helps clarify the connection between moral reasoning and moral action.

Moral Atmosphere

Kohlberg (1980, 1985a) created the concept of *moral atmosphere* to refer to a community's moral climate or moral culture, by which he primarily meant a community's shared expectations and normative values. Kohlberg was coming to understand that the primary context for the development of a moral person is the group. At the same time, Kohlberg's stage theory was being criticized for his emphasis on the individual reasoner and upon individual rights, at the expense of the needs of the community. Communitarian ethical values are rare in Kohlberg's scoring manual, especially at the postconventional level, although cross-gender, cross-class, and cross-cultural studies have shown that higher-stage reasoning can be articulated in terms of communitarian values (Snarey, 1982). Those who are socialized in groups in which communitarian values prevail tend to express moral reasoning in terms of those values (e.g., altruism rather than individualism).

Kohlberg's conception of moral atmosphere was a vigorous answer to his critics. His new understanding was based in part on Emile Durkheim's well-known idea that groups themselves have qualities that are not simply the aggregation of the qualities of their individuals but that the group is greater than the sum of its individual members. Kohlberg sought to characterize the added value of groups that would be the most relevant to moral cognition, development, and behavior. Drawing on Durkheim's concept that the unit of education is the group, Kohlberg concluded that changes in the school's moral culture should have the most profound impact on an individual's moral formation. Kohlberg specified that the most beneficial social unit for moral development is a democratically governed group, one that recognizes the rights and responsibilities of each to each other and to the group as a whole. Thus, a simple focus on the developmental promotion of moral reasoning was not enough; to foster moral ideals, goals, and actions as well as promote moral reasoning, the school would need to be governed democratically. The promotion of moral development has to include the collective socialization of moral content, based on group decision making (Power, Higgins, & Kohlberg, 1989).

Kohlberg (1985a) made the sociological concept of moral atmosphere operational by describing an array of complex variables that, taken together, provide a detailed map of a school's moral climate. The two major variables in this approach are (1) *levels of institutional valuing* and (2) *phases of the collective norm*. The levels of institutional valuing includes four levels, ranging from "instrumental extrinsic valuing" (the school is valued because it helps individuals meet their own needs) to "normative community" (the school is valued for its own sake; it can obligate its members in special ways and, in turn, members can expect others to uphold group norms). The phases of the collective norm include seven phases, ranging from groups in which no collective norms exist to groups in which the collective norm is expected and upheld through persuasion and reporting. In general, the first moral atmosphere model focuses on the valuing of the school as a social entity, and the second model focuses on the phases of commitment to the collective norm. Furthermore, Kohlberg noted that the element of institutional value and the collective norm "correspond to two of Durkheim's goals of moral education: *discipline* and *attachment to the group*" (Power et al., 1989, p. 116). Going beyond Durkheim's sociological conception of autonomy, however, Kohlberg placed a much stronger emphasis on rational "autonomy" to avoid abuses that could result from "immoral use" of the power of the "collectivist model" (Power et al., 1989, pp. 116–117). Furthermore, Kohlberg (1985a) supplemented Durkheim's concept of "loyalty" to one's society with "loyalty to universal principles of justice and responsibility as the solution to problems" (p. 41).

Kohlberg's analysis of social-moral atmosphere demonstrated the profound impact that socialization has on the content of moral reasoning and on an individual's moral concepts. Thus, Kohlberg advanced the idea that a school's social-moral atmosphere should emphasize a sense of community, democratic values, personal autonomy, individual rights and responsibilities, a sense of fair play, and collective responsibility. Kohlberg had again launched a revolutionary understanding within moral psychology—the group will provide the dilemma of enculturation, the content of which will be rethought or resolved, following an invariant sequence of increasingly complex stages of moral reasoning. Variations among social environments, such as opportunities for civic participation, have substantial effects on the structure of moral development as well as on the content of socialization to enhance moral principles. Kohlberg integrated socialization with development in a way that gave priority to the power of the community yet also protected the rights of individual community members. His approach to moral formation was not merely developmental but can be characterized as a "developmental socialization." Within this developmental-socialization approach, Kohlberg employed three distinct pedagogical methods, which will be discussed in the following section on moral education.

THE DEVELOPMENT OF KOHLBERG'S MORAL PEDAGOGY

Lawrence Kohlberg began an intense reflection on moral education in the late 1960s, when he became convinced that achieving a just society would require proactive intervention to help children become more likely to reach higher stages of moral development. The center of Kohlberg's moral identity, in fact, became that of a moral educator. He believed that what promotes a person's moral development is having rich experiences in the social-moral realm. While rooted in his structural-developmental psychology, Kohlberg's three pedagogical methods include all of the critical learning experiences according to cultural learning theory: (1) moral exemplars are a type of learning by imitation; (2) dilemma discussions are a prime example of collaborative learning; and (3) the just community approach employs direct instruction along with collaborative learning and imitation.

Moral Exemplars

Attending to moral exemplars was, in effect, Kohlberg's first method of moral education. In his collected works, Kohlberg (1981, 1984) demonstrates that he intuitively understood that examining the lives of those who practice universal moral principles is a more direct method of moral education than teaching about an abstract theory could even hope to be. Kohlberg believed that *public moral exemplars*, through their insights and actions, "drew" persons' development toward higher stages of moral reasoning. Public moral exemplars, therefore, are *moral educators* because they make real the ideal of universal principles of justice through their words and deeds and allow those who are not reasoning with those principles to comprehend them intuitively.

In one of the concluding chapters of *Essays on Moral Development, Vol. II*, Kohlberg and chapter coauthor Ann Higgins (1984) highlighted the example of a 32-year-old woman named Joan. Her ability to frame moral dilemmas as a dialogue of competing claims, coupled with her capacity to take the role of each person in the dilemma, in turn, appeared to be an example of principled moral reasoning. This was confirmed for Kohlberg by Joan's life story. In her job working with juvenile wards of the court for a local judge, Joan assisted one of the wards in her care by allowing her to escape to a better situation at a halfway house in another state, and, furthermore, she provided her with bus money for the journey. This action was a clear violation of her responsibilities as outlined by the law, and Joan lost her job. Joan's words and actions suggest a form of reasoning that posits a universal respect for the rights and dignity of persons, regardless of the dictates of the law. Her example can be unsettling to those using conventional reasoning and herein, Kohlberg believed, lies the vital role of moral exemplars.

Kohlberg did not consider himself to be a moral exemplar, however. Rather, he identified 13 people as his moral exemplars—people from whom he sought to learn and whom he held up as examples for others also to consider. His two-volume collected works on moral philosophy (1981) and moral psychology (1984) include six separate lists with a total of nine moral exemplars, plus four other persons who are cited individually. *Socrates* (469–399 BCE) and *Martin Luther King, Jr.* (1929–1968) are on five of his six lists and, of the 13 exemplars he mentioned, he cited Dr. King the most frequently.

Kohlberg (1981) observed in the writings and actions of King the universal principle of justice (p. 392). In brief, he believed that moral exemplars are those whose lives illustrate a statement from King's 1963 "Letter from a Birmingham Jail." Dr. King had been asked by some fellow pastors how he could possibly condone breaking the law. King replied, "The answer lies in the fact that there are two types of laws: just and unjust. I would be the first to advocate obeying just laws. One has not only a legal but a moral responsibility to obey just laws. Conversely, one has a moral responsibility to disobey unjust laws." Kohlberg continued to quote King when he said, "I would agree with St. Augustine that 'an unjust law is no law at all'" (p. 392). Kohlberg saw that Dr. King was a prime example of the highest stage of moral reasoning because of his willingness to take the perspective of all the actors in the struggle for human rights, from the most oppressed and economically disadvantaged person to the most racist and privileged person. King argued from a universal and principled stance that granting civil rights to African Americans would lift all people to a higher, more just, and freer existence. Kohlberg observed that King elevated the moral atmosphere of the United States and provided an example for oppressed societies around the world.

In addition to King and Socrates, *Abraham Lincoln* was included in two of Kohlberg's lists, and another six exemplars were each included in one of the six lists: *Marcus Aurelius* (121–180 CE)—Roman emperor and stoic philosopher; humanitarian and protector of the poor, especially of orphans and minors; *Baruch Spinoza* (1632–1677)—stoic philosopher, ethicist, and moral educator; *Thomas More* (1478–1535)—lawyer and Lord Chancellor to Henry VIII, courageous humanist who was executed by beheading; *Henry David Thoreau* (1817–1862)—naturalist and author, nonviolent abolitionist whose philosophy of "civil disobedience" influenced Tolstoy, Gandhi, and M. L. King, Jr.; *Janusz Korczak* (1878–1942)—pediatrician and children's writer, director of Jewish and Catholic orphanages in Poland who defied Nazis and was murdered in the Holocaust; and Andrea Simpson (1898–1992)—mental health worker and antiwar activist. Furthermore, Kohlberg spoke of at least three other individuals in such a way as to suggest membership in his pantheon of moral exemplars—"*Joan*," as well as *William Brennan* (1906–1997), Supreme Court Justice, and *Archibald Cox* (1912–2004), special prosecutor for the Watergate hearings. Finally, Kohlberg named India's civil rights leader *Mohandas Gandhi* (1869–1948) as one of his moral exemplars in a lengthy case study appendix to his collected works, although the publisher declined to include the Mahatma addendum because of page limitations (Kohlberg, 1985b).

Kohlberg regarded all thirteen exemplars to be, broadly speaking, "moral educators." What makes the lives of these persons worthy of being considered moral exemplars and valuable public models for moral education today? Beyond their consummate moral reasoning and superlative moral empathy, Kohlberg observed, they all took direct and tangible *moral action*, including, for example, the use of nonviolent public dissent, critical speeches, or protest marches. These moral exemplars engaged in *public moral education* through their incarnation of moral principles and through their actions. While Kohlberg had many philosophical conversation partners (e.g., Plato, Aristotle, Kant, John Dewey, John Rawls), the only one he elevated to moral sainthood was Socrates. While he cites several theologians with respectful admiration (Paul Tillich, Martin Luther King, Jr., Teilhard de Chardin) and four saints of the Catholic Church (Saint Thomas Aquinas, Saint Augustine, Saint Thomas More, Saint Paul), Kohlberg only spoke of two of these seven as moral exemplars—Saint Thomas More and Martin Luther King, Jr. Socrates, More, and King, had to pay the ultimate price for their individual moral positions. In fact, almost half of Kohlberg's exemplars died as martyrs for their moral stance. Kohlberg (1981) selected Saint Thomas More to illustrate a post-conventional moral conscience at Stage 5 and, of course, More "chose death over denouncing his faith" (p. 382). Martin Luther King, Jr., who exemplified the use of post-conventional justice reasoning at Stage 6, chose prison as an extension of his nonviolent civil disobedience and was assassinated for his stand against racism and injustice (pp. 382–383).

Finally, Kohlberg always understood that moral exemplars are still flawed human beings, as well as products of their particular historical contexts. In relation to increasing ethical clarity regarding slavery, Kohlberg (1981) commented that "Socrates was more accepting of slavery than was Lincoln, who was more accepting of it than King" (p. 129). Similarly, one could add that the male exemplars' views of women were not as enlightened as those of Andrea Simpson, the feminist and Quaker antiwar activist in Kohlberg's list. Inevitably, of course, the same historical partiality was true of Kohlberg himself. In terms of race and gender, his 13 exemplars included nine White men, two White women, and two men of color.

Dilemma Discussions

About a decade after the debut of Kohlberg's (1958) moral stage model, the first genuine Kohlbergian venture into moral education began with an experiment completed in 1969 by Moshe Blatt, one of Kohlberg's doctoral students, who attempted to facilitate moral stage development among sixth-grade students through weekly classroom discussions of hypothetical moral dilemmas. Blatt found that over one-third of the students in the experimental group advanced in stage of moral development during the year, whereas few of the students in a control group exhibited any stage change.

Subsequently, Kohlberg and his colleagues implemented this method by integrating dilemma discussions into the curricula of school classes on the humanities (e.g., literature) and social studies (e.g., history). In preparation for these dilemma-discussion interventions, Kohlberg and colleagues taught teachers how to lead moral dilemma discussions (Fenton & Kohlberg, 1976; Kohlberg & Lickona, 1987). Some of the discussion questions were quite similar to those used in a standard moral judgment interview, that is, they focused on asking students to clarify their reasoning about "why" they held a certain position. Other questions were aimed at asking students to make their meaning clear, ensuring a shared understanding, or promoting peer interaction, especially perspective taking. Additionally, attention was given to questions designed to promote Socratic discussion (e.g., Is it ever right to break a law? What would happen if everyone broke laws when it pleased them?).

Early research results showed that children and adolescents who participated in moral dilemma discussion made significant and positive gains in moral stage scores. Beyond statistical significance, however, Kohlberg asked, how psychologically significant are the statistical gains promoted by participation in dilemma discussions? Subsequent comparison studies of approaches to moral education, and several reviews of moral education research and programs using moral dilemmas, answered Kohlberg's question. Quantitative meta-analyses of prior studies showed that dilemma discussions produce moderate and significant educational effects on moral development, whereas other types of intervention programs produce smaller effects, and individual academic courses in the humanities produce even weaker effects. Qualitative analyses of prior studies similarly concluded that the most effective interventions for promoting moral stage change are those that involve discussions of real (rather than hypothetical) dilemmas that naturally occur in small groups, whether the family or class, in which all participants are given the power to voice their perspective in the discussion.

It is not just the method or experience of moral dilemma discussion that can influence moral development but also the peer context. Kohlberg hypothesized that the ideal situation for advancement in moral reasoning is to be involved in a discussion with another person who reasons at the level next higher (+1) than one's own. Blatt and Kohlberg (1975) engaged a group whose participants expressed reasoning at various levels in a dilemma discussion. The discussion facilitator (experimenter) then chose the argument that was one stage above the level of most of the participants and supported it, emphasizing its strengths and encouraging participants to engage in thinking along these lines. This method led to significant increases in moral maturity scores. Subsequent reviews of the effectiveness of moral development interventions using the +1 strategy have confirmed what Kohlberg's termed "the Blatt effect," although other similar strategies (+2 and +1/3 stage differentials) also proved effective under different circumstances. Overall, Kohlberg believed, students learn best from a person who performs at a level just above the student's level.

The research on educational intervention programs conducted by Kohlberg and his colleagues allowed them to draw several conclusions: (1) dilemma discussion is a useful method for moral development education; (2) real-life dilemmas, especially those drawn from personal experience, are more efficacious for moral development than are hypothetical dilemmas; (3) a zone of proximal development exists in which dilemma discussions advance moral development maximally; and, thus, (4) peers are the best teachers or conversation partners. Beyond moral exemplar role models and moral dilemma small-group discussions, however, Kohlberg's third method of moral education would make the most effective use of peers.

Just Community Schools

In 1973 Kohlberg's thinking about moral education within schools broke new ground when he recognized a limitation of the moral dilemma discussion method and began to perceive schools as ethics education communities. As Kohlberg (1978) later put it, the school is a context "in which one cannot wait until children reach" Stage 5 of moral development "to deal directly with moral behavior" (p. 15). Yet now Kohlberg faced a pedagogical dilemma: how to teach moral values without imposing them on children or compromising their moral autonomy. Moreover, Kohlberg had theorized (and his research findings had supported) that children are perhaps best equipped to help each other advance in moral reasoning since they often reason within a stage of one another, and their interaction provides optimal dilemmas for discussion and resolution. The challenge then is even more refined: how to help children promote each other's development toward universal moral principles.

Kohlberg had theorized that this dilemma is solvable because he understood that the principles of reasoning present in higher stages (4, 5, and 6), such as reciprocity, respect, and justice, are present in some immature form from Stage 1 onward (Kohlberg, 1980). His idea for educating children toward moral maturity was for the teacher to promote the development of the children's native sense of fairness and, in so doing, prepare them to understand better and then appropriate the principle of justice toward which moral development reaches. The goal was to achieve a "balance [of] 'justice' and 'community'; to introduce the powerful appeal of the collective while both protecting the rights of individual students and promoting their moral growth" (Power et al., 1989, p. 53). Kohlberg acknowledged that his turn to educational democracy within a communitarian mode was inspired by his 1948 residence on an Israeli *kibbutz* and by his subsequent professional research on another *kibbutz* (Snarey, 1982; Snarey et al., 1985).

Kohlberg founded the first "just community school" in spring 1974. He had received funding to train high school teachers in developmental moral education. At the same time in Cambridge, Massachusetts, plans for a new alternative high school were under way, and Kohlberg was invited to consult in its planning. Students, parents, teachers, and Kohlberg met together to design the new school. The end result was the Cluster School (operating within a larger Cambridge high school), which was governed by the following principles (Power et al., 1989, p. 64):

1. "Students and teachers would have the same basic rights, including freedom of expression, respect of others, and freedom from physical or verbal harm."
2. "A social contract would be drawn between members which would define everyone's rights and responsibilities."
3. "The school would be governed by direct democracy."

Direct participatory democracy was implemented through two primary governance structures—*community meetings* and *standing committees*. The keystone of the just community approach was the weekly community meeting (also known as town meeting), a gathering of students and staff to decide school policies and practices that dealt with issues of fairness and community. All community members (students and teachers) would have one vote to contribute to the decision-making process. The school would also have a number of standing committees, each of which consisted of one teacher-advisor and 1/5 of the students. The standing committees met weekly on the day before the community meeting. Kohlberg believed that these small group meetings "set the stage" for the larger community meetings as well as provided an opportunity for students and their advisors to get to know each other and share more personal concerns than could be dealt with in the larger meeting. The agenda for the community meeting would be discussed, and the small group would often debate the issues and try to achieve consensus or agreement on majority and minority proposals to bring to the next day's meeting.

All of these meetings functioned as a context for moral discussion and a place to build community. The general aim was for students to achieve a sense of community solidarity—to create a "moral atmosphere"—through the practice of democratic governance (i.e., coming to fair decisions, carrying out these decisions and, as necessary, democratically changing their decisions). Direct participatory democracy, furthermore, functioned to protect the rights of the student, to limit the power of group solidarity to coerce conformity in order to maintain the possibility for alternative conceptions of the good to be voiced. Just as important, the teachers' role was similar to that of a *kibbutz* youth leader—they served as moral leaders by advocating their own positions within the constraints of one person, one vote, and by being invested in "what" students decided to do and "why" they decided to do it.

Later, Kohlberg and his colleagues would have an opportunity to apply the just community approach at the upper and upper-middle class suburban Scarsdale Alternative High School in Westchester County, New York, and at the semiurban middle-class School-Within-a-School in Brookline High School, Brookline, Massachusetts. Kohlberg and colleagues' comparative analysis of the first three just community schools (i.e., Cambridge, Scarsdale, and Brookline) documented that the students in each of the three intervention schools scored significantly higher than their contemporaries attending the parent high schools on all measures of moral atmosphere, including the level of institutional valuing, stage of community valuing, and phase of collective norm. The results on individual moral judgment were also in the expected direction; the average moral stage scores for the students in the just community programs were significantly higher than for the students in their companion traditional high schools. The stage gains were not large but still worthwhile (cf. Power et al., 1989).

In Kohlberg's last just community endeavor, he, his partner Ann Higgins, and several graduate students implemented three just community programs in New York City: two in one of the five worst city schools and one in an exam school with high-performing students. Other schools have adopted the principles of just community schools, at least in part, to promote moral development. Kohlberg's idea of "the adolescent as citizen" was as revolutionary as his earlier idea of "the child as philosopher." His approach to moral education provided a way for teachers and administrators to embody justice and care in their treatment of students and each other and a way for students to develop these moral values and to practice living them out in their daily behavior.

CONTRIBUTION TO DEVELOPMENTAL PSYCHOLOGY

Lawrence Kohlberg's personal experiences during boyhood and early adulthood helped set the direction of his professional ideas. He was a developmental psychologist who had a deep personal effect on a great many people and academic fields. He made morality a central concern in psychology, and he remains the person most often identified as a founding figure in the field of moral psychology, including moral cognition, moral development, and moral education. Kohlberg understood that children and adolescents, as well as adults, are *developing* moral philosophers, capable of forming their own moral judgments and capable of revising them. He is best known among psychologists for his six-stage model of moral cognition and development, which he buttressed with research on moral types and social-moral atmosphere. He is best known among educators for developing three methods of moral pedagogy: adult role models as moral exemplars, peer interaction through moral dilemma discussions, and democratic participation in a morally grounded democratic school community. Kohlberg created lasting frameworks for approaching the study of moral cognition and development and inspired educational programs to prepare citizens for living in a participatory democracy.

SUGGESTED READINGS

Colby, A., & Kohlberg, L. (1987). *The measurement of moral judgment* (2 volumes). New York: Cambridge University Press.

  This is the final standardized version of Kohlberg's scoring manual, which is the gold standard for the measurement of stages of moral judgment. Volume one includes instructions for moral dilemma interviewing and scoring as well as information on measurement reliability and validity. Volume two is the actual scoring manual, with scoring examples for all three versions of the standardized Moral Judgment Interview (MJI).

Colby, A., Kohlberg, L., Gibbs, J. C., & Lieberman, M. (1983). A longitudinal study of moral judgment. *Monographs of the Society for Research in Child Development, 48*(1–2, Serial No. 200).

  Beginning with his dissertation, Kohlberg conducted a 20-year longitudinal study of moral development. The final results are published in this monograph.

Kohlberg, L. (1963). The development of children's orientations toward a moral order: Sequence in the development of moral thought. *Vita Humana, 6,* 11–33.

  This article is the first published report of Kohlberg's dissertation research. It is often cited and reprinted because it was one of those rare studies that changed psychology. The academic psychology journal in which it appeared, *Vita Humana,* was renamed *Human Development* in 1964, the year after Kohlberg's article was published.

Kohlberg, L. (1981). *Essays on moral development: Volume I, The philosophy of moral development: The nature and validity of moral stages.* San Francisco: Harper & Row.

  The first volume of his collected works includes several of his philosophy journal articles, including such classics as "Development as the Aim of Education" (Chapter 3), "From Is to Ought" (Chapter 4), and "Moral Development, Religious Thinking, and the Question of the Seventh Stage" (Chapter 9).

Kohlberg, L. (1984). *Essays on moral development: Volume II, The psychology of moral development: The nature and validity of moral stages.* San Francisco: Harper & Row.

  The second volume of his collected works includes such highly cited psychology articles as "Stage and Sequence" (Chapter 1), "Moral Stages and Moralization" (Chapter 2), "The Relationship of Moral Judgment to Moral Action" (Chapter 7), and "Cultural Universality of Moral Judgment Stages" (Chapter 9).

REFERENCES

Blatt, M., & Kohlberg, L. (1975). The effects of classroom moral discussion upon children's level of moral judgment. *Journal of Moral Education, 4,* 129–161. doi:10.1080/0305724750040207

Brabeck, M. (2000). Lawrence Kohlberg. In A. Kazdin (Ed.), *Encyclopedia of psychology* (vol. 4, pp. 453–454). Washington, DC: American Psychological Association.

Colby, A., & Kohlberg, L. (1987). *The measurement of moral judgment* (2 volumes). New York: Cambridge University Press.

Colby, A., Kohlberg, L., Gibbs, J., & Lieberman, M. (1983). A longitudinal study of moral judgment. *Monographs of the Society for Research in Child Development, 48*(1–2, Serial No. 200).

Fenton, E., & Kohlberg, L. (Eds.). (1976). *Teacher training in values education.* New York: Guidance Associates.

Fowler, J., Snarey, J., & DeNicola, K. (Eds.) (1988). *Remembrances of Lawrence Kohlberg.* Atlanta, GA: Emory University Center for Research in Faith and Moral Development.

Gibbs, J. C. (2010). *Moral development and reality: Beyond the theories of Kohlberg and Hoffman.* New York: Allyn & Bacon.

Havens, L. (1993). Failure and tragedy. Chapter 3 in *Coming to live* (pp. 45–58). Cambridge, MA: Harvard University Press.

Herzstein, R. (2006). *Alfred Kohlberg: Global entrepreneur and hyper-nationalist.* Paper presented at The Historical Society, University of North Carolina, Chapel Hill.

Keeley, J. (1969). *The China lobby man: The story of Alfred Kohlberg.* New Rochelle, NY: Arlington.

Kohlberg, L. (1948, Autumn). Beds for bananas: A first-hand story of the S. S. Redemption. *Menorah Journal*, 285–399.

Kohlberg, L. (1958). *The development of modes of thinking and choice in years 10 to 16.* Unpublished doctoral dissertation, University of Chicago, Chicago, IL.

Kohlberg, L. (1963). The development of children's orientations toward a moral order: Sequence in the development of moral thought. *Vita Humana*, 6, 11–33.

Kohlberg, L. (1968). The child as a moral philosopher. *Psychology Today*, 7, 25–30.

Kohlberg, L. (1978). Moral education reappraised. *Humanist*, 38, 13–15.

Kohlberg, L. (1980). *The meaning and measurement of moral development.* Worcester, MA: Clark University Press.

Kohlberg, L. (1981). *Essays on moral development: Volume I, The philosophy of moral development: The nature and validity of moral stages.* San Francisco: Harper & Row Publishers.

Kohlberg, L. (1984). *Essays on moral development: Volume II, The psychology of moral development: The nature and validity of moral stages.* San Francisco: Harper & Row.

Kohlberg, L. (1985a). The just community approach to moral education in theory and practice. In M. Berkowitz & F. Oser (Eds.), *Moral education* (pp. 27–86). Hillsdale, NJ: Erlbaum.

Kohlberg, L. (1985b). *My personal search for universal morality.* Paper presented at the Institute of Morology, Tokyo, Japan in October. Reprinted (1991) in L. Kuhmerker (Ed.), *The Kohlberg legacy for the helping professions* (pp. 11–17). Birmingham, AL: Religious Education Press.

Kohlberg, L., & Lickona, T. (1987). Moral discussion and the class meeting. In. R. DeVries & L. Kohlberg (Eds.), *Programs of early education: The constructivist view* (pp. 143–181). New York: Longman.

Levine, C., Hewer, A., & Kohlberg, L. (1983). *Moral stages: A current formulation and a response to critics.* New York: Karger.

Milgram, S. (1974). *Obedience to authority.* New York: Harper & Row.

Morrison, W. N. (2007). Off and running with Larry Kohlberg. In *Pieces of eight* (pp. 141–173). Raleigh, NC: Lulu.

Power, F. C., Higgins, A., & Kohlberg, L. (1989). *Lawrence Kohlberg's approach to moral education.* New York: Columbia University Press.

Reed, D. (1997). *Following Kohlberg: Liberalism and the practice of democratic community.* Notre Dame, IN: University of Notre Dame Press.

Rest, J., Power, F. C., & Brabeck, M. (1988). Lawrence Kohlberg (1927–1987). *American Psychologist*, 43(5), 399–400. doi:10.1037/h0091958

Schrader, D., Tappan, M., Kohlberg, L., & Armon, C. (1987). Assessing heteronomous and autonomous moral types: Instructions and manual. In A. Colby & L. Kohlberg, (Eds.), *The measurement of moral judgment, Volume I: Theoretical foundations and research validation* (pp. 909–997). New York: Cambridge University Press.

Siddle-Walker, V., & Snarey, J. (2004). *Race-ing moral formation: African American perspectives on care and justice.* New York: Teachers College Press.

Snarey, J. (1982). *The social and moral development of kibbutz founders and sabras: A longitudinal and cross-sectional cross-cultural study*. Doctoral dissertation, Harvard University, Cambridge, MA, 392 pp., UMI Doctoral Dissertations 83-02-435, Ann Arbor, MI.

Snarey, J., Reimer, J., & Kohlberg, L. (1985). The kibbutz as a model for moral education: A longitudinal study. *Journal of Applied Developmental Psychology, 6*, 151–172. doi:10.1016/0193-3973(85)90057-7

Tappan, M., Kohlberg, L., Schrader, D., Higgins, A., Armon, C., & Lei, T. (1987). Heteronomy and autonomy in moral development: Two types of moral judgment. In A. Colby & L. Kohlberg, (Eds.), *The measurement of moral judgment, Volume I: Theoretical foundations and research validation* (pp. 315–380). New York: Cambridge University Press.

Eyes on the Prize:
Psychologists and Human Development

WADE E. PICKREN

Ryerson University

One of the take-home messages from this volume is the incredible richness of human experience as evidenced by the diverse paths of human psychological development. This diversity is also found, as we have seen, in the history of developmental psychology. The pioneers portrayed in this volume each found a way to work with materials of the human life span, or some portion of it, to explicate some facet of the human experience. The first focus of the nascent field was on infant and child development, which paved the way for later studies of adult and lifespan development.

As noted in the introductory essay, it was in the period between the two world wars that the field of scientific study of human development became an important part of American psychology while also gaining attention in other countries. Although its greatest growth did not come for another 2 decades, these years were critical. Of the psychologists found in this volume, many of them received their training or became active during this period, including Mamie Phipps Clark (Chapter 15), Eleanor Gibson (Chapter 14), Lois Barclay Murphy (Chapter 8), Joseph McVicker Hunt (Chapter 11), Robert W. White (Chapter 10), Florence Goodenough (Chapter 2), Roger Barker (Chapter 9), Sidney Bijou (Chapter 12), and John Paul Scott (Chapter 13). Although the contexts and rationales were different, many of our other subjects in the volume also began their careers in this period, such as Lev Vygotsky in Russia (Chapter 7), Jean Piaget in Switzerland (Chapter 6), Heinz Werner in Germany (Chapter 3), Charlotte Bühler in Austria (Chapter 5), and Helena Antipoff in Brazil (Chapter 4).

For some of our pioneers, theories about children's development were central to their work. Thus, in the accounts of Lev Vygotsky, Jean Piaget, and Lawrence

Kohlberg we see how they attempted to test ideas about some facet of human development to understand a larger theoretical issue. For example, in the work of Jean Piaget, he studied children to understand how reasoning develops, especially the kind of reasoning that makes scientific work possible. Kohlberg, on the other hand, felt a sense of urgency in understanding the moral dimensions of human development.

For other pioneers, the application of psychological theory and research to social problems or concerns was paramount. Helena Antipoff in Brazil, for example, sought to use the ideas about children's cognitive and social development to improve education there. Drawing upon the work of Eduard Claparède, Lev Vygotsky, and Jean Piaget, she envisioned the child as one who learns through activity. Mamie Phipps Clark, in her graduate work but primarily through her professional role as founder and developer of the Northside Center for Child Development in New York City, sought to improve the lives of children and their families in a variety of ways, from direct clinical interventions to advocacy before the Board of Education.

As the field of developmental psychology grew, there were psychologists who chose to focus on children's strengths and the importance of appropriate environments for development. Lois Barclay Murphy, who came to psychology from an unorthodox background, was one of the early pioneers who thought outside the box of conventional approaches and topics. She stressed the positive aspects of children's development, especially how children develop a sense of identification with others, mutual care, and the need for ethical behavior. To study these topics, she was innovative in her methods and her interpretations. Mamie Phipps Clark had a similar focus on the strengths and abilities of children. This was especially important in her work at the Northside Center, as many of the children she and her staff served there were racial and ethnic minorities who faced structural barriers in New York City schools and of poverty and paucity of opportunity. Joseph McVicker Hunt, who came late to the formal study of children's development, had a profound impact on how we understand children's abilities and the importance of the environment in maximizing those abilities. It is interesting that the wide range of his experiences prior to his formal engagement with the field may have been especially important as an environmental stimulus to his own scientific development as a midcareer scientist at the University of Illinois. He was among a small cohort of psychologists and other child specialists who played a central role in creating Head Start, which has certainly been critically important in providing opportunities for the appropriate early development of hundreds of thousands of children in the United States.

Environment and the general context were also important in the work of Roger Barker. His large-scale studies of entire towns and the interplay of contexts and people provided a new understanding of the ecology of human development. A new field within psychology was stimulated by Barker and his colleagues, environmental psychology. Robert W. White was also focused on the larger context of development. White argued for the importance of understanding the whole life of a person. His careful and detailed studies of lives in context have not only generated a rich understanding of the human life span but have also spurred the creation of new narrative methodologies that have given new generations of psychologists an enlarged toolkit to explore the nuances of human development. One should not be surprised that White was so innovative and not afraid to explore new approaches. His mentor and colleague for many years at Harvard was Henry Murray, who encouraged his students and staff to be creative and to pursue ideas and methods wherever they led.

Three of our pioneers were more traditional scientists. Florence Goodenough studied with Lewis Terman and was greatly influenced by his view of the development of human abilities. She was fortunate to be hired at the then new Institute of Child Welfare (now Institute of Child Development) at the University of Minnesota, which was one of the institutes funded by the Laura Spelman Rockefeller Memorial, as detailed in the volume's introduction. She spent her career there, gradually becoming a noted scientist, eventually perhaps America's best-known woman psychologist of her day. She was innovative in developing new methods for assessing children's abilities. Her textbooks, tests, and salient position made her a symbol of American psychological science in the mid-20th century. Eleanor Gibson, on the other hand, took a less traditional route to becoming a noted scientist. After a bright career as an undergraduate at Smith College, she married one of her professors, J. J. Gibson, and together and individually they developed a rich body of work on perception. However, due to nepotism rules, it was not until relatively late in her career that Eleanor was able to gain a full appointment as a professor at Cornell. Her research on perceptual learning and the visual cliff have become icons of American psychological science. John Paul Scott is perhaps best known as one of the founders of behavioral genetics. He is unique in this volume because his research subjects were nonhuman animals. With a variety of animals, albeit with dogs as his favorite subjects, Scott investigated the development of sociality and from his work generated the hypothesis of a "critical period" of development that has been important in a number of fields within psychology. What is most striking about Scott is his sincere desire to use scientific research to help enhance the possibilities for peace among nations and among people.

For almost all of the pioneers whose lives and contributions have been documented in this volume, an added dimension is that they were mentors to younger scientists and to their colleagues. Lev Vygotsky, in his relatively brief life and even briefer career, gathered around him a brilliant group of students and colleagues who carried on many aspects of his work under very difficult conditions in the Soviet Union. It is only in recent years that Western scientists are beginning to understand the richness of his contributions. One of Florence Goodenough's strengths was her mentoring, as noted in the chapter. She was a demanding mentor with very high standards, yet she was capable of helping her students develop their potential while offering genuine support. Similar stories can be told about most of our pioneers, though the details differ, of course. For example, when one looks at the growth of qualitative approaches in contemporary psychology around the world, it is important to recall that it was Robert W. White and the network of students for several generations who have played such an important role in bringing qualitative approaches to the fore.

This volume began with a statement about how developmental research has revealed many aspects of the richness of human experience. Of course, only a small slice of this richness has been touched upon in the vignettes found here. Today, the field of developmental psychology is vast, with greatly expanded methodological and topical toolkits. The field has also expanded well beyond its initial European and North American boundaries, so that some of the most interesting and important research is now being done in places such as India, South Africa, and Brazil. The lives portrayed here can indicate why developmental psychology has grown and diversified over the course of the last 100-plus years. It has succeeded because it has found a way to keep its eyes on the prize: the richness of human life.

Author Index

Subject Index

Note: *f* indicates figures.

A

AAAP (American Association for Applied Psychology), 194
Abnormal Psychology, The (White), 178
Abstract logic, 100–102
Accommodation, 93, 97
Achievement
    measurement of, 209
    racism and, 265, 266
Acquired distinctiveness of cues, 251
Active School methods (École Active)
    Antipoff and, 54, 58–59
    exceptional children and, 61
Adolescence
    Hall and, xv, 94
    Kohlberg and, 293
Affordances, perception of, 255, 256, 258
African Americans, *see* Blacks
Age norms, 9
Age-related stages, *see* Stages of development
Aggression
    Barclay Murphy and, 141
    Scott and, 238, 241, 243, 244, 299
Agonistic behavior, 235, 236, 238
Allee, Warder Clyde, 231
American Association for Applied Psychology (AAAP), 194
American Men of Science, 21, 31
American Psychological Association (APA)
    growth of, 193
    Hunt and, 194–195
Anger of children, 25
Animal Behavior (Scott), 242
Animal Behavior Society, 240–241
Animal research
    dog program, 233–235, 236
    Gibson and, 253
    house mice, 235, 236
    rats, 191, 253
    Scott and, 229–230, 233–235, 236, 238, 240–241, 243
Animism
    empirical tests of, 101, 102
    Hall and, 94
    Piaget and, 98–99, 100
Antipoff, Helena, 51–63, 51*f*
    education in Russia and Europe, 52–53

exceptional children, 60–63
family, 56
Geneva to Brazil, 57–58
psychology and education studies, 53–55
science and reconstruction of Russia, 55–57
work as psychologist and educator, 58–60, 298
APA (American Psychological Association), 193, 194–195
Applied behavior analysis, 215–217
Appropriation, 119
Articulation of parts, 38–39, 39*f*, 40*f*
Assimilation, 97
Audiogenic seizures in mice, 235
Autism, 216–217
Autonomy and heteronomy subtypes, 284–285

B

Baldwin, James Mark
    accommodation and, 93, 97
    on dialectic of personal growth, xv
    on quantitative methods, 39
Bar Harbor program, *see* Jackson Laboratory
Barclay Murphy, Lois, *see* Murphy, Lois Barclay
Barker, Roger, 151–167, 151*f*
    additional contributions, 154–155
    awards and honors, 151–152
    behavior setting theory, 151, 152–154, 161–163, 166
    early academic career, 158–160
    early history, education, mentoring, 156–158
    ecological psychology, 152, 163, 164, 166–167, 298
    ecological work after Field Station, 165–166
    family, 157
    legacy, 164, 165, 166–167
    the man, 155–156
    Midwest Psychological Field Station, 159, 160–165, 298
Basic stage of development, 221
Behavior, definition of, 211–212; *see also* Responses
Behavior analysis theory of development, 219–221
Behavior disorders, 190–192
Behavior episodes, 161